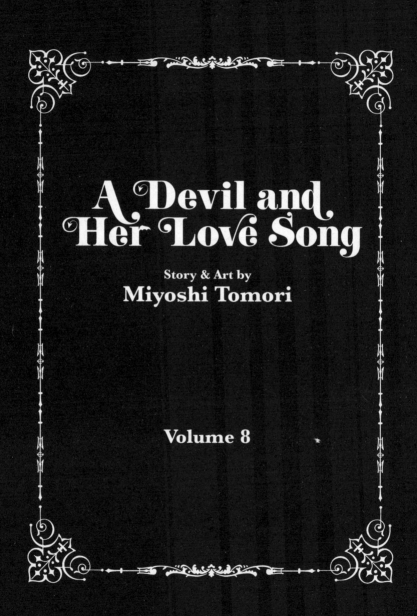

A Devil and Her Love Song

**Story & Art by
Miyoshi Tomori**

Volume 8

A Devil and Her Love Song

Volume 8

CONTENTS

The devil makes me LOVELY!!!

STORY THUS FAR

Shin tries to distance himself from Maria to keep her from being reminded of the pain in her past. Yusuke, on the other hand, takes her in his arms and tells her that he's in love with her, triggering the memories Shin was hoping to keep at bay.

Meanwhile, Anna finally shares her true feelings with Maria—that she wants to sing. While Maria is devastated by the realization that she is unable to help Anna, Anna drops out of St. Katria and vanishes, leaving behind only a cross identical to the one Maria wears.

4

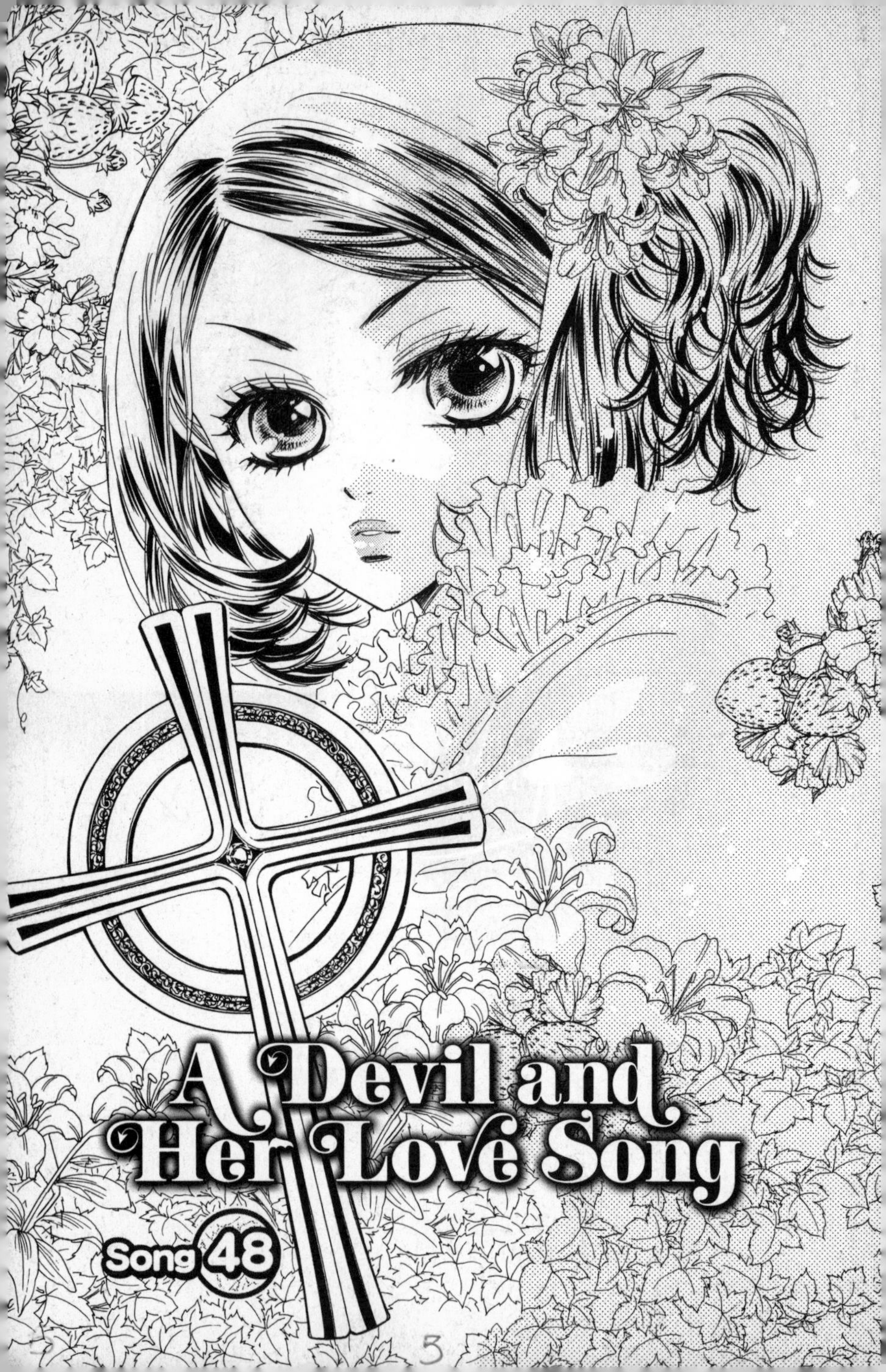
A Devil and Her Love Song
Song 48

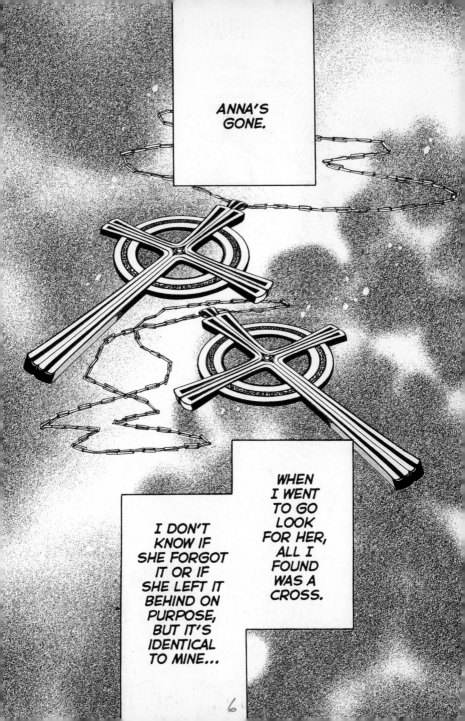

ANNA'S GONE.

WHEN I WENT TO GO LOOK FOR HER, ALL I FOUND WAS A CROSS.

I DON'T KNOW IF SHE FORGOT IT OR IF SHE LEFT IT BEHIND ON PURPOSE, BUT IT'S IDENTICAL TO MINE...

6

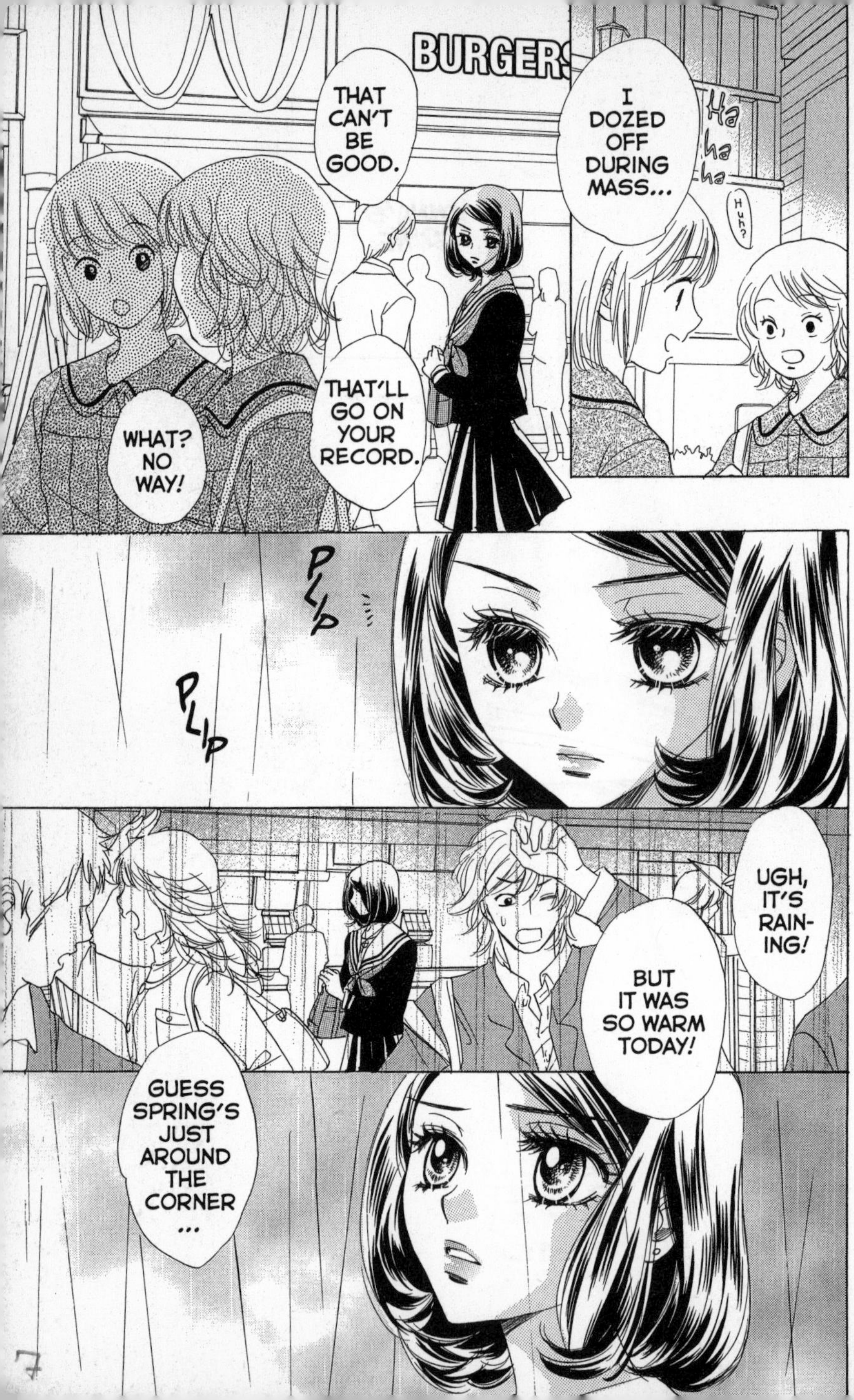
BURGERS
I DOZED OFF DURING MASS...
Ha ha ha
Huh?
THAT CAN'T BE GOOD.
THAT'LL GO ON YOUR RECORD.
WHAT? NO WAY!
PLIP
PLIP
UGH, IT'S RAIN-ING!
BUT IT WAS SO WARM TODAY!
GUESS SPRING'S JUST AROUND THE CORNER...

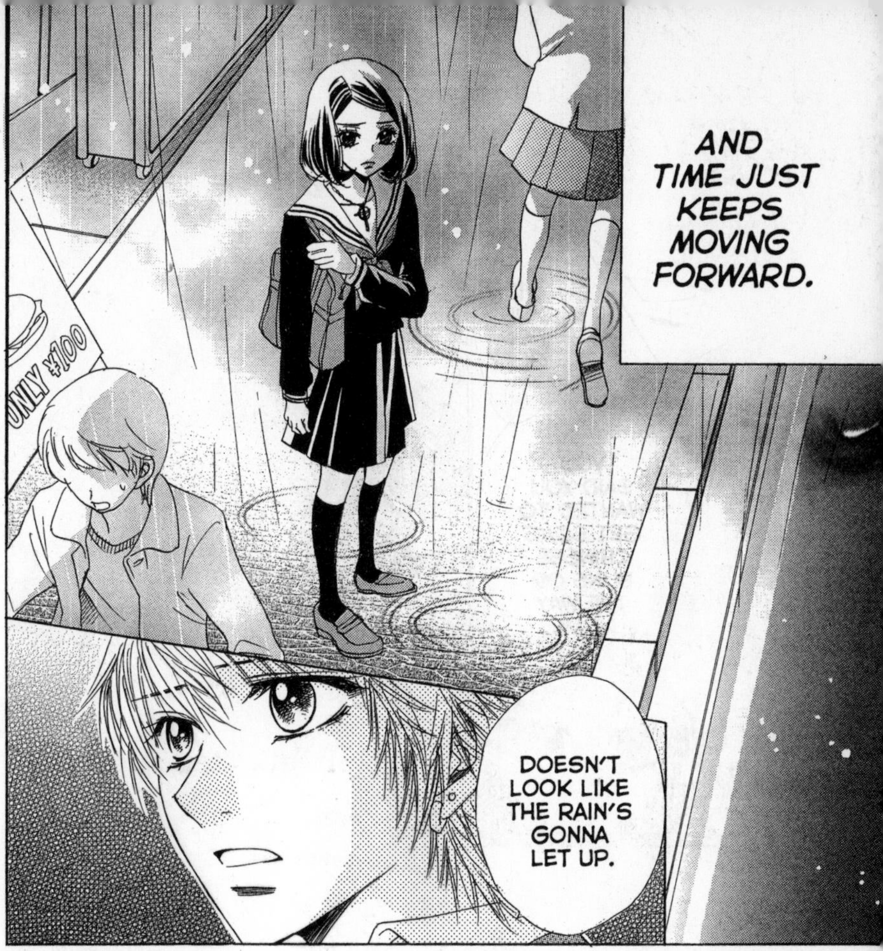
AND TIME JUST KEEPS MOVING FORWARD.
ONLY ¥100
DOESN'T LOOK LIKE THE RAIN'S GONNA LET UP.

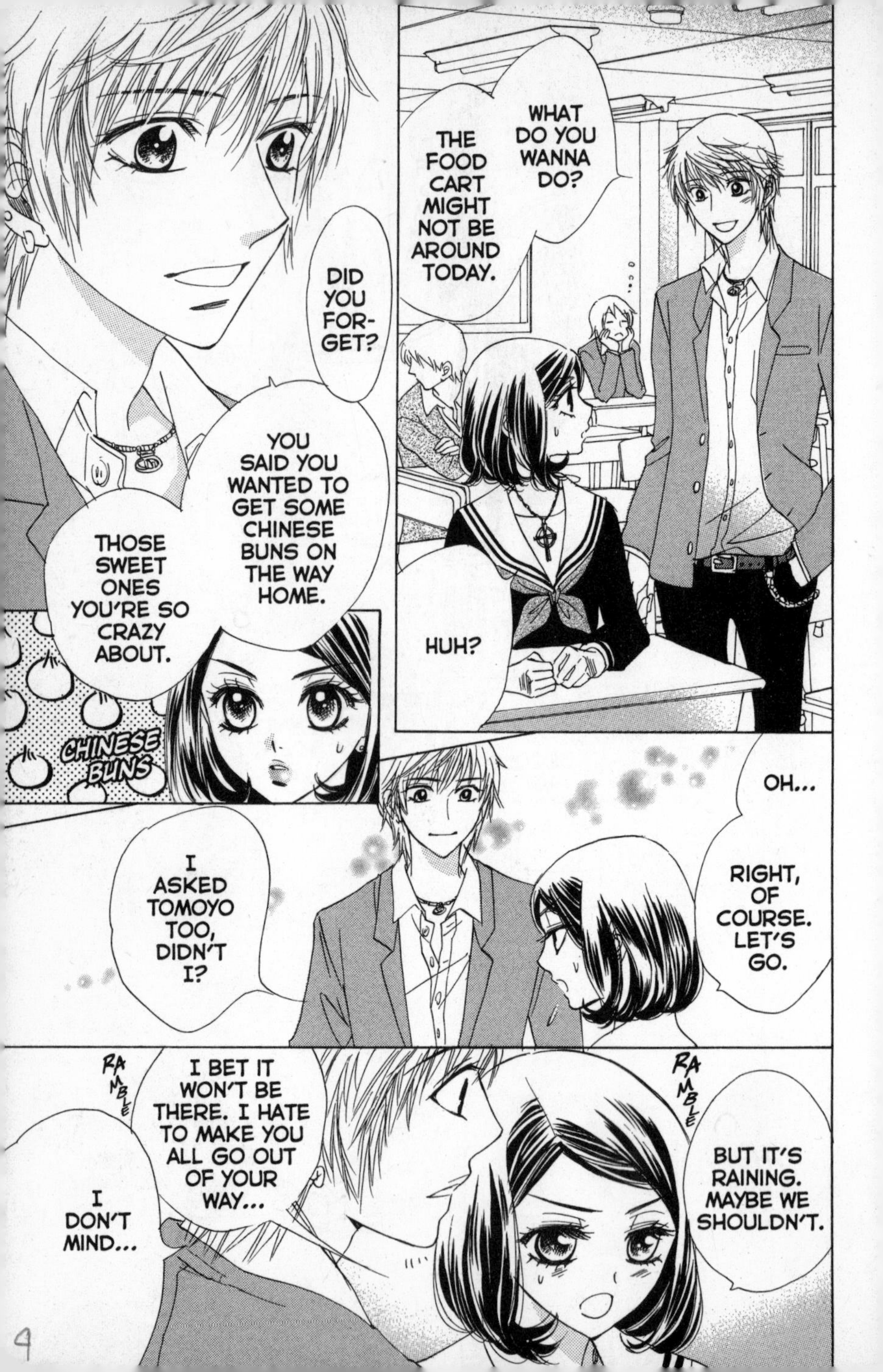
WHAT DO YOU WANNA DO?
THE FOOD CART MIGHT NOT BE AROUND TODAY.
HUH?
DID YOU FOR-GET?
YOU SAID YOU WANTED TO GET SOME CHINESE BUNS ON THE WAY HOME.
THOSE SWEET ONES YOU'RE SO CRAZY ABOUT.
CHINESE BUNS
OH...
RIGHT, OF COURSE. LET'S GO.
I ASKED TOMOYO TOO, DIDN'T I?
RAMBLE
BUT IT'S RAINING. MAYBE WE SHOULDN'T.
RAMBLE
I BET IT WON'T BE THERE. I HATE TO MAKE YOU ALL GO OUT OF YOUR WAY...
I DON'T MIND...

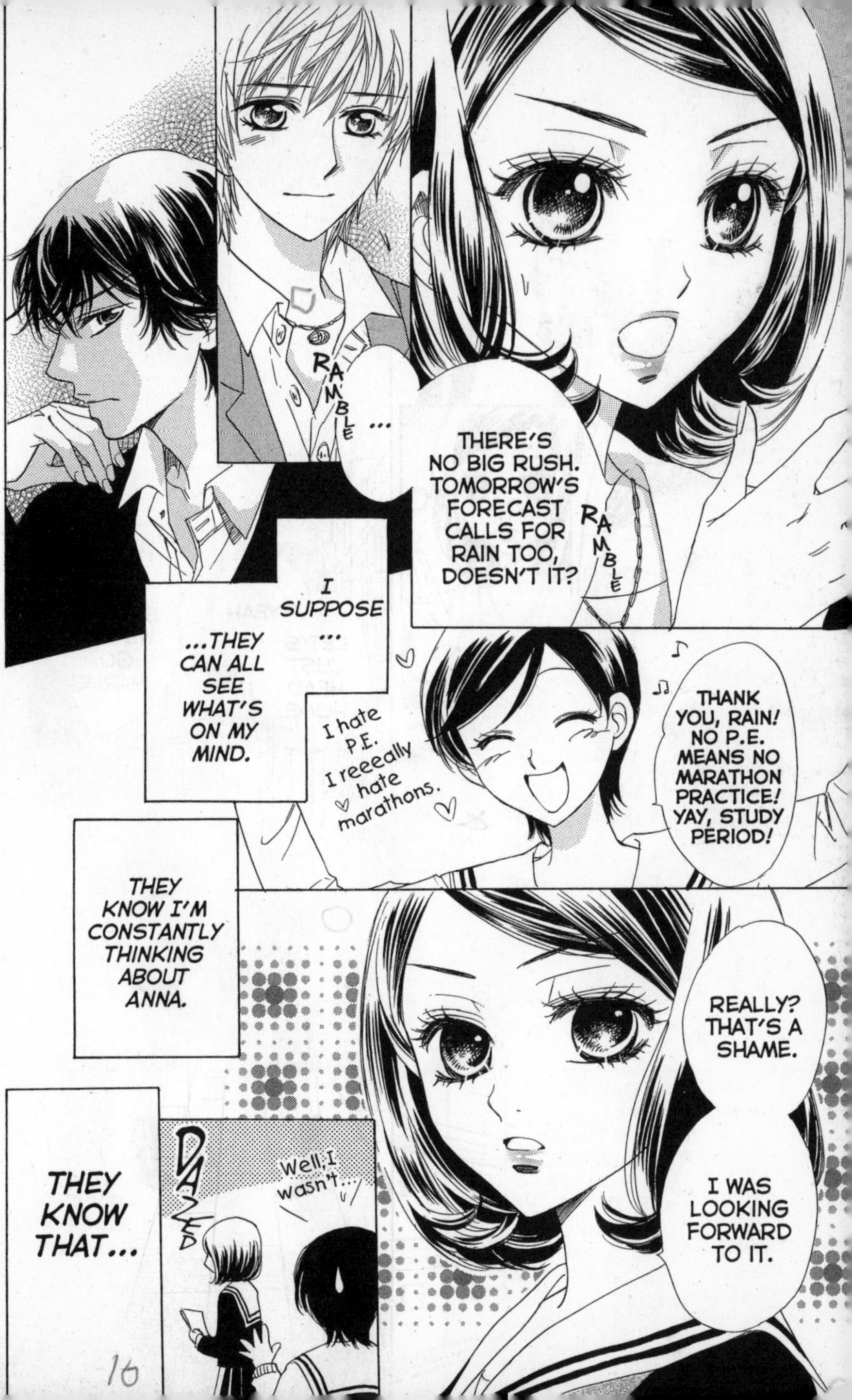
THERE'S NO BIG RUSH. TOMORROW'S FORECAST CALLS FOR RAIN TOO, DOESN'T IT?
RAMBLE
RAMBLE...
I SUPPOSE...
...THEY CAN ALL SEE WHAT'S ON MY MIND.
THANK YOU, RAIN! NO P.E. MEANS NO MARATHON PRACTICE! YAY, STUDY PERIOD!
I hate P.E. I reeeally hate marathons.
REALLY? THAT'S A SHAME.
I WAS LOOKING FORWARD TO IT.
THEY KNOW I'M CONSTANTLY THINKING ABOUT ANNA.
DAZED
Well, I wasn't...
THEY KNOW THAT...

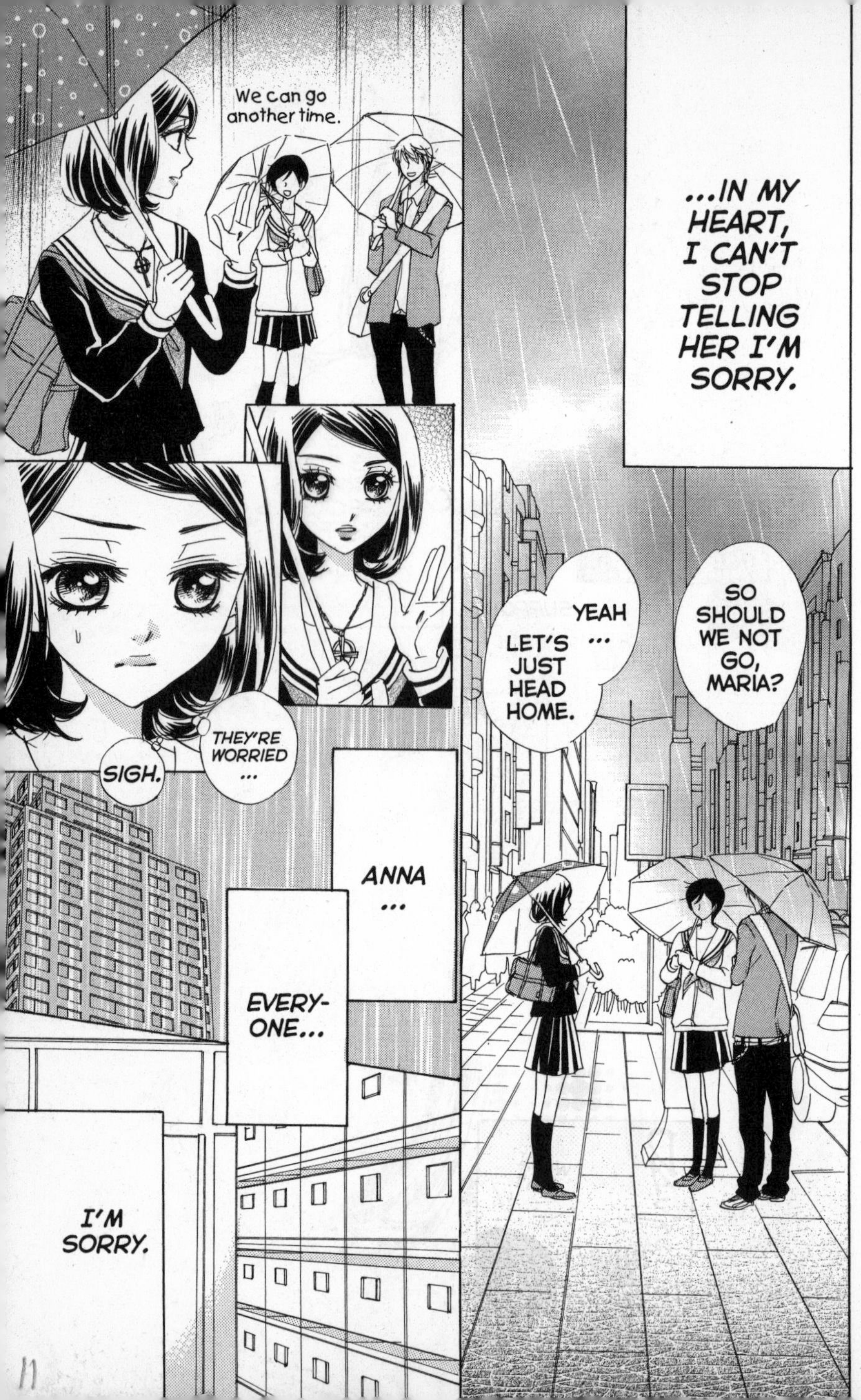
...IN MY HEART, I CAN'T STOP TELLING HER I'M SORRY.
SO SHOULD WE NOT GO, MARIA?
YEAH ...
LET'S JUST HEAD HOME.
We can go another time.
THEY'RE WORRIED ...
SIGH.
ANNA ...
EVERY-ONE...
I'M SORRY.

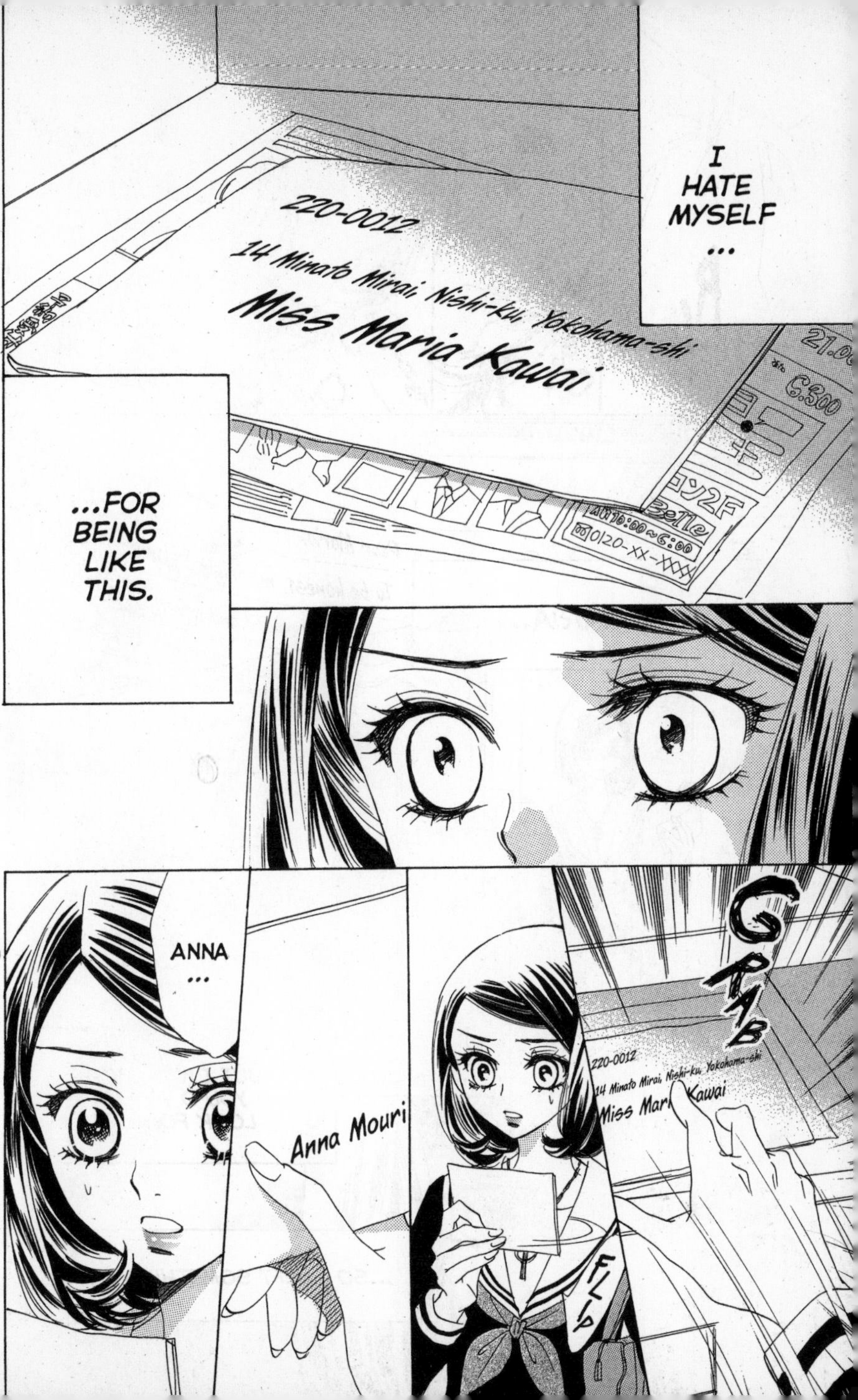
I HATE MYSELF ...
220-0012
14 Minato Mirai, Nishi-ku, Yokohama-shi
Miss Maria Kawai
...FOR BEING LIKE THIS.
GRAB
220-0012
14 Minato Mirai, Nishi-ku, Yokohama-shi
Miss Mari Kawai
FLIP
Anna Mouri
ANNA ...

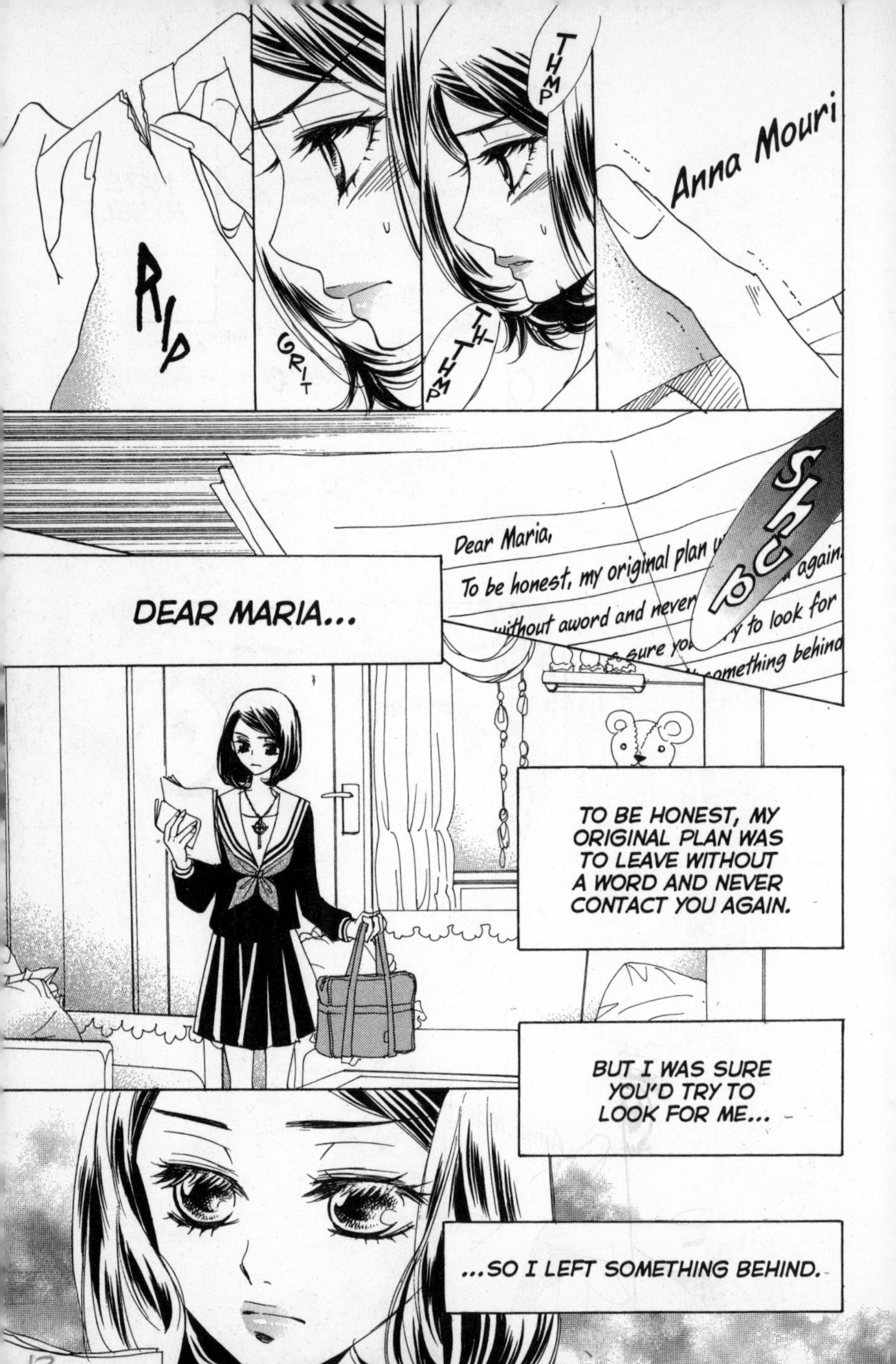
Anna Mouri
THMP
TH-THMP
GRIT
RIP
Shup
Dear Maria,
To be honest, my original plan w
again.
without aword and never
y to look for
sure you
something behind
DEAR MARIA...
TO BE HONEST, MY ORIGINAL PLAN WAS TO LEAVE WITHOUT A WORD AND NEVER CONTACT YOU AGAIN.
BUT I WAS SURE YOU'D TRY TO LOOK FOR ME...
...SO I LEFT SOMETHING BEHIND.

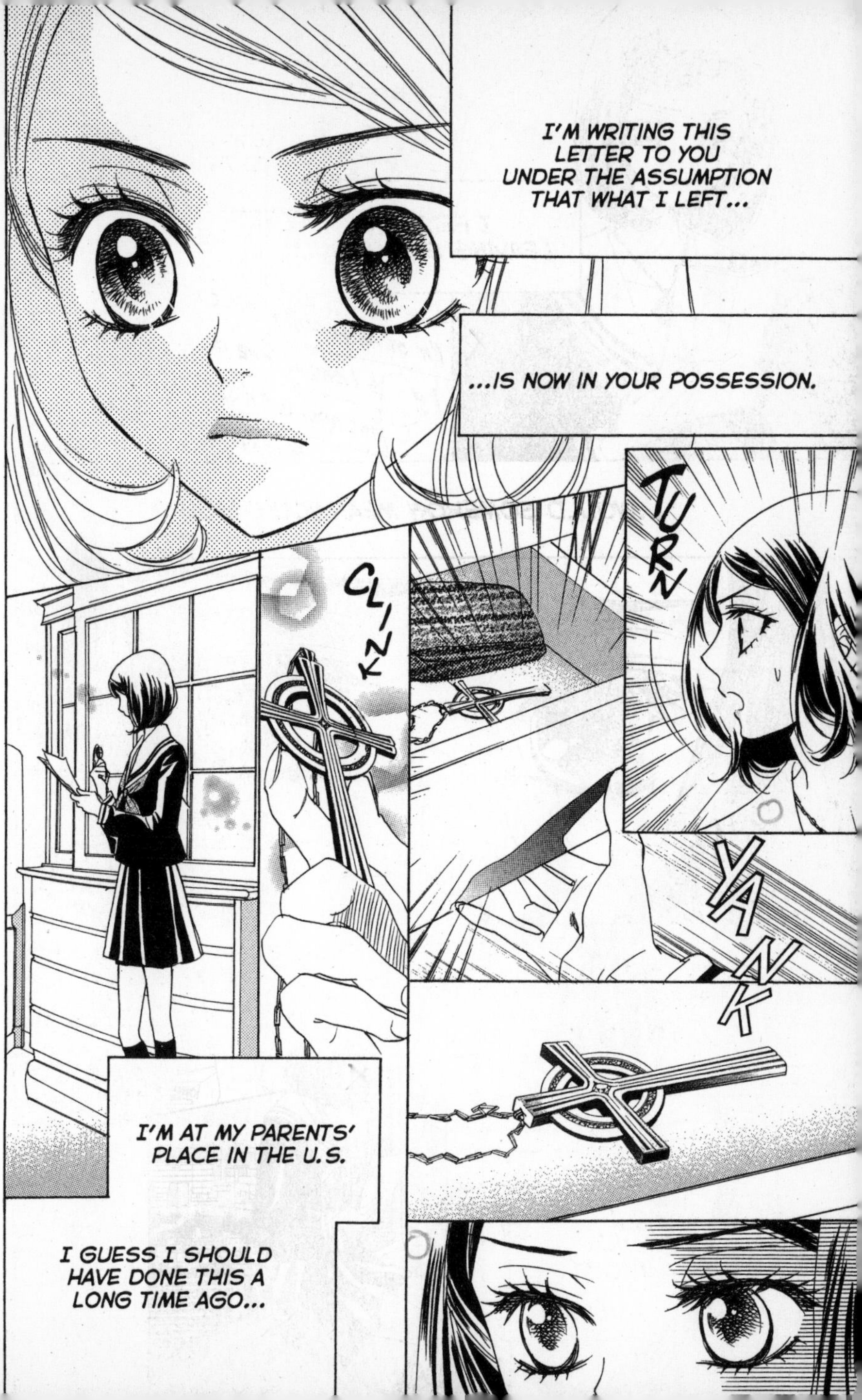
I'M WRITING THIS LETTER TO YOU UNDER THE ASSUMPTION THAT WHAT I LEFT...
...IS NOW IN YOUR POSSESSION.
TURN
YANK
CLINK
I'M AT MY PARENTS' PLACE IN THE U.S.
I GUESS I SHOULD HAVE DONE THIS A LONG TIME AGO...

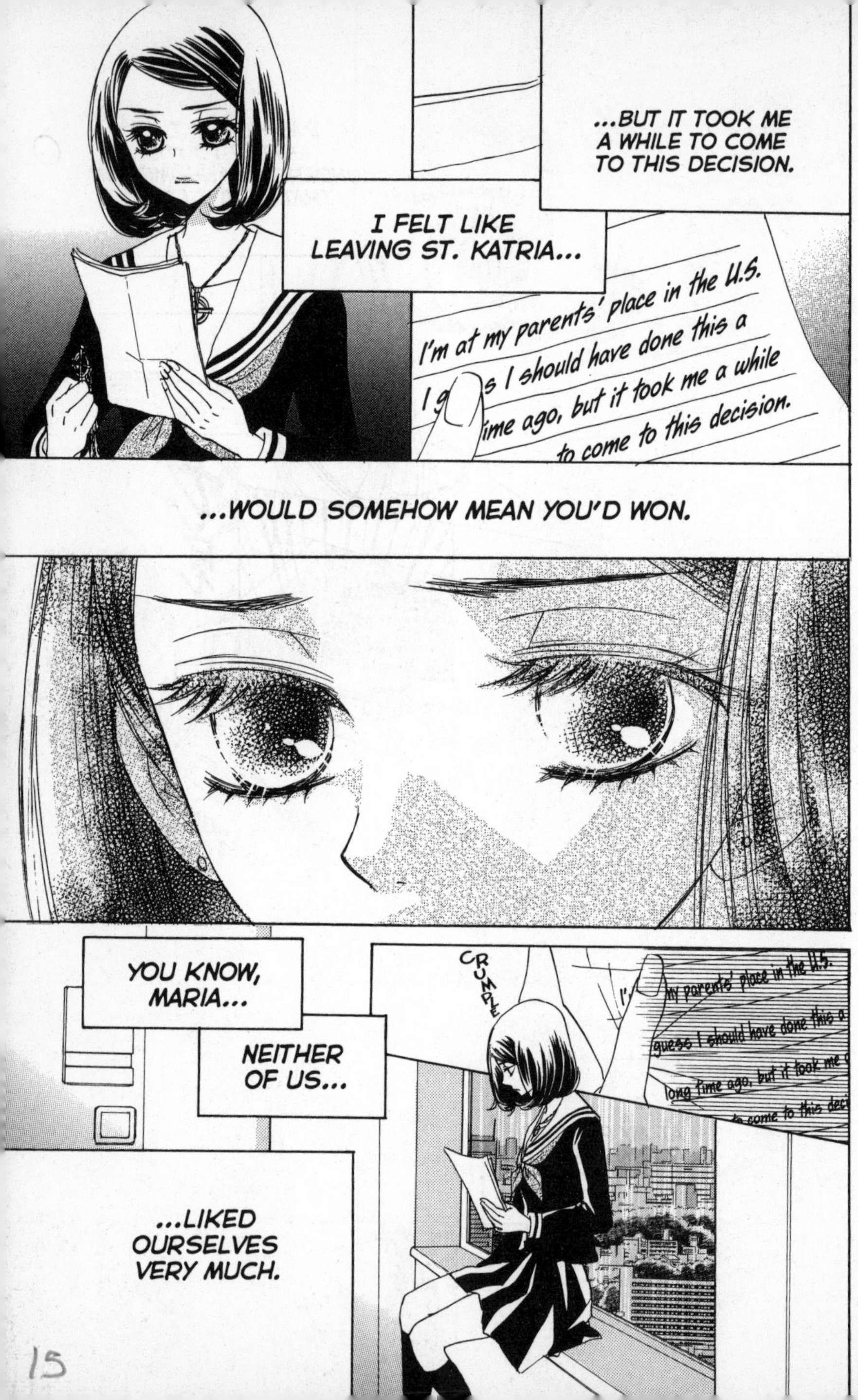
...BUT IT TOOK ME A WHILE TO COME TO THIS DECISION.
I'm at my parents' place in the U.S.
s I should have done this a
ime ago, but it took me a while
to come to this decision.
I FELT LIKE LEAVING ST. KATRIA...
...WOULD SOMEHOW MEAN YOU'D WON.
CRUMPLE
my parents' place in the U.S.
guess I should have done this a
long time ago, but it took me
to come to this deci
YOU KNOW, MARIA...
NEITHER OF US...
...LIKED OURSELVES VERY MUCH.

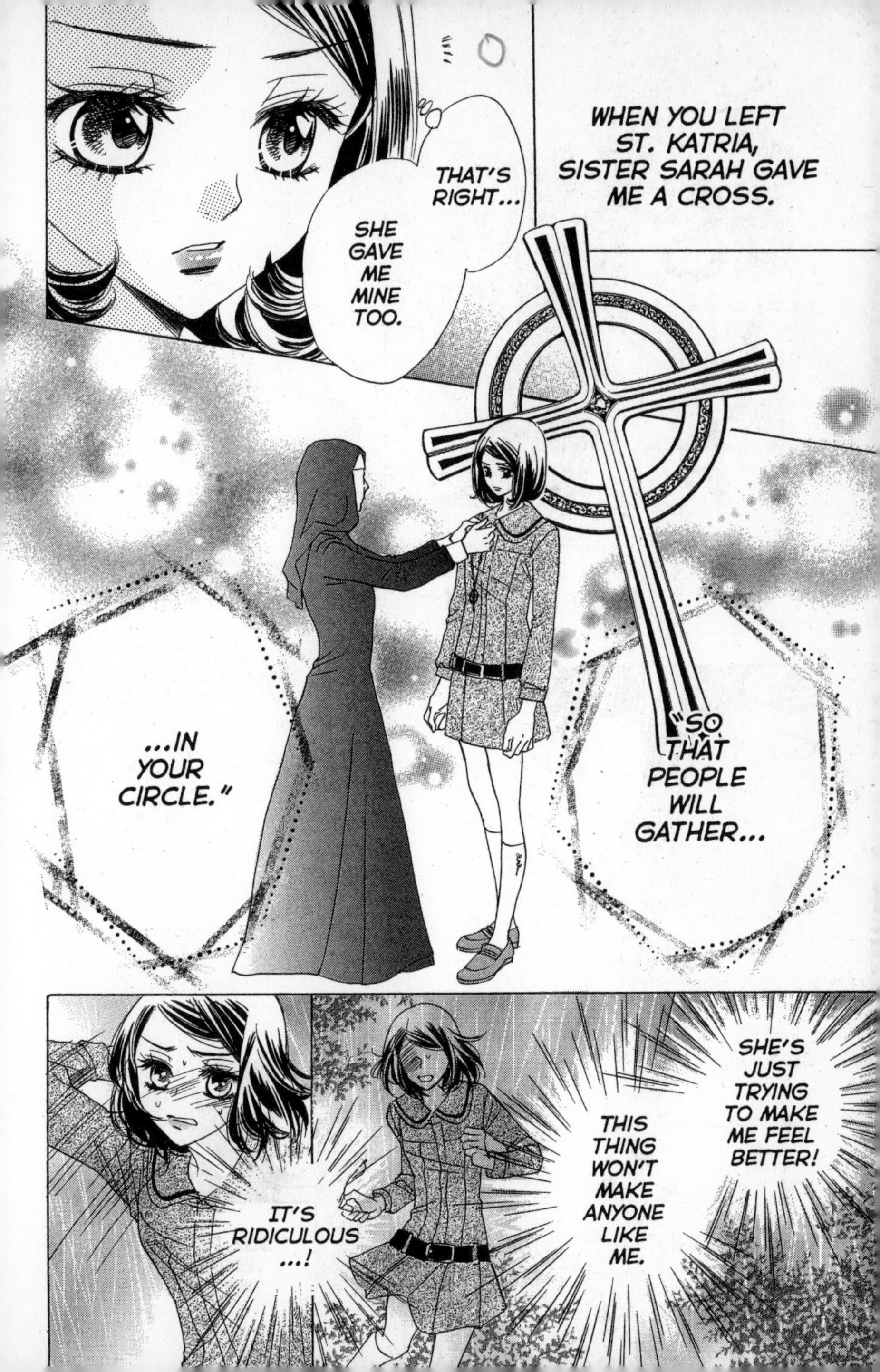
WHEN YOU LEFT ST. KATRIA, SISTER SARAH GAVE ME A CROSS.
THAT'S RIGHT...
SHE GAVE ME MINE TOO.
"SO THAT PEOPLE WILL GATHER...
...IN YOUR CIRCLE."
SHE'S JUST TRYING TO MAKE ME FEEL BETTER!
THIS THING WON'T MAKE ANYONE LIKE ME.
IT'S RIDICULOUS...!

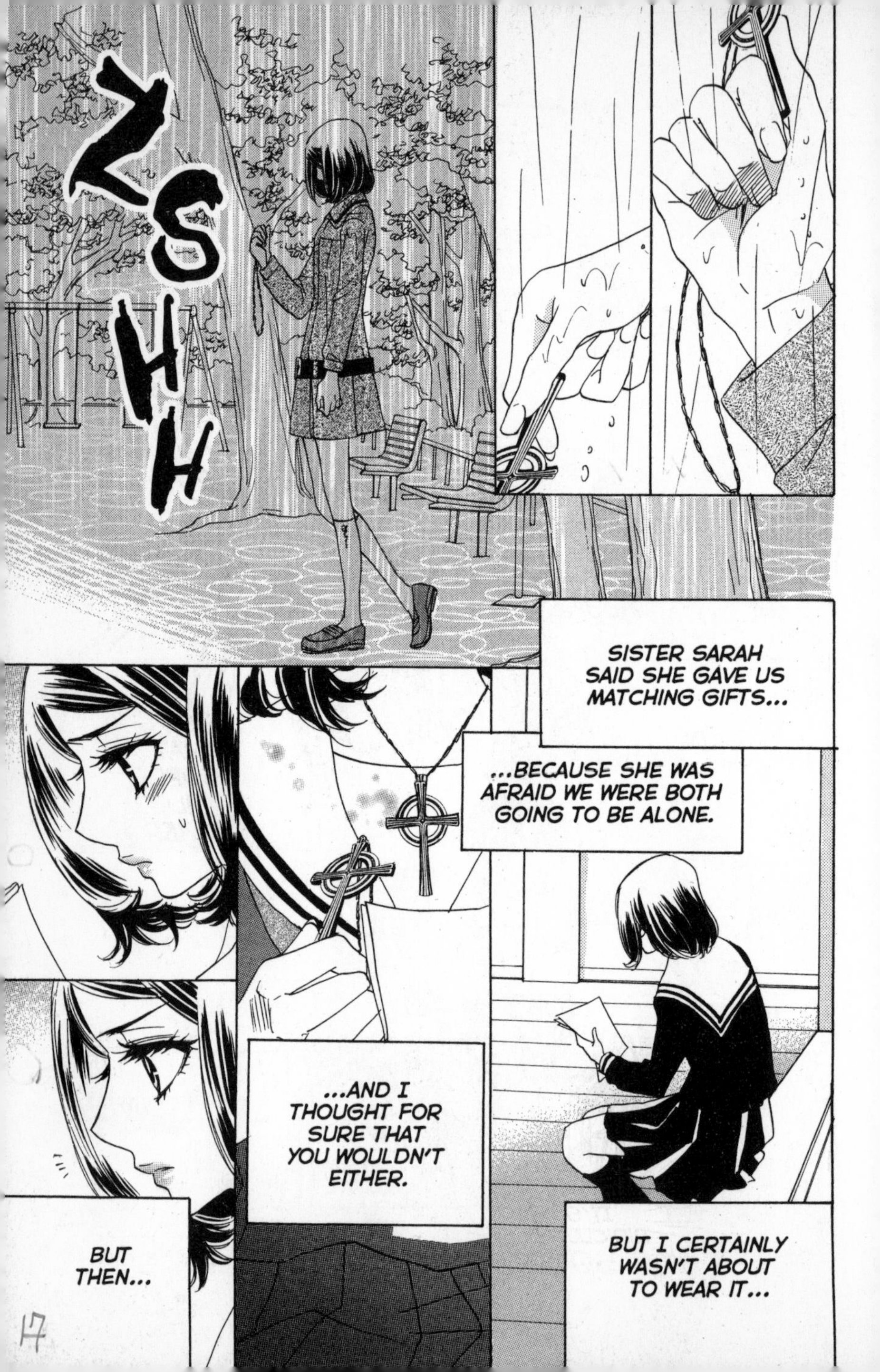
ZSHHH
SISTER SARAH SAID SHE GAVE US MATCHING GIFTS...
...BECAUSE SHE WAS AFRAID WE WERE BOTH GOING TO BE ALONE.
BUT I CERTAINLY WASN'T ABOUT TO WEAR IT...
...AND I THOUGHT FOR SURE THAT YOU WOULDN'T EITHER.
BUT THEN...

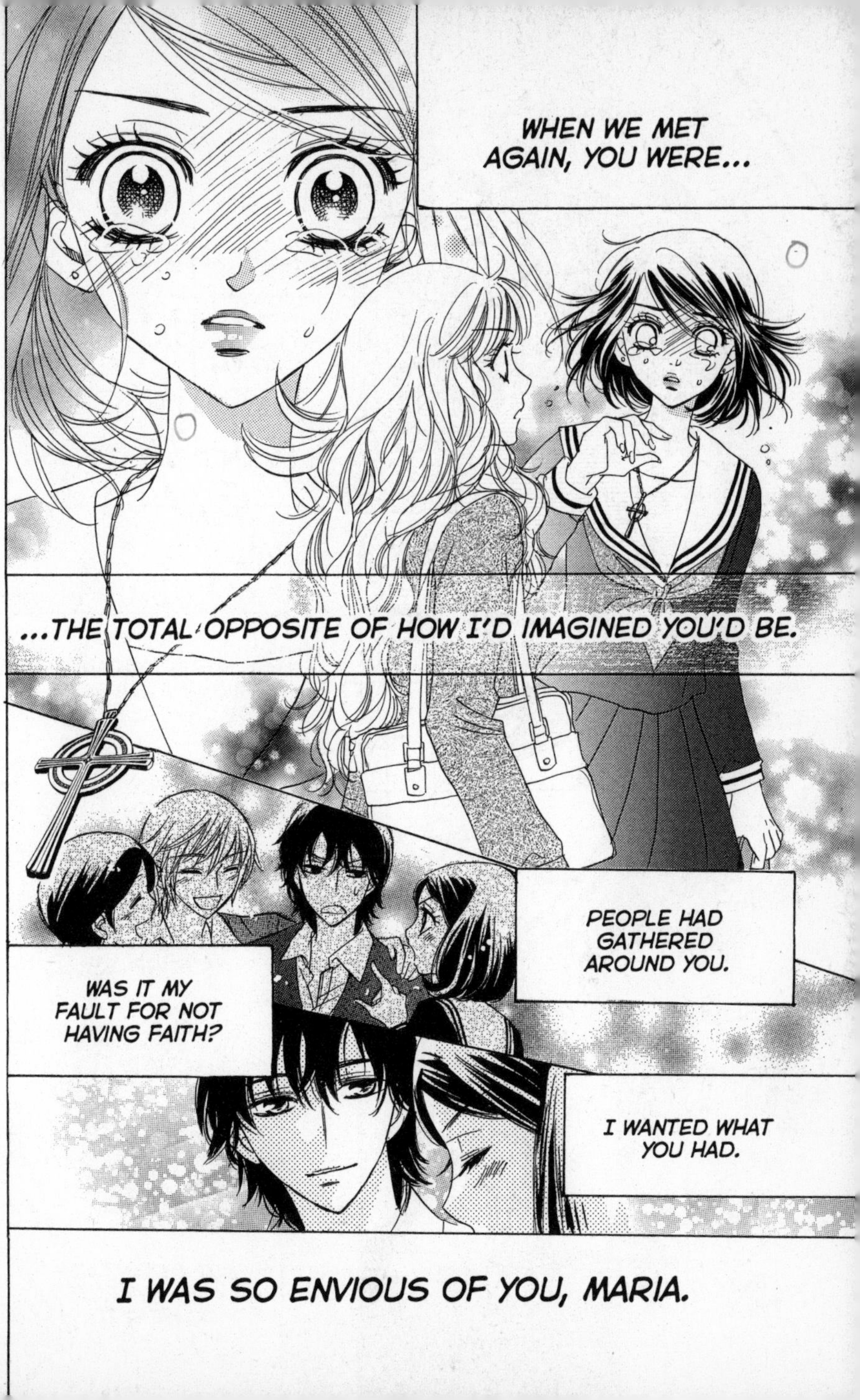
WHEN WE MET AGAIN, YOU WERE...
...THE TOTAL OPPOSITE OF HOW I'D IMAGINED YOU'D BE.
PEOPLE HAD GATHERED AROUND YOU.
WAS IT MY FAULT FOR NOT HAVING FAITH?
I WANTED WHAT YOU HAD.
I WAS SO ENVIOUS OF YOU, MARIA.

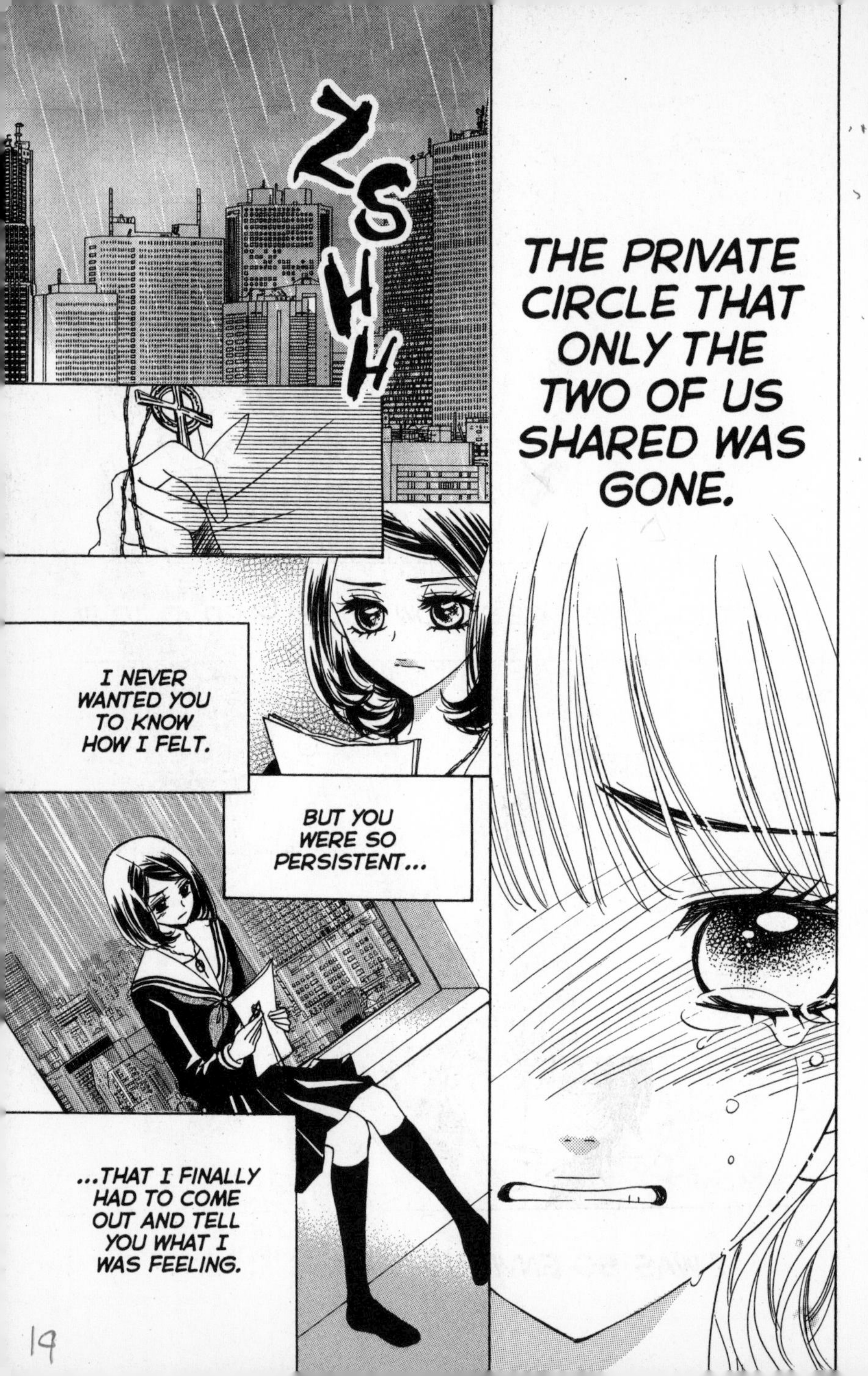
THE PRIVATE CIRCLE THAT ONLY THE TWO OF US SHARED WAS GONE.
ZSHH
I NEVER WANTED YOU TO KNOW HOW I FELT.
BUT YOU WERE SO PERSISTENT...
...THAT I FINALLY HAD TO COME OUT AND TELL YOU WHAT I WAS FEELING.

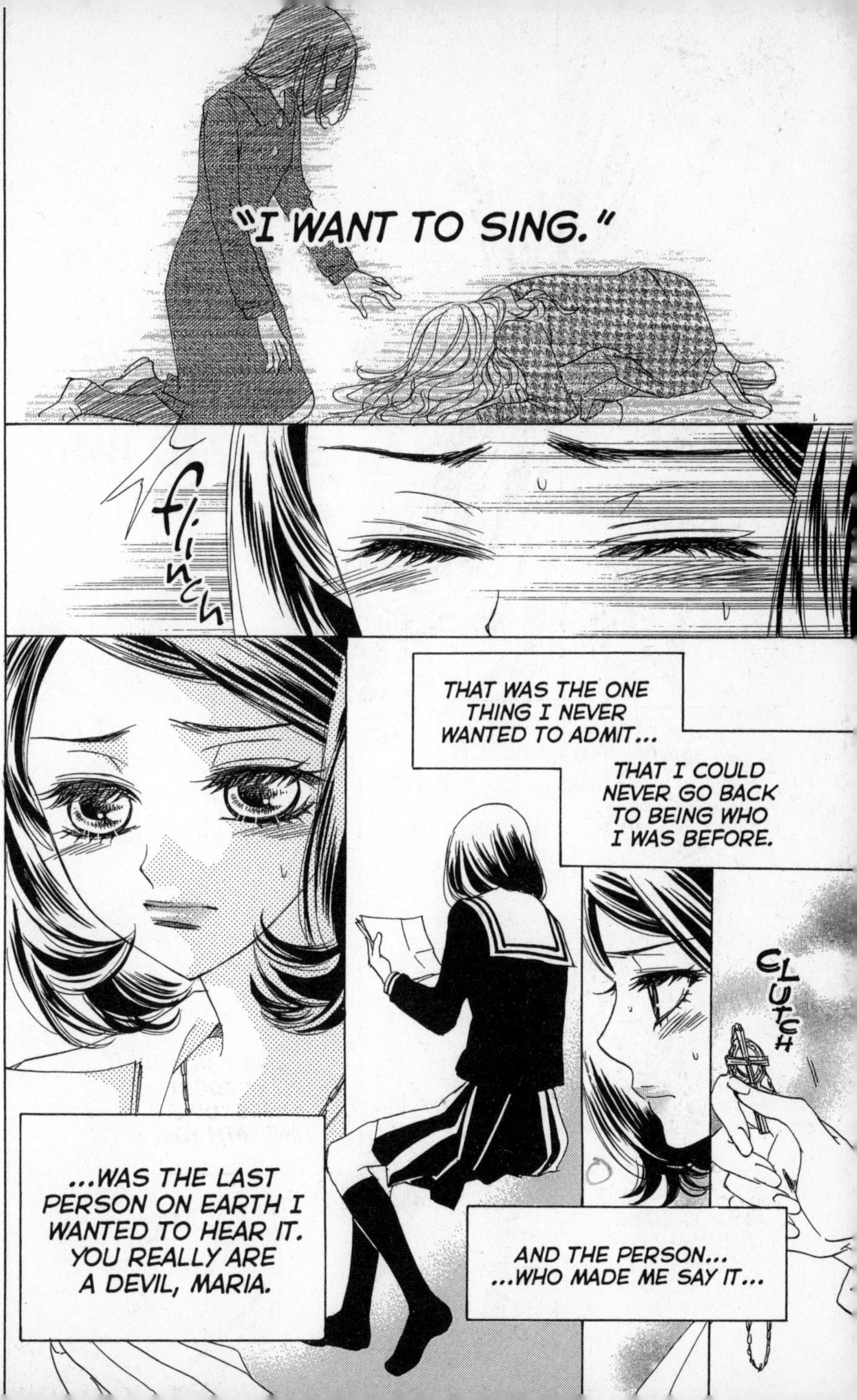
"I WANT TO SING."
flinch
THAT WAS THE ONE THING I NEVER WANTED TO ADMIT...
THAT I COULD NEVER GO BACK TO BEING WHO I WAS BEFORE.
CLUTCH
AND THE PERSON... ...WHO MADE ME SAY IT...
...WAS THE LAST PERSON ON EARTH I WANTED TO HEAR IT. YOU REALLY ARE A DEVIL, MARIA.

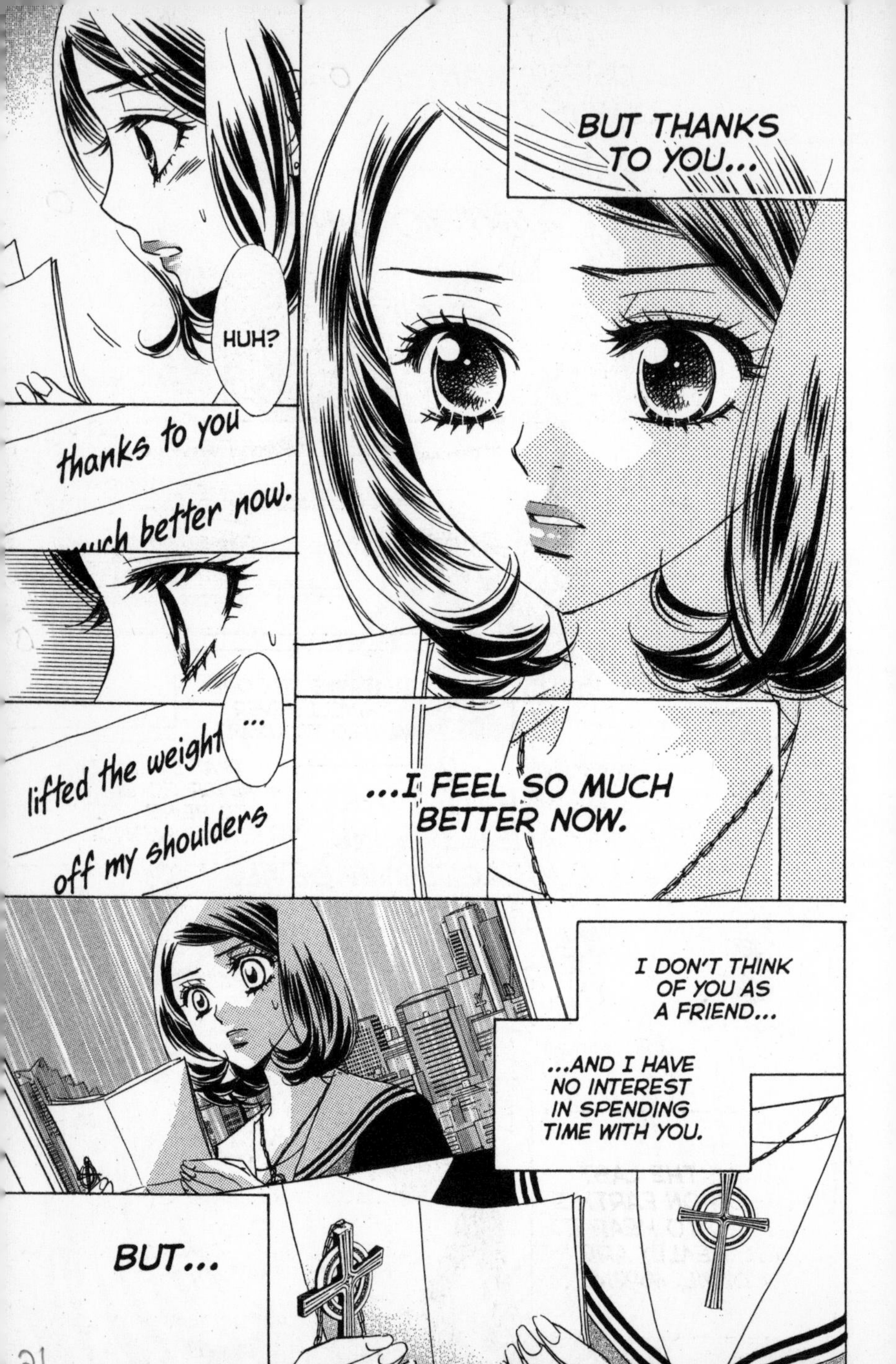
BUT THANKS TO YOU...
...I FEEL SO MUCH BETTER NOW.
HUH?
thanks to you
better now.
...
lifted the weight
off my shoulders
I DON'T THINK OF YOU AS A FRIEND...
...AND I HAVE NO INTEREST IN SPENDING TIME WITH YOU.
BUT...

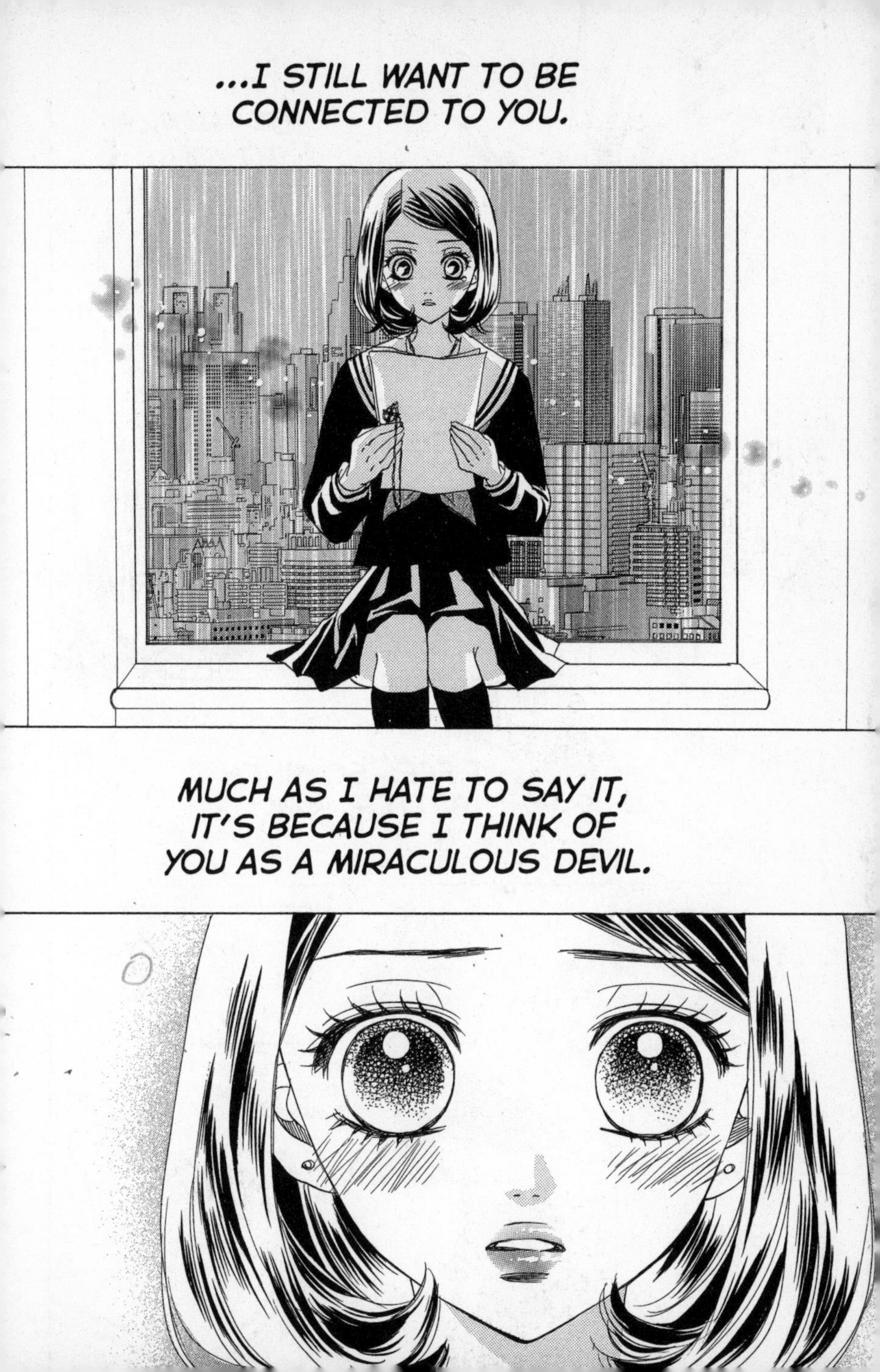
...I STILL WANT TO BE CONNECTED TO YOU.
MUCH AS I HATE TO SAY IT, IT'S BECAUSE I THINK OF YOU AS A MIRACULOUS DEVIL.

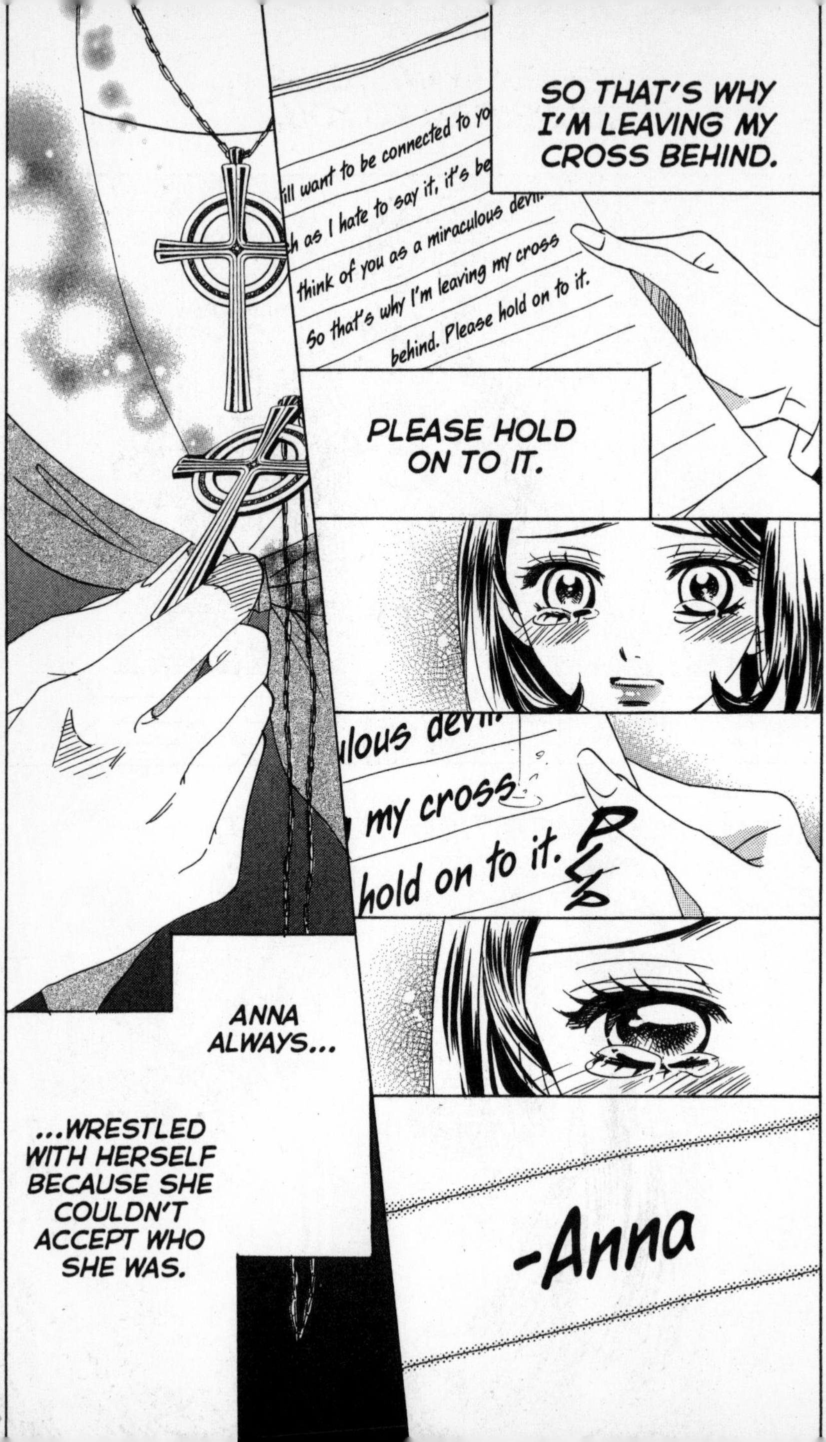
SO THAT'S WHY I'M LEAVING MY CROSS BEHIND.
ill want to be connected to yo
h as I hate to say it, it's be
think of you as a miraculous devil.
So that's why I'm leaving my cross
behind. Please hold on to it.
PLEASE HOLD ON TO IT.
ulous devil.
my cross
hold on to it.
-Anna
ANNA ALWAYS...
...WRESTLED WITH HERSELF BECAUSE SHE COULDN'T ACCEPT WHO SHE WAS.

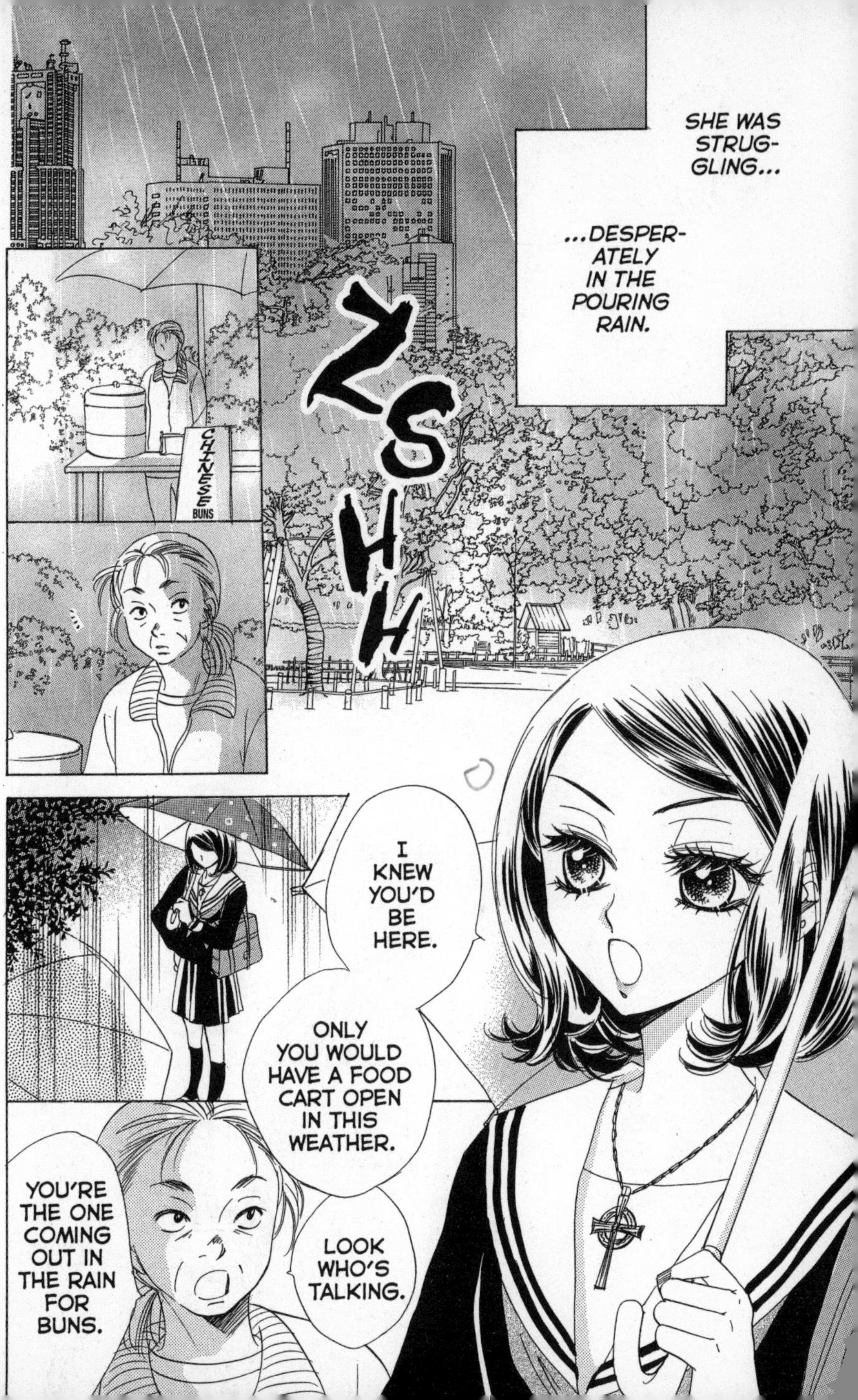
SHE WAS STRUGGLING...
...DESPERATELY IN THE POURING RAIN.
ZSHH
CHINESE BUNS
I KNEW YOU'D BE HERE.
ONLY YOU WOULD HAVE A FOOD CART OPEN IN THIS WEATHER.
LOOK WHO'S TALKING.
YOU'RE THE ONE COMING OUT IN THE RAIN FOR BUNS.

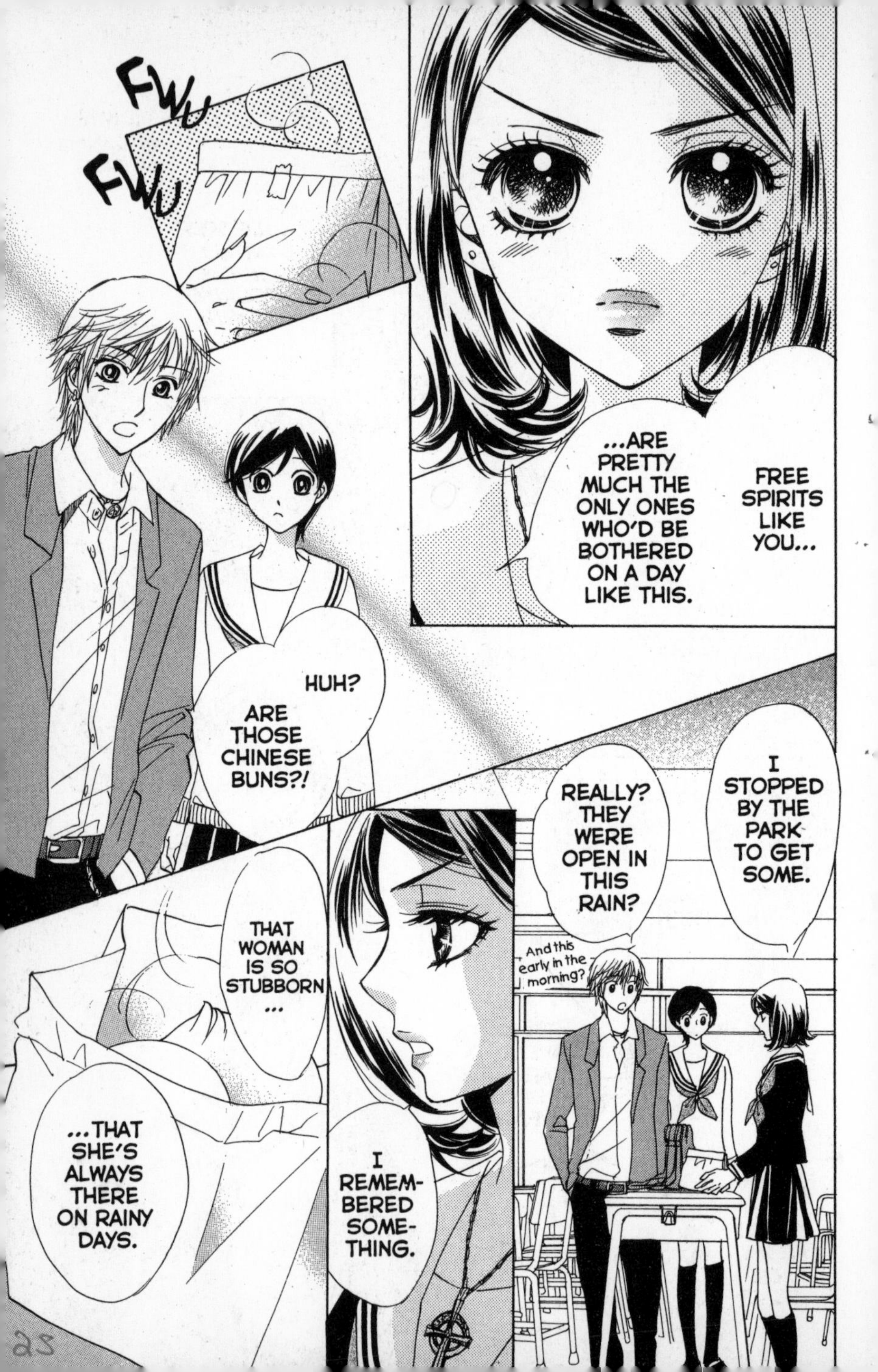
FREE SPIRITS LIKE YOU...
...ARE PRETTY MUCH THE ONLY ONES WHO'D BE BOTHERED ON A DAY LIKE THIS.
FWU FWU
HUH?
ARE THOSE CHINESE BUNS?!
I STOPPED BY THE PARK TO GET SOME.
REALLY? THEY WERE OPEN IN THIS RAIN?
And this early in the morning?
THAT WOMAN IS SO STUBBORN...
I REMEMBERED SOMETHING.
...THAT SHE'S ALWAYS THERE ON RAINY DAYS.

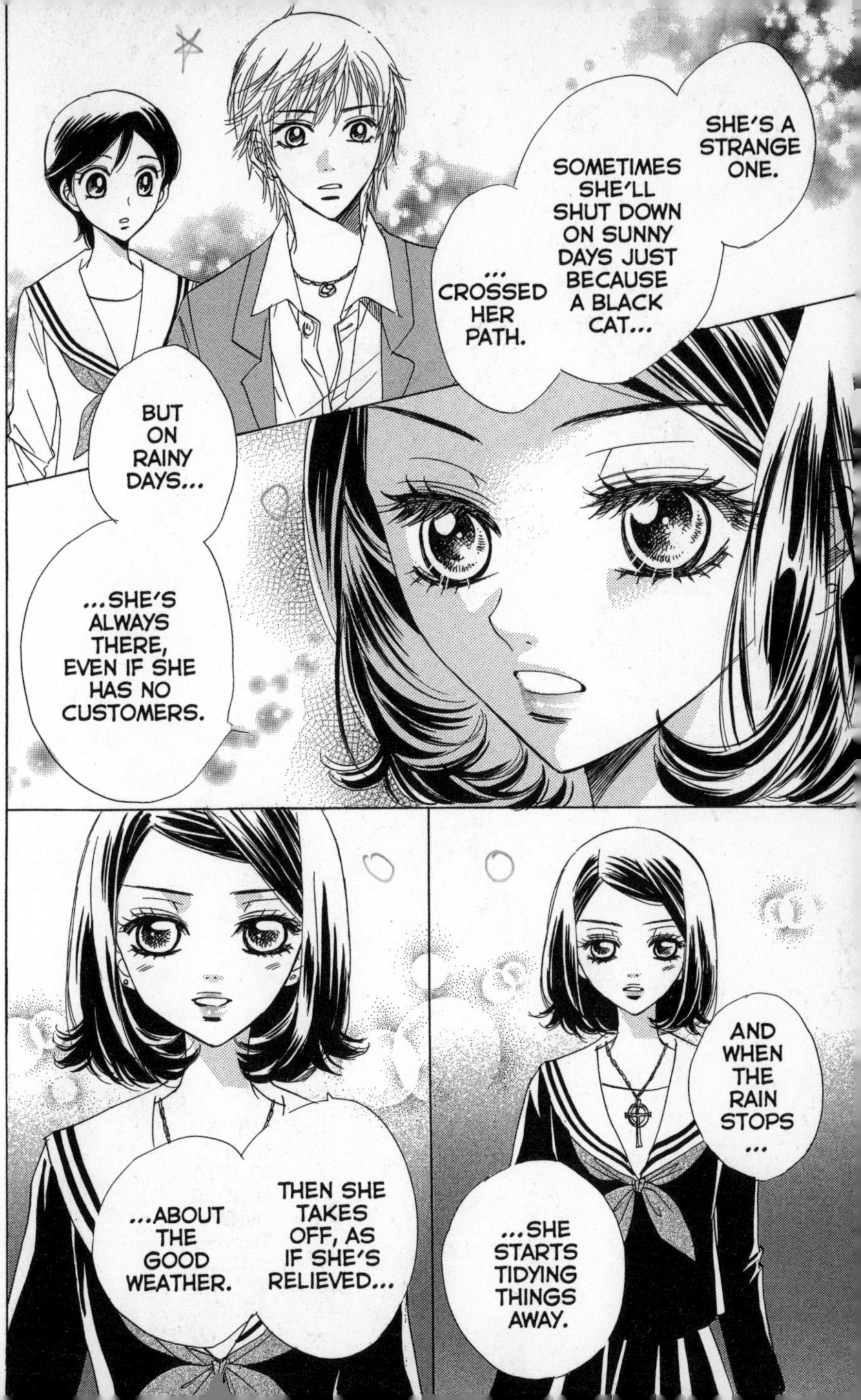
SHE'S A STRANGE ONE.
SOMETIMES SHE'LL SHUT DOWN ON SUNNY DAYS JUST BECAUSE A BLACK CAT...
...CROSSED HER PATH.
BUT ON RAINY DAYS...
...SHE'S ALWAYS THERE, EVEN IF SHE HAS NO CUSTOMERS.
AND WHEN THE RAIN STOPS...
...SHE STARTS TIDYING THINGS AWAY.
THEN SHE TAKES OFF, AS IF SHE'S RELIEVED...
...ABOUT THE GOOD WEATHER.

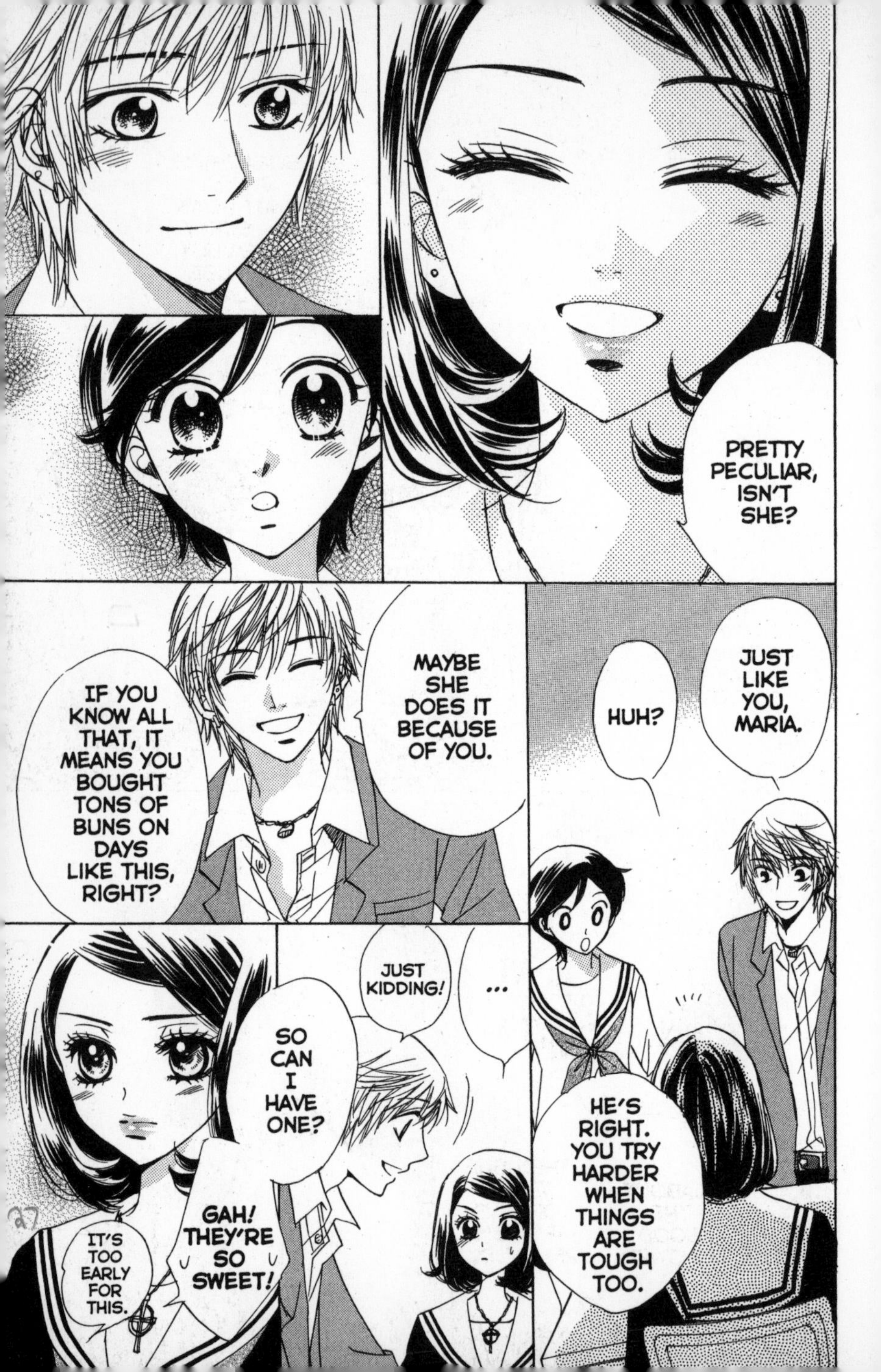
PRETTY PECULIAR, ISN'T SHE?
JUST LIKE YOU, MARIA.
HUH?
HE'S RIGHT. YOU TRY HARDER WHEN THINGS ARE TOUGH TOO.
MAYBE SHE DOES IT BECAUSE OF YOU.
IF YOU KNOW ALL THAT, IT MEANS YOU BOUGHT TONS OF BUNS ON DAYS LIKE THIS, RIGHT?
...
JUST KIDDING!
SO CAN I HAVE ONE?
GAH! THEY'RE SO SWEET!
IT'S TOO EARLY FOR THIS.

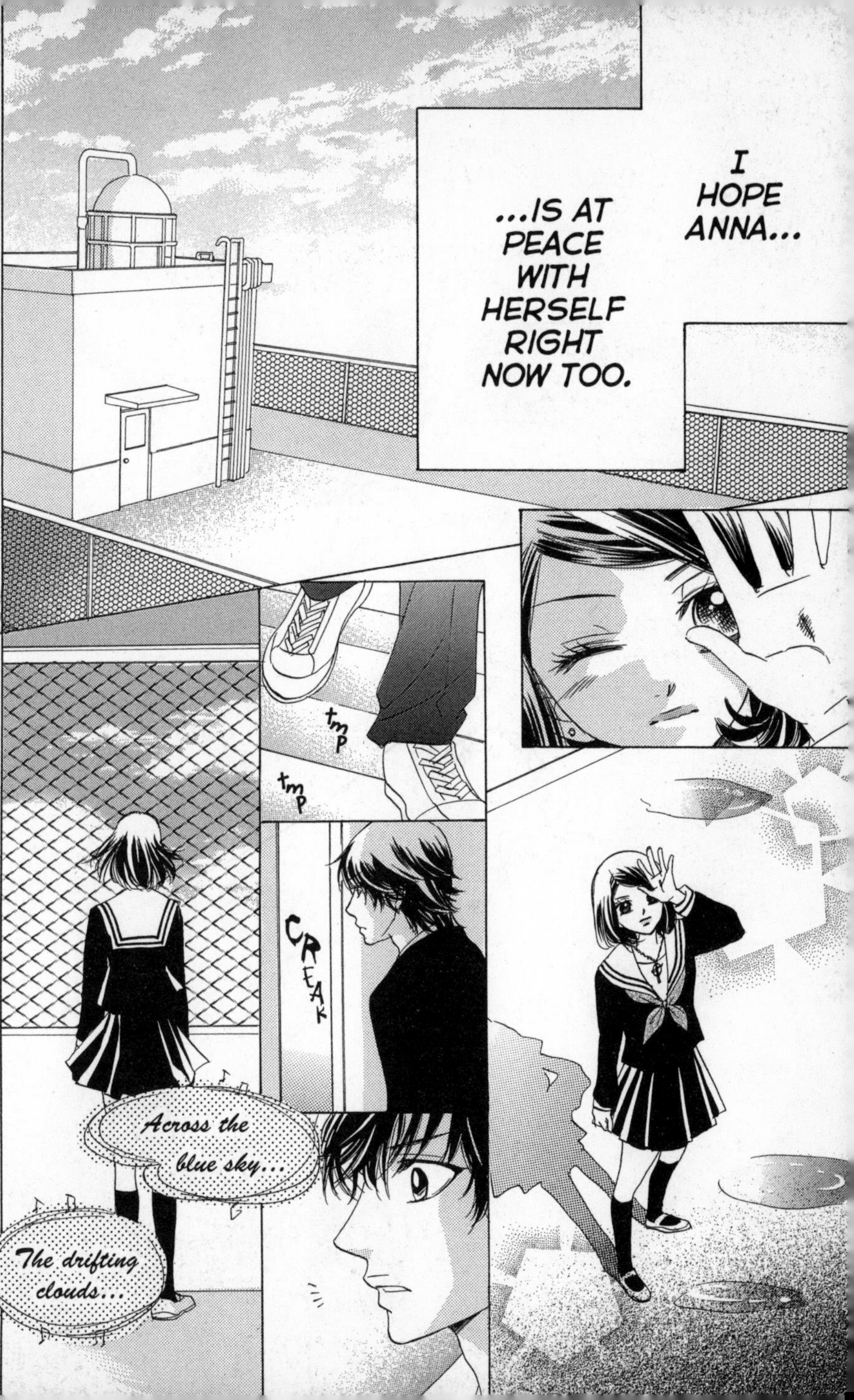
I HOPE ANNA...
...IS AT PEACE WITH HERSELF RIGHT NOW TOO.
tmp
tmp
CREAK
Across the blue sky...
The drifting clouds...

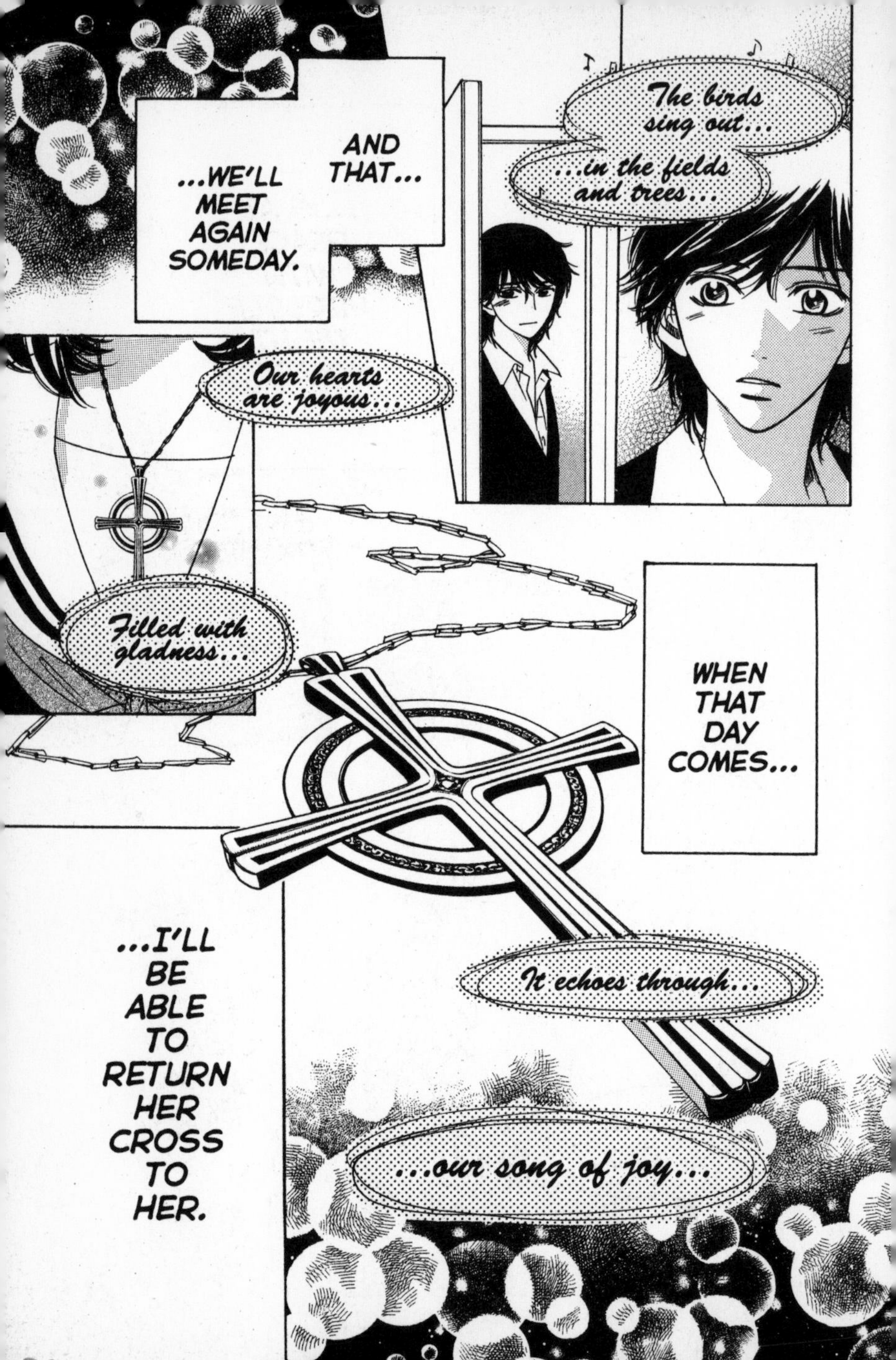
The birds sing out...
...in the fields and trees...
AND THAT...
...WE'LL MEET AGAIN SOMEDAY.
Our hearts are joyous...
Filled with gladness...
WHEN THAT DAY COMES...
It echoes through...
...our song of joy...
...I'LL BE ABLE TO RETURN HER CROSS TO HER.

A Devil and
Her Love Song

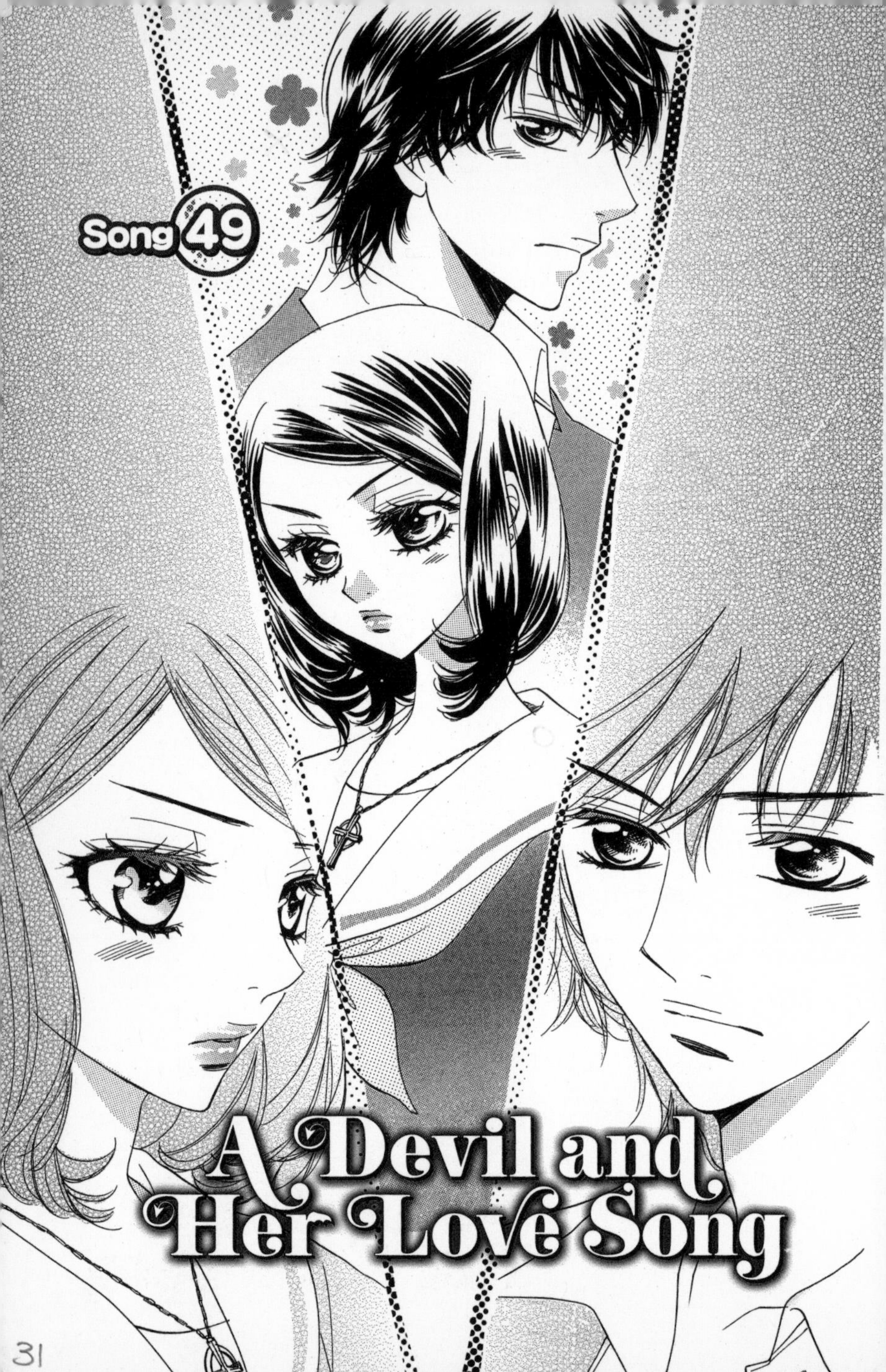
Song 49
A Devil and Her Love Song

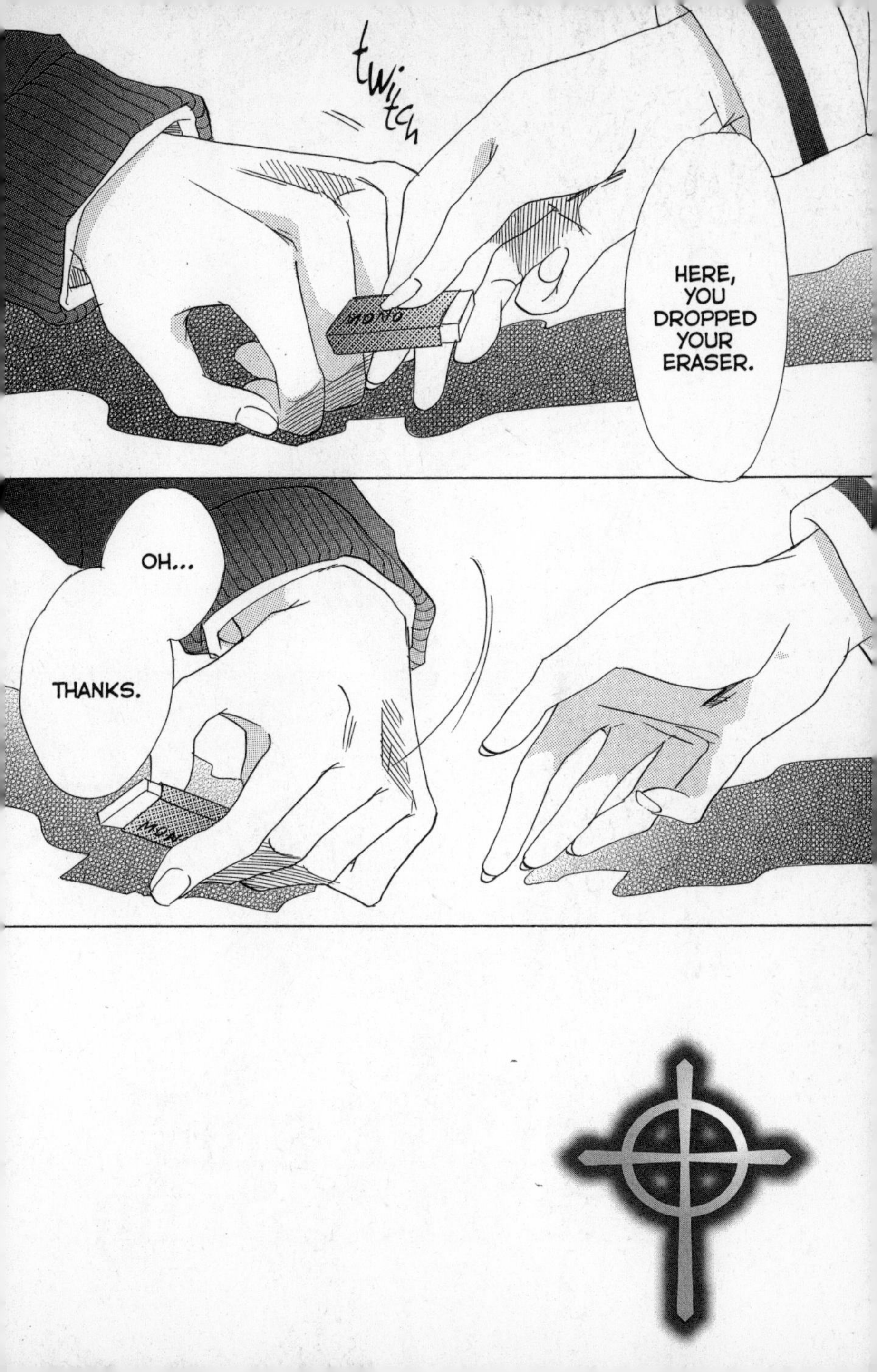
twitch
HERE, YOU DROPPED YOUR ERASER.
OH...
THANKS.

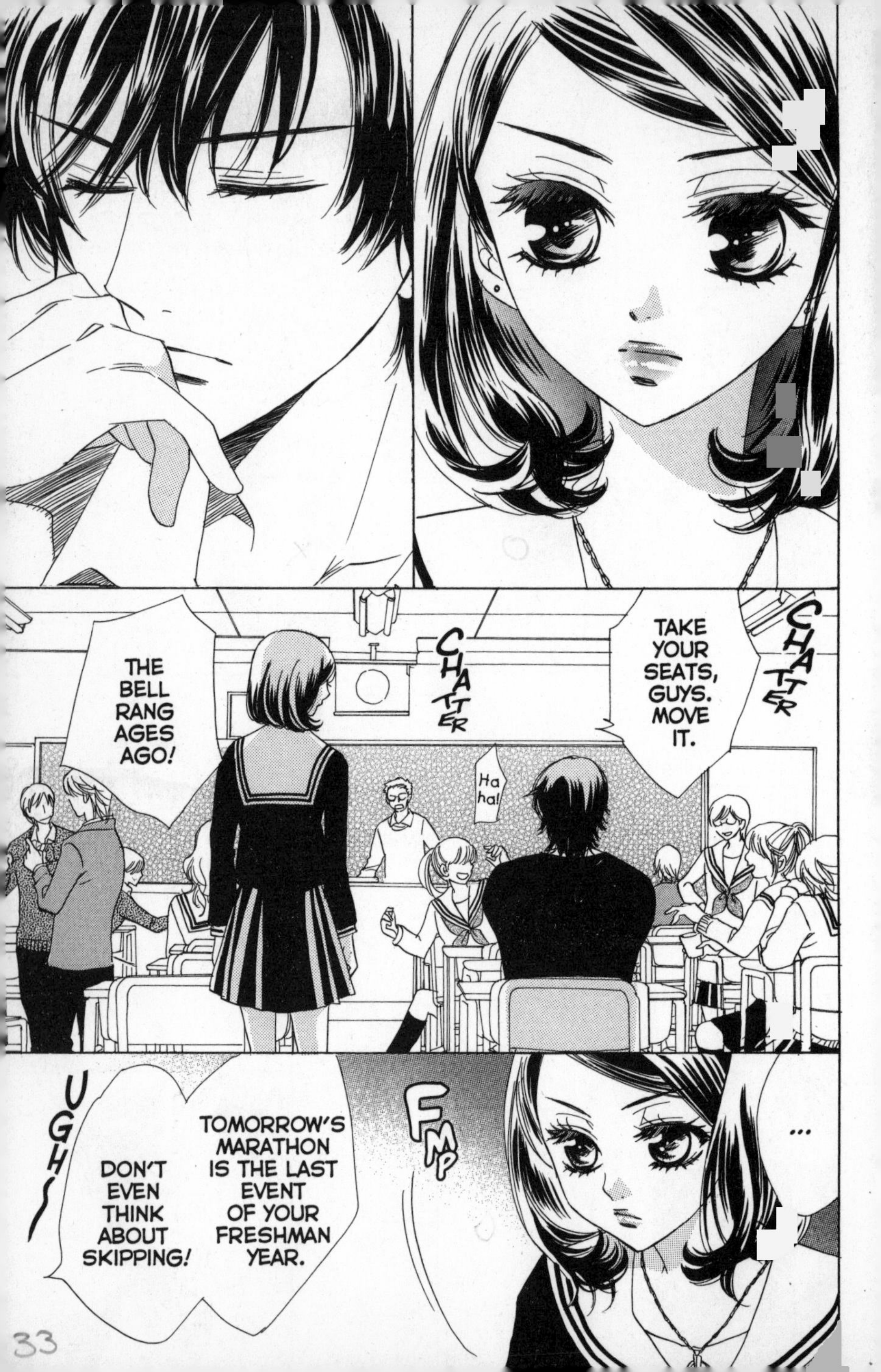
CHATTER
TAKE YOUR SEATS, GUYS. MOVE IT.
CHATTER
Ha ha!
THE BELL RANG AGES AGO!
...
FMP
TOMORROW'S MARATHON IS THE LAST EVENT OF YOUR FRESHMAN YEAR.
DON'T EVEN THINK ABOUT SKIPPING!
UGH~

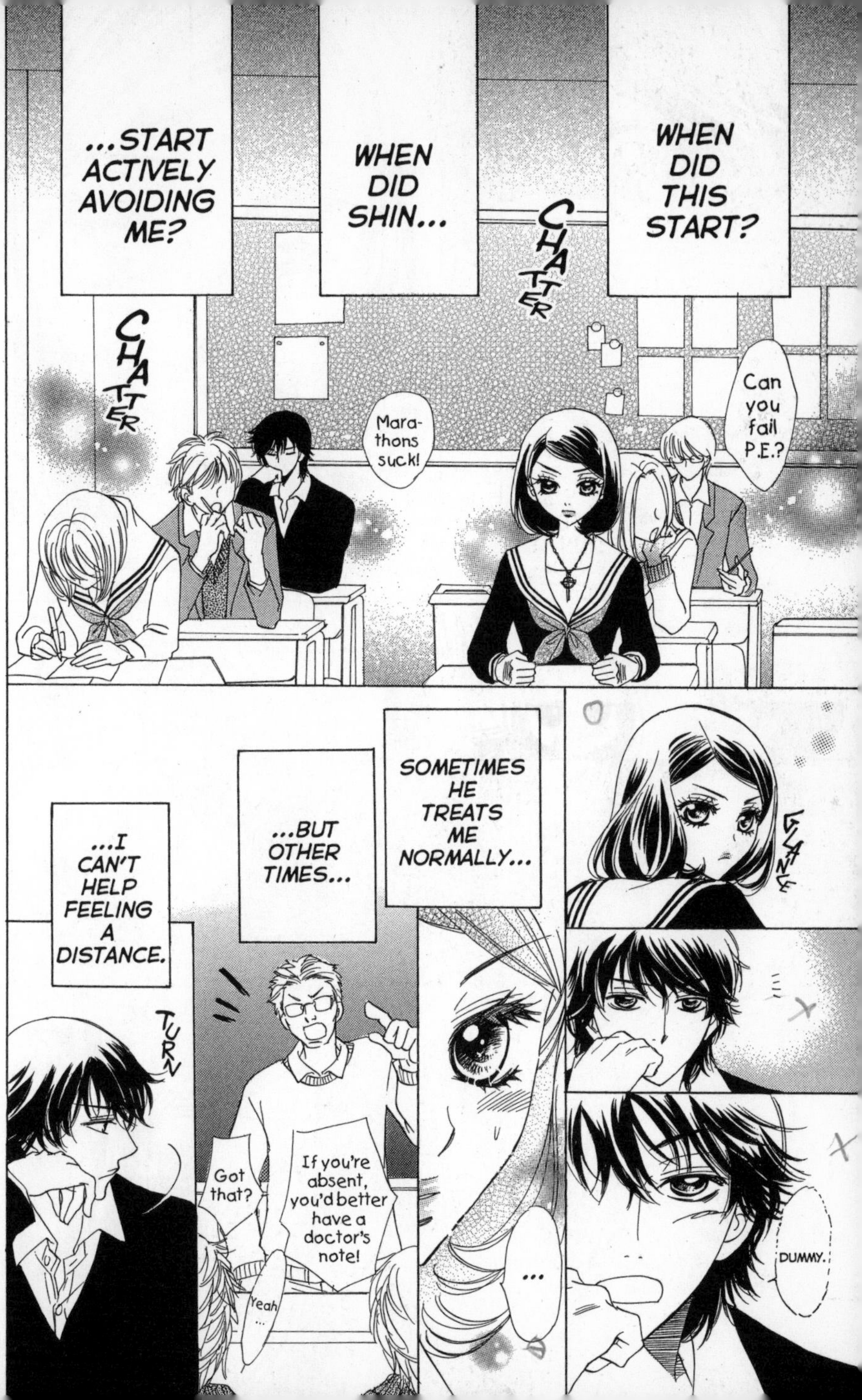
WHEN DID THIS START?
CHATTER
WHEN DID SHIN...
...START ACTIVELY AVOIDING ME?
Can you fail P.E.?
Mara-thons suck!
CHATTER
GLANCE
SOMETIMES HE TREATS ME NORMALLY...
...BUT OTHER TIMES...
...I CAN'T HELP FEELING A DISTANCE.
DUMMY.
...
TURN
If you're absent, you'd better have a doctor's note!
Got that?
Yeah...

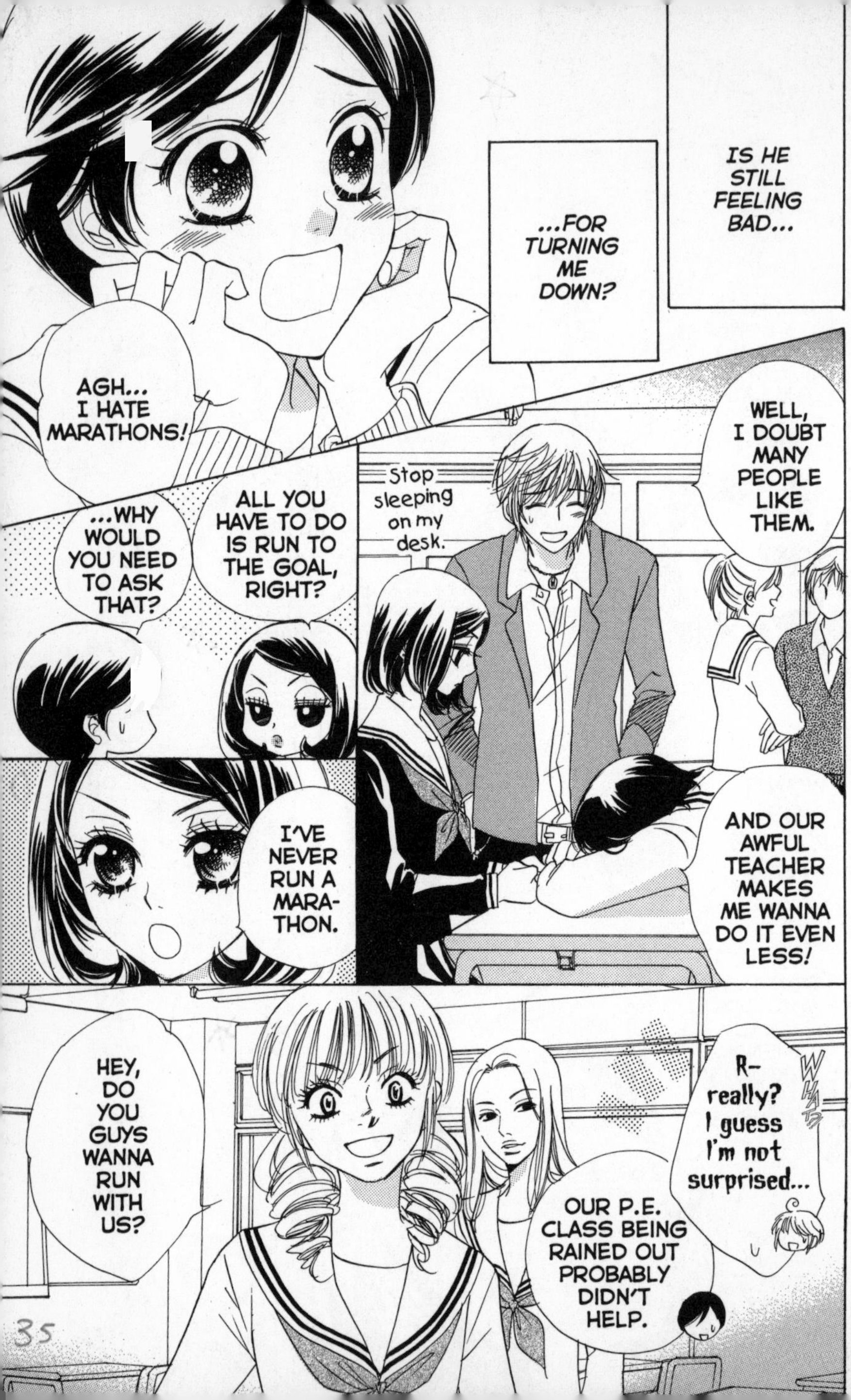
IS HE STILL FEELING BAD...
...FOR TURNING ME DOWN?
AGH... I HATE MARATHONS!
WELL, I DOUBT MANY PEOPLE LIKE THEM.
Stop sleeping on my desk.
AND OUR AWFUL TEACHER MAKES ME WANNA DO IT EVEN LESS!
ALL YOU HAVE TO DO IS RUN TO THE GOAL, RIGHT?
...WHY WOULD YOU NEED TO ASK THAT?
I'VE NEVER RUN A MARA-THON.
WHAT!?
R- really? I guess I'm not surprised...
OUR P.E. CLASS BEING RAINED OUT PROBABLY DIDN'T HELP.
HEY, DO YOU GUYS WANNA RUN WITH US?

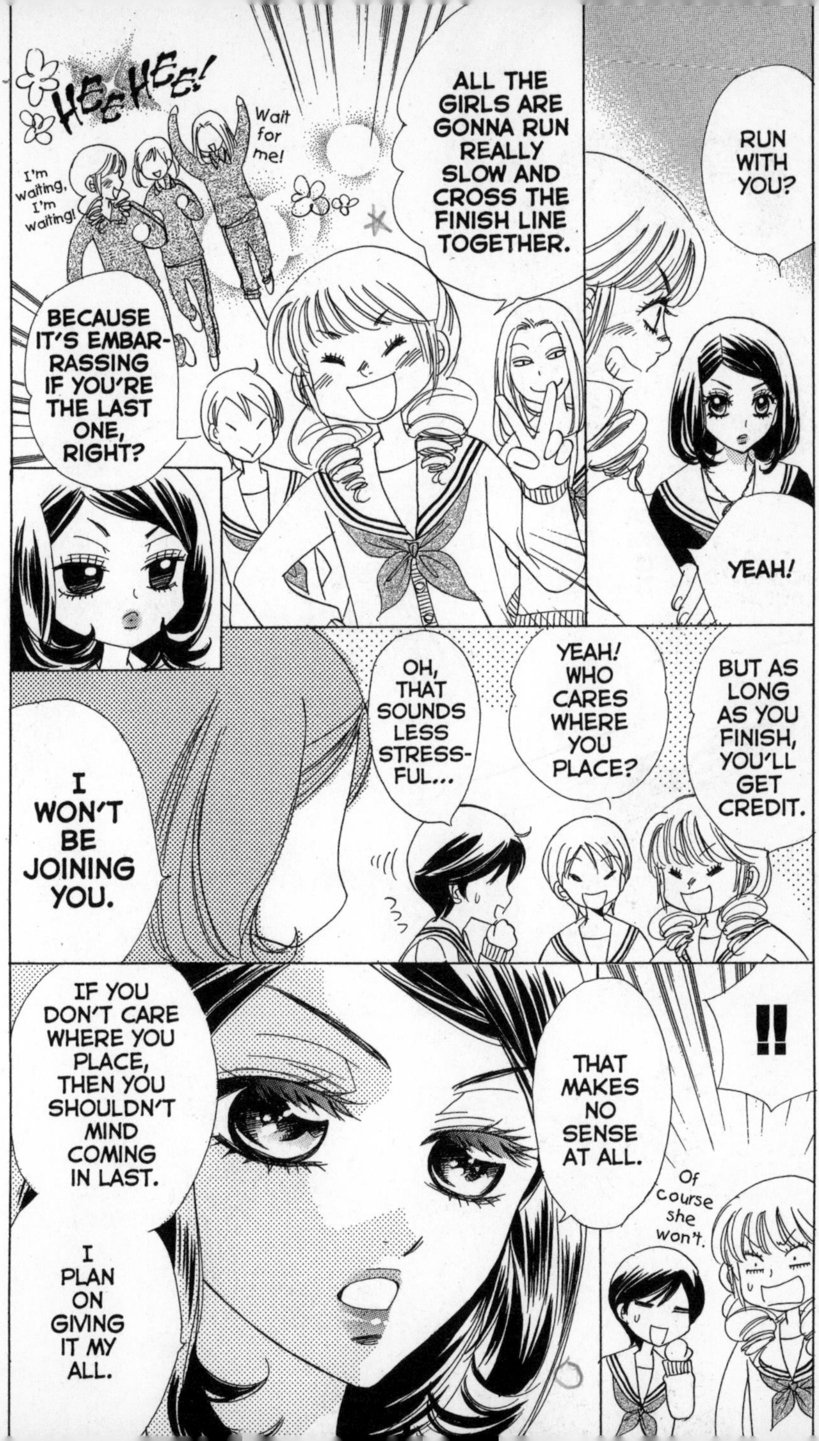
RUN WITH YOU?
YEAH!
ALL THE GIRLS ARE GONNA RUN REALLY SLOW AND CROSS THE FINISH LINE TOGETHER.
HEE HEE!
Wait for me!
I'm waiting, I'm waiting!
BECAUSE IT'S EMBAR-RASSING IF YOU'RE THE LAST ONE, RIGHT?
BUT AS LONG AS YOU FINISH, YOU'LL GET CREDIT.
YEAH! WHO CARES WHERE YOU PLACE?
OH, THAT SOUNDS LESS STRESS-FUL...
I WON'T BE JOINING YOU.
!!
Of course she won't.
THAT MAKES NO SENSE AT ALL.
IF YOU DON'T CARE WHERE YOU PLACE, THEN YOU SHOULDN'T MIND COMING IN LAST.
I PLAN ON GIVING IT MY ALL.

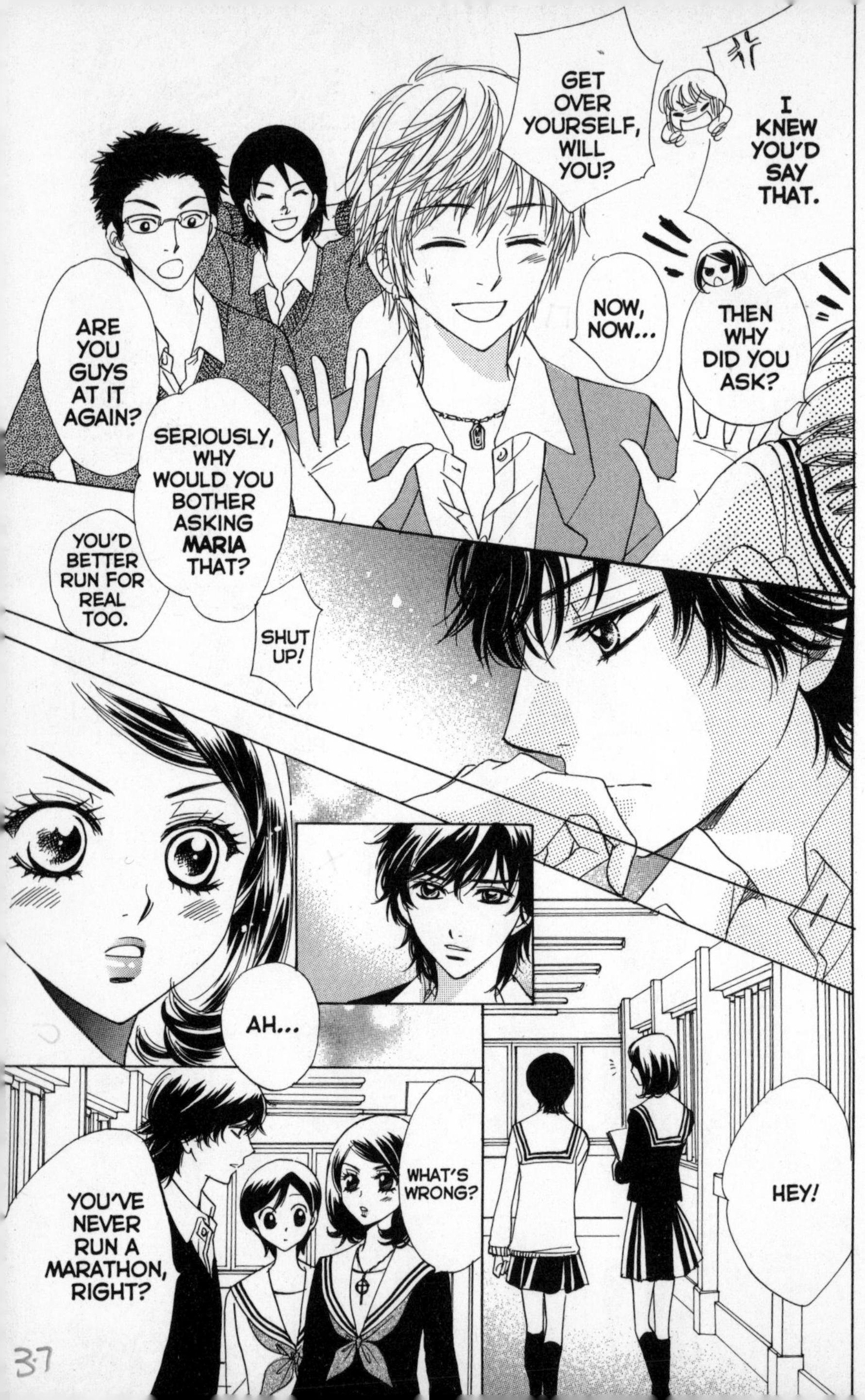
I KNEW YOU'D SAY THAT.
GET OVER YOURSELF, WILL YOU?
THEN WHY DID YOU ASK?
NOW, NOW...
ARE YOU GUYS AT IT AGAIN?
SERIOUSLY, WHY WOULD YOU BOTHER ASKING MARIA THAT?
SHUT UP!
YOU'D BETTER RUN FOR REAL TOO.
AH...
HEY!
WHAT'S WRONG?
YOU'VE NEVER RUN A MARATHON, RIGHT?

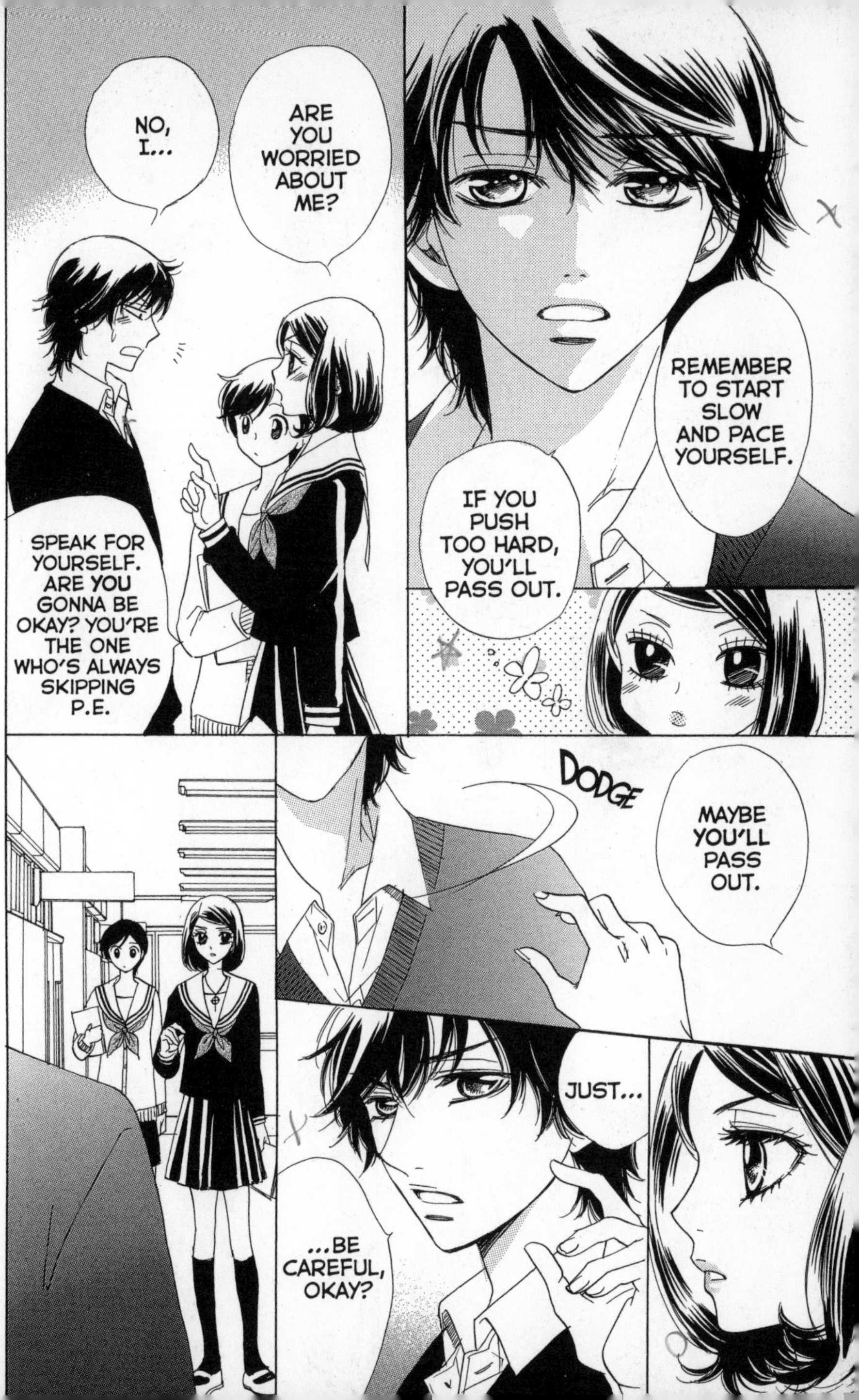
REMEMBER TO START SLOW AND PACE YOURSELF.
IF YOU PUSH TOO HARD, YOU'LL PASS OUT.
ARE YOU WORRIED ABOUT ME?
NO, I...
SPEAK FOR YOURSELF. ARE YOU GONNA BE OKAY? YOU'RE THE ONE WHO'S ALWAYS SKIPPING P.E.
MAYBE YOU'LL PASS OUT.
DODGE
JUST...
...BE CAREFUL, OKAY?

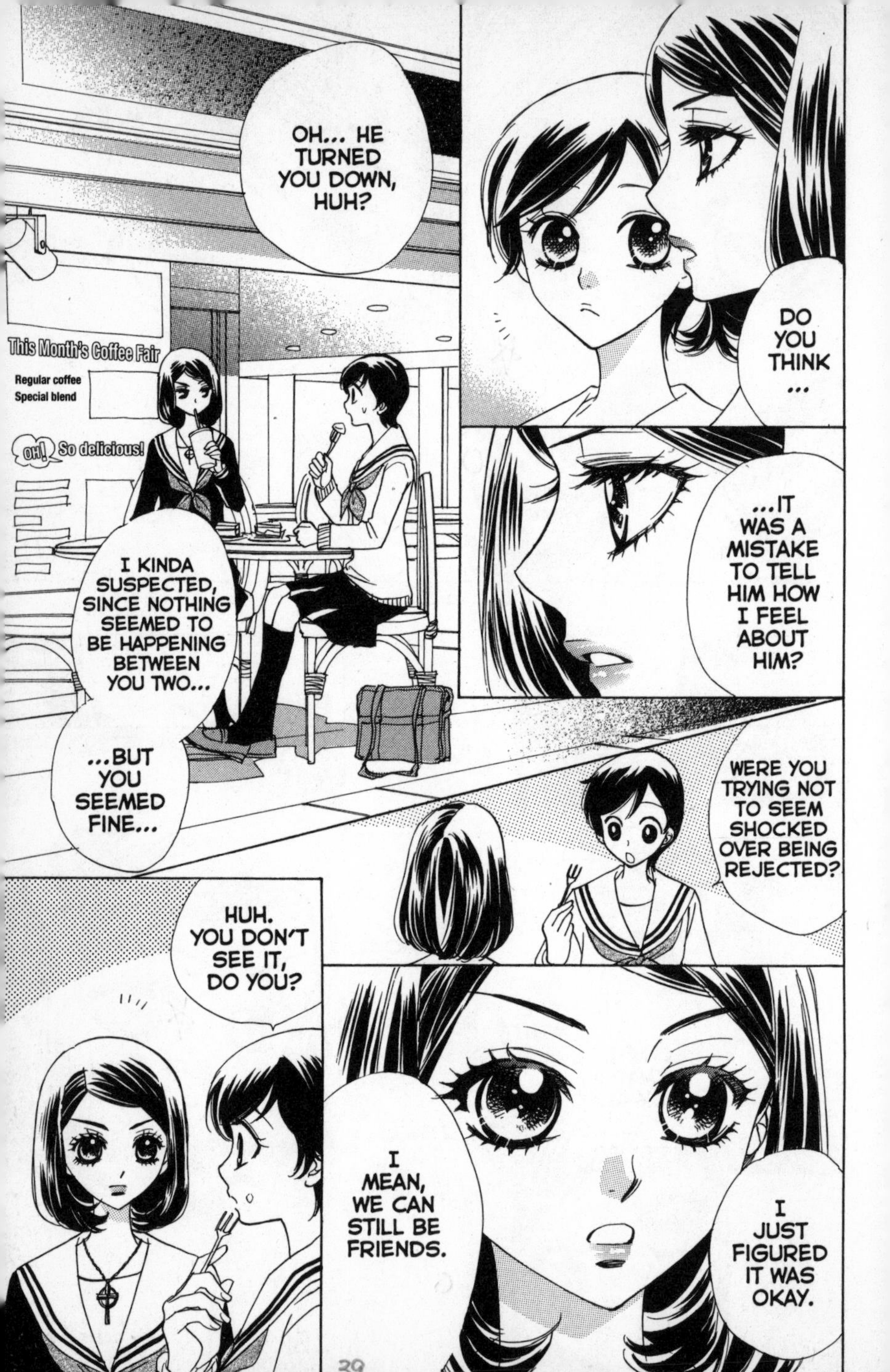
DO YOU THINK ...
...IT WAS A MISTAKE TO TELL HIM HOW I FEEL ABOUT HIM?
OH... HE TURNED YOU DOWN, HUH?
This Month's Coffee Fair
Regular coffee
Special blend
OH! So delicious!
I KINDA SUSPECTED, SINCE NOTHING SEEMED TO BE HAPPENING BETWEEN YOU TWO...
...BUT YOU SEEMED FINE...
WERE YOU TRYING NOT TO SEEM SHOCKED OVER BEING REJECTED?
I JUST FIGURED IT WAS OKAY.
I MEAN, WE CAN STILL BE FRIENDS.
HUH. YOU DON'T SEE IT, DO YOU?

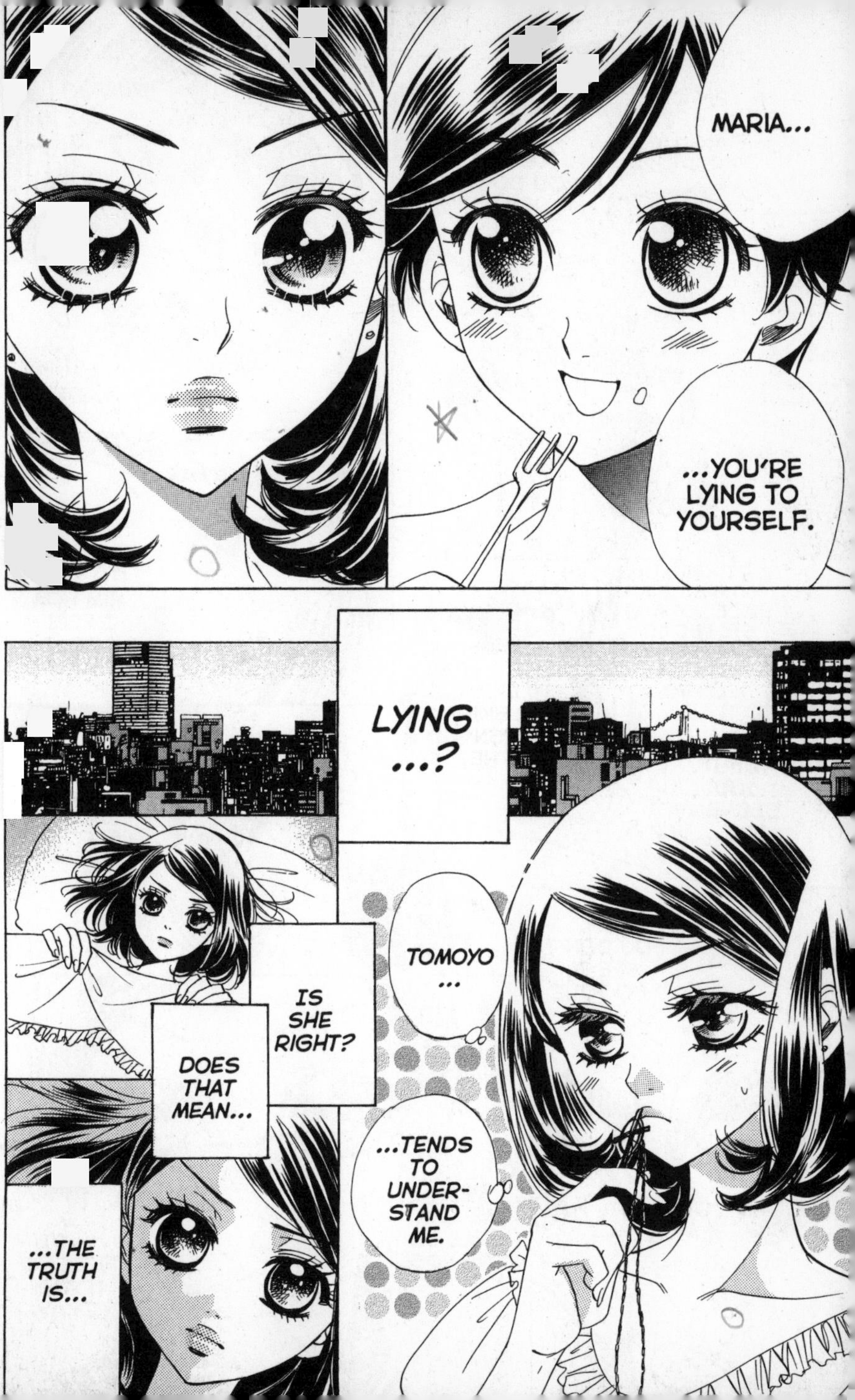
MARIA...
...YOU'RE LYING TO YOURSELF.
LYING ...?
TOMOYO ...
...TENDS TO UNDER-STAND ME.
IS SHE RIGHT?
DOES THAT MEAN...
...THE TRUTH IS...

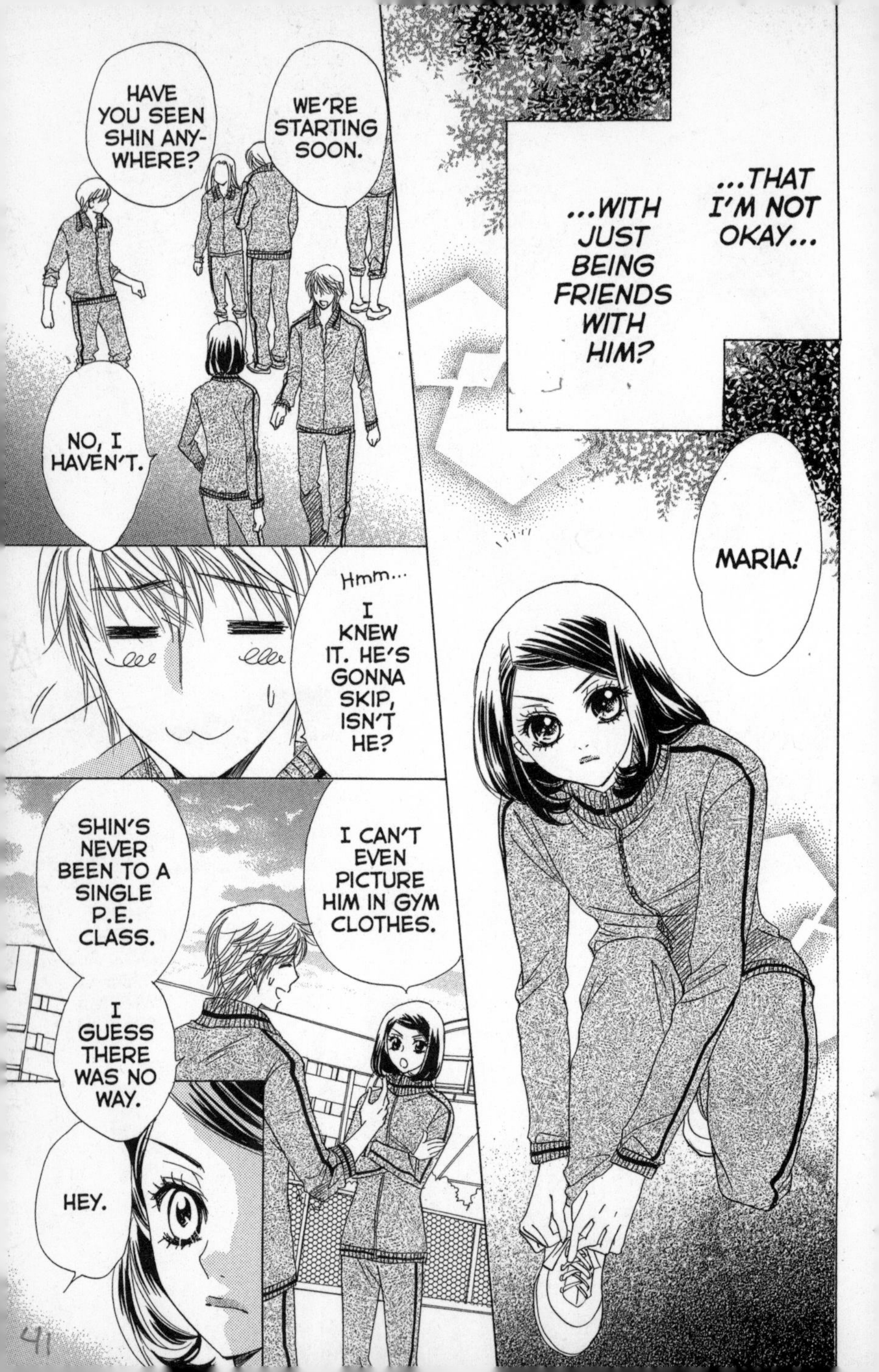
...THAT I'M NOT OKAY...
...WITH JUST BEING FRIENDS WITH HIM?
MARIA!
WE'RE STARTING SOON.
HAVE YOU SEEN SHIN ANY-WHERE?
NO, I HAVEN'T.
Hmm...
I KNEW IT. HE'S GONNA SKIP, ISN'T HE?
I CAN'T EVEN PICTURE HIM IN GYM CLOTHES.
SHIN'S NEVER BEEN TO A SINGLE P.E. CLASS.
I GUESS THERE WAS NO WAY.
HEY.

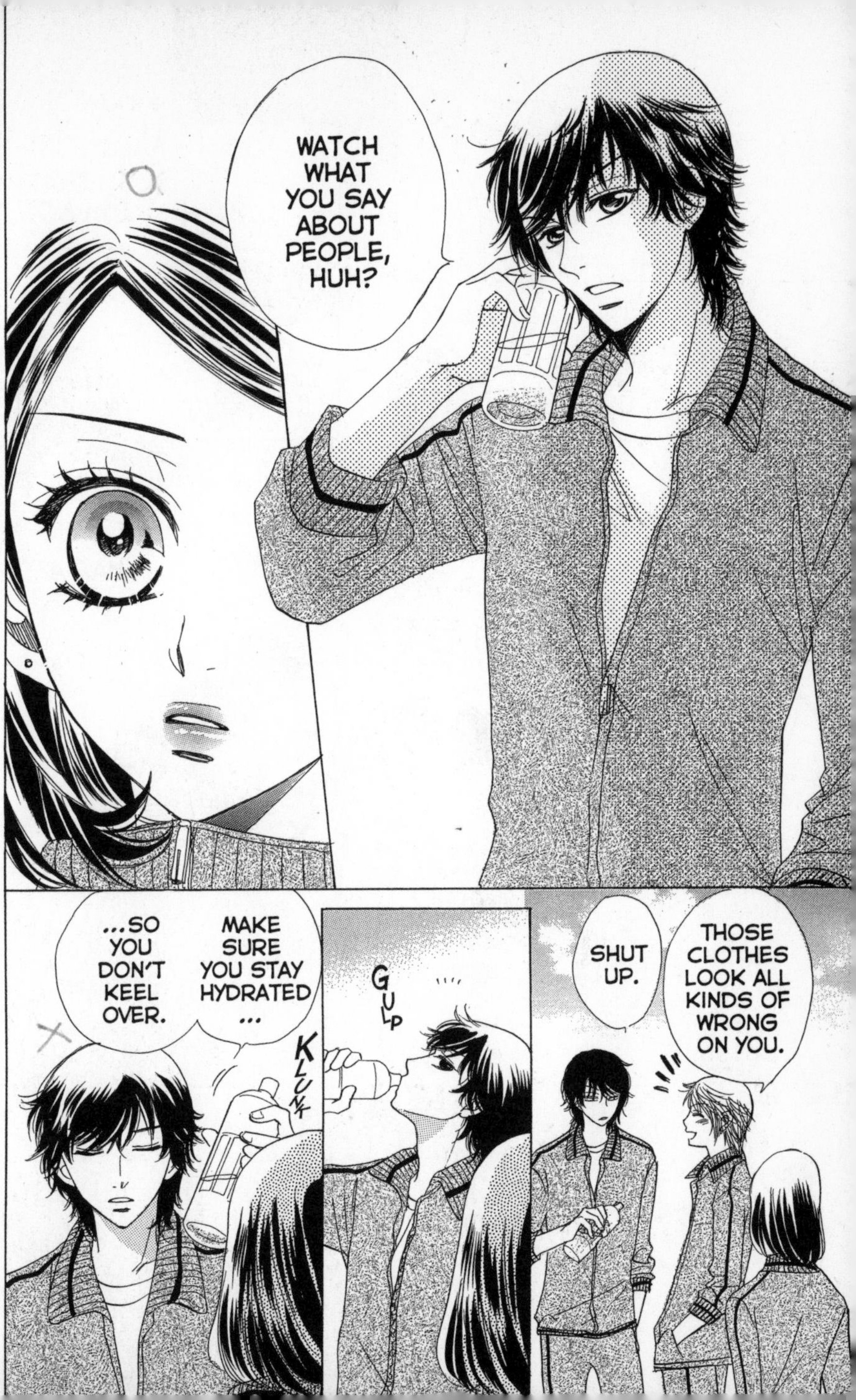
WATCH WHAT YOU SAY ABOUT PEOPLE, HUH?
THOSE CLOTHES LOOK ALL KINDS OF WRONG ON YOU.
SHUT UP.
GULP
MAKE SURE YOU STAY HYDRATED...
...SO YOU DON'T KEEL OVER.
KLUNK

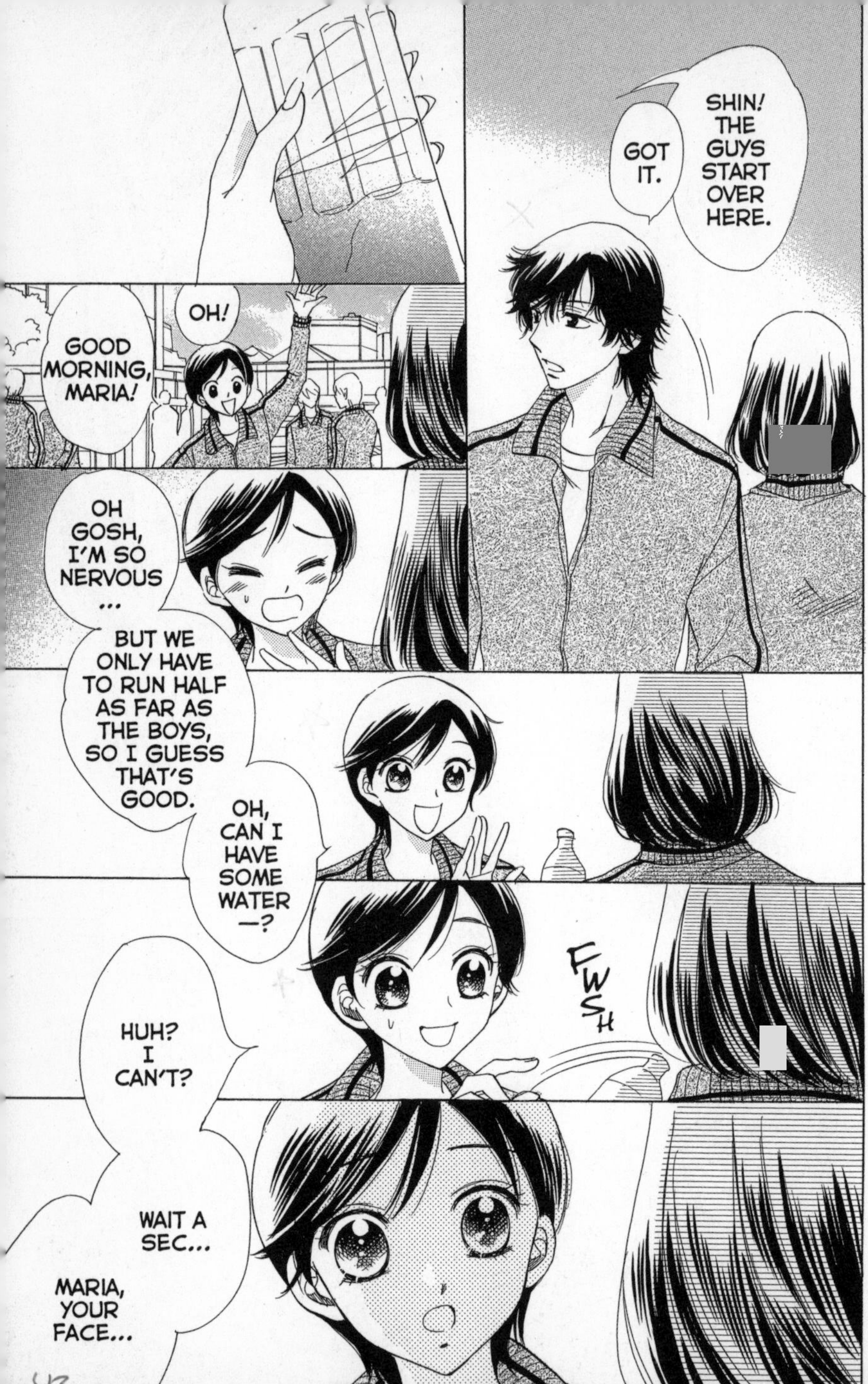
SHIN! THE GUYS START OVER HERE.
GOT IT.
OH!
GOOD MORNING, MARIA!
OH GOSH, I'M SO NERVOUS ...
BUT WE ONLY HAVE TO RUN HALF AS FAR AS THE BOYS, SO I GUESS THAT'S GOOD.
OH, CAN I HAVE SOME WATER —?
FWSH
HUH? I CAN'T?
WAIT A SEC...
MARIA, YOUR FACE...

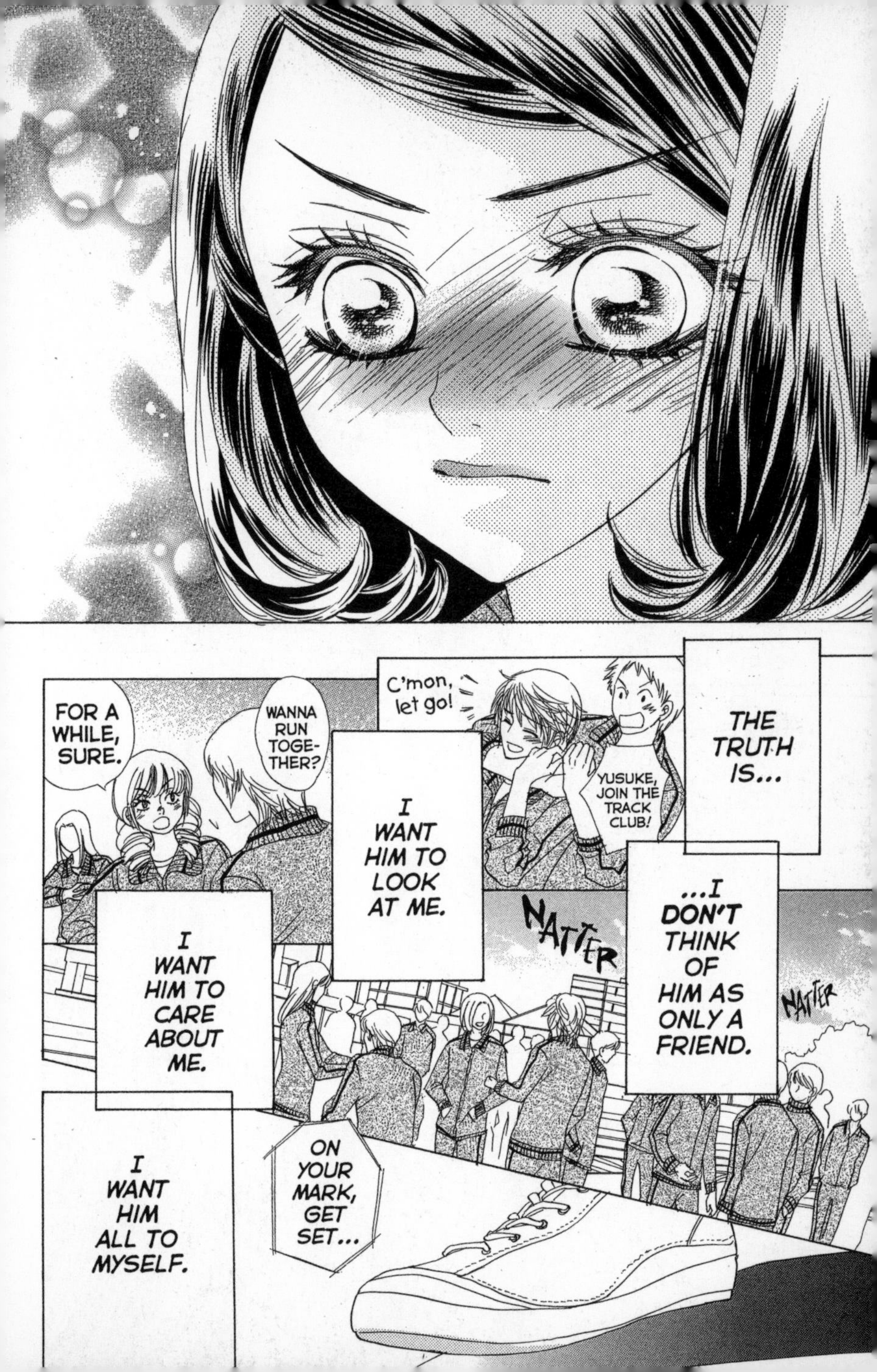
THE TRUTH IS...
YUSUKE, JOIN THE TRACK CLUB!
C'mon, let go!
I WANT HIM TO LOOK AT ME.
WANNA RUN TOGE-THER?
FOR A WHILE, SURE.
...I DON'T THINK OF HIM AS ONLY A FRIEND.
NATTER
NATTER
I WANT HIM TO CARE ABOUT ME.
ON YOUR MARK, GET SET...
I WANT HIM ALL TO MYSELF.

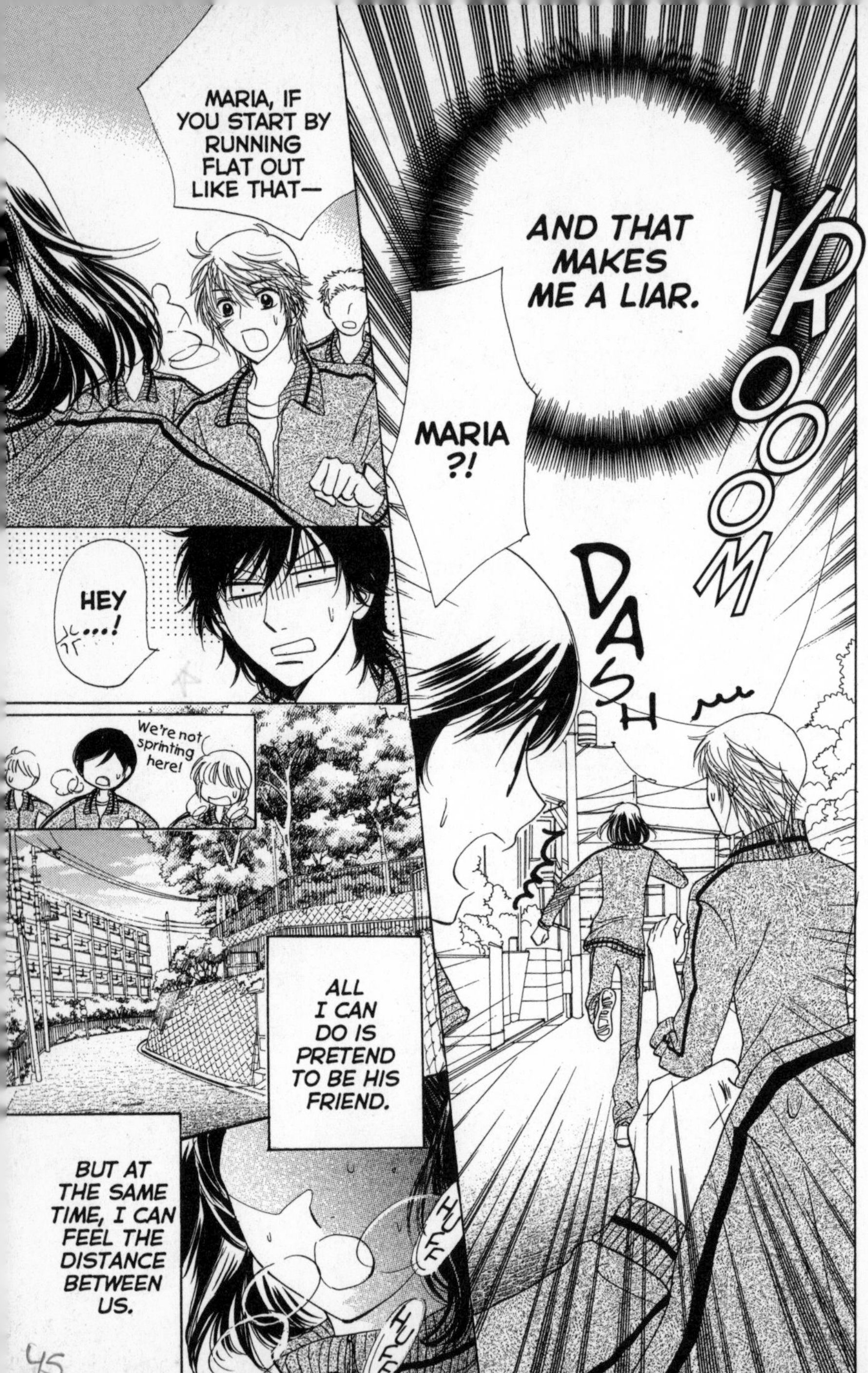
AND THAT MAKES ME A LIAR.
VROOOOM
MARIA ?!
DASH
MARIA, IF YOU START BY RUNNING FLAT OUT LIKE THAT—
HEY...!
We're not sprinting here!
ALL I CAN DO IS PRETEND TO BE HIS FRIEND.
BUT AT THE SAME TIME, I CAN FEEL THE DISTANCE BETWEEN US.
HUFF
HUFF

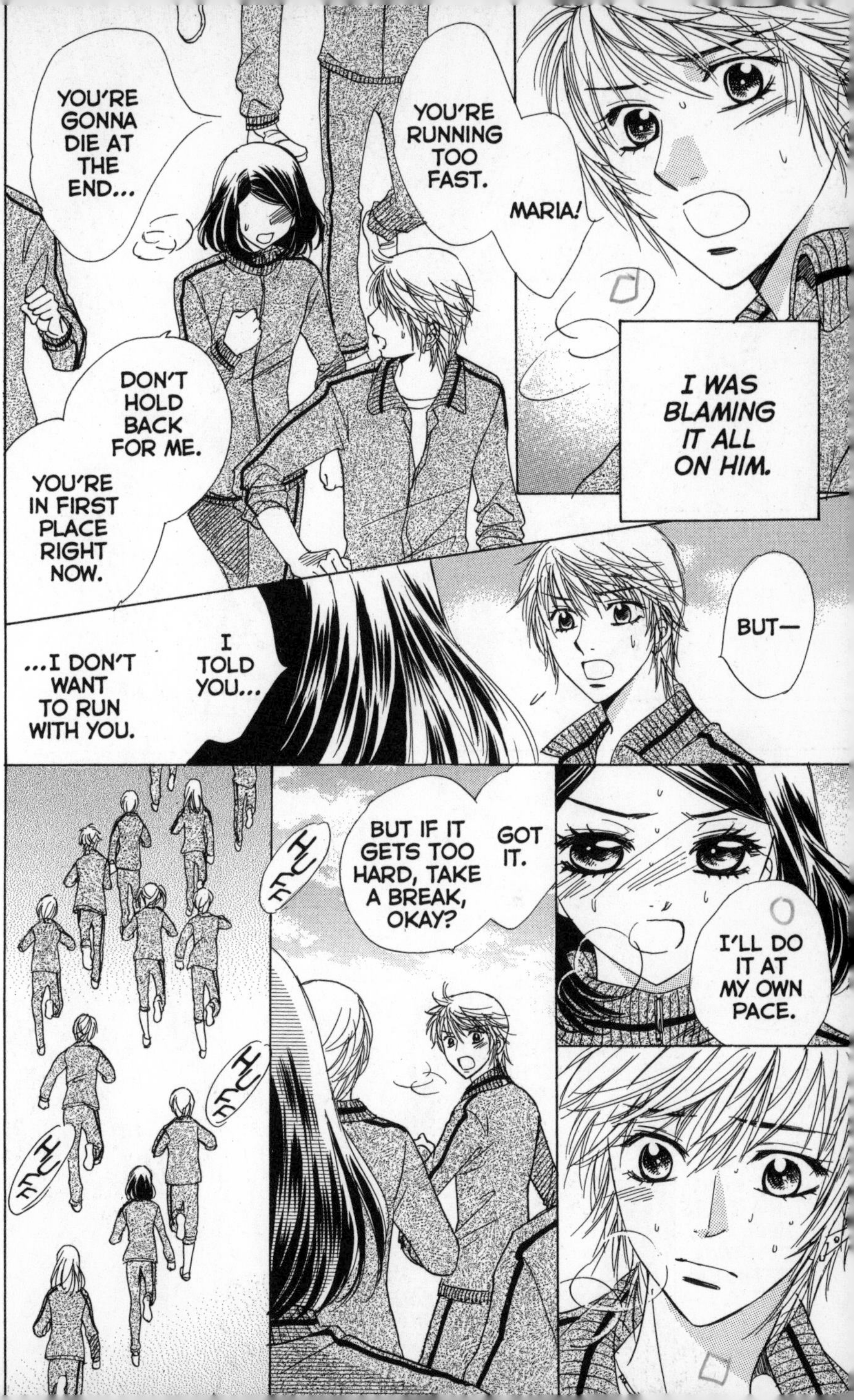
MARIA!
I WAS BLAMING IT ALL ON HIM.
YOU'RE RUNNING TOO FAST.
YOU'RE GONNA DIE AT THE END...
DON'T HOLD BACK FOR ME.
YOU'RE IN FIRST PLACE RIGHT NOW.
BUT—
I TOLD YOU...
...I DON'T WANT TO RUN WITH YOU.
I'LL DO IT AT MY OWN PACE.
GOT IT.
BUT IF IT GETS TOO HARD, TAKE A BREAK, OKAY?
HUFF
HUFF
HUFF

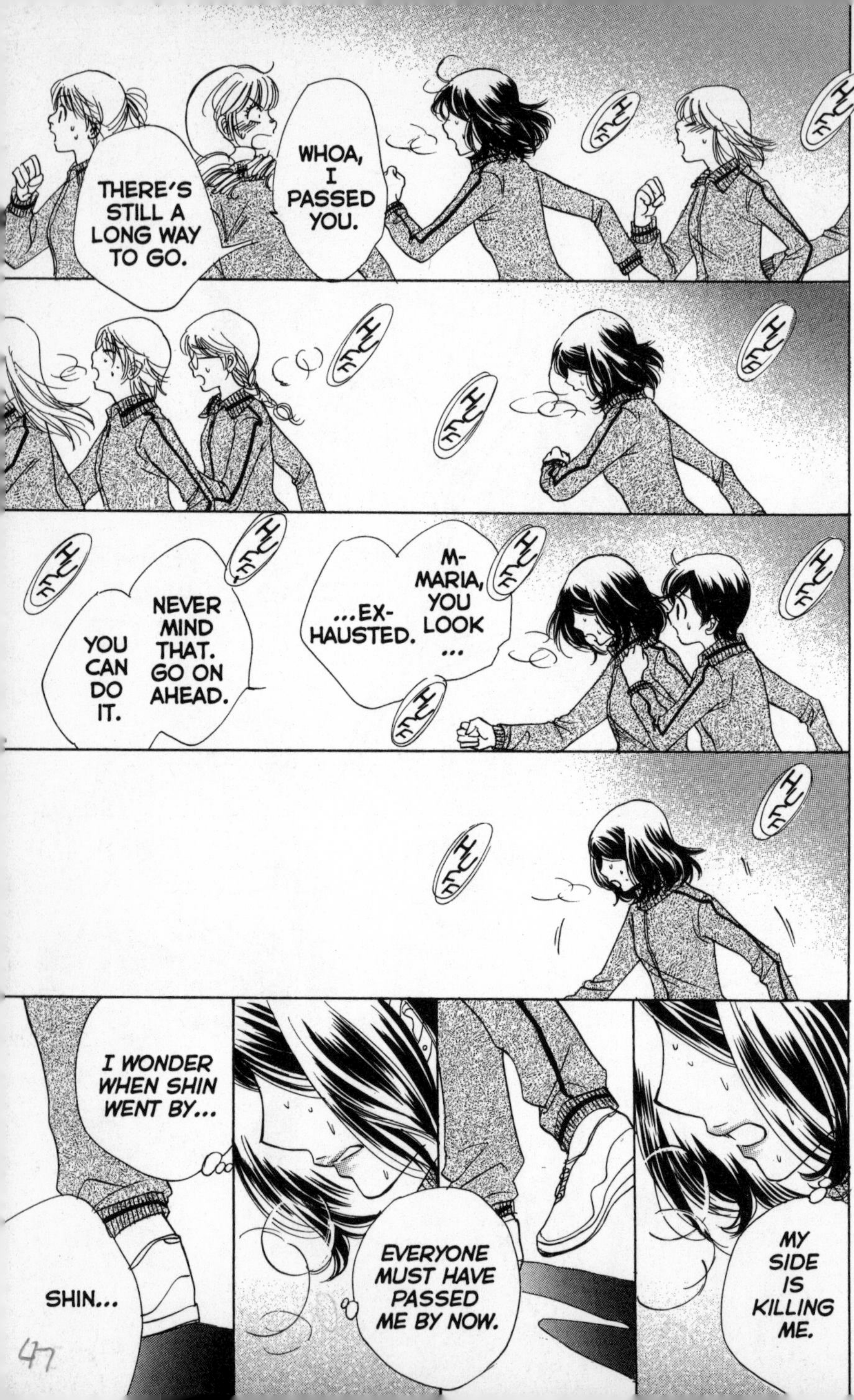
HUFF
HUFF
WHOA, I PASSED YOU.
THERE'S STILL A LONG WAY TO GO.
HUFF
HUFF
HUFF
HUFF
HUFF
M-MARIA, YOU LOOK ...
...EX-HAUSTED.
HUFF
HUFF
NEVER MIND THAT. GO ON AHEAD.
YOU CAN DO IT.
HUFF
HUFF
HUFF
MY SIDE IS KILLING ME.
EVERYONE MUST HAVE PASSED ME BY NOW.
I WONDER WHEN SHIN WENT BY...
SHIN...

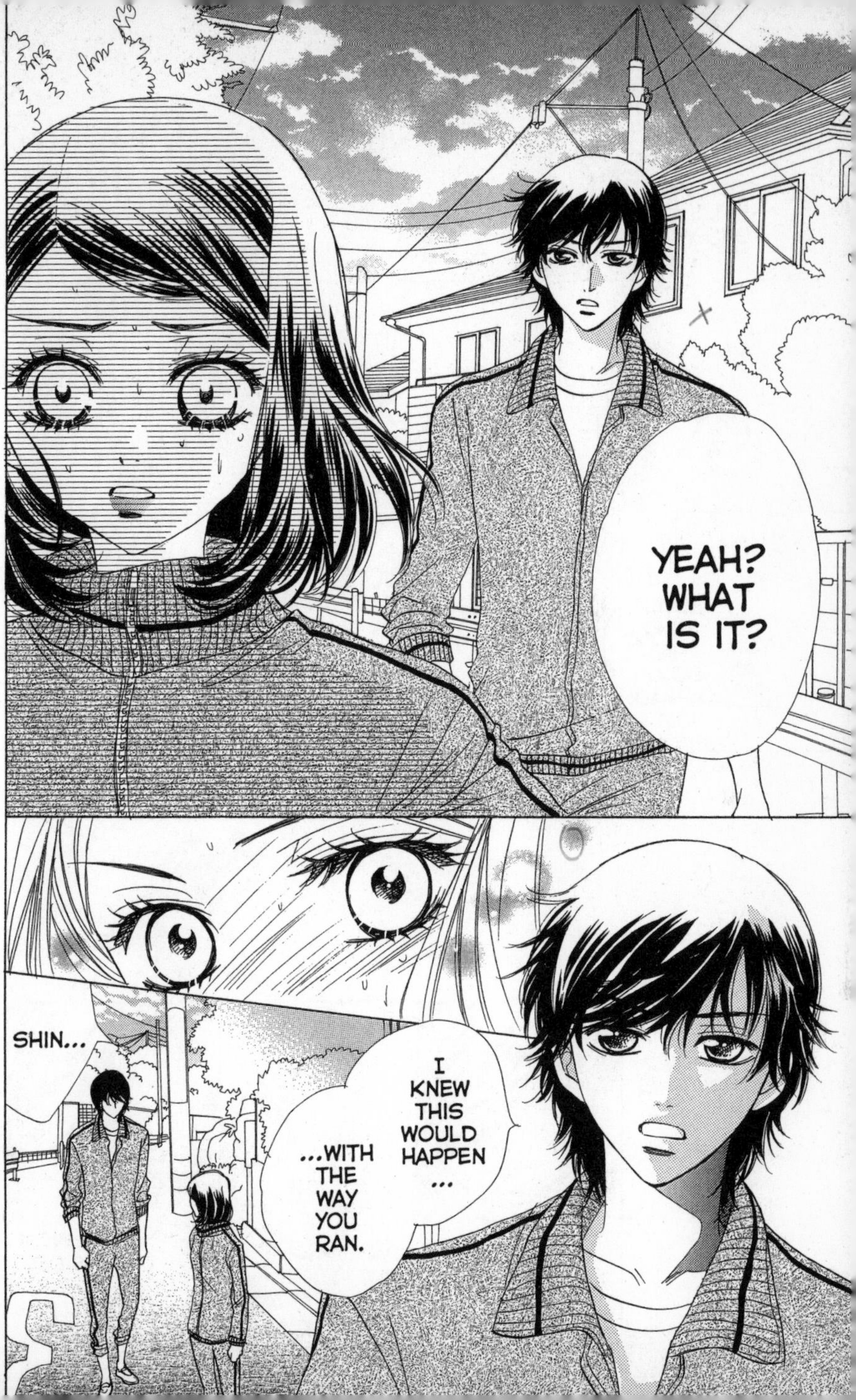
YEAH? WHAT IS IT?
I KNEW THIS WOULD HAPPEN...
...WITH THE WAY YOU RAN.
SHIN...

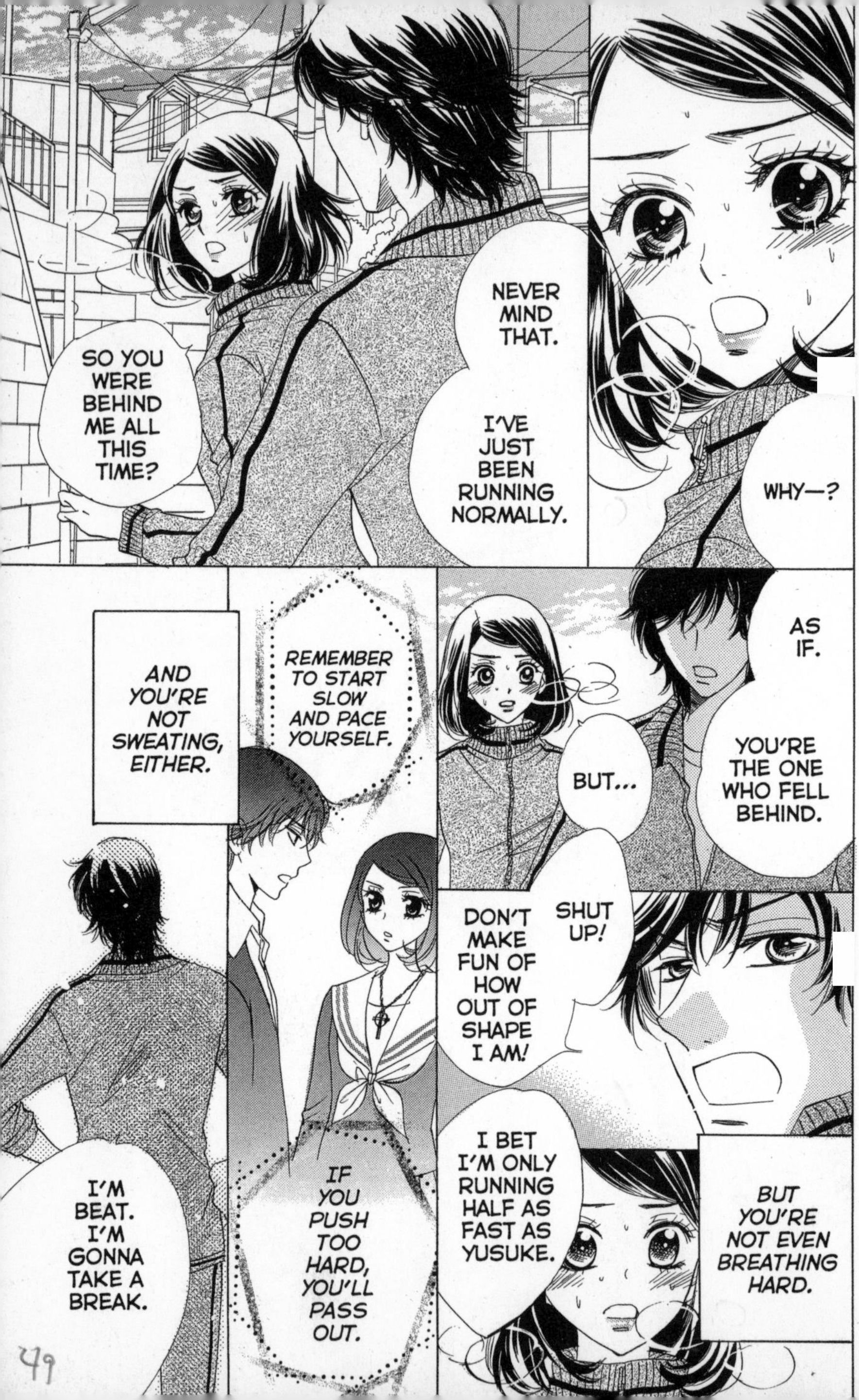
WHY—?
NEVER MIND THAT.
I'VE JUST BEEN RUNNING NORMALLY.
SO YOU WERE BEHIND ME ALL THIS TIME?
AS IF.
YOU'RE THE ONE WHO FELL BEHIND.
BUT...
SHUT UP!
DON'T MAKE FUN OF HOW OUT OF SHAPE I AM!
BUT YOU'RE NOT EVEN BREATHING HARD.
I BET I'M ONLY RUNNING HALF AS FAST AS YUSUKE.
REMEMBER TO START SLOW AND PACE YOURSELF.
IF YOU PUSH TOO HARD, YOU'LL PASS OUT.
AND YOU'RE NOT SWEATING, EITHER.
I'M BEAT. I'M GONNA TAKE A BREAK.

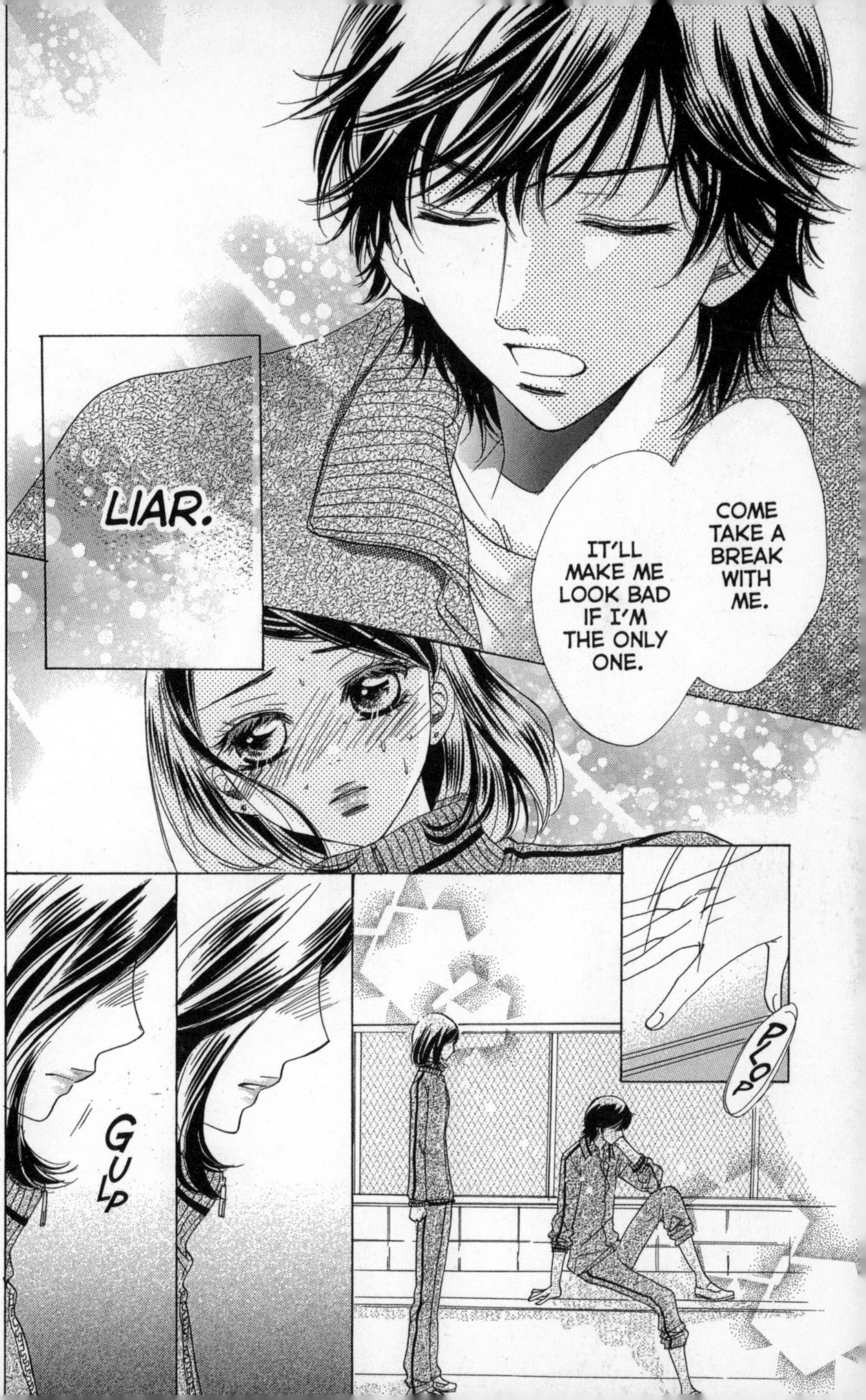
COME TAKE A BREAK WITH ME.
IT'LL MAKE ME LOOK BAD IF I'M THE ONLY ONE.
LIAR.
PLOP
GULP

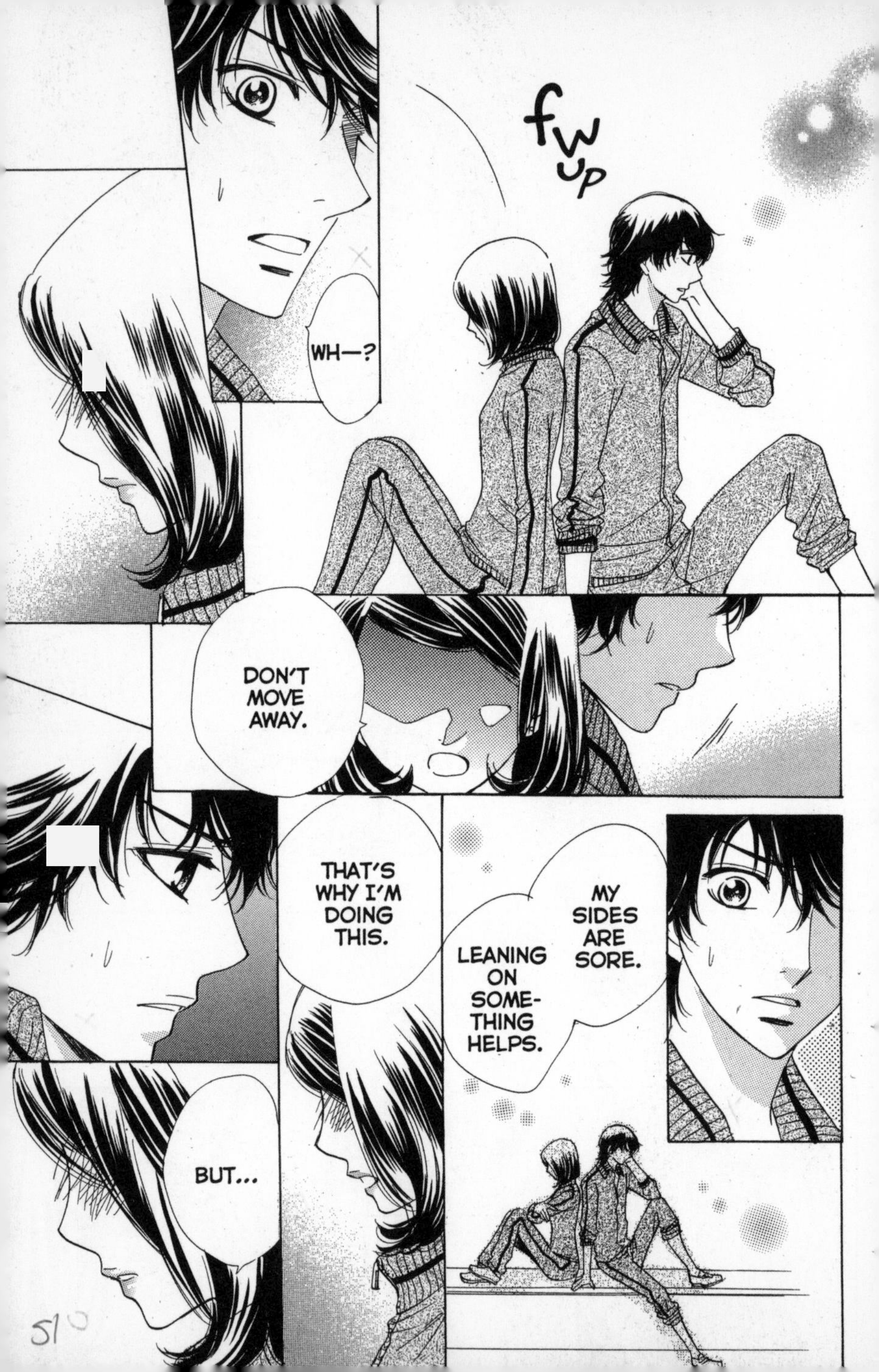
fwup
WH—?
DON'T MOVE AWAY.
MY SIDES ARE SORE.
LEANING ON SOME-THING HELPS.
THAT'S WHY I'M DOING THIS.
BUT...

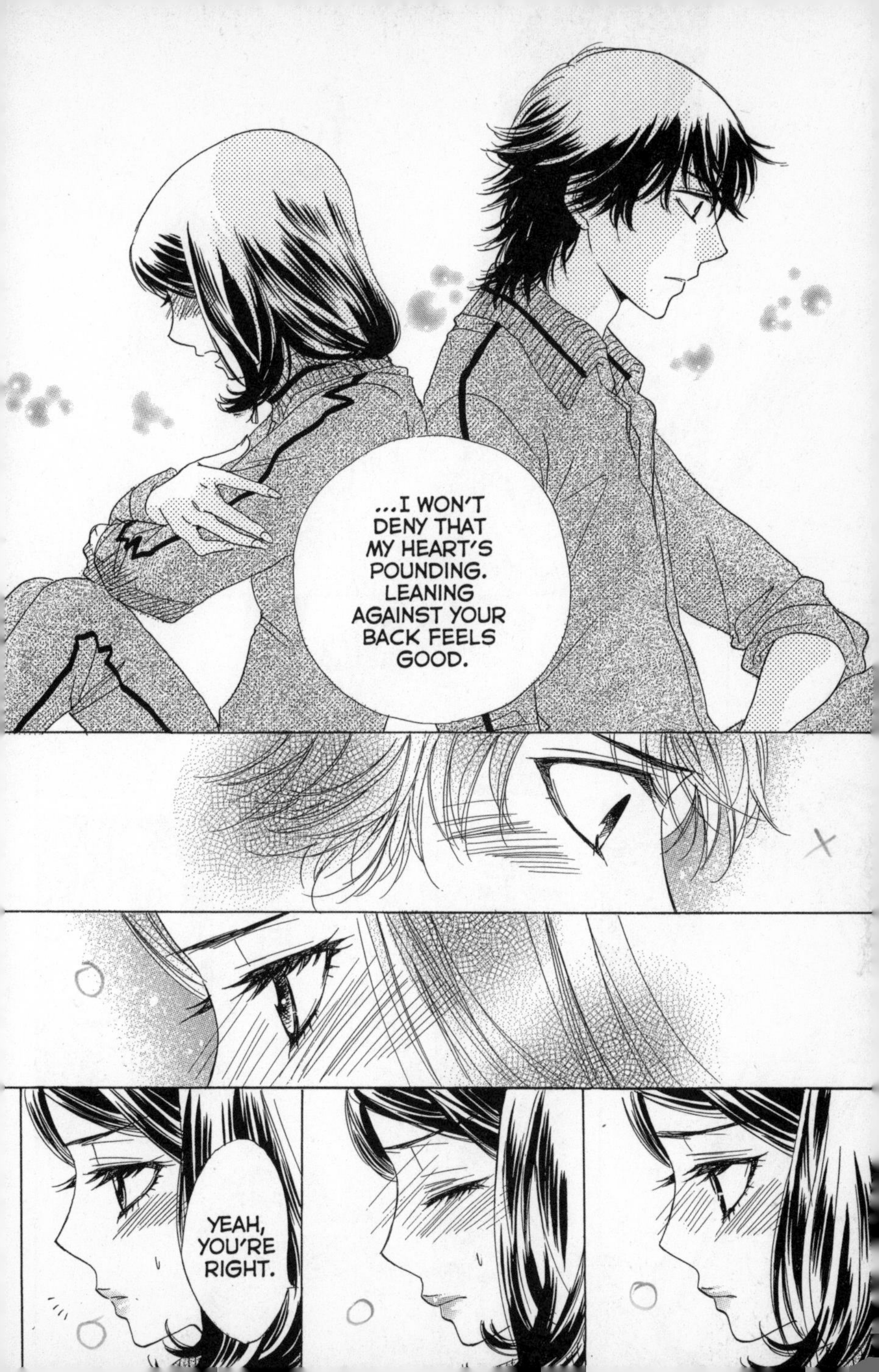
...I WON'T DENY THAT MY HEART'S POUNDING. LEANING AGAINST YOUR BACK FEELS GOOD.
YEAH, YOU'RE RIGHT.

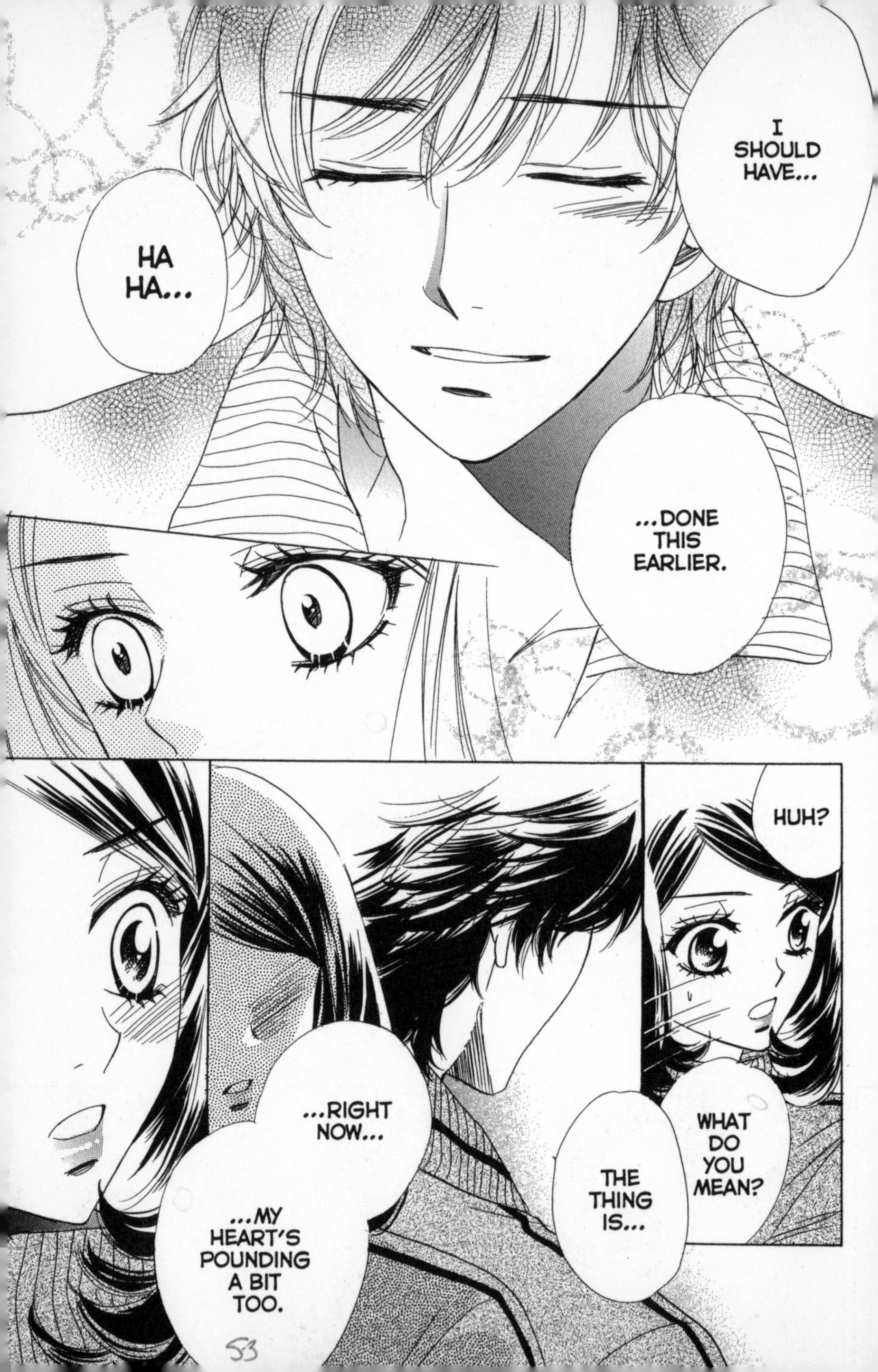
I SHOULD HAVE...
HA HA...
...DONE THIS EARLIER.
HUH?
WHAT DO YOU MEAN?
THE THING IS...
...RIGHT NOW...
...MY HEART'S POUNDING A BIT TOO.

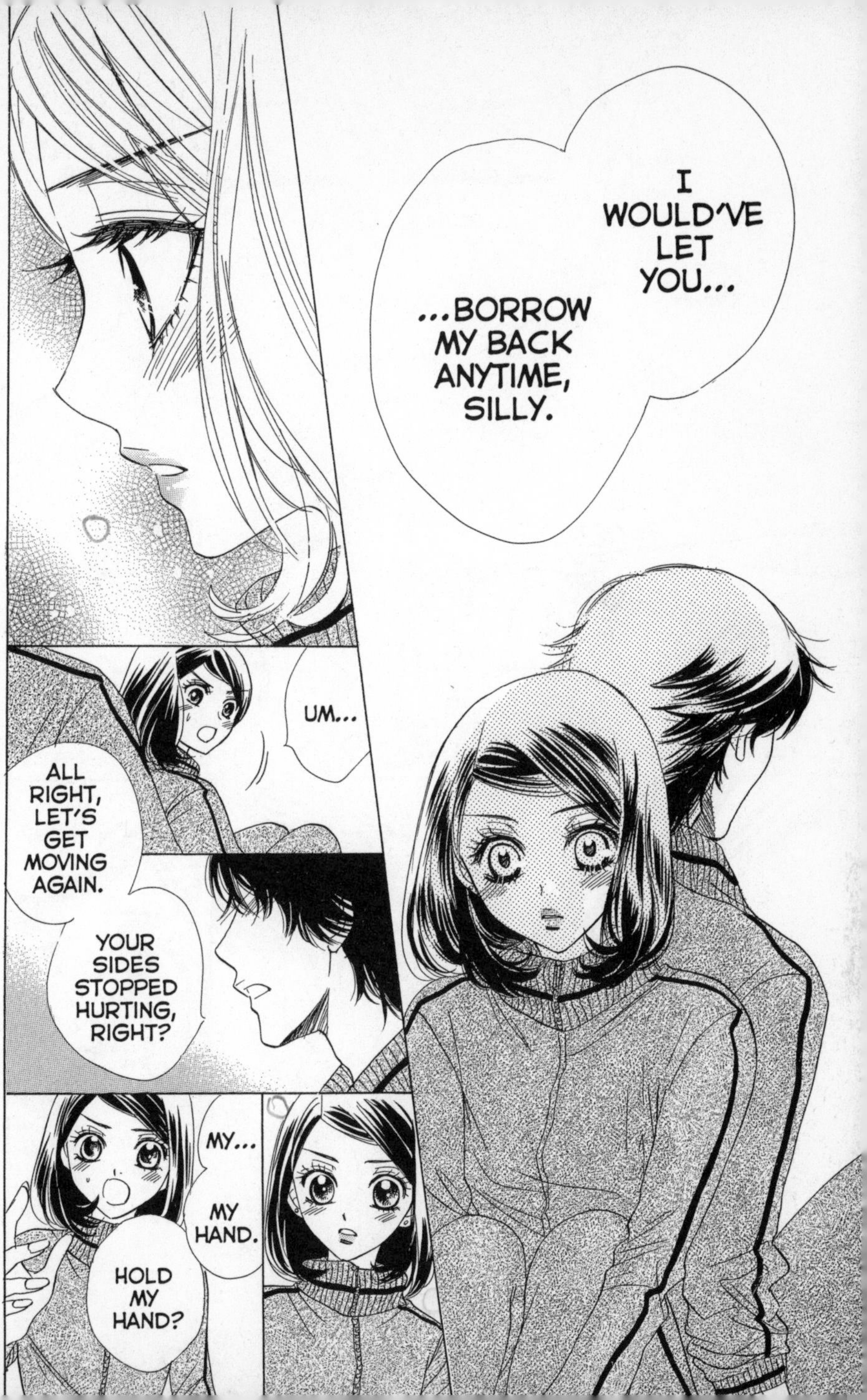
I WOULD'VE LET YOU...
...BORROW MY BACK ANYTIME, SILLY.
UM...
ALL RIGHT, LET'S GET MOVING AGAIN.
YOUR SIDES STOPPED HURTING, RIGHT?
MY...
MY HAND.
HOLD MY HAND?

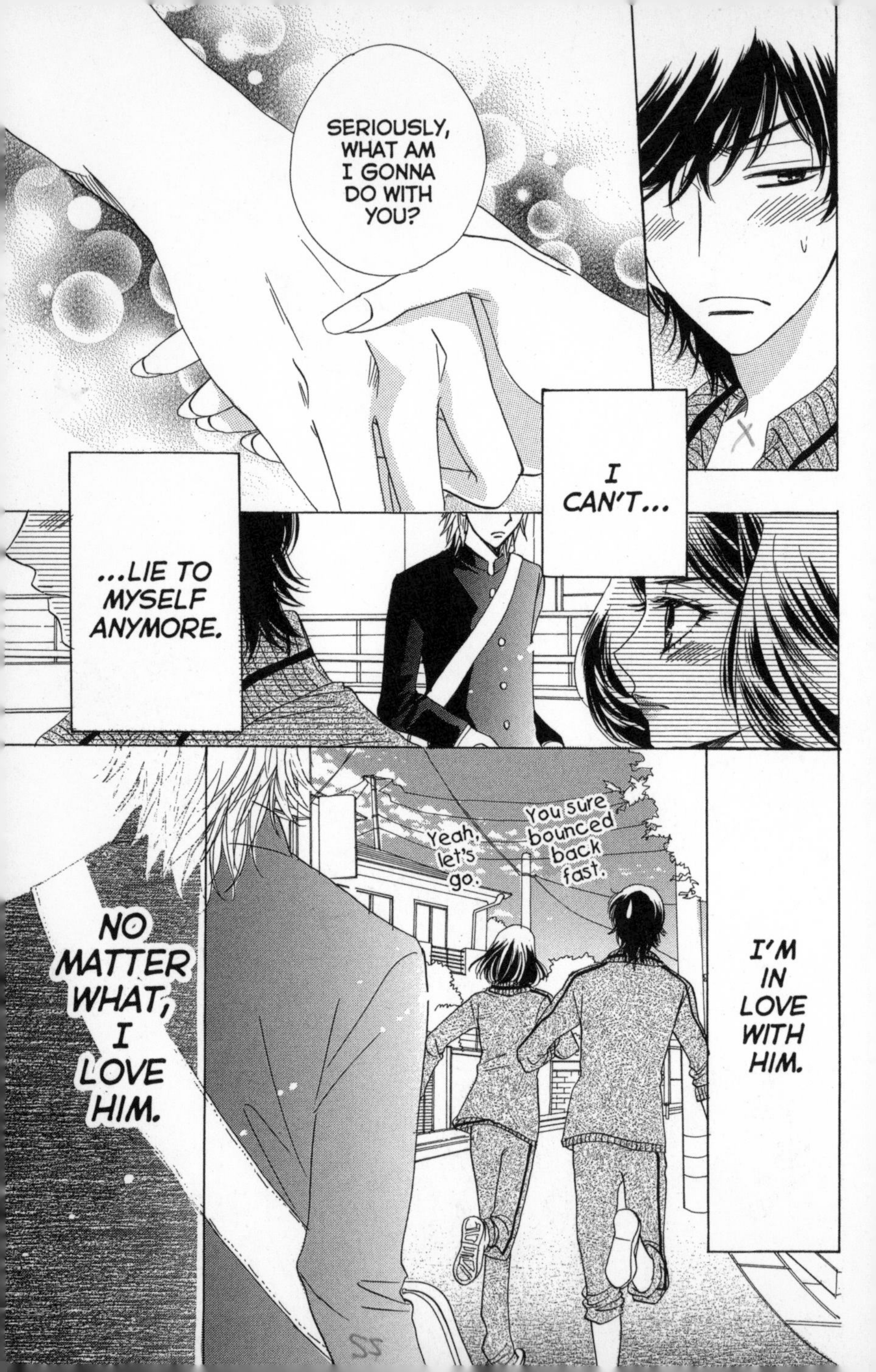
SERIOUSLY, WHAT AM I GONNA DO WITH YOU?
I CAN'T...
...LIE TO MYSELF ANYMORE.
I'M IN LOVE WITH HIM.
You sure bounced back fast.
Yeah, let's go.
NO MATTER WHAT, I LOVE HIM.

A Devil and Her Love Song

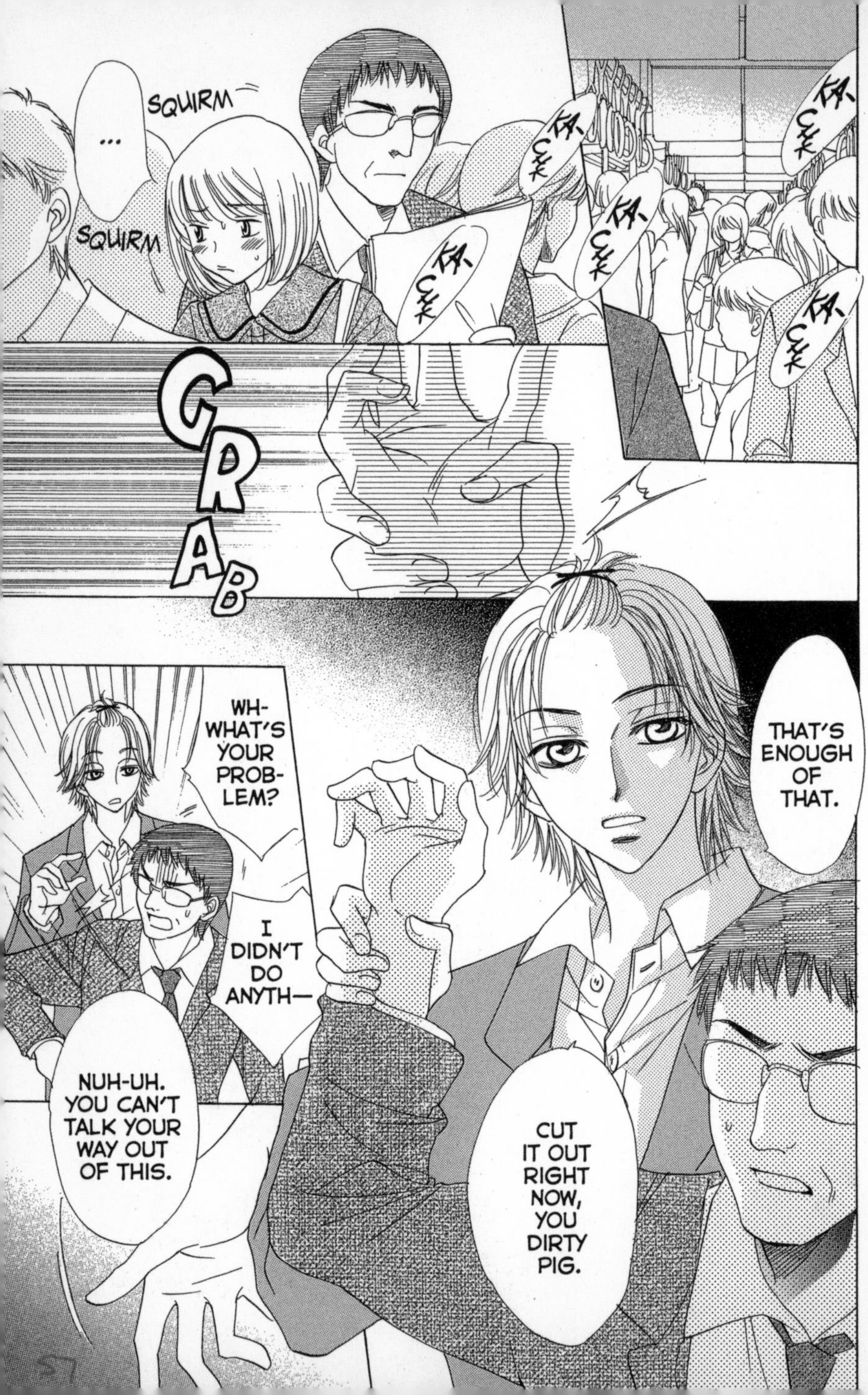
KA-CHK
KA-CHK
KA-CHK
KA-CHK
...
SQUIRM
SQUIRM
KA-CHK
GRAB
THAT'S ENOUGH OF THAT.
CUT IT OUT RIGHT NOW, YOU DIRTY PIG.
WH-WHAT'S YOUR PROB-LEM?
I DIDN'T DO ANYTH—
NUH-UH. YOU CAN'T TALK YOUR WAY OUT OF THIS.

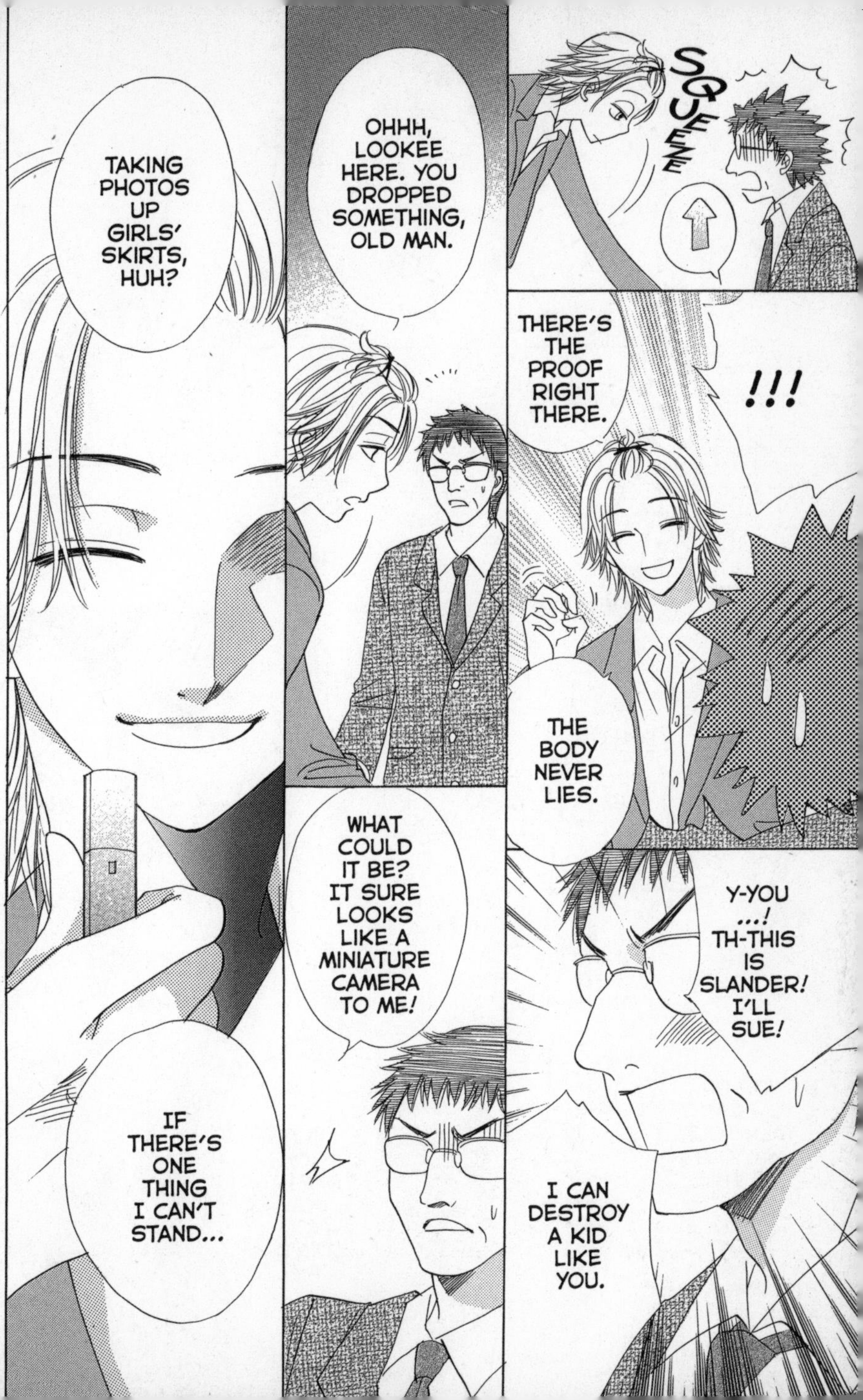
SQUEEZE
THERE'S THE PROOF RIGHT THERE.
!!!
THE BODY NEVER LIES.
Y-YOU ...! TH-THIS IS SLANDER! I'LL SUE!
I CAN DESTROY A KID LIKE YOU.
OHHH, LOOKEE HERE. YOU DROPPED SOMETHING, OLD MAN.
WHAT COULD IT BE? IT SURE LOOKS LIKE A MINIATURE CAMERA TO ME!
TAKING PHOTOS UP GIRLS' SKIRTS, HUH?
IF THERE'S ONE THING I CAN'T STAND...

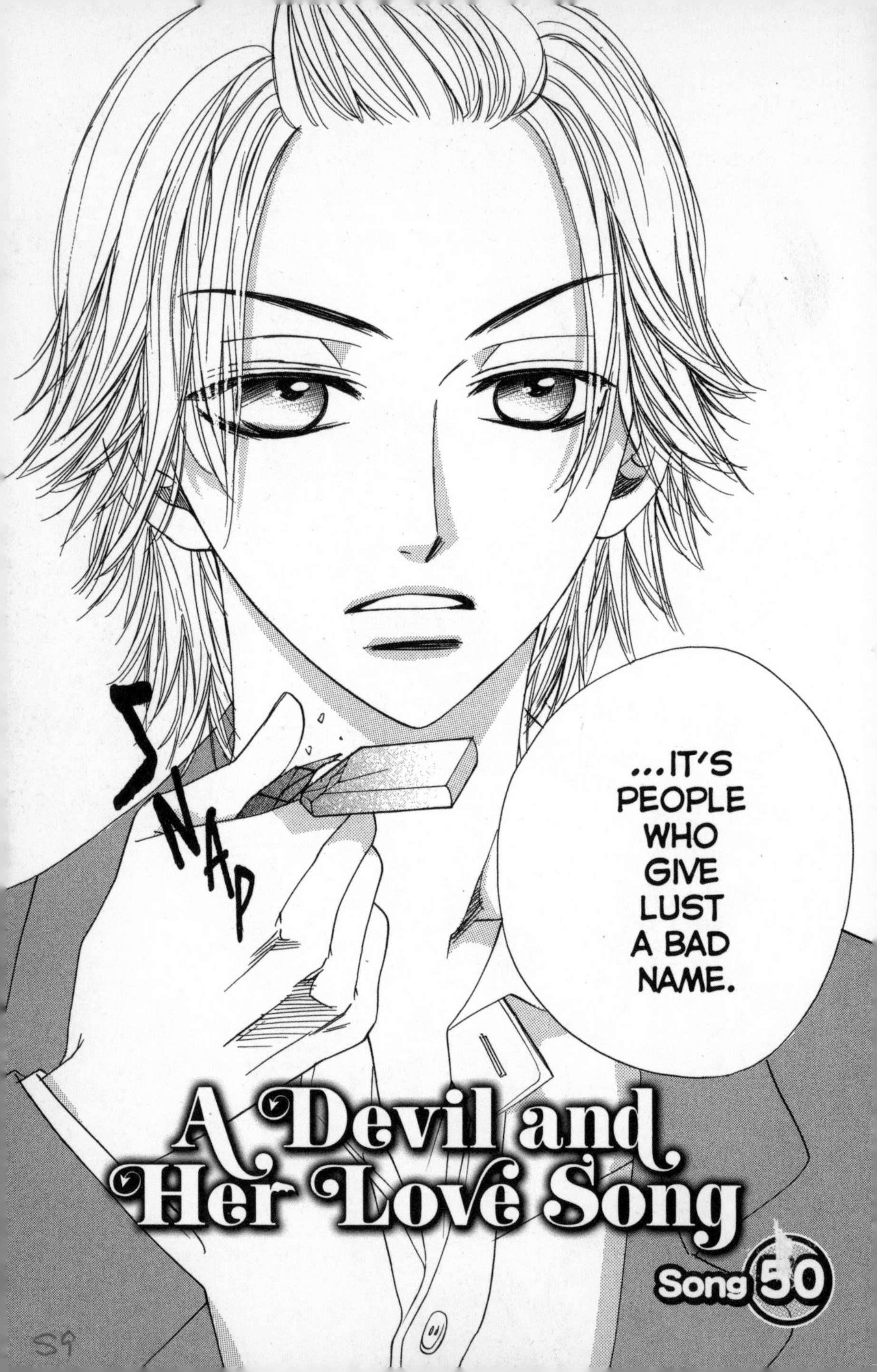
...IT'S PEOPLE WHO GIVE LUST A BAD NAME.
SNAP
A Devil and Her Love Song
Song 50

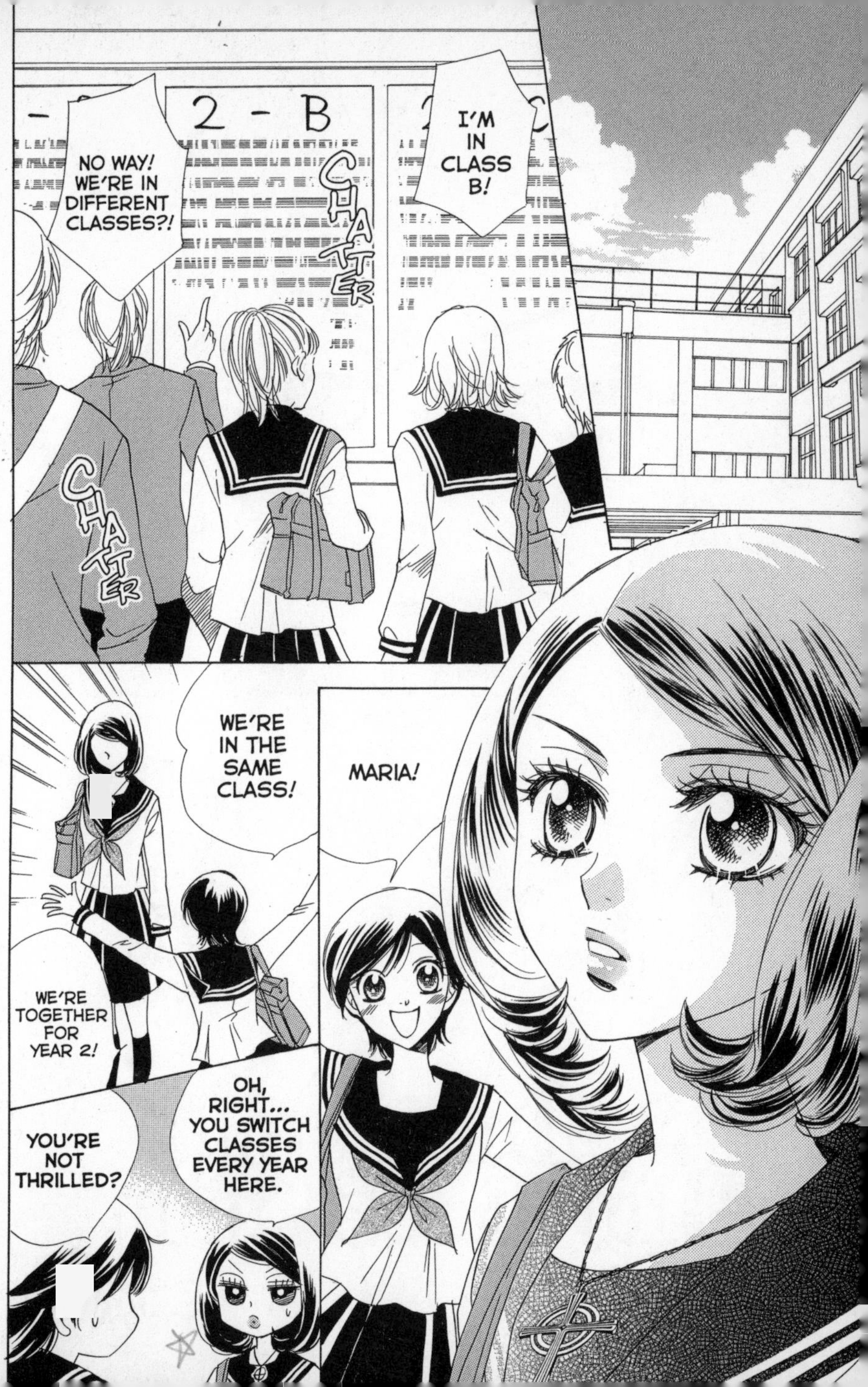
2 - B
I'M IN CLASS B!
CHATTER
NO WAY! WE'RE IN DIFFERENT CLASSES?!
CHATTER
MARIA!
WE'RE IN THE SAME CLASS!
WE'RE TOGETHER FOR YEAR 2!
OH, RIGHT... YOU SWITCH CLASSES EVERY YEAR HERE.
YOU'RE NOT THRILLED?

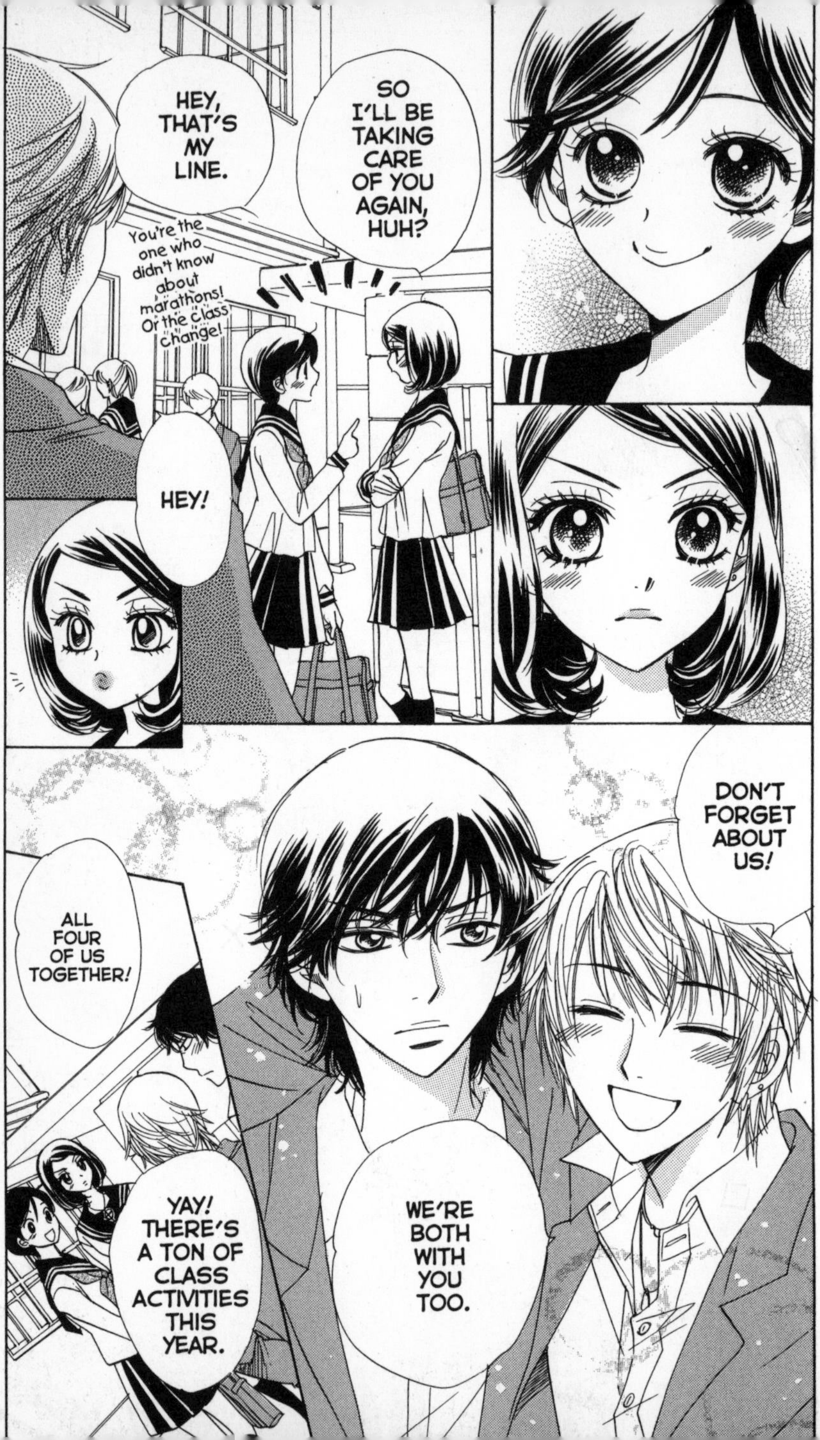
SO I'LL BE TAKING CARE OF YOU AGAIN, HUH?
HEY, THAT'S MY LINE.
You're the one who didn't know about marathons! Or the class change!
HEY!
DON'T FORGET ABOUT US!
WE'RE BOTH WITH YOU TOO.
ALL FOUR OF US TOGETHER!
YAY! THERE'S A TON OF CLASS ACTIVITIES THIS YEAR.

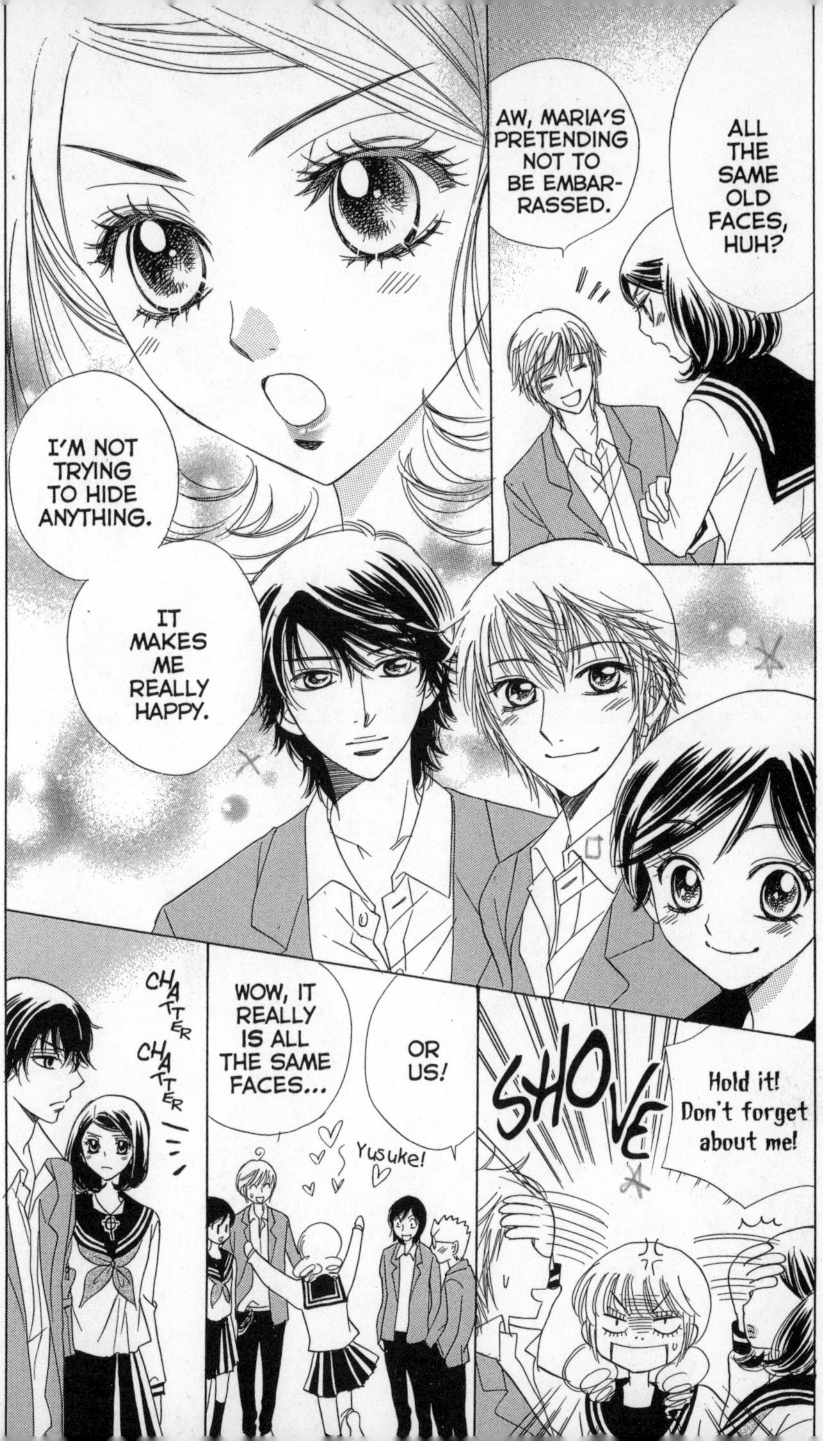
ALL THE SAME OLD FACES, HUH?
AW, MARIA'S PRETENDING NOT TO BE EMBARRASSED.
I'M NOT TRYING TO HIDE ANYTHING.
IT MAKES ME REALLY HAPPY.
Hold it! Don't forget about me!
SHOVE
WOW, IT REALLY IS ALL THE SAME FACES...
OR US!
Yusuke!
CHATTER
CHATTER

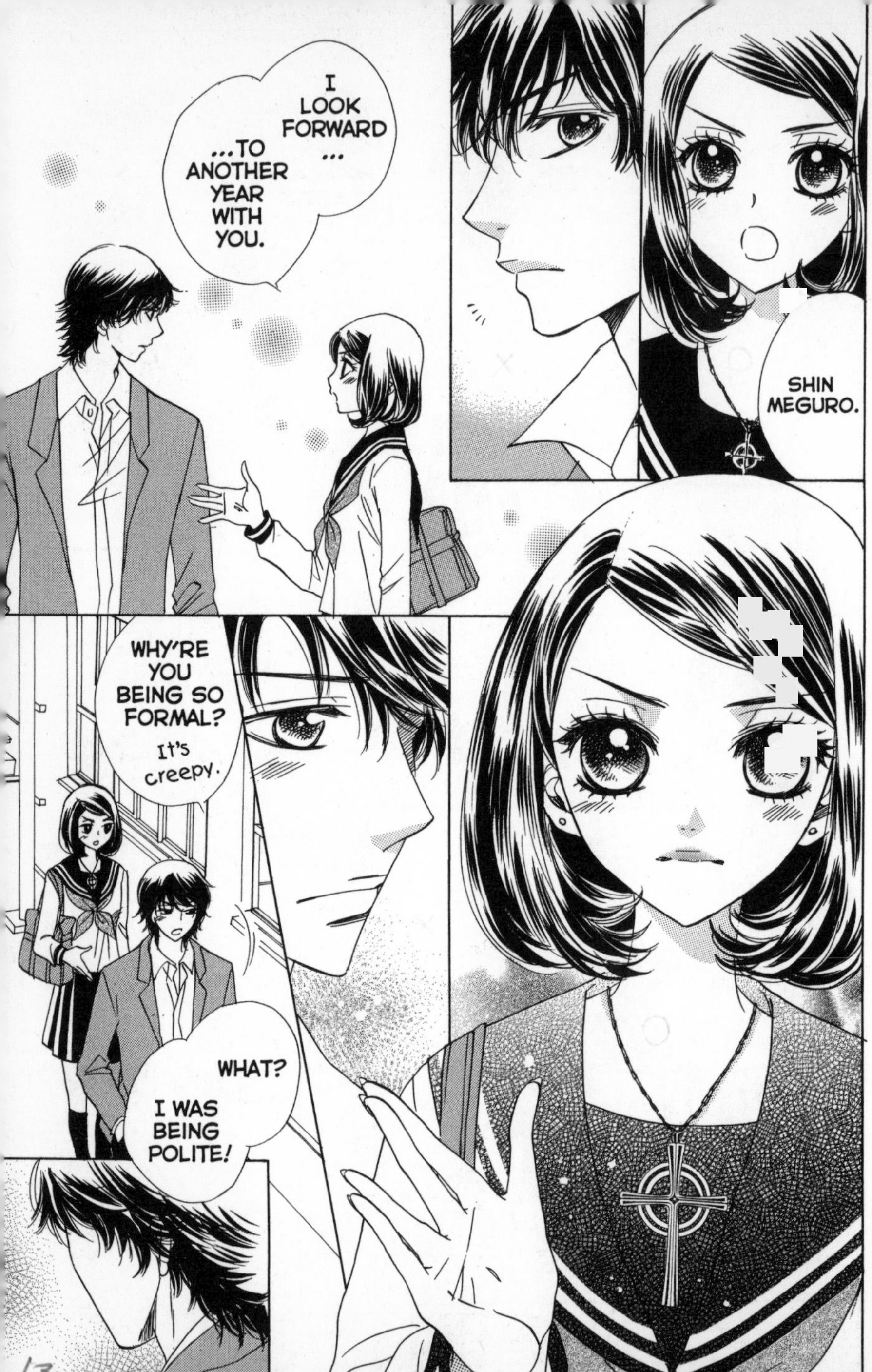
SHIN MEGURO.
I LOOK FORWARD...
...TO ANOTHER YEAR WITH YOU.
WHY'RE YOU BEING SO FORMAL?
It's creepy.
WHAT?
I WAS BEING POLITE!

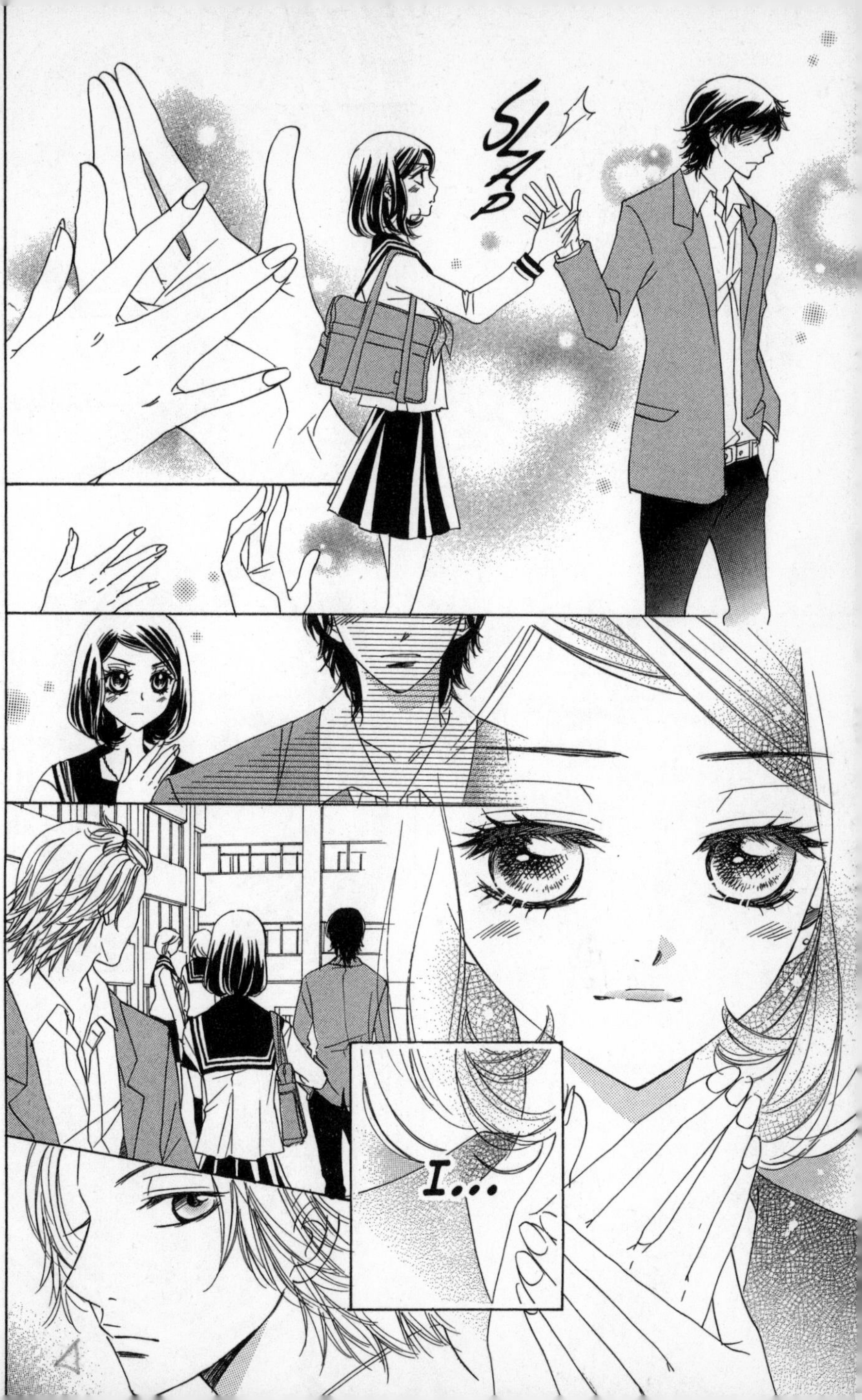
SLAP
I...

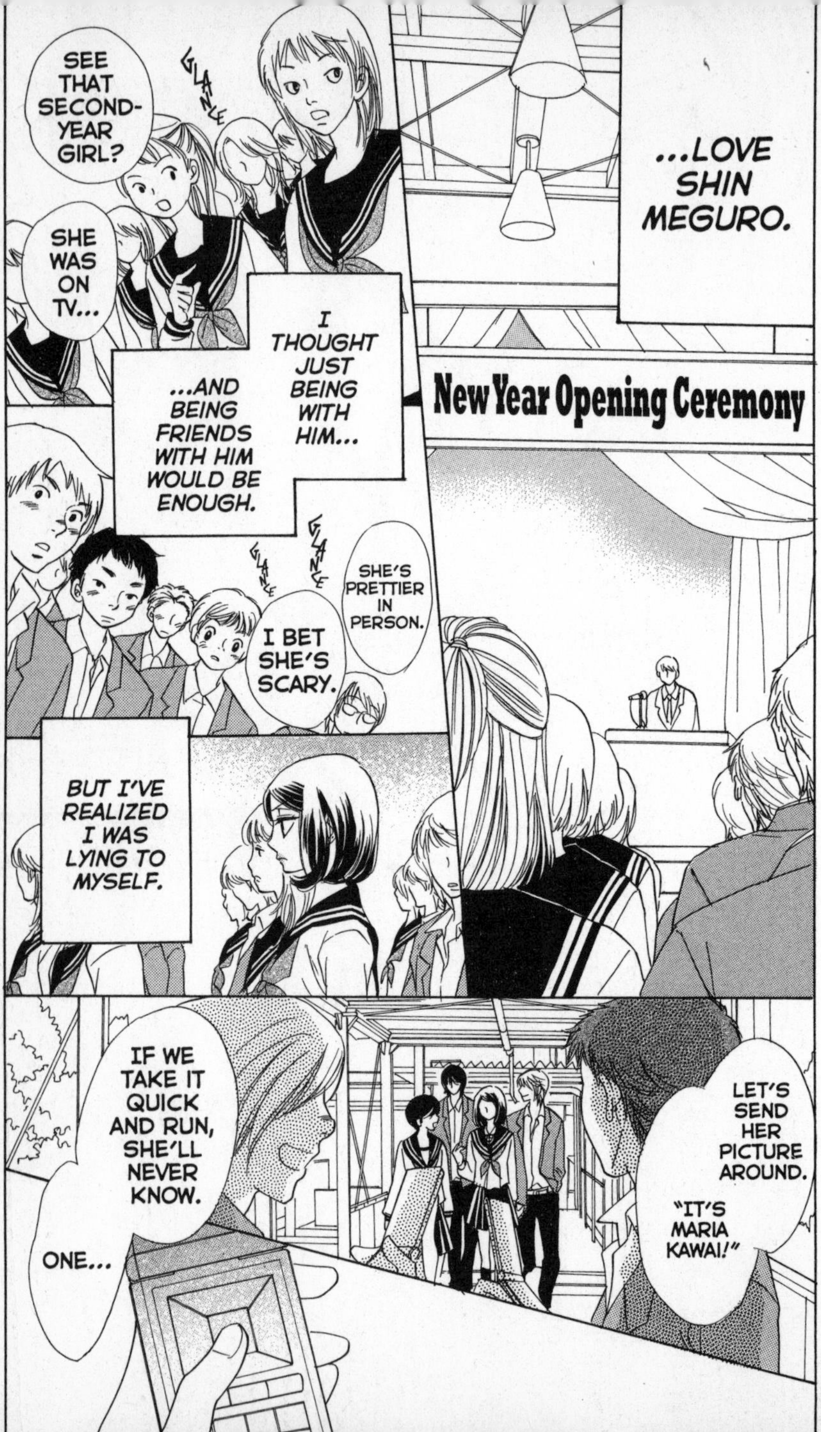
...LOVE SHIN MEGURO.
New Year Opening Ceremony
SEE THAT SECOND-YEAR GIRL?
GLANCE
SHE WAS ON TV...
I THOUGHT JUST BEING WITH HIM...
...AND BEING FRIENDS WITH HIM WOULD BE ENOUGH.
GLANCE
GLANCE
SHE'S PRETTIER IN PERSON.
I BET SHE'S SCARY.
BUT I'VE REALIZED I WAS LYING TO MYSELF.
LET'S SEND HER PICTURE AROUND.
"IT'S MARIA KAWAI!"
IF WE TAKE IT QUICK AND RUN, SHE'LL NEVER KNOW.
ONE...

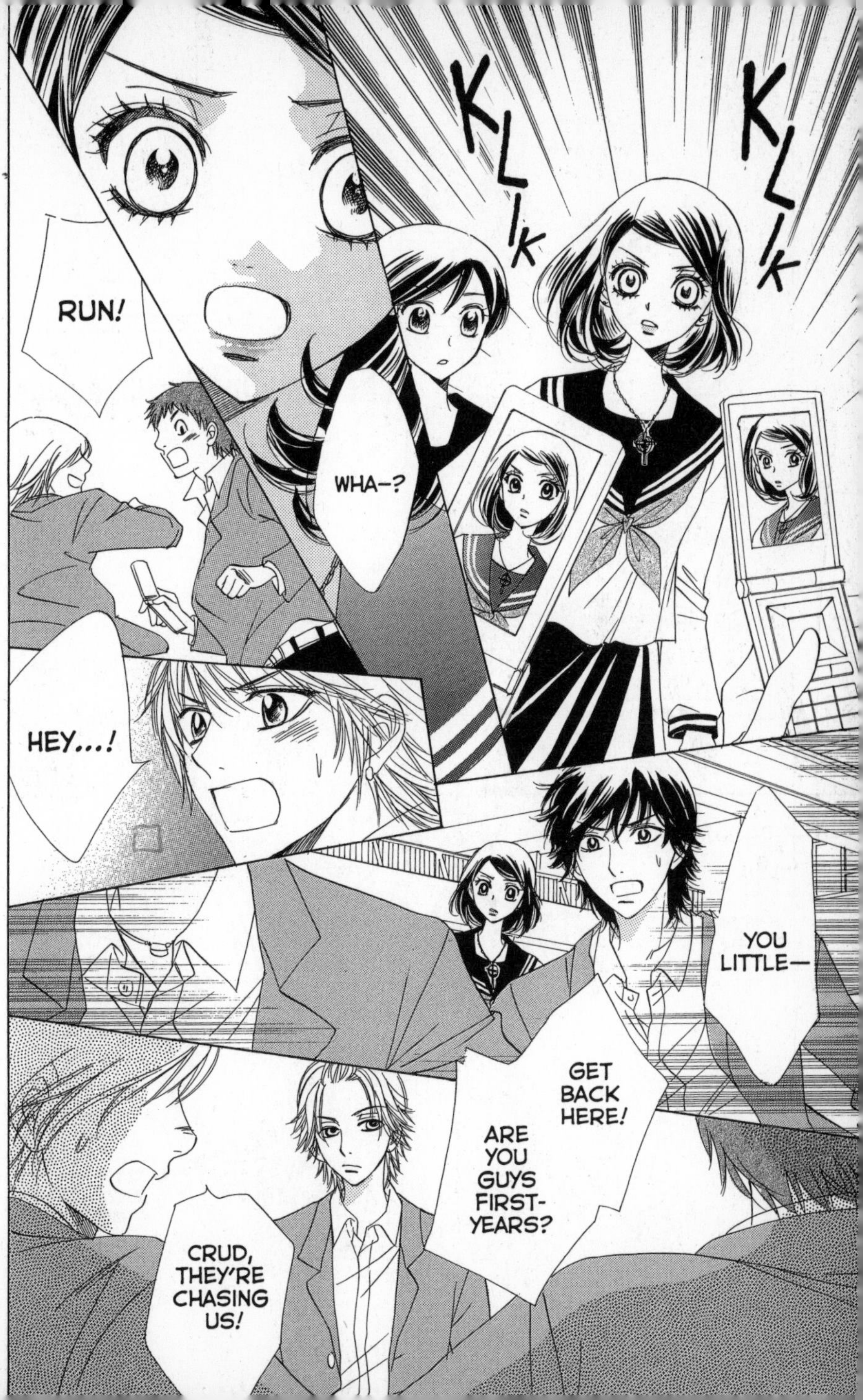
KLIK
KLIK
WHA-?
RUN!
YOU LITTLE—
HEY...!
GET BACK HERE!
ARE YOU GUYS FIRST-YEARS?
CRUD, THEY'RE CHASING US!

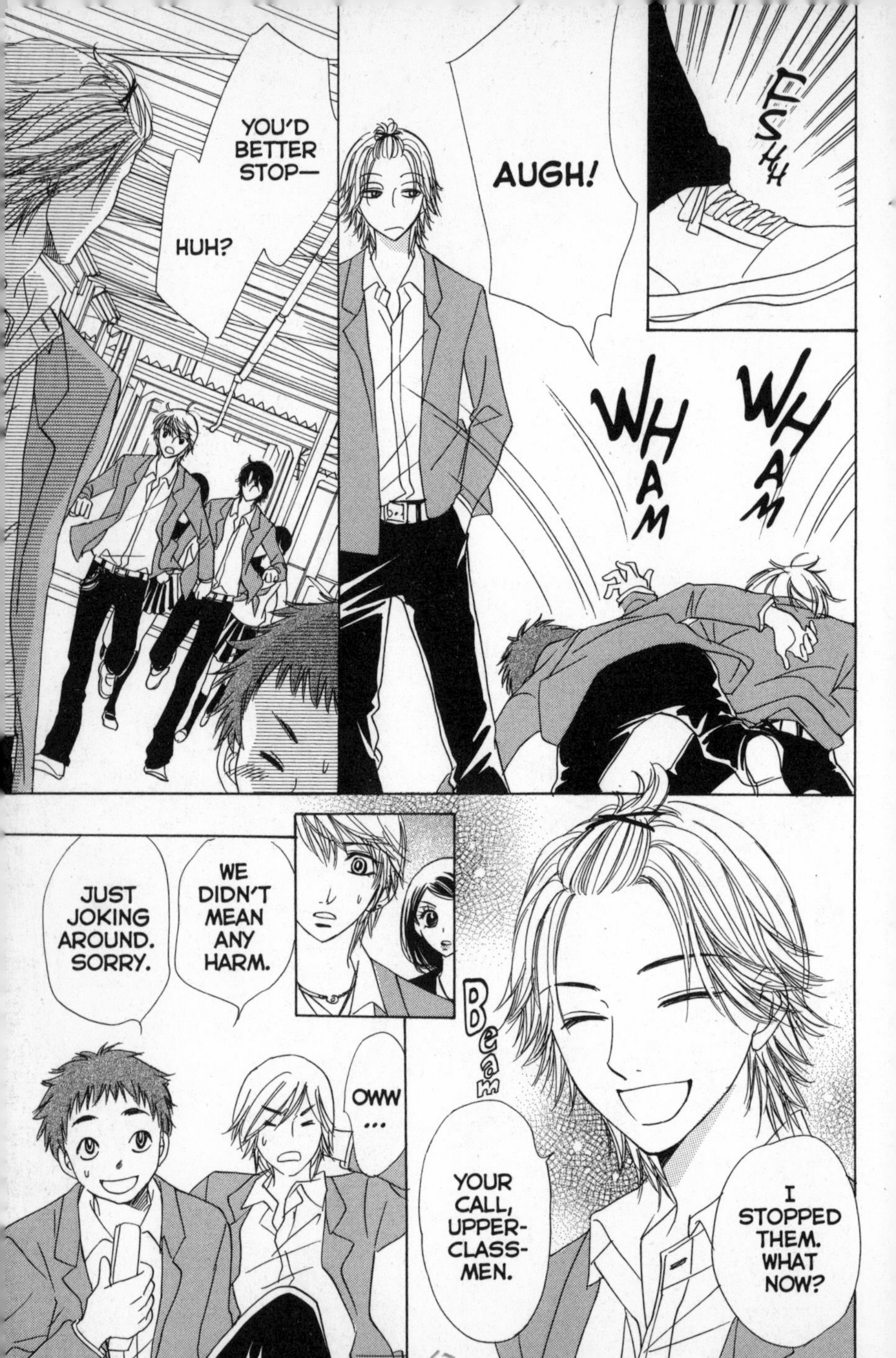
FSHH
AUGH!
WHAM
WHAM
YOU'D BETTER STOP—
HUH?
Beam
I STOPPED THEM. WHAT NOW?
YOUR CALL, UPPER-CLASSMEN.
WE DIDN'T MEAN ANY HARM.
JUST JOKING AROUND. SORRY.
OWW ...

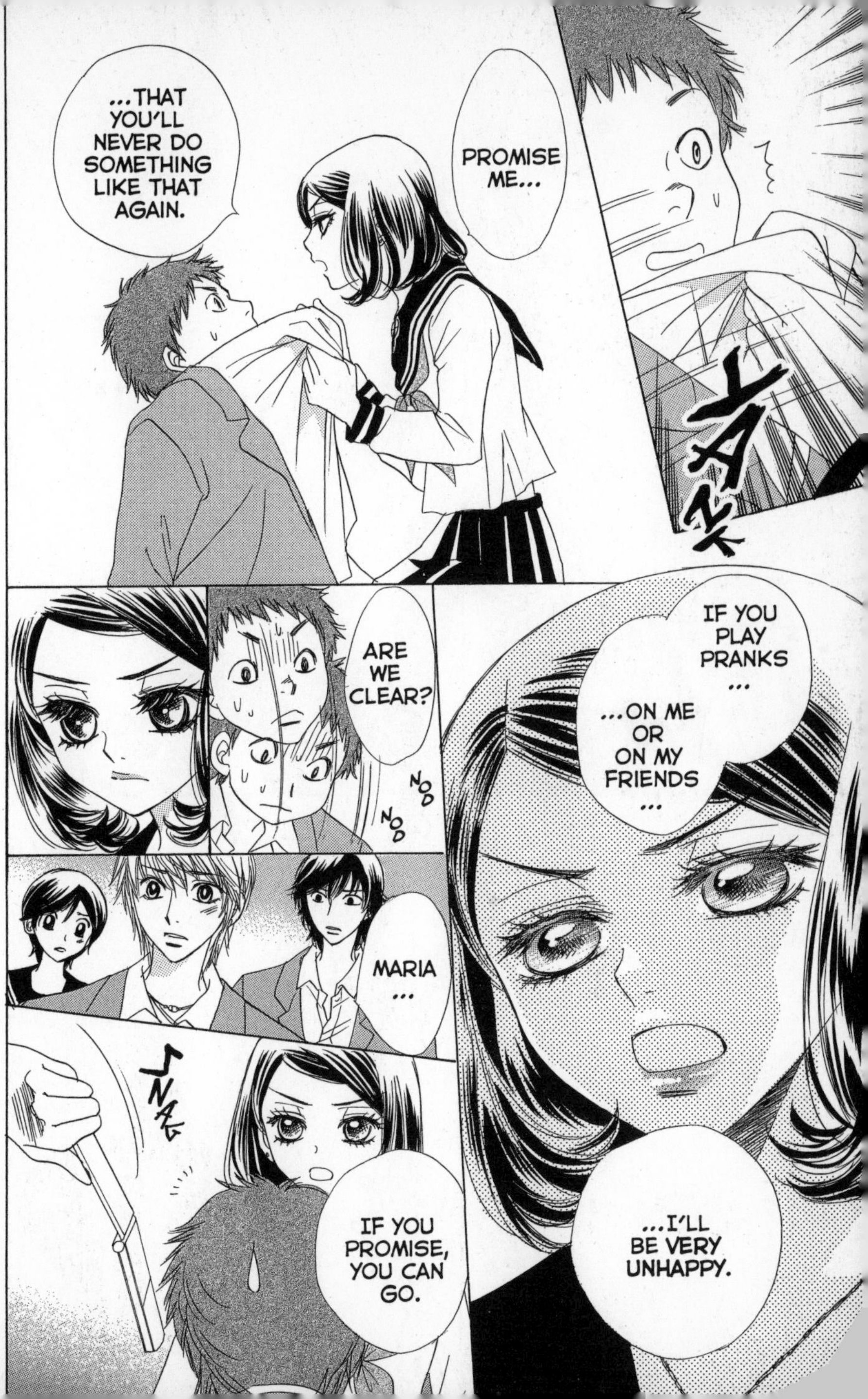
PROMISE ME...
...THAT YOU'LL NEVER DO SOMETHING LIKE THAT AGAIN.
IF YOU PLAY PRANKS ...
...ON ME OR ON MY FRIENDS ...
...I'LL BE VERY UNHAPPY.
ARE WE CLEAR?
NOD
NOD
MARIA ...
SNAG
IF YOU PROMISE, YOU CAN GO.

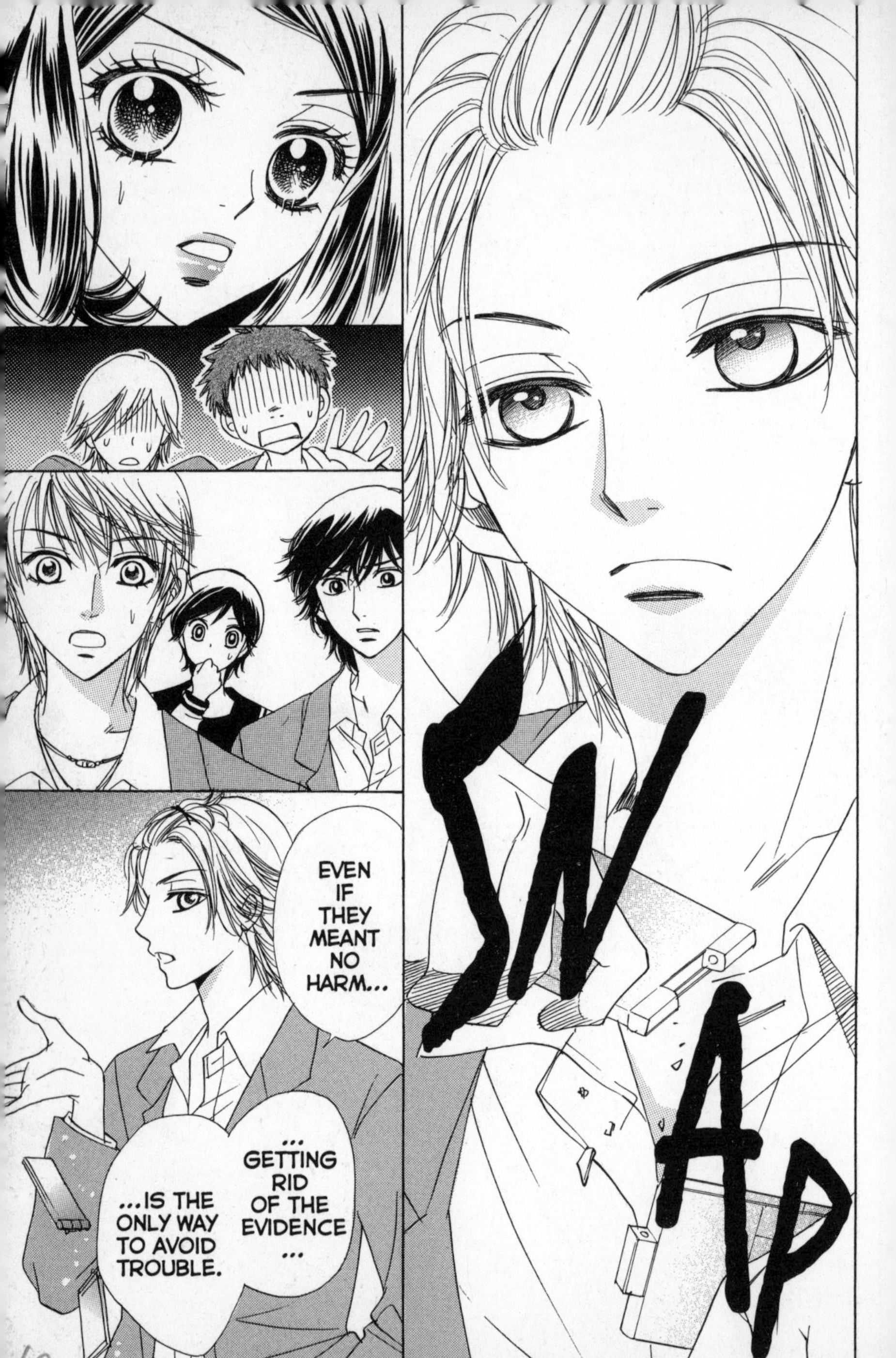
SNAP
EVEN IF THEY MEANT NO HARM...
...GETTING RID OF THE EVIDENCE...
...IS THE ONLY WAY TO AVOID TROUBLE.

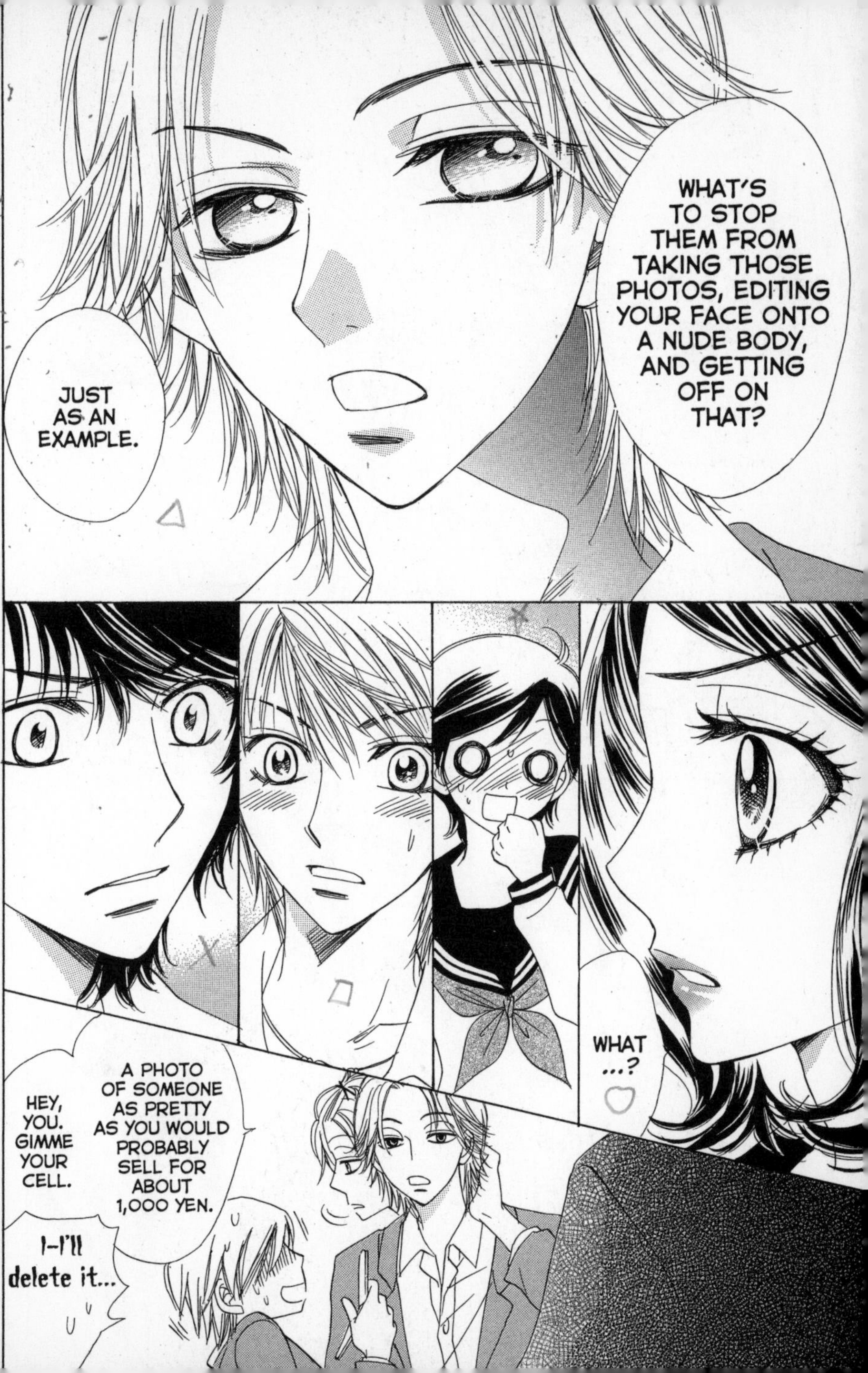
WHAT'S TO STOP THEM FROM TAKING THOSE PHOTOS, EDITING YOUR FACE ONTO A NUDE BODY, AND GETTING OFF ON THAT?
JUST AS AN EXAMPLE.
WHAT ...?
A PHOTO OF SOMEONE AS PRETTY AS YOU WOULD PROBABLY SELL FOR ABOUT 1,000 YEN.
HEY, YOU. GIMME YOUR CELL.
I-I'll delete it...

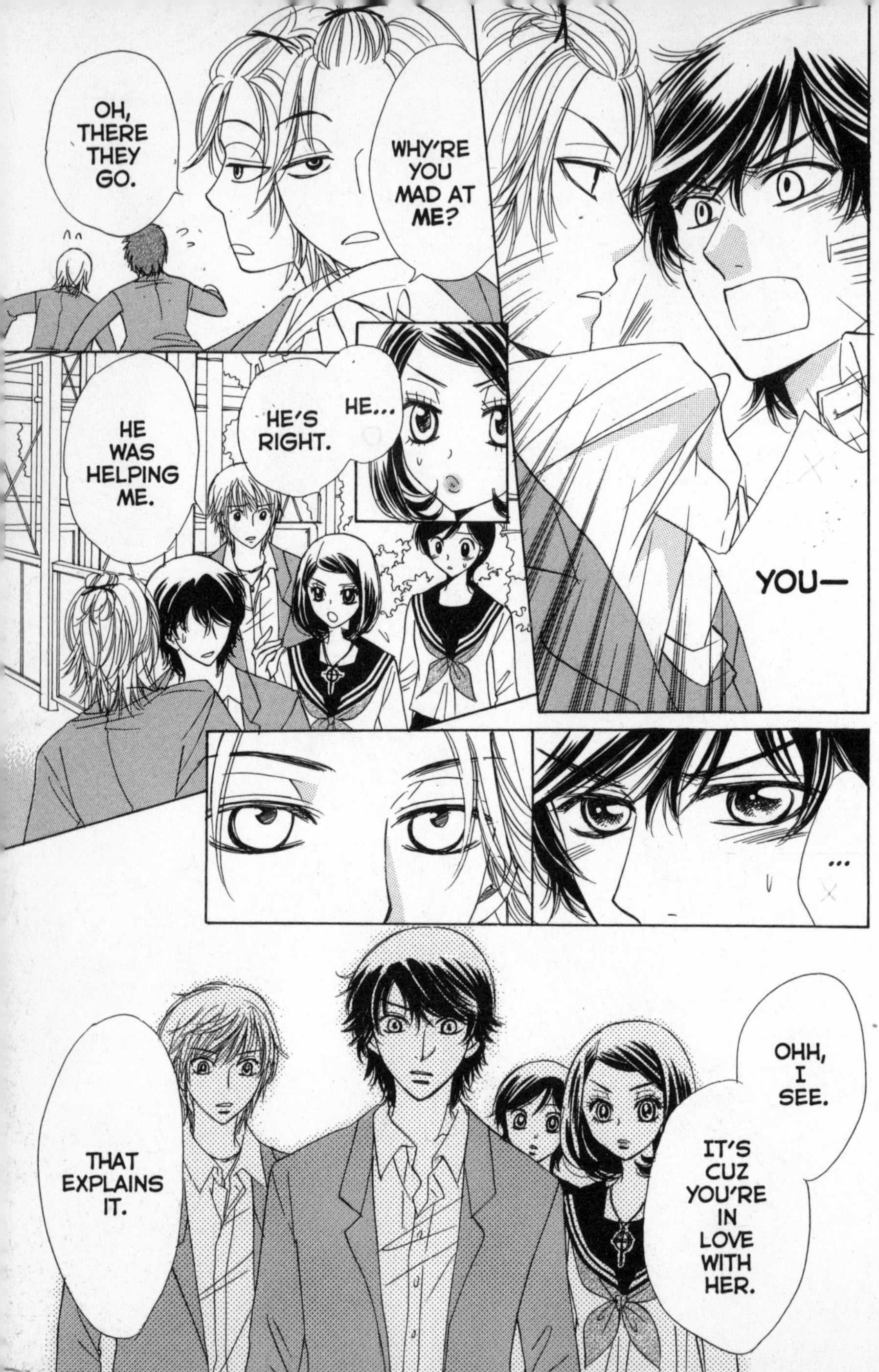
YOU—
WHY'RE YOU MAD AT ME?
OH, THERE THEY GO.
HE...
HE'S RIGHT.
HE WAS HELPING ME.
...
OHH, I SEE.
IT'S CUZ YOU'RE IN LOVE WITH HER.
THAT EXPLAINS IT.

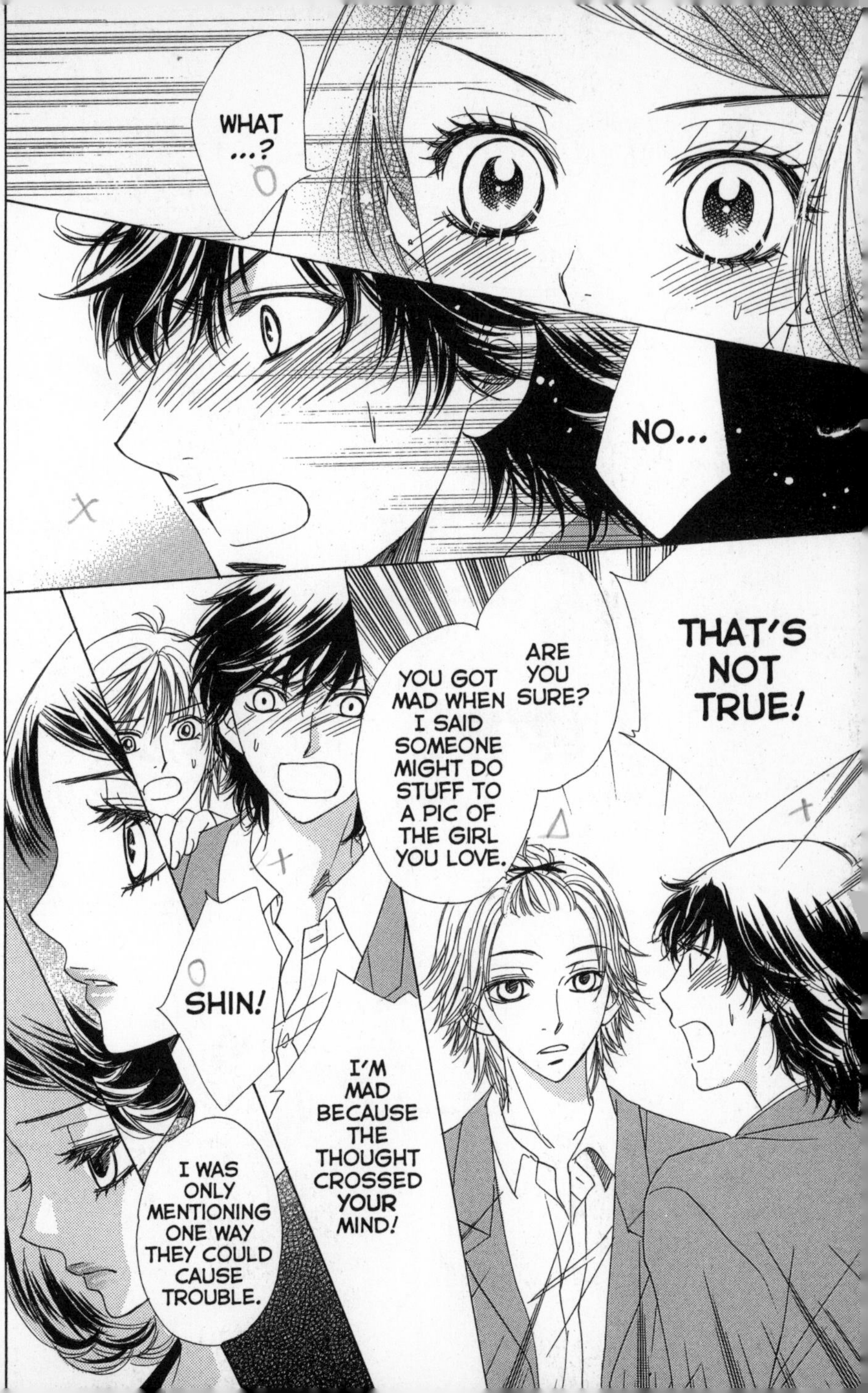
WHAT ...?
NO...
THAT'S NOT TRUE!
ARE YOU SURE? YOU GOT MAD WHEN I SAID SOMEONE MIGHT DO STUFF TO A PIC OF THE GIRL YOU LOVE.
SHIN!
I'M MAD BECAUSE THE THOUGHT CROSSED YOUR MIND!
I WAS ONLY MENTIONING ONE WAY THEY COULD CAUSE TROUBLE.

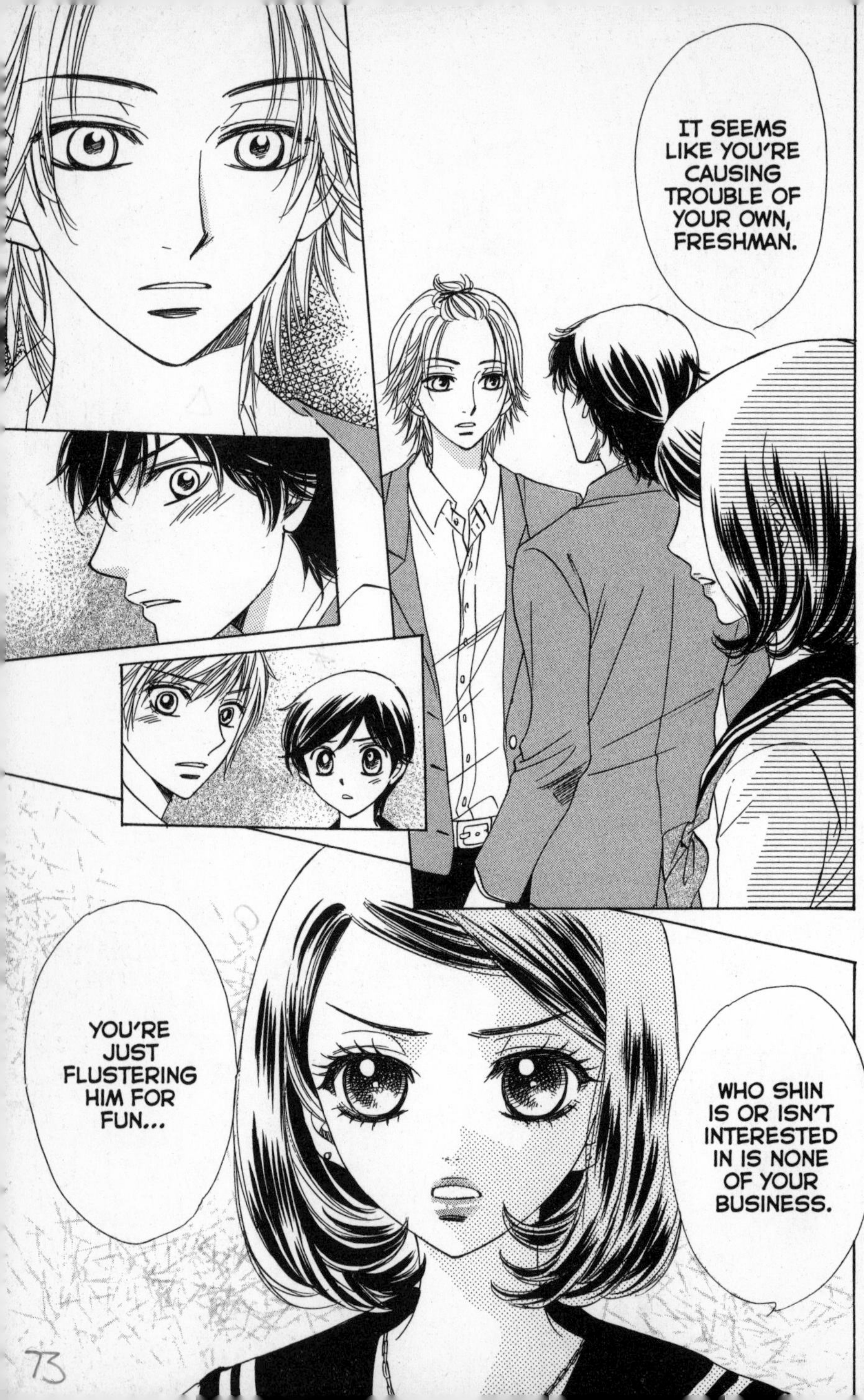
IT SEEMS LIKE YOU'RE CAUSING TROUBLE OF YOUR OWN, FRESHMAN.
WHO SHIN IS OR ISN'T INTERESTED IN IS NONE OF YOUR BUSINESS.
YOU'RE JUST FLUSTERING HIM FOR FUN...

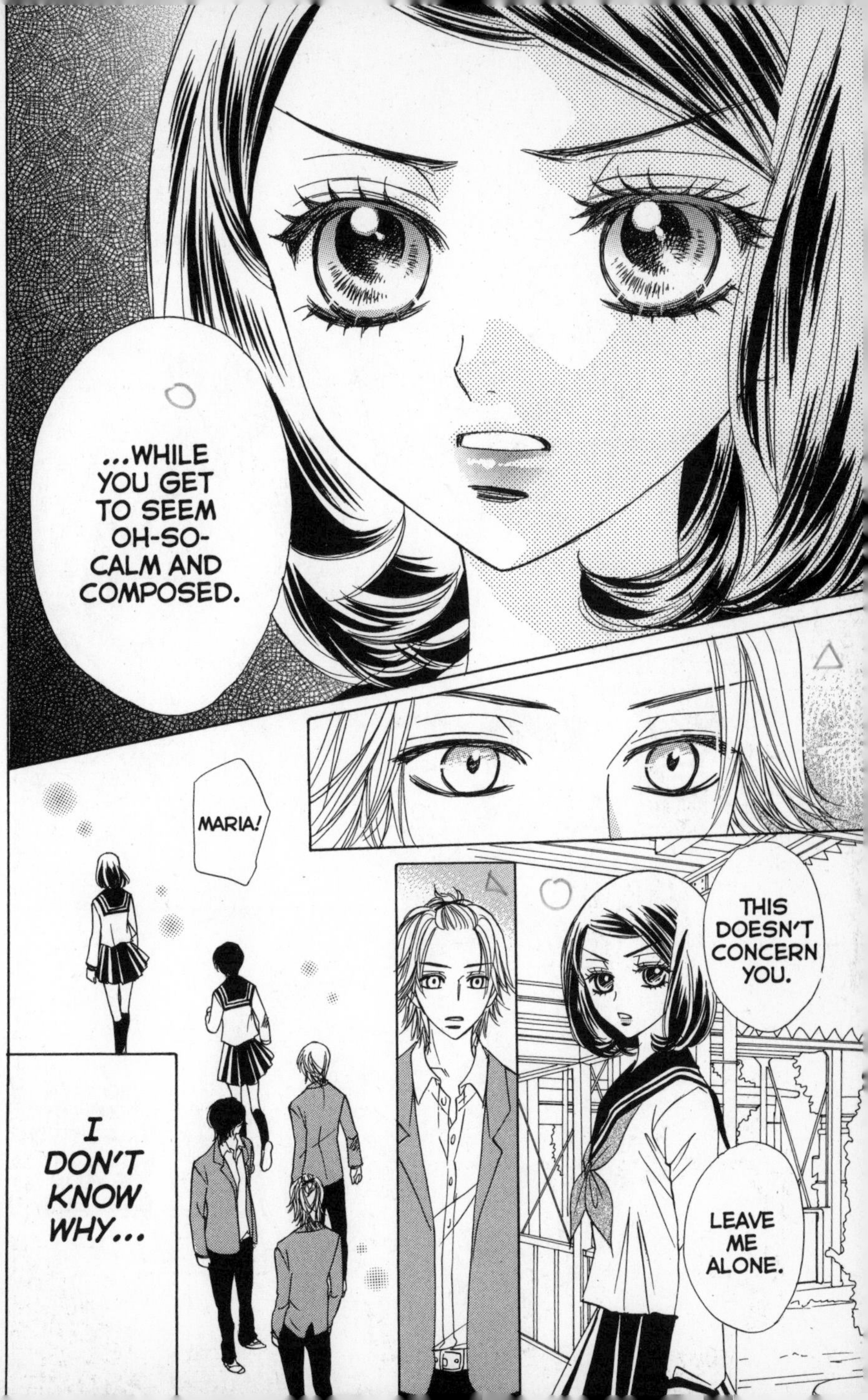
...WHILE YOU GET TO SEEM OH-SO-CALM AND COMPOSED.
THIS DOESN'T CONCERN YOU.
LEAVE ME ALONE.
MARIA!
I DON'T KNOW WHY...

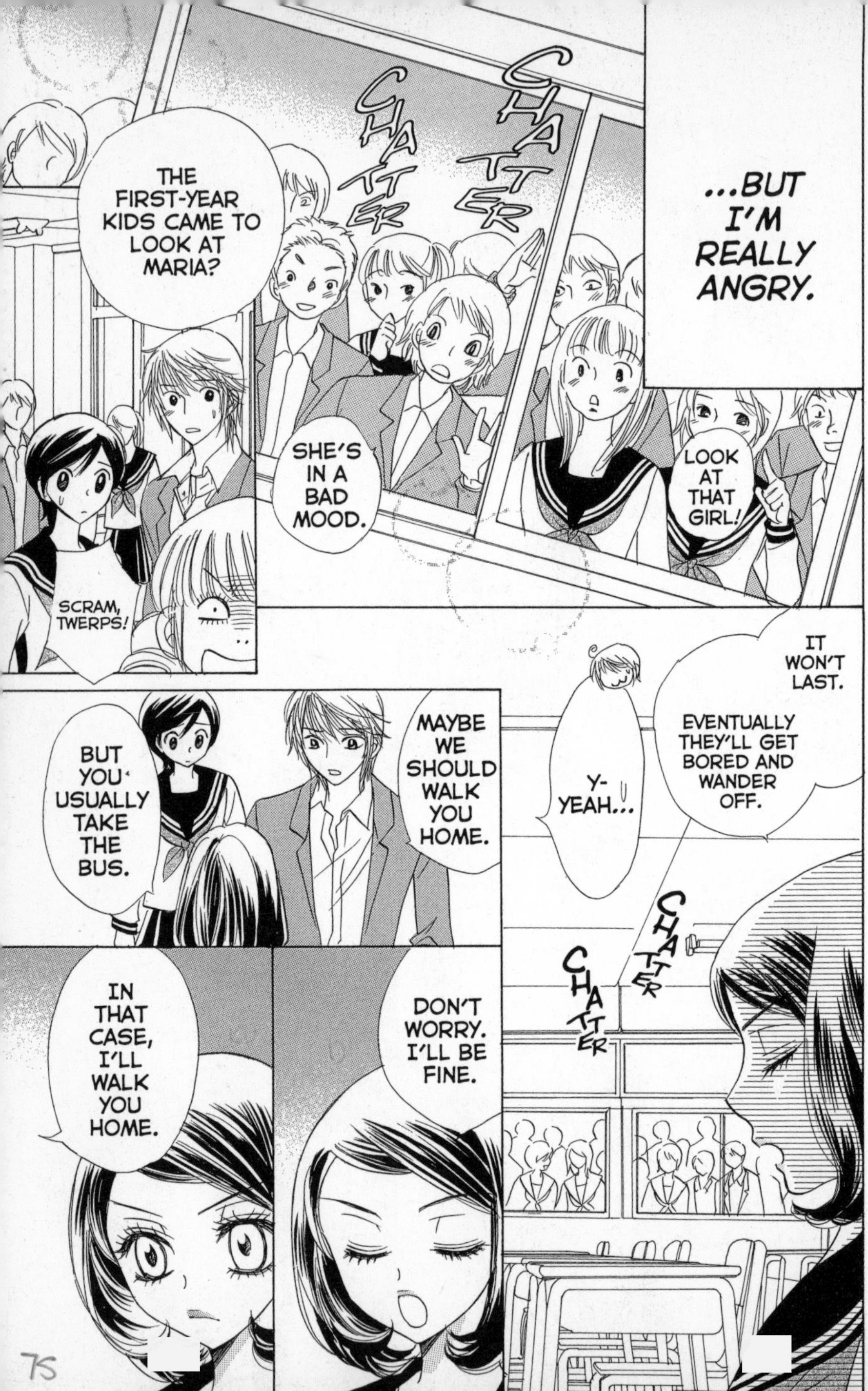
...BUT I'M REALLY ANGRY.
CHATTER
CHATTER
THE FIRST-YEAR KIDS CAME TO LOOK AT MARIA?
LOOK AT THAT GIRL!
SHE'S IN A BAD MOOD.
SCRAM, TWERPS!
IT WON'T LAST.
EVENTUALLY THEY'LL GET BORED AND WANDER OFF.
Y-YEAH...
CHATTER
CHATTER
MAYBE WE SHOULD WALK YOU HOME.
BUT YOU USUALLY TAKE THE BUS.
DON'T WORRY. I'LL BE FINE.
IN THAT CASE, I'LL WALK YOU HOME.

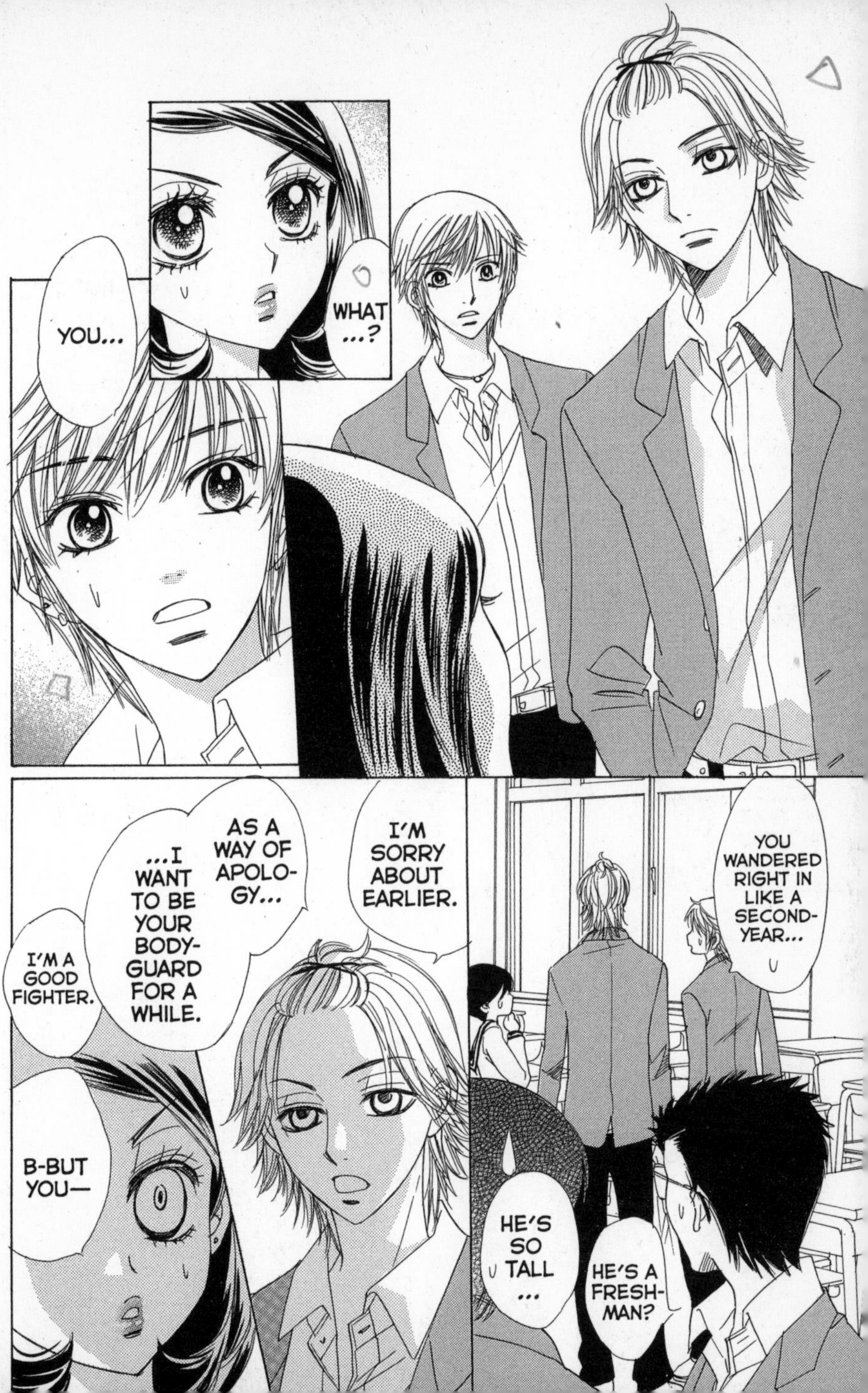
WHAT ...?
YOU...
YOU WANDERED RIGHT IN LIKE A SECOND-YEAR...
HE'S A FRESHMAN?
HE'S SO TALL ...
I'M SORRY ABOUT EARLIER.
AS A WAY OF APOLOGY...
...I WANT TO BE YOUR BODYGUARD FOR A WHILE.
I'M A GOOD FIGHTER.
B-BUT YOU—

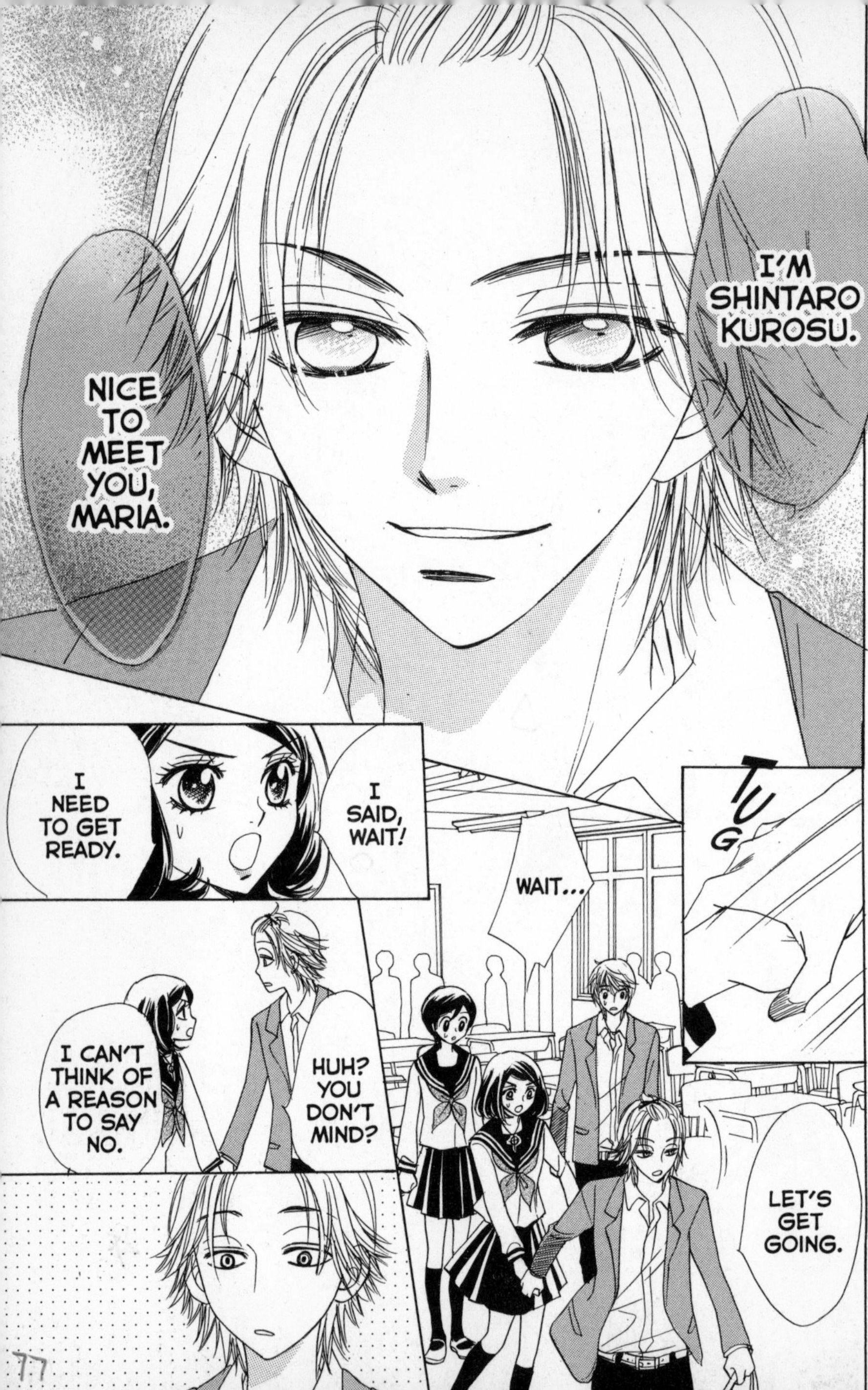
I'M SHINTARO KUROSU.
NICE TO MEET YOU, MARIA.
TUG
WAIT...
I SAID, WAIT!
I NEED TO GET READY.
HUH? YOU DON'T MIND?
I CAN'T THINK OF A REASON TO SAY NO.
LET'S GET GOING.

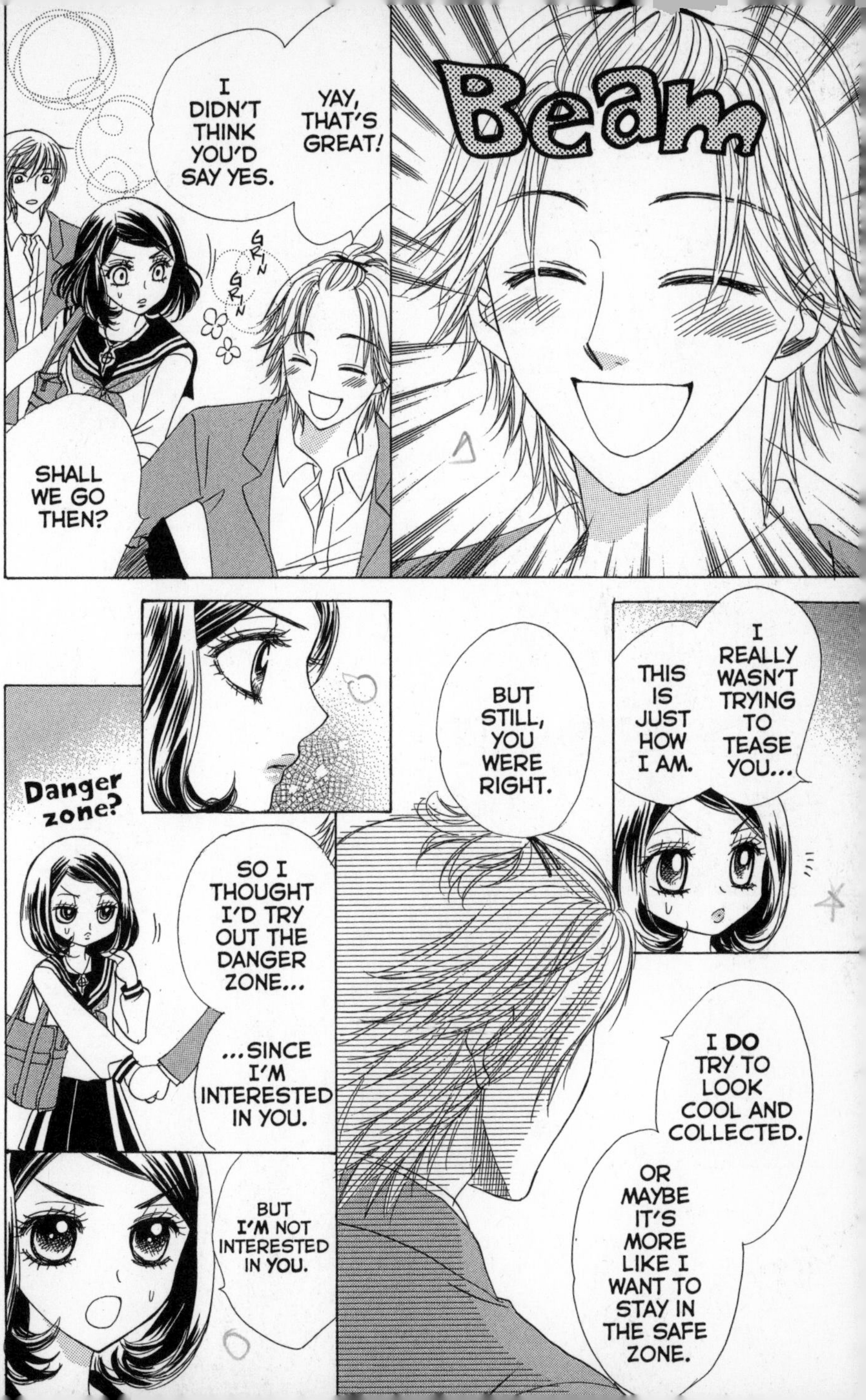
Beam
YAY, THAT'S GREAT!
I DIDN'T THINK YOU'D SAY YES.
GRIN GRIN
SHALL WE GO THEN?
I REALLY WASN'T TRYING TO TEASE YOU...
THIS IS JUST HOW I AM.
BUT STILL, YOU WERE RIGHT.
I **DO** TRY TO LOOK COOL AND COLLECTED.
OR MAYBE IT'S MORE LIKE I WANT TO STAY IN THE SAFE ZONE.
Danger zone?
SO I THOUGHT I'D TRY OUT THE DANGER ZONE...
...SINCE I'M INTERESTED IN YOU.
BUT **I'M** NOT INTERESTED IN **YOU**.

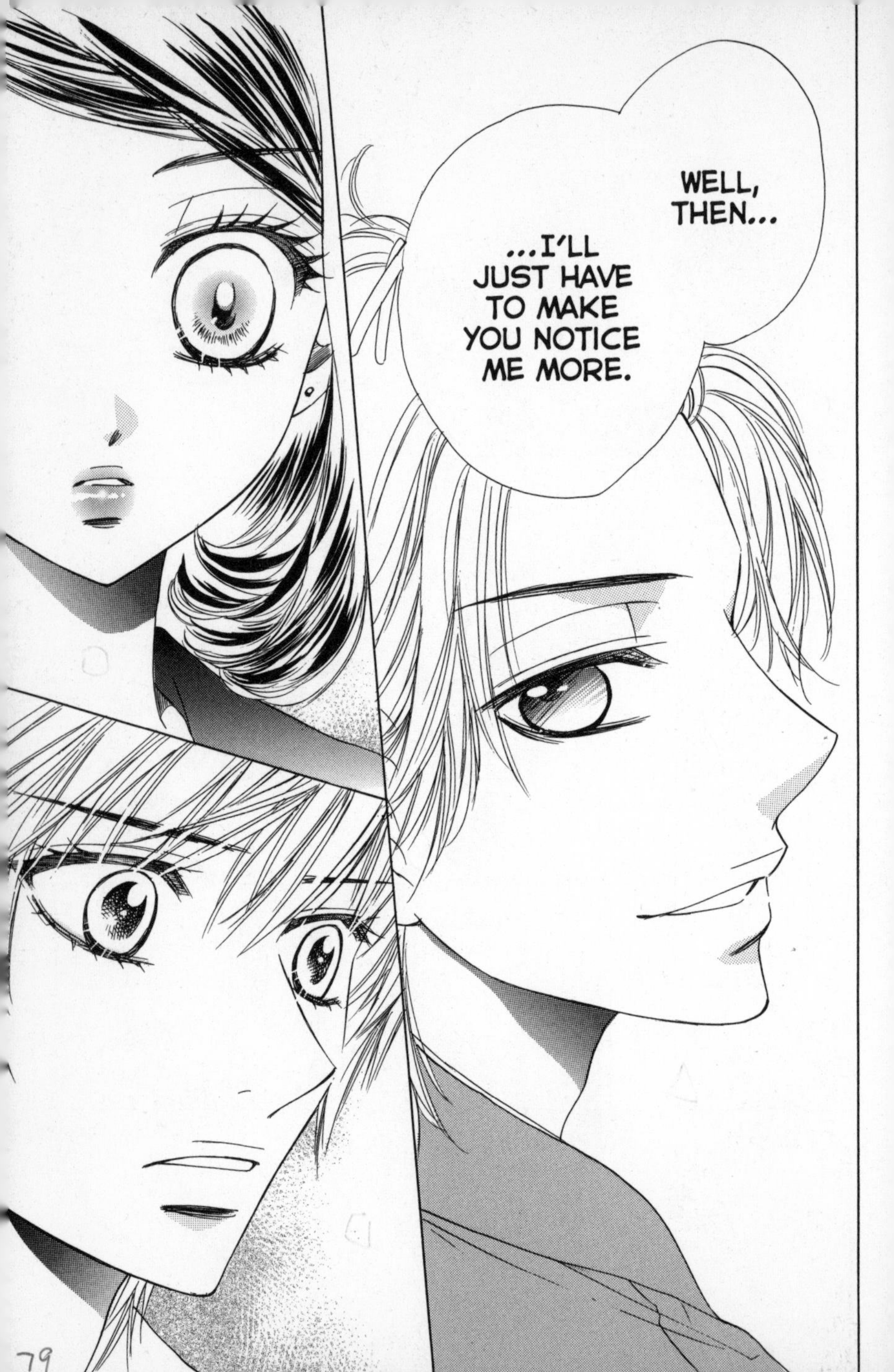
WELL, THEN...
...I'LL JUST HAVE TO MAKE YOU NOTICE ME MORE.

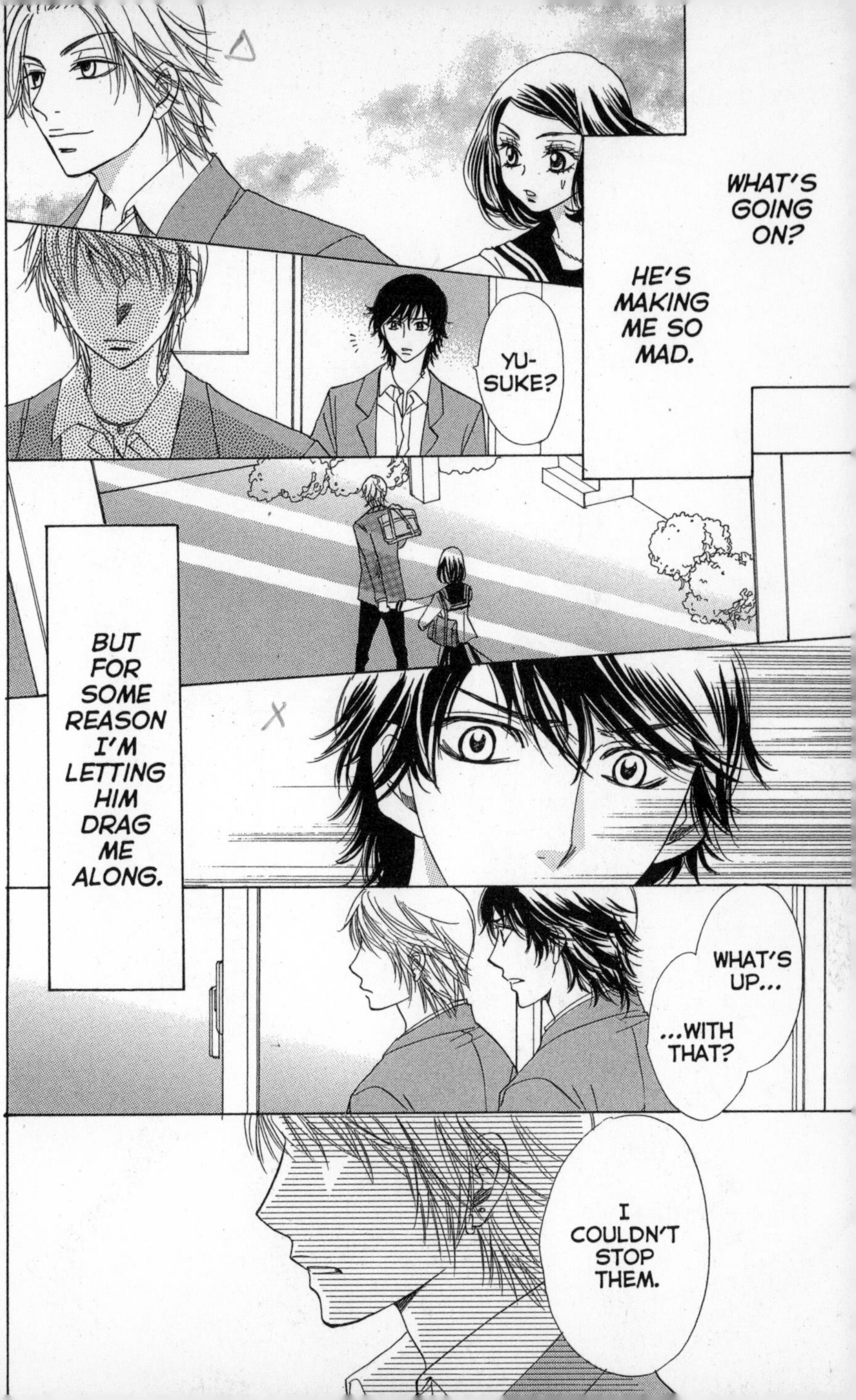
WHAT'S GOING ON?
HE'S MAKING ME SO MAD.
YU-SUKE?
BUT FOR SOME REASON I'M LETTING HIM DRAG ME ALONG.
WHAT'S UP...
...WITH THAT?
I COULDN'T STOP THEM.

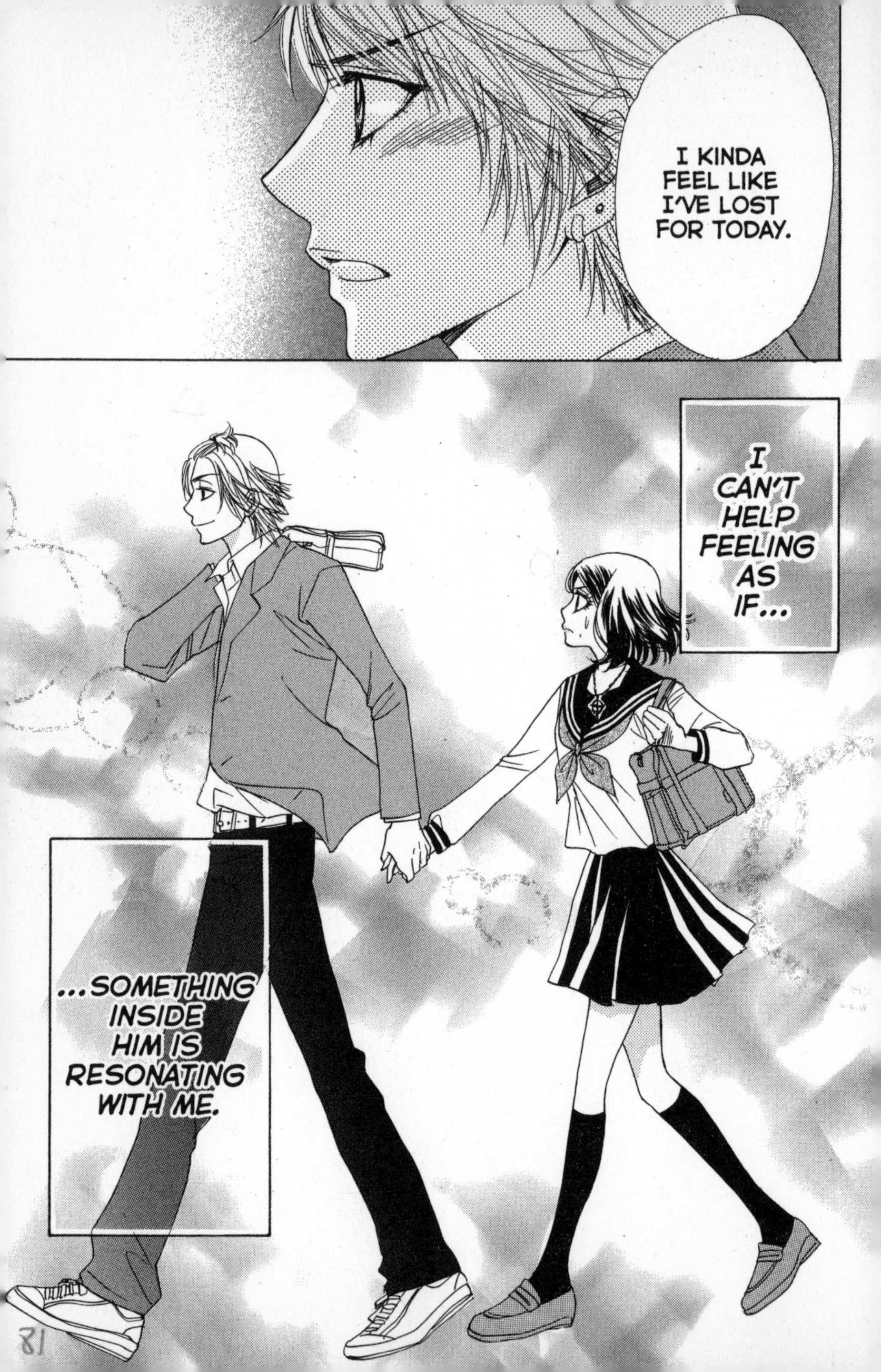
I KINDA FEEL LIKE I'VE LOST FOR TODAY.
I CAN'T HELP FEELING AS IF...
...SOMETHING INSIDE HIM IS RESONATING WITH ME.

A Devil and
Her Love Song

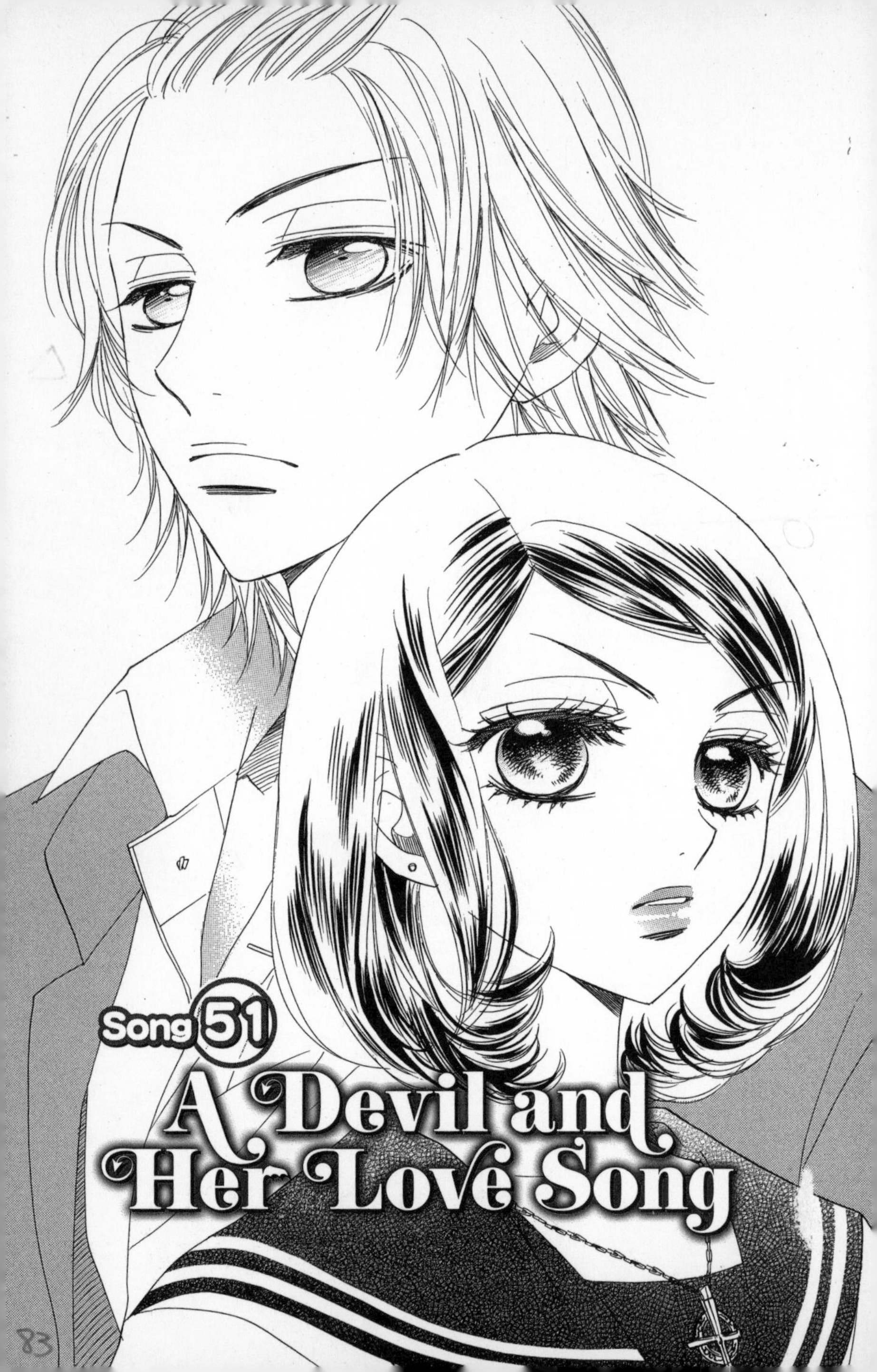
Song 51
A Devil and Her Love Song

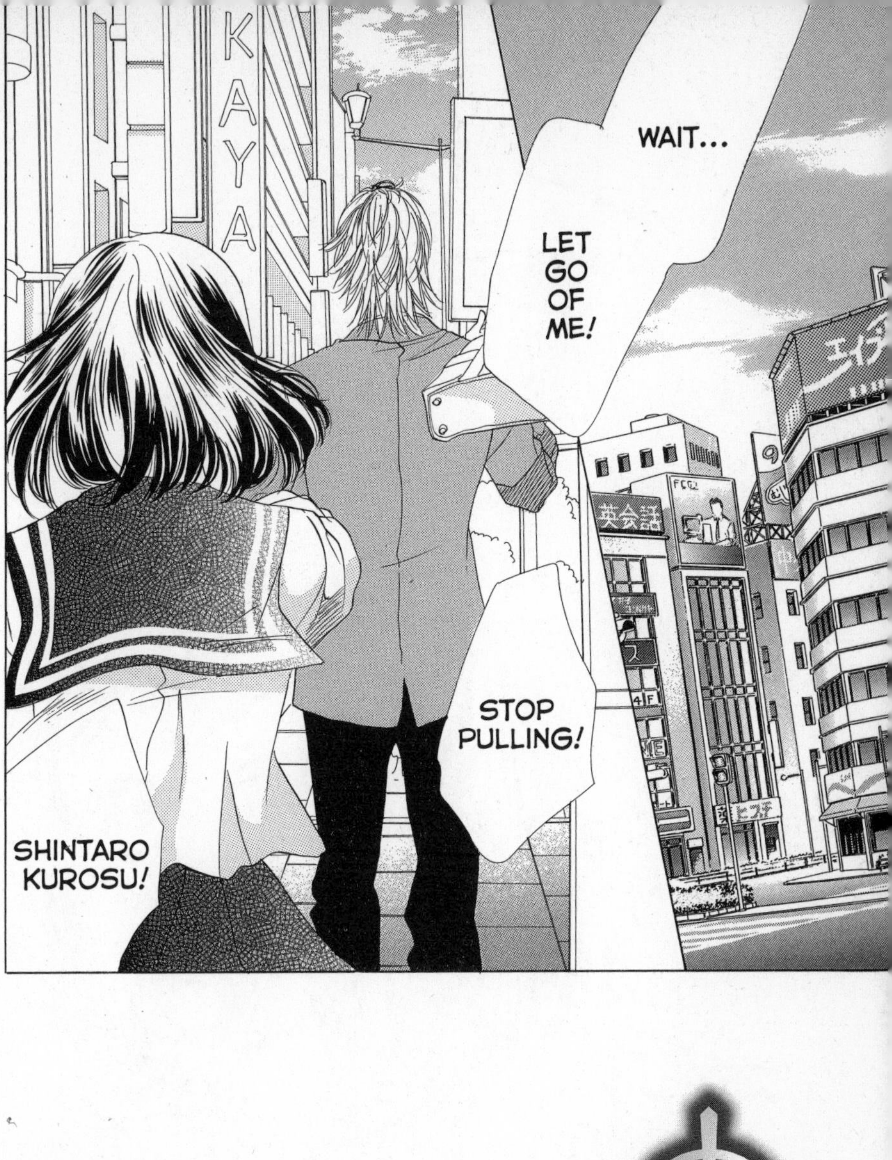
WAIT...
LET GO OF ME!
STOP PULLING!
SHINTARO KUROSU!
KAYA
英会話

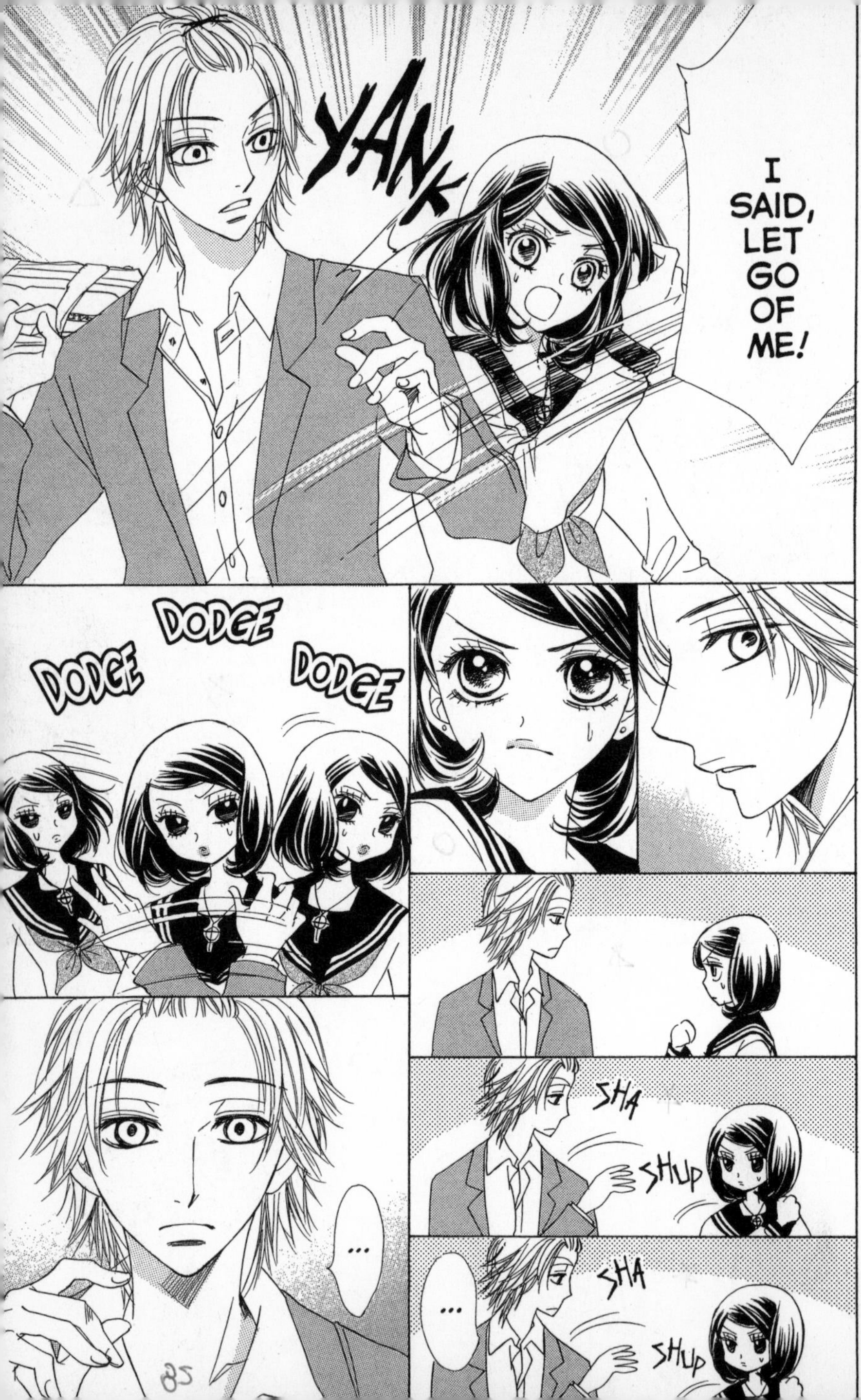
I SAID, LET GO OF ME!
YANK
SHA
SHUP
...
SHA
SHUP
DODGE
DODGE
DODGE
...

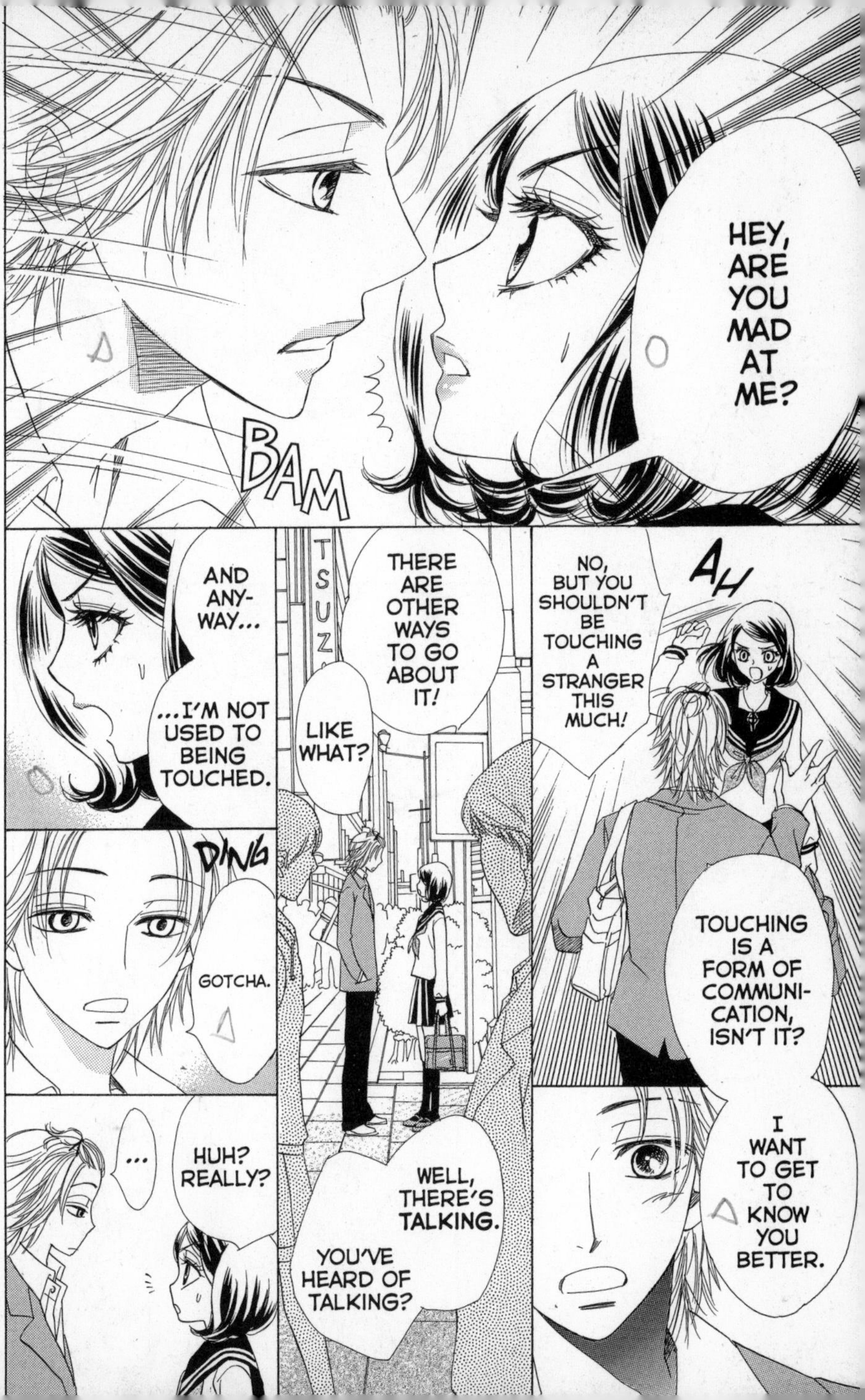
HEY, ARE YOU MAD AT ME?
BAM
AH
NO, BUT YOU SHOULDN'T BE TOUCHING A STRANGER THIS MUCH!
TOUCHING IS A FORM OF COMMUNICATION, ISN'T IT?
I WANT TO GET TO KNOW YOU BETTER.
TSUZ
THERE ARE OTHER WAYS TO GO ABOUT IT!
LIKE WHAT?
WELL, THERE'S TALKING.
YOU'VE HEARD OF TALKING?
AND ANY-WAY...
...I'M NOT USED TO BEING TOUCHED.
DING
GOTCHA.
HUH? REALLY?
...

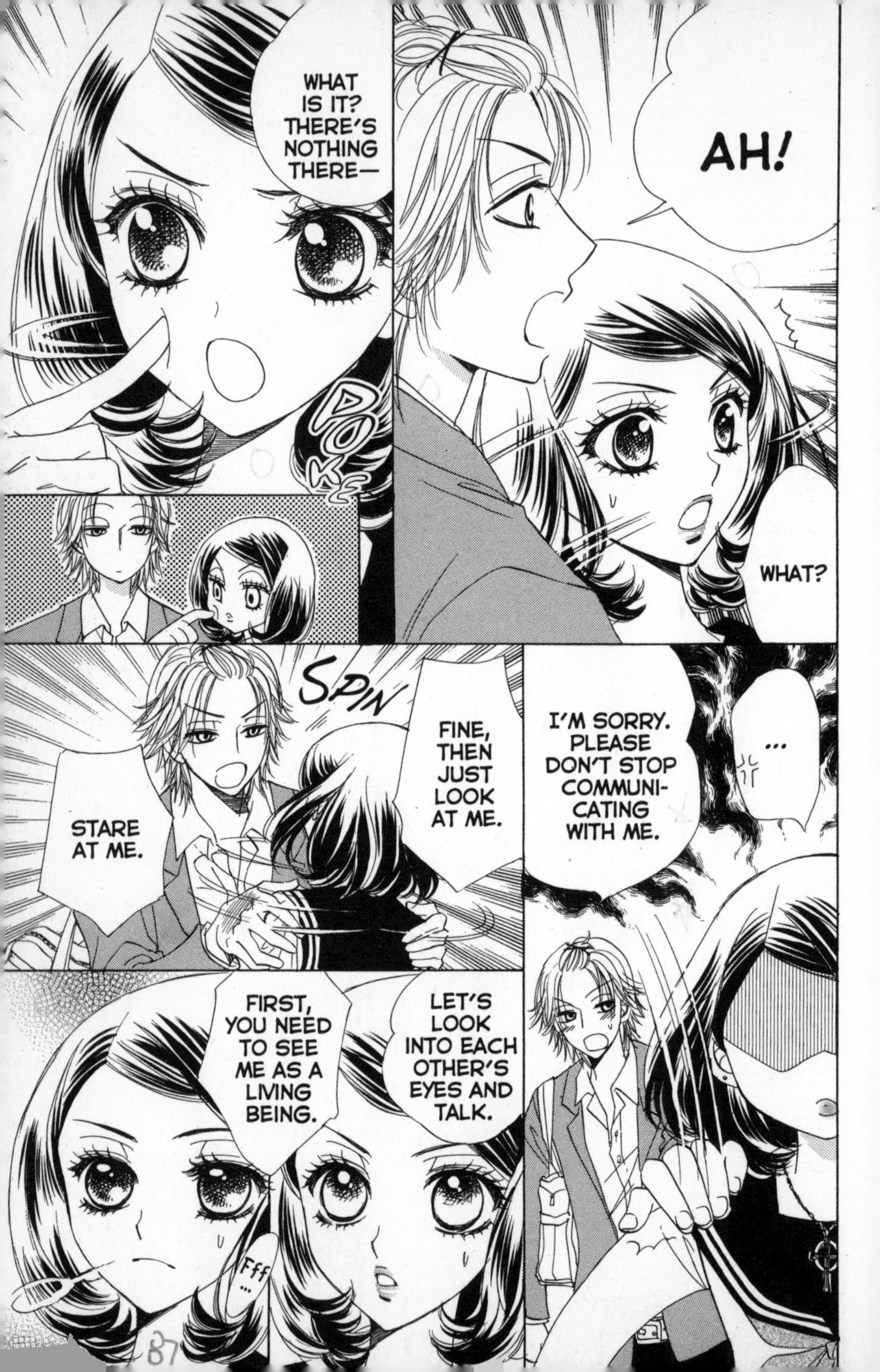
AH!
WHAT?
WHAT IS IT? THERE'S NOTHING THERE—
POKE
...
I'M SORRY. PLEASE DON'T STOP COMMUNICATING WITH ME.
SPIN
FINE, THEN JUST LOOK AT ME.
STARE AT ME.
LET'S LOOK INTO EACH OTHER'S EYES AND TALK.
FIRST, YOU NEED TO SEE ME AS A LIVING BEING.
Fff...

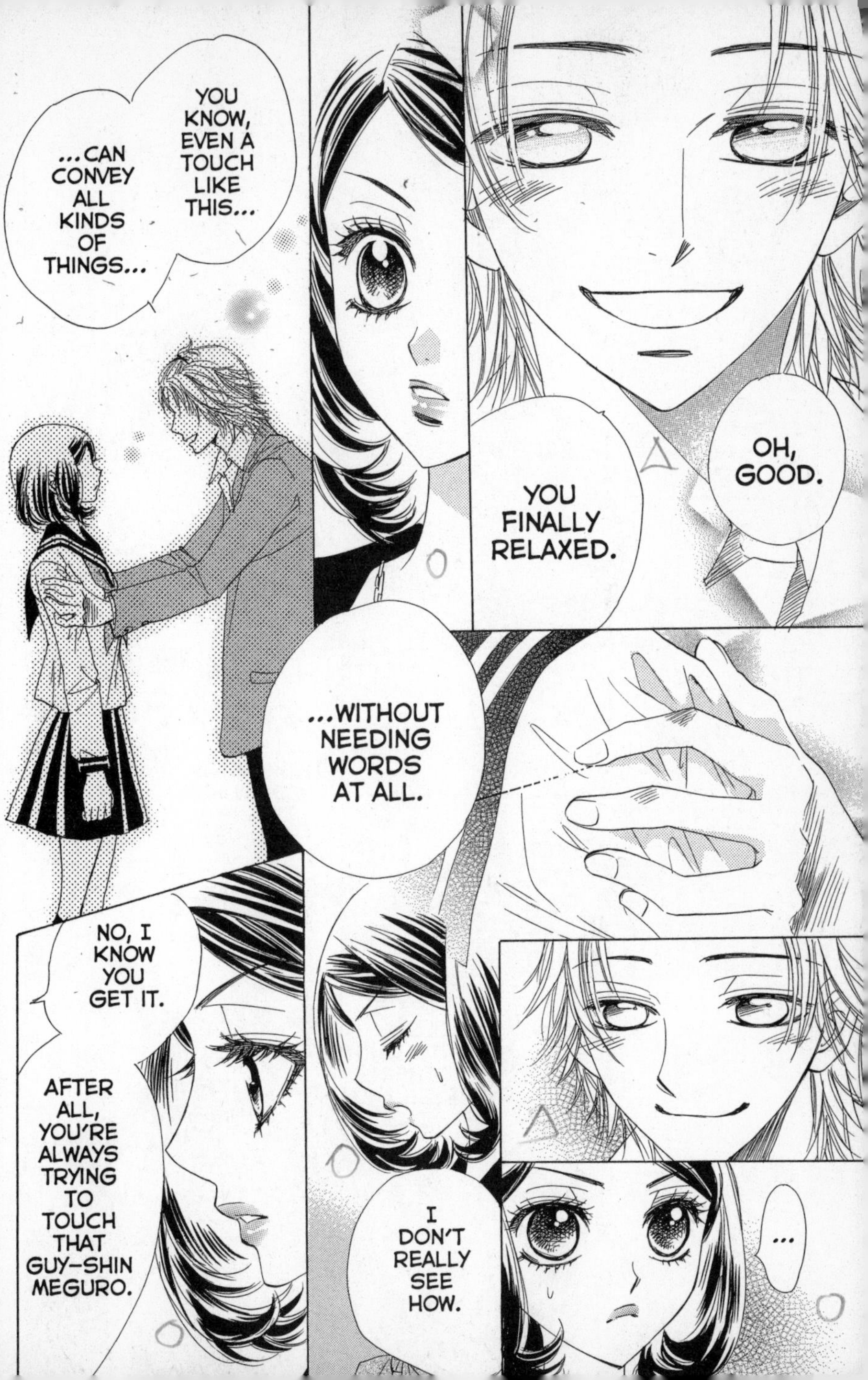
OH, GOOD.
YOU FINALLY RELAXED.
YOU KNOW, EVEN A TOUCH LIKE THIS...
...CAN CONVEY ALL KINDS OF THINGS...
...WITHOUT NEEDING WORDS AT ALL.
...
I DON'T REALLY SEE HOW.
NO, I KNOW YOU GET IT.
AFTER ALL, YOU'RE ALWAYS TRYING TO TOUCH THAT GUY—SHIN MEGURO.

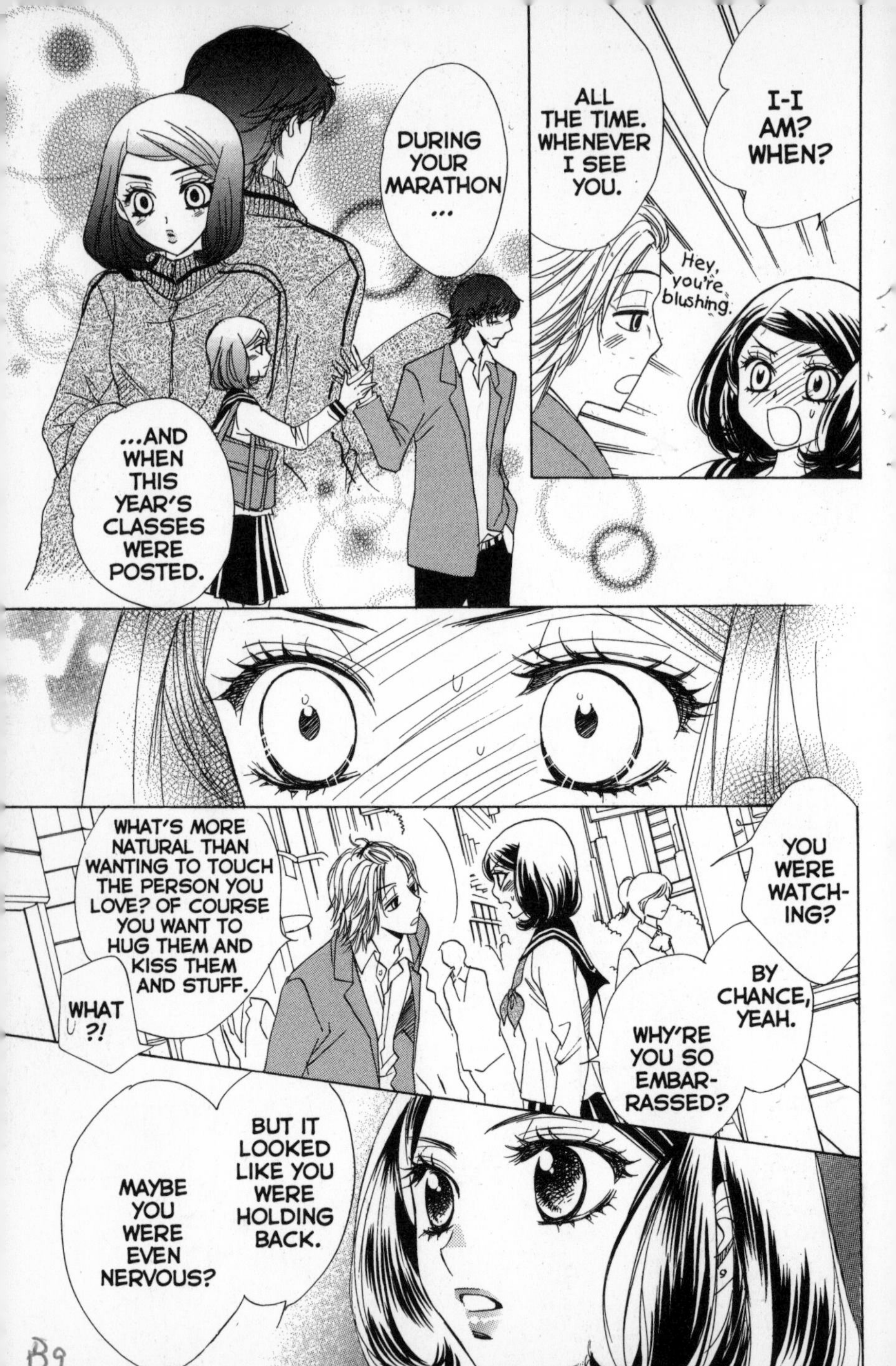
I-I AM? WHEN?
ALL THE TIME. WHENEVER I SEE YOU.
Hey, you're blushing.
DURING YOUR MARATHON...
...AND WHEN THIS YEAR'S CLASSES WERE POSTED.
YOU WERE WATCHING?
BY CHANCE, YEAH.
WHY'RE YOU SO EMBARRASSED?
WHAT'S MORE NATURAL THAN WANTING TO TOUCH THE PERSON YOU LOVE? OF COURSE YOU WANT TO HUG THEM AND KISS THEM AND STUFF.
WHAT ?!
BUT IT LOOKED LIKE YOU WERE HOLDING BACK.
MAYBE YOU WERE EVEN NERVOUS?

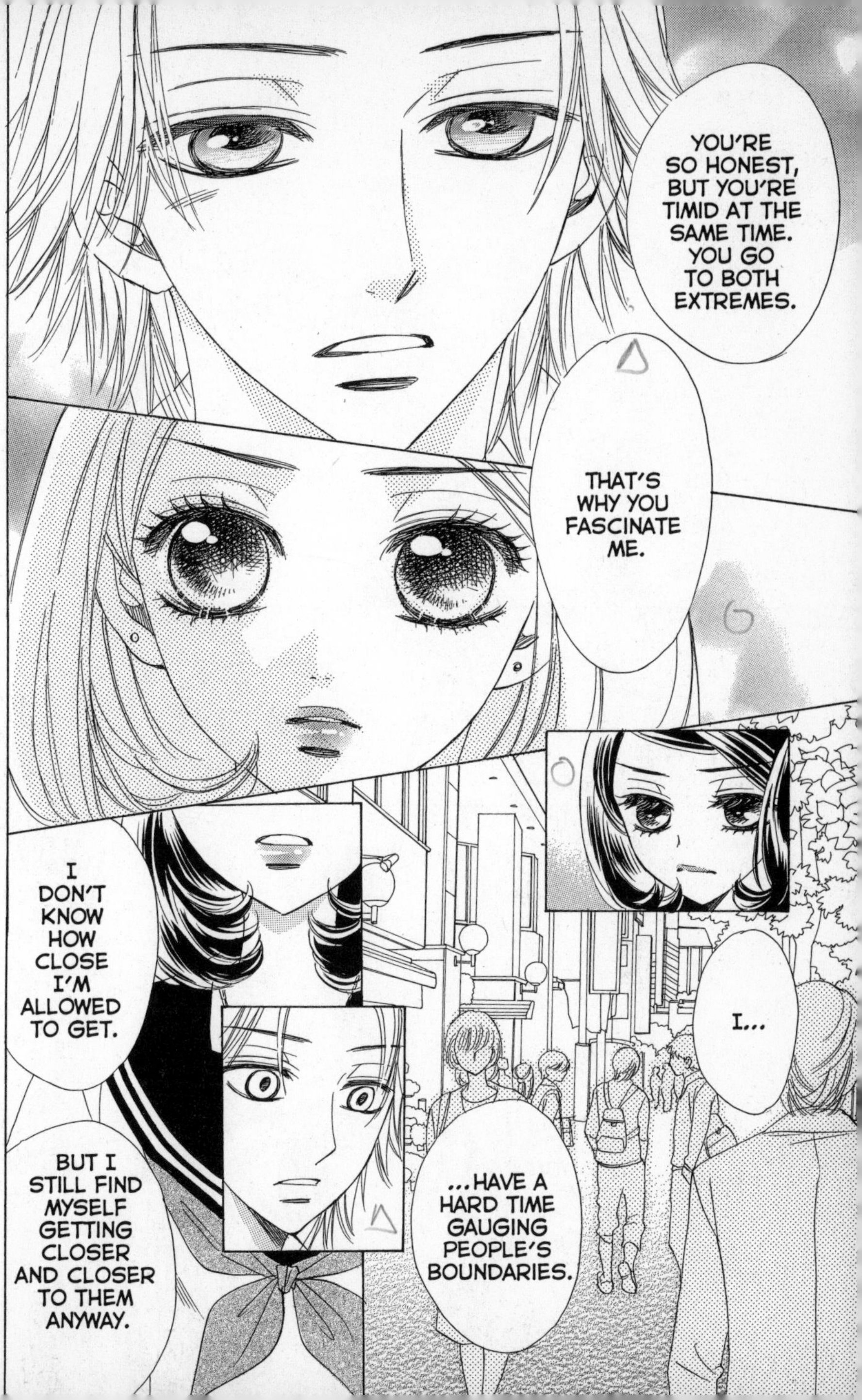
YOU'RE SO HONEST, BUT YOU'RE TIMID AT THE SAME TIME. YOU GO TO BOTH EXTREMES.
THAT'S WHY YOU FASCINATE ME.
I...
I DON'T KNOW HOW CLOSE I'M ALLOWED TO GET.
...HAVE A HARD TIME GAUGING PEOPLE'S BOUNDARIES.
BUT I STILL FIND MYSELF GETTING CLOSER AND CLOSER TO THEM ANYWAY.

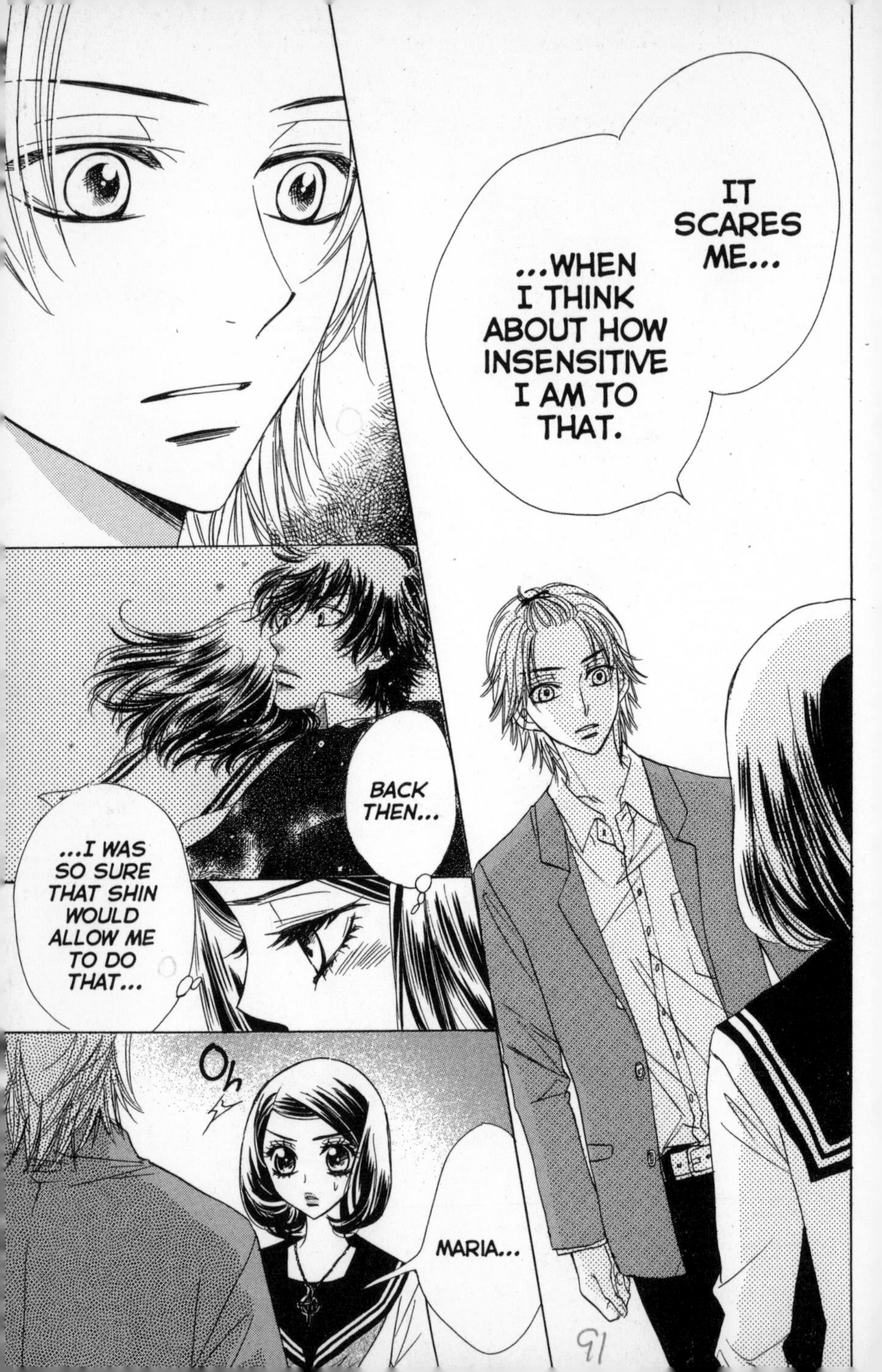
IT SCARES ME...
...WHEN I THINK ABOUT HOW INSENSITIVE I AM TO THAT.
BACK THEN...
...I WAS SO SURE THAT SHIN WOULD ALLOW ME TO DO THAT...
Oh
MARIA...

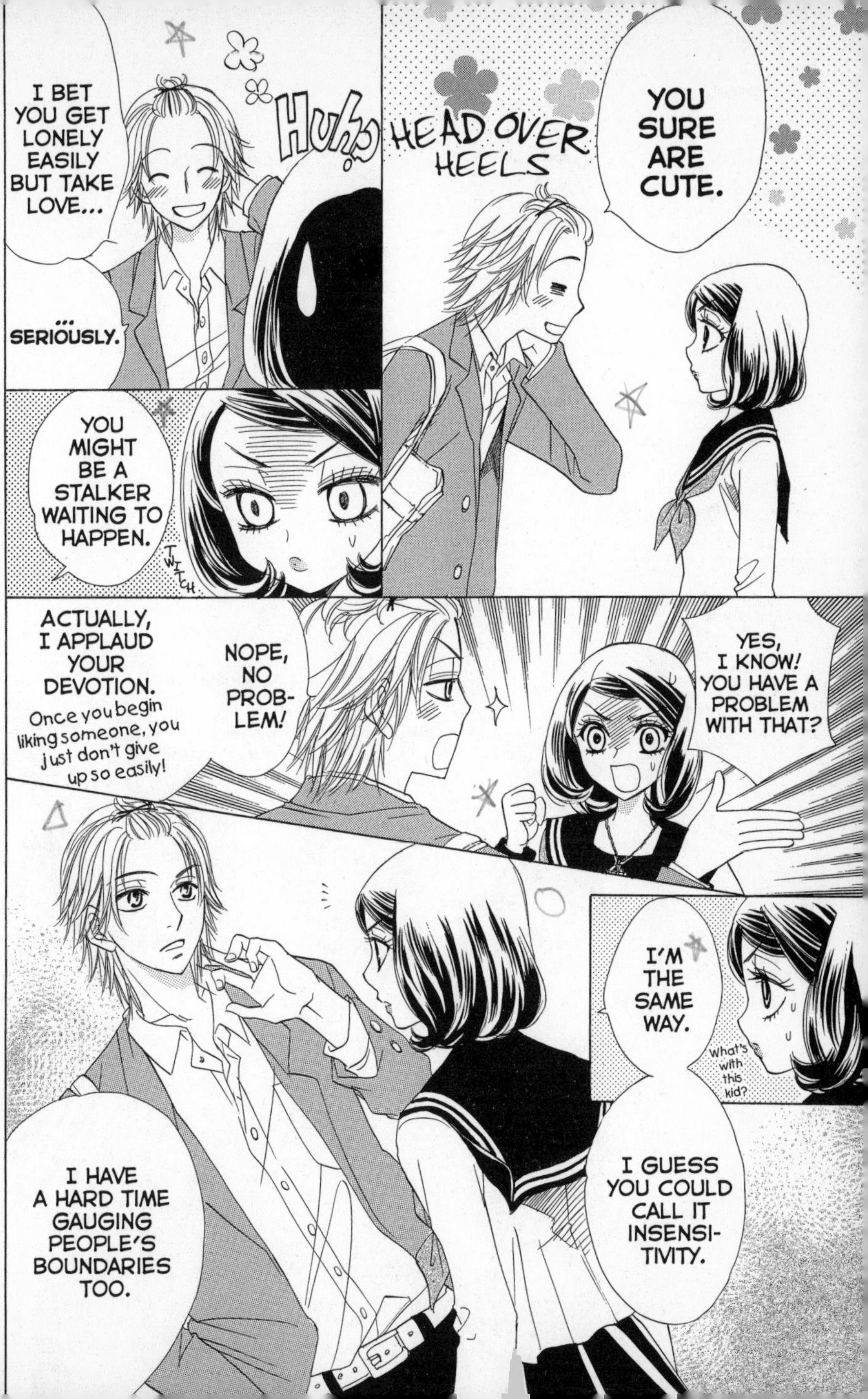
HEAD OVER HEELS
YOU SURE ARE CUTE.
I BET YOU GET LONELY EASILY BUT TAKE LOVE...
Huh?
... SERIOUSLY.
YOU MIGHT BE A STALKER WAITING TO HAPPEN.
TWITCH
YES, I KNOW! YOU HAVE A PROBLEM WITH THAT?
NOPE, NO PROB-LEM!
ACTUALLY, I APPLAUD YOUR DEVOTION.
Once you begin liking someone, you just don't give up so easily!
I'M THE SAME WAY.
What's with this kid?
I GUESS YOU COULD CALL IT INSENSI-TIVITY.
I HAVE A HARD TIME GAUGING PEOPLE'S BOUNDARIES TOO.

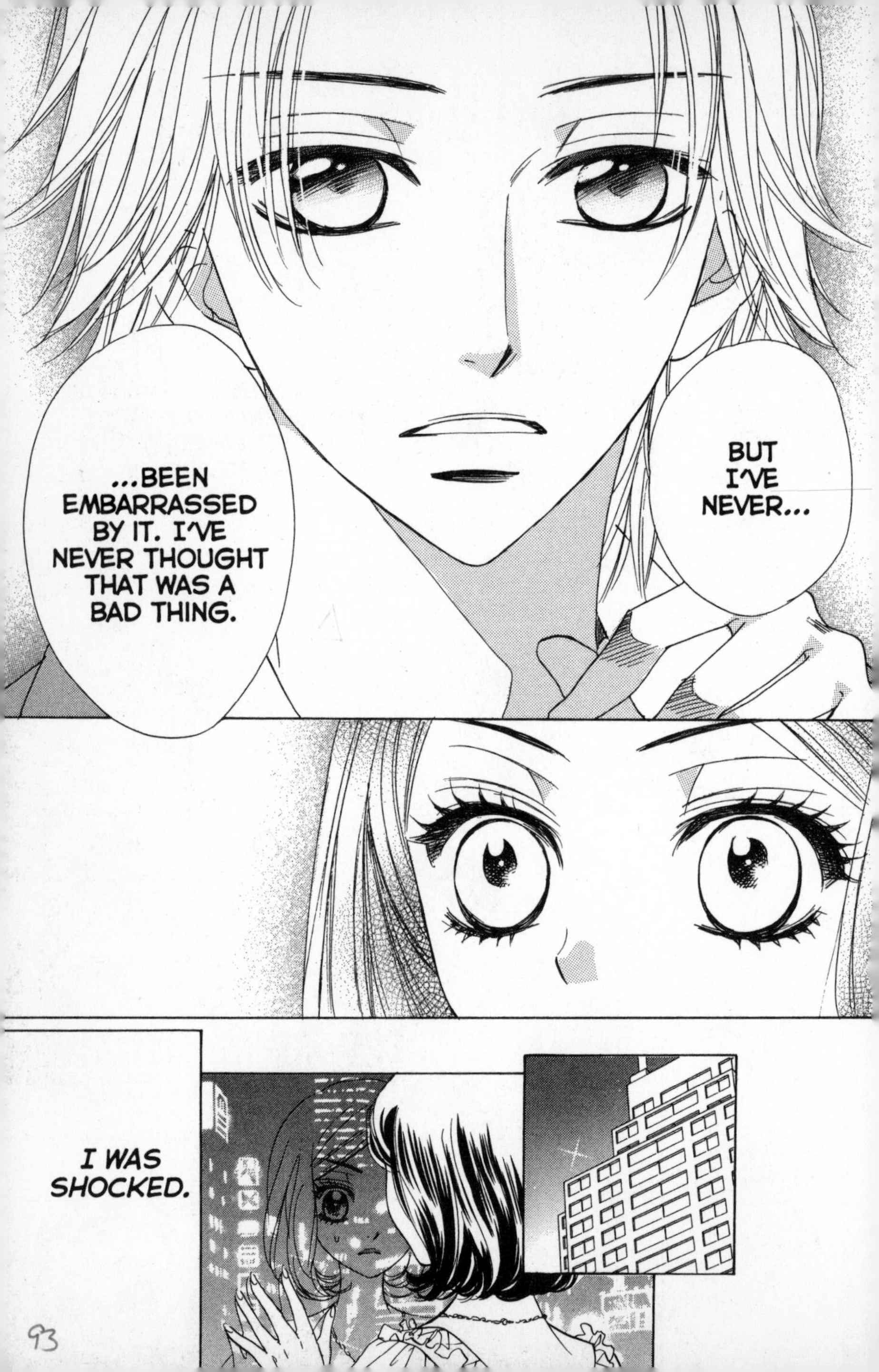
BUT I'VE NEVER...
...BEEN EMBARRASSED BY IT. I'VE NEVER THOUGHT THAT WAS A BAD THING.
I WAS SHOCKED.

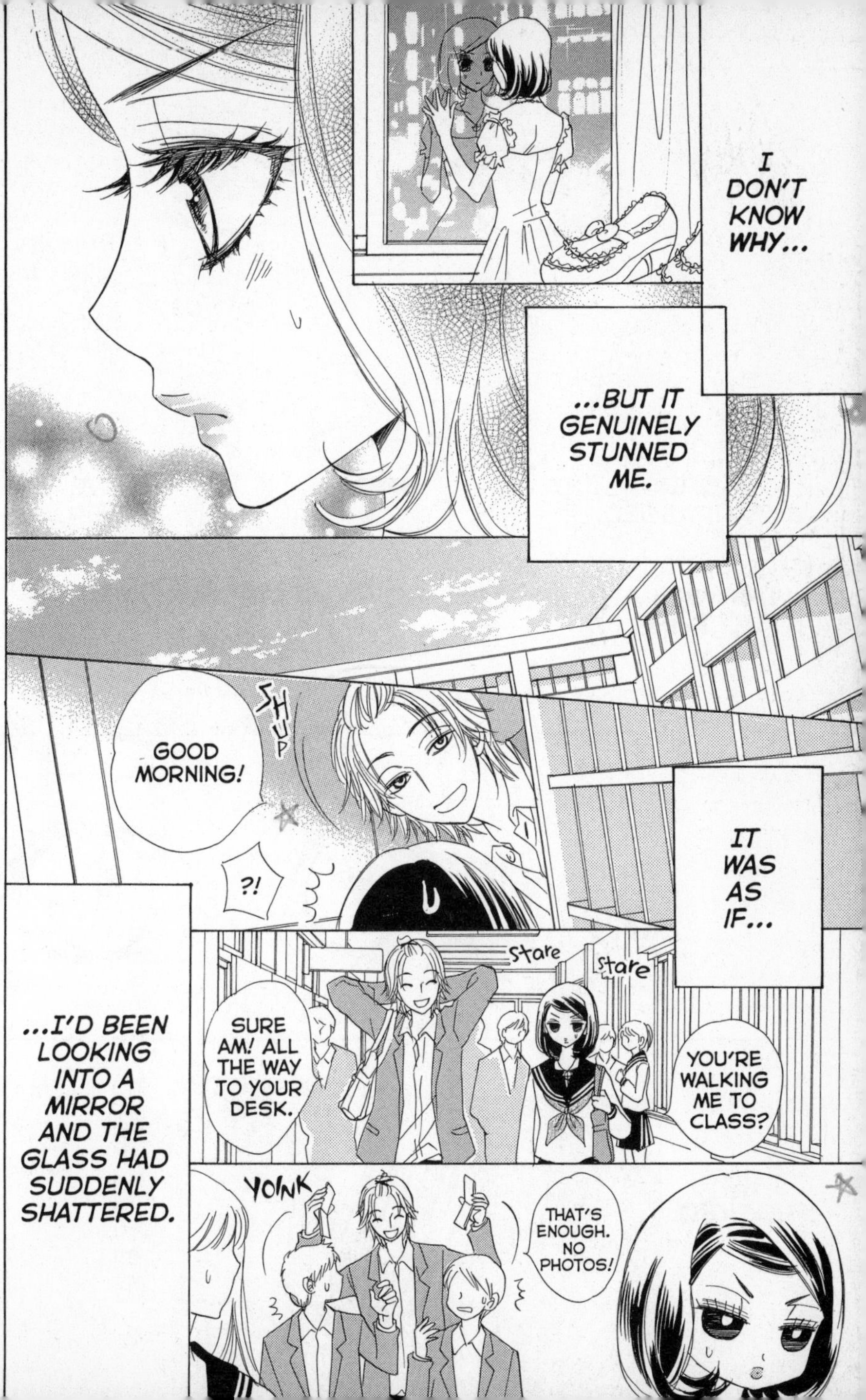
I DON'T KNOW WHY...
...BUT IT GENUINELY STUNNED ME.
IT WAS AS IF...
SHUP
GOOD MORNING!
?!
Stare
Stare
YOU'RE WALKING ME TO CLASS?
SURE AM! ALL THE WAY TO YOUR DESK.
THAT'S ENOUGH. NO PHOTOS!
YOINK
...I'D BEEN LOOKING INTO A MIRROR AND THE GLASS HAD SUDDENLY SHATTERED.

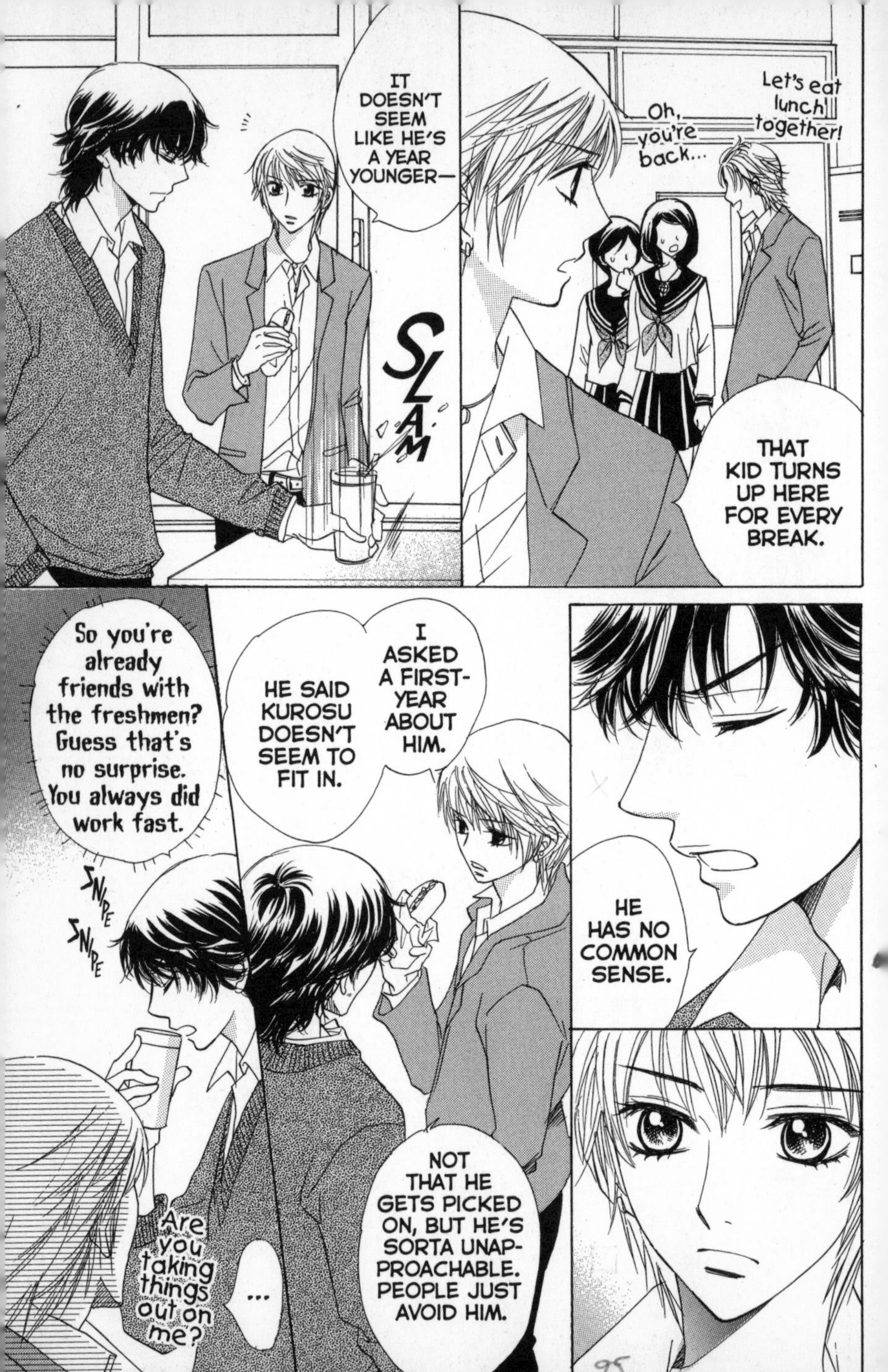
Let's eat lunch together!
Oh, you're back...
THAT KID TURNS UP HERE FOR EVERY BREAK.
IT DOESN'T SEEM LIKE HE'S A YEAR YOUNGER—
SLAM
HE HAS NO COMMON SENSE.
I ASKED A FIRST-YEAR ABOUT HIM.
HE SAID KUROSU DOESN'T SEEM TO FIT IN.
NOT THAT HE GETS PICKED ON, BUT HE'S SORTA UNAPPROACHABLE. PEOPLE JUST AVOID HIM.
So you're already friends with the freshmen? Guess that's no surprise. You always did work fast.
SNIPE SNIPE
...
Are you taking things out on me?

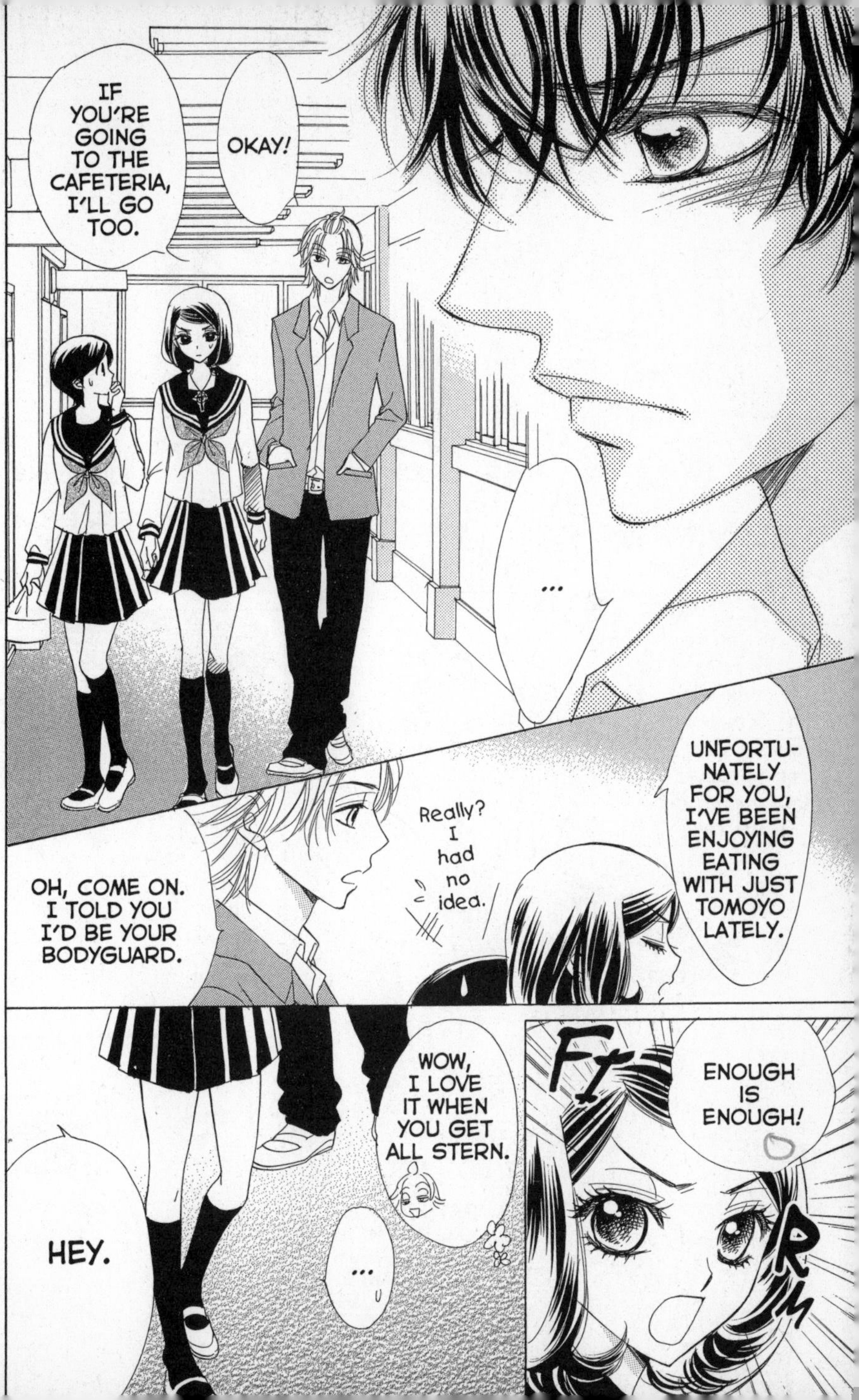
...
OKAY!
IF YOU'RE GOING TO THE CAFETERIA, I'LL GO TOO.
UNFORTUNATELY FOR YOU, I'VE BEEN ENJOYING EATING WITH JUST TOMOYO LATELY.
Really? I had no idea.
OH, COME ON. I TOLD YOU I'D BE YOUR BODYGUARD.
FT
ENOUGH IS ENOUGH!
RM
WOW, I LOVE IT WHEN YOU GET ALL STERN.
...
HEY.

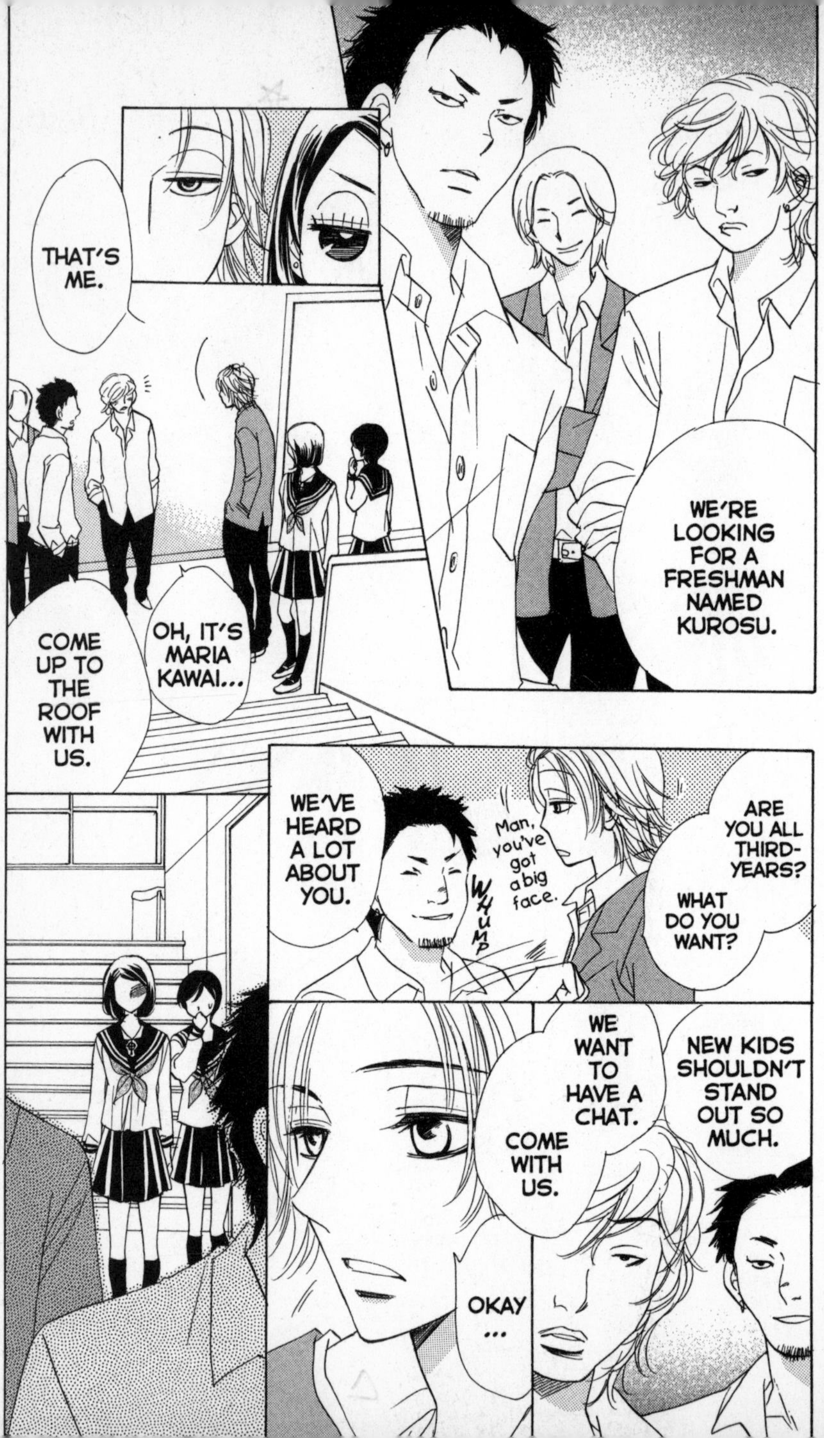
WE'RE LOOKING FOR A FRESHMAN NAMED KUROSU.
THAT'S ME.
OH, IT'S MARIA KAWAI...
COME UP TO THE ROOF WITH US.
ARE YOU ALL THIRD-YEARS?
WHAT DO YOU WANT?
WE'VE HEARD A LOT ABOUT YOU.
Man, you've got a big face.
WHUMP
NEW KIDS SHOULDN'T STAND OUT SO MUCH.
WE WANT TO HAVE A CHAT.
COME WITH US.
OKAY ...

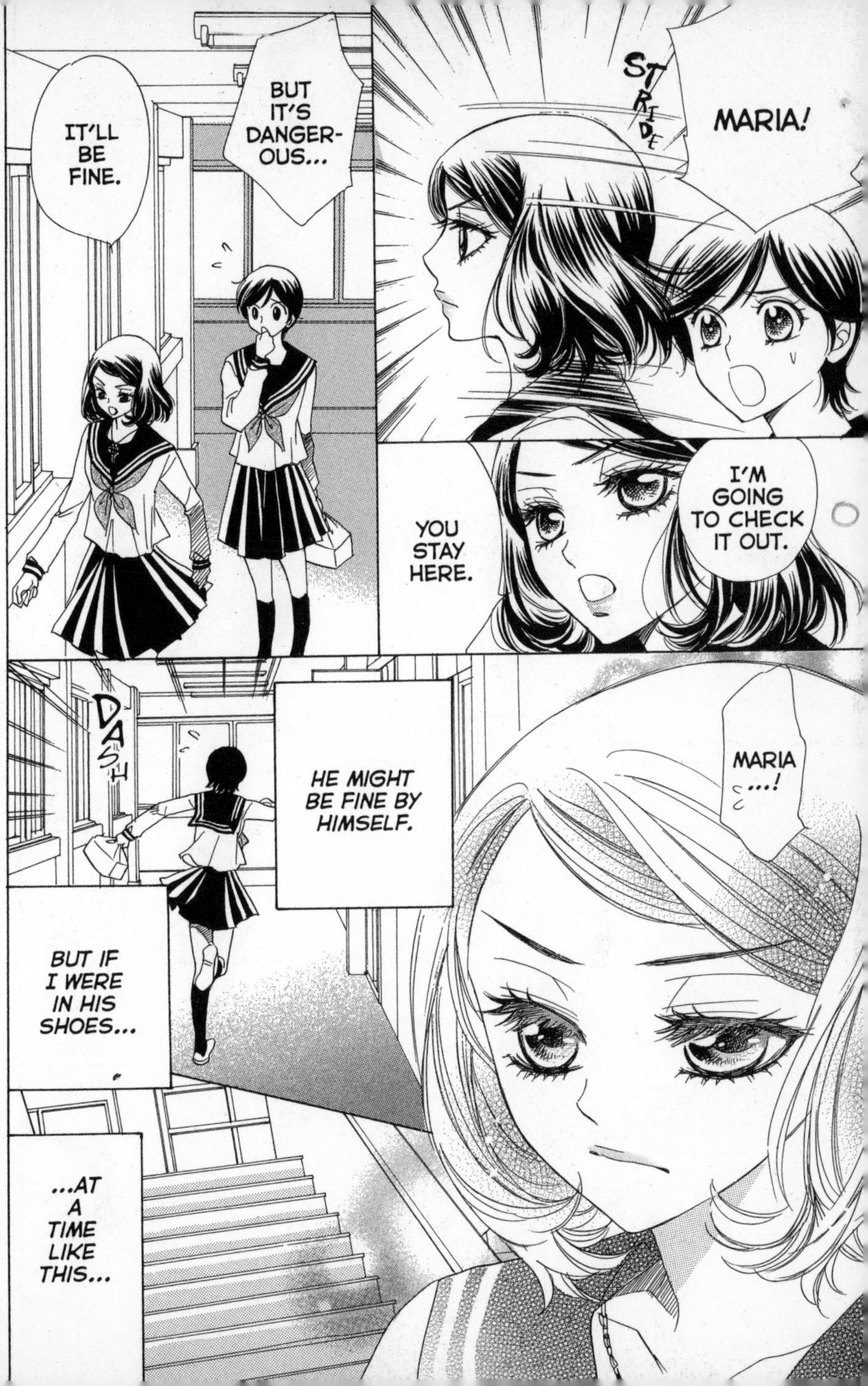
MARIA!
STRIDE
I'M GOING TO CHECK IT OUT.
YOU STAY HERE.
BUT IT'S DANGER-OUS...
IT'LL BE FINE.
MARIA...!
HE MIGHT BE FINE BY HIMSELF.
DASH
BUT IF I WERE IN HIS SHOES...
...AT A TIME LIKE THIS...

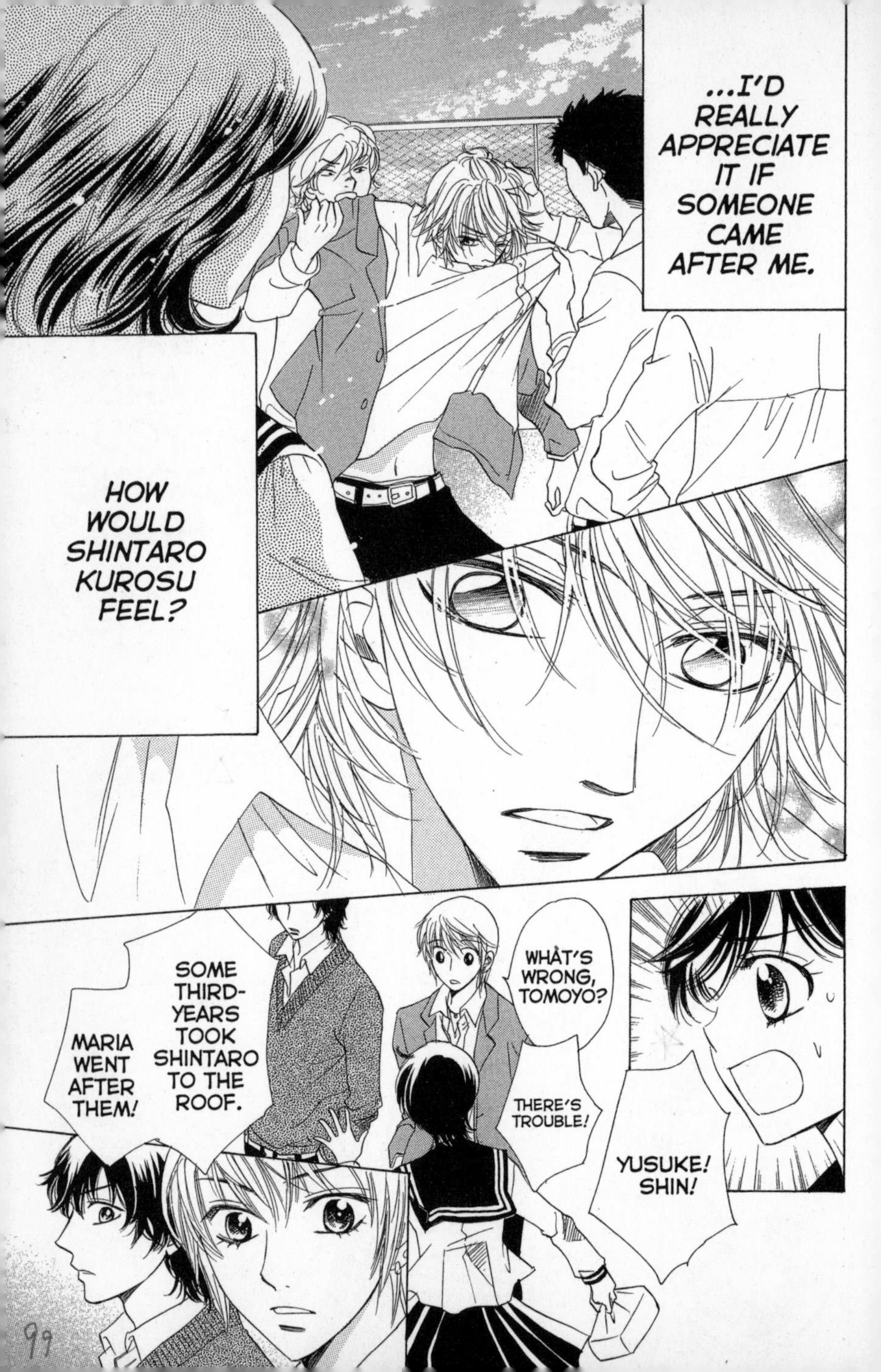
...I'D REALLY APPRECIATE IT IF SOMEONE CAME AFTER ME.
HOW WOULD SHINTARO KUROSU FEEL?
YUSUKE! SHIN!
WHAT'S WRONG, TOMOYO?
THERE'S TROUBLE!
SOME THIRD-YEARS TOOK SHINTARO TO THE ROOF.
MARIA WENT AFTER THEM!

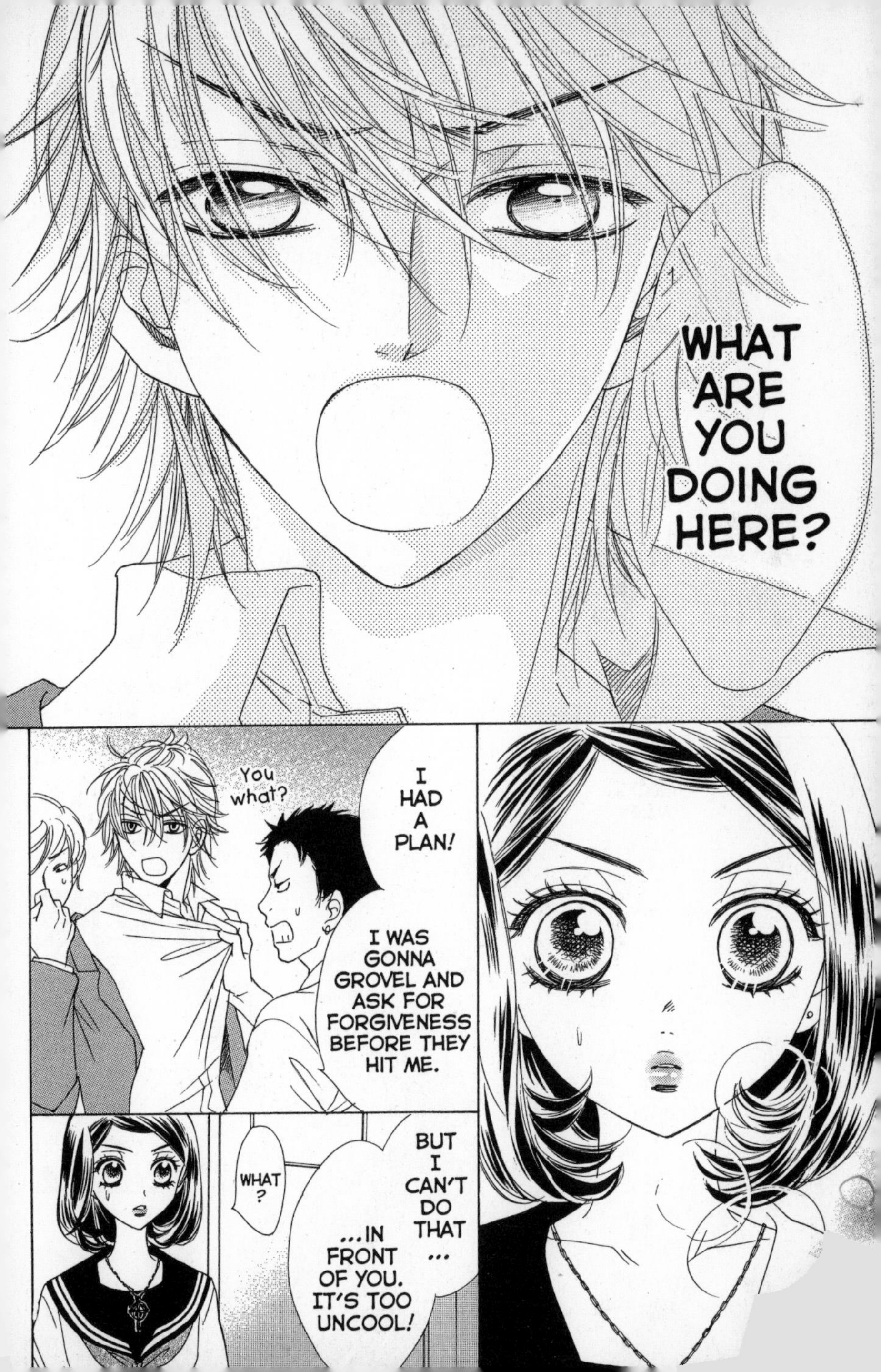
WHAT ARE YOU DOING HERE?
I HAD A PLAN!
You what?
I WAS GONNA GROVEL AND ASK FOR FORGIVENESS BEFORE THEY HIT ME.
BUT I CAN'T DO THAT...
...IN FRONT OF YOU. IT'S TOO UNCOOL!
WHAT?

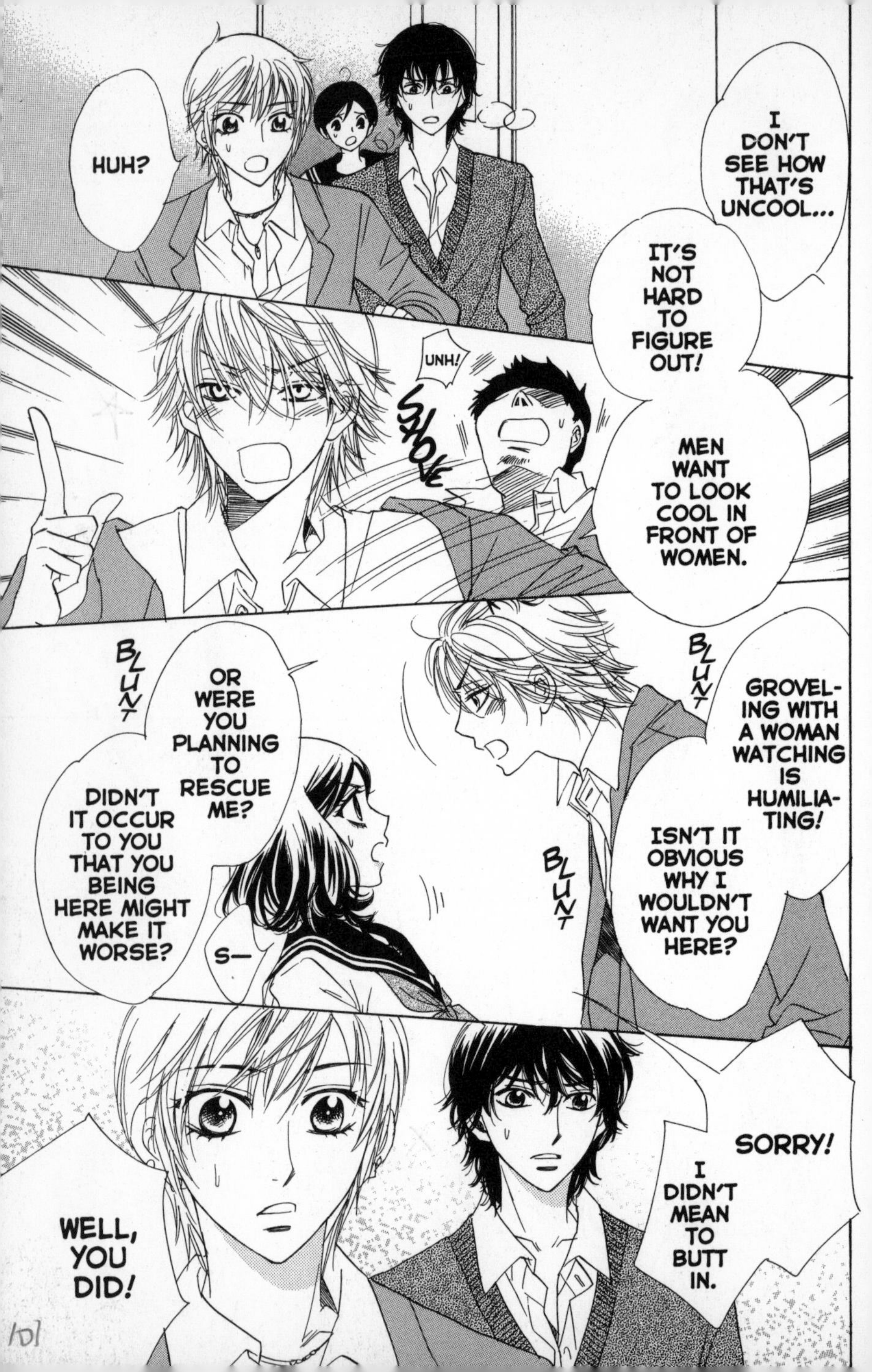
I DON'T SEE HOW THAT'S UNCOOL...
HUH?
IT'S NOT HARD TO FIGURE OUT!
MEN WANT TO LOOK COOL IN FRONT OF WOMEN.
UNH!
SHOVE
GROVELING WITH A WOMAN WATCHING IS HUMILIATING!
BLUNT
ISN'T IT OBVIOUS WHY I WOULDN'T WANT YOU HERE?
BLUNT
OR WERE YOU PLANNING TO RESCUE ME?
BLUNT
DIDN'T IT OCCUR TO YOU THAT YOU BEING HERE MIGHT MAKE IT WORSE?
S—
SORRY!
I DIDN'T MEAN TO BUTT IN.
WELL, YOU DID!

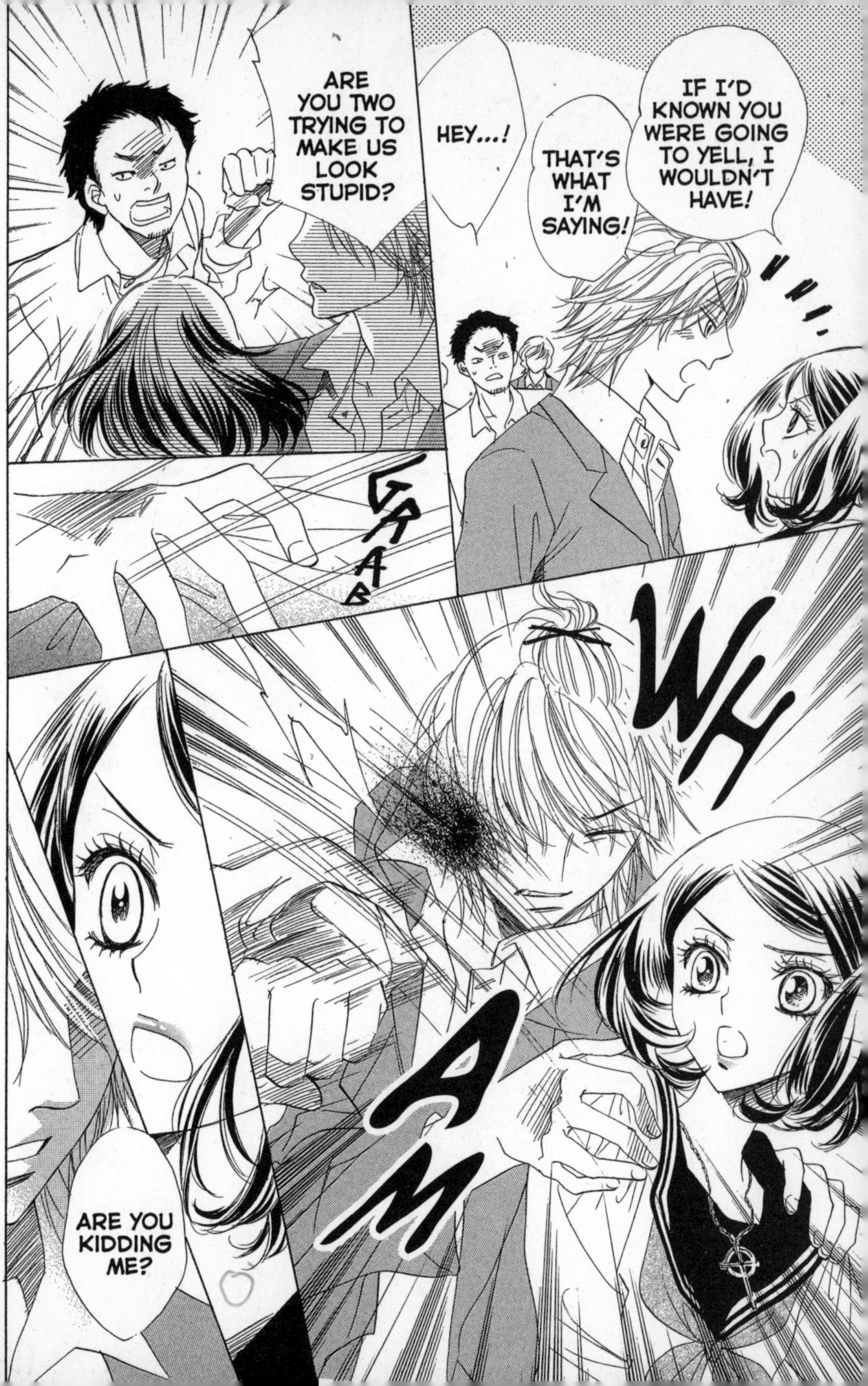
IF I'D KNOWN YOU WERE GOING TO YELL, I WOULDN'T HAVE!
THAT'S WHAT I'M SAYING!
HEY...!
ARE YOU TWO TRYING TO MAKE US LOOK STUPID?
GRAB
WHAM
ARE YOU KIDDING ME?

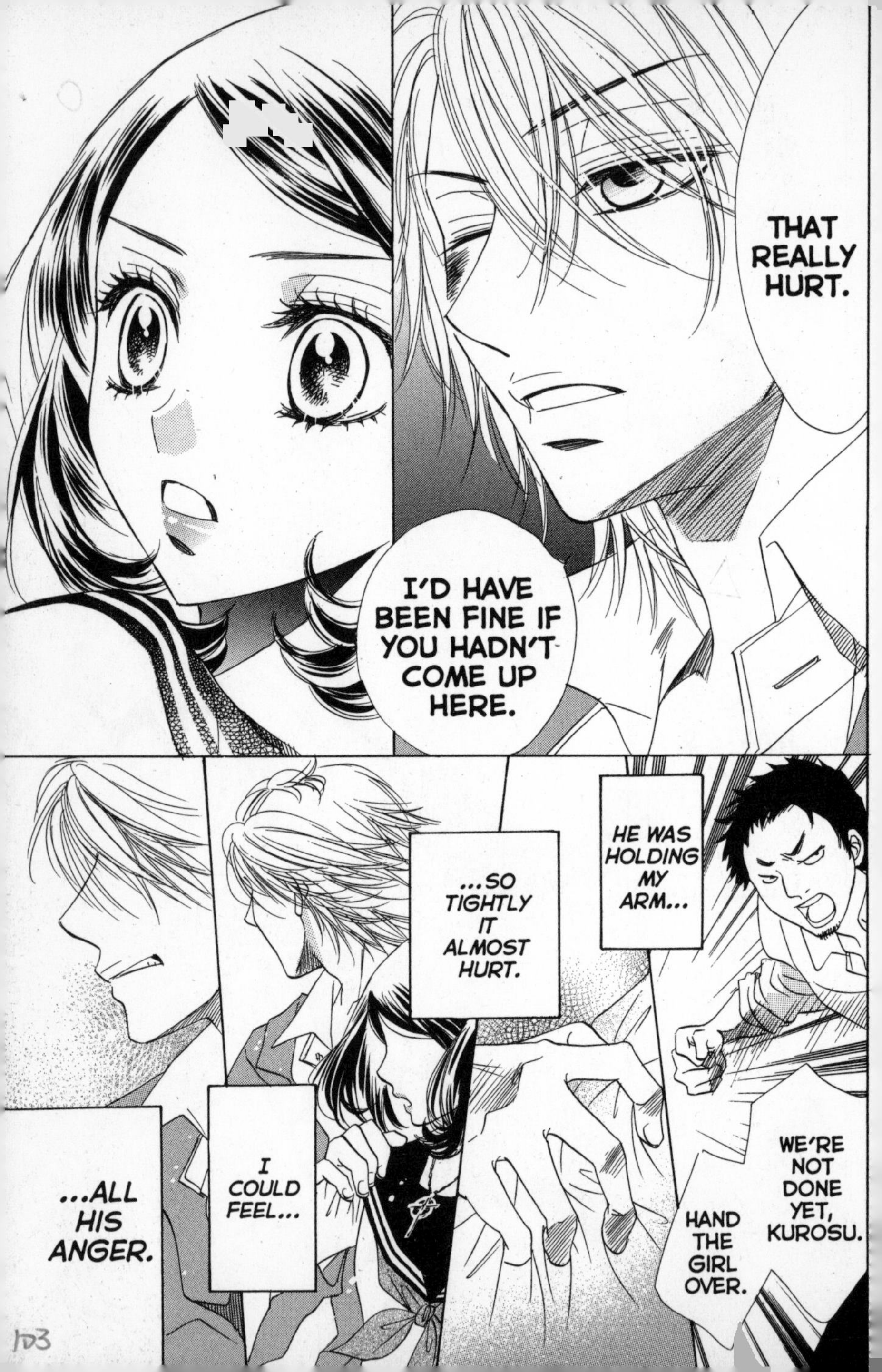
THAT REALLY HURT.
I'D HAVE BEEN FINE IF YOU HADN'T COME UP HERE.
WE'RE NOT DONE YET, KUROSU.
HAND THE GIRL OVER.
HE WAS HOLDING MY ARM...
...SO TIGHTLY IT ALMOST HURT.
I COULD FEEL...
...ALL HIS ANGER.

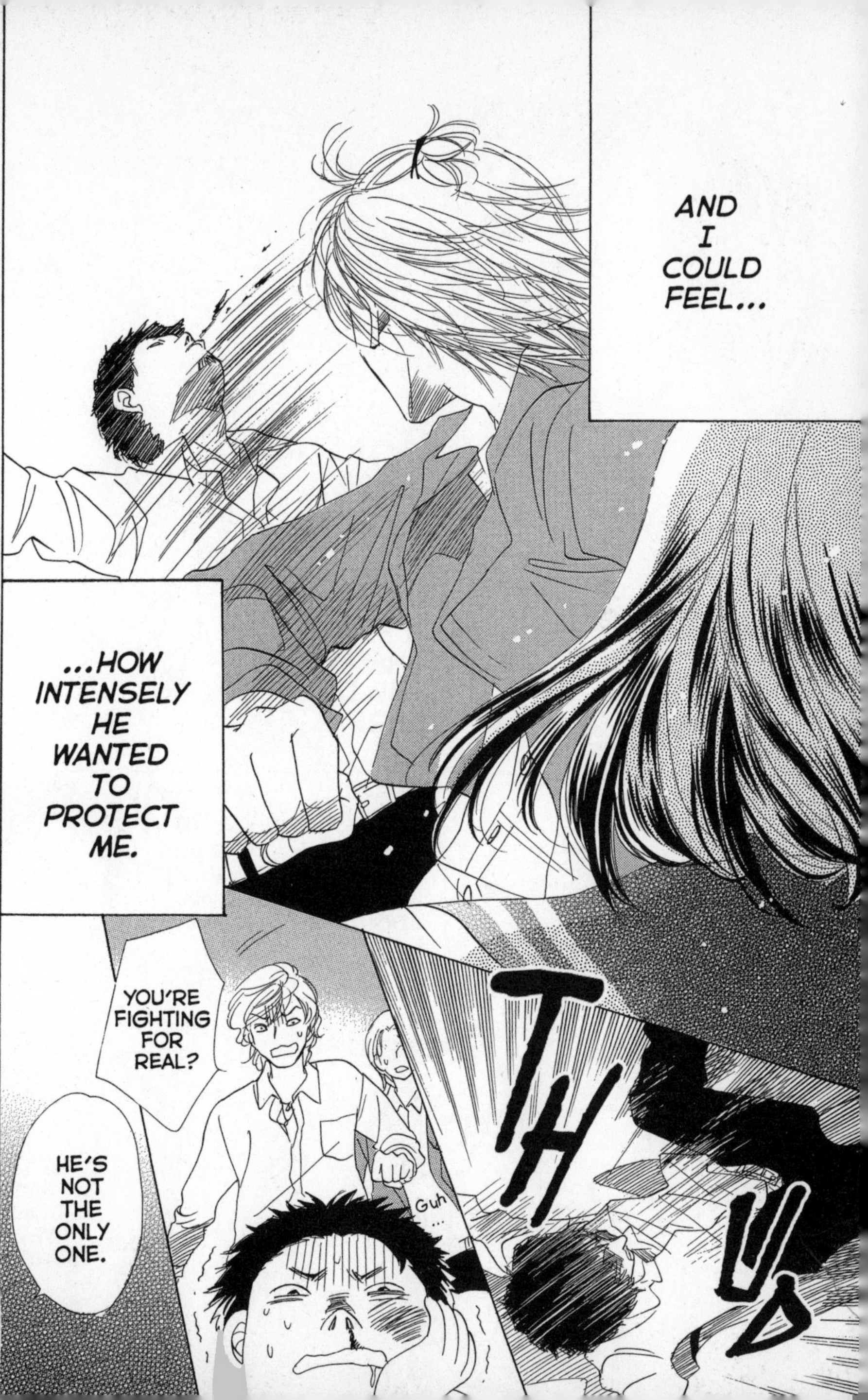
AND I COULD FEEL...
...HOW INTENSELY HE WANTED TO PROTECT ME.
THUD
YOU'RE FIGHTING FOR REAL?
HE'S NOT THE ONLY ONE.
Guh...

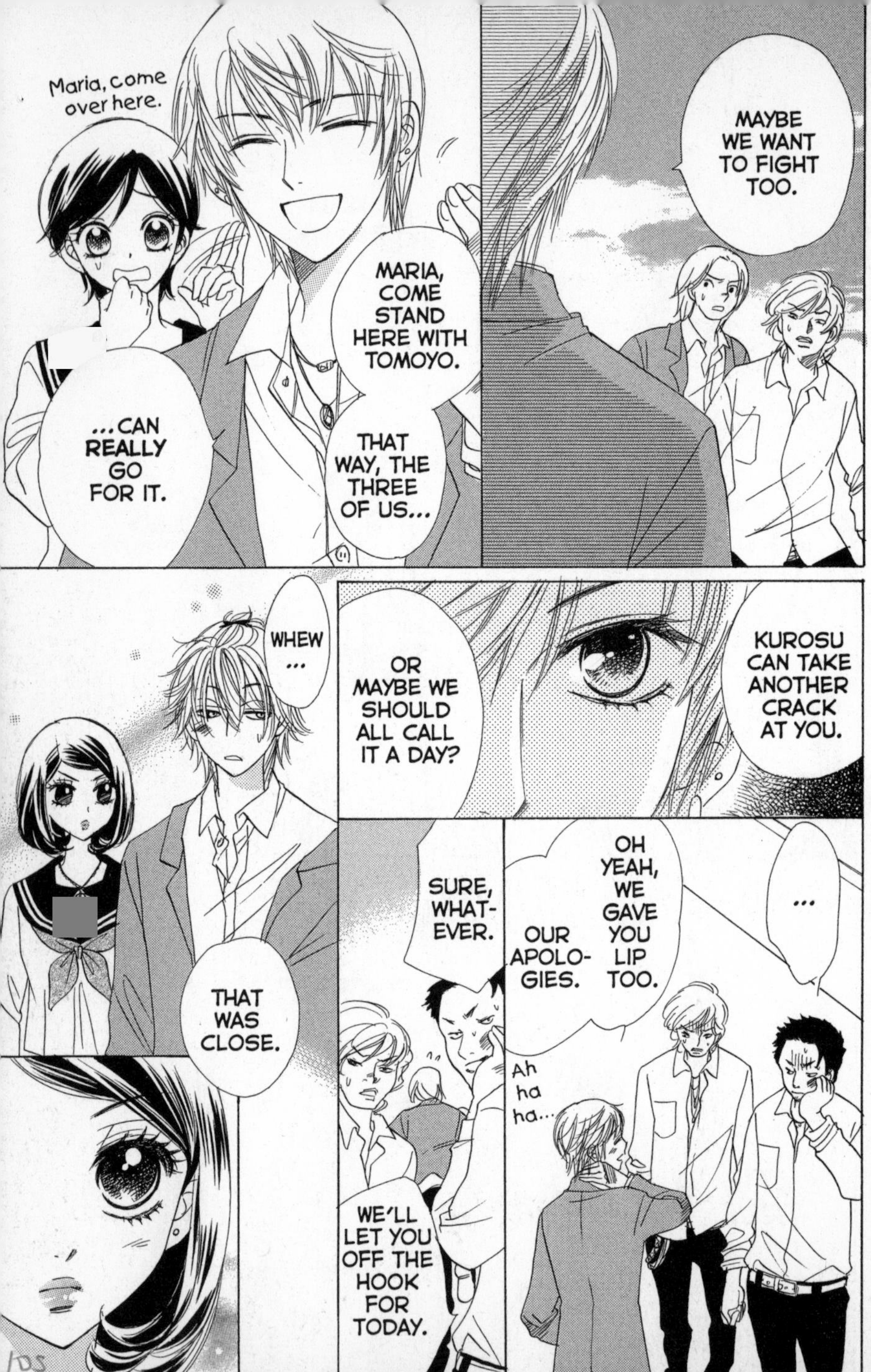
MAYBE WE WANT TO FIGHT TOO.
Maria, come over here.
MARIA, COME STAND HERE WITH TOMOYO.
THAT WAY, THE THREE OF US...
...CAN REALLY GO FOR IT.
KUROSU CAN TAKE ANOTHER CRACK AT YOU.
OR MAYBE WE SHOULD ALL CALL IT A DAY?
...
OH YEAH, WE GAVE YOU LIP TOO.
OUR APOLOGIES.
Ah ha ha...
SURE, WHATEVER.
WE'LL LET YOU OFF THE HOOK FOR TODAY.
WHEW...
THAT WAS CLOSE.

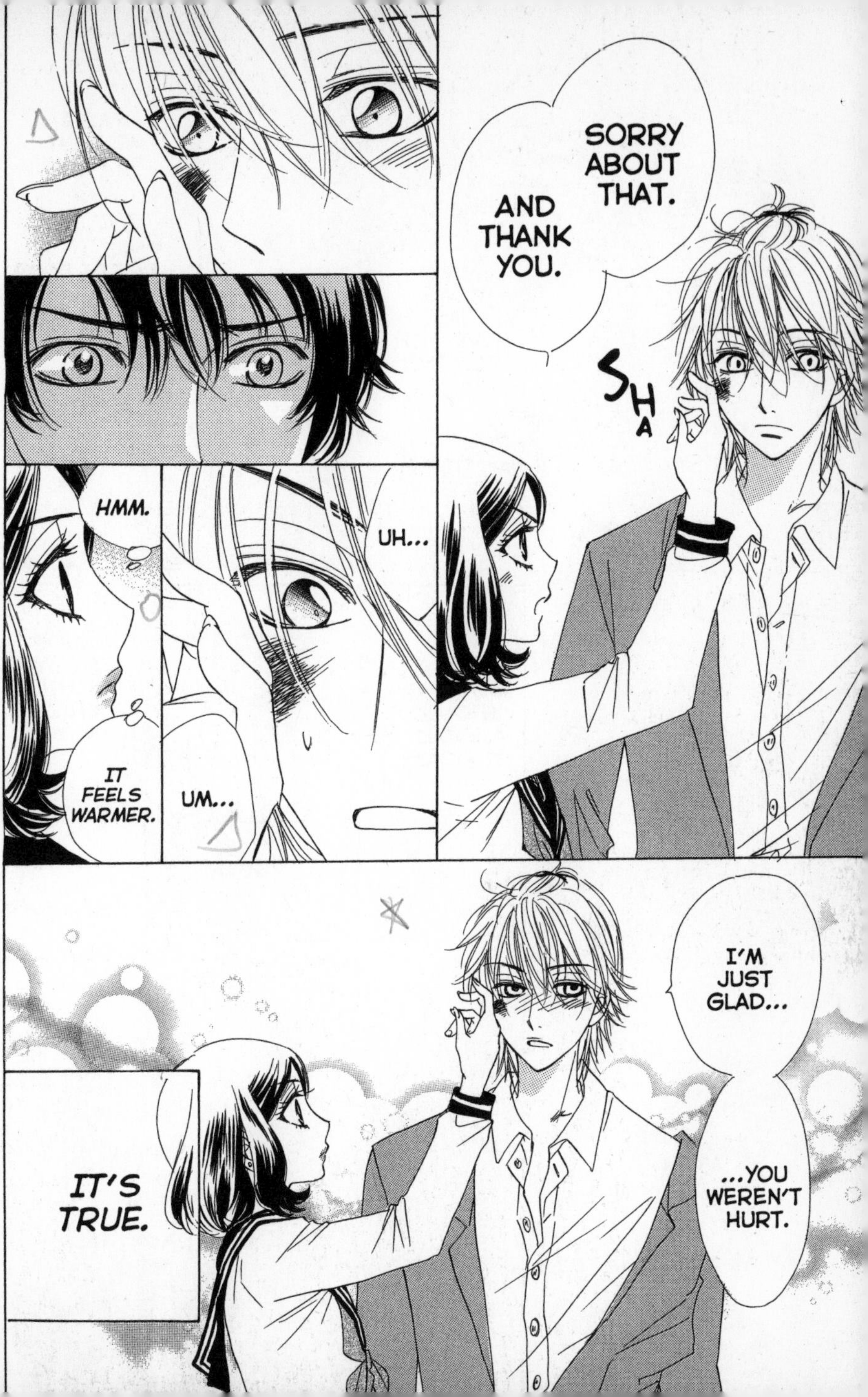
SORRY ABOUT THAT.
AND THANK YOU.
SHA
UH...
UM...
HMM.
IT FEELS WARMER.
I'M JUST GLAD...
...YOU WEREN'T HURT.
IT'S TRUE.

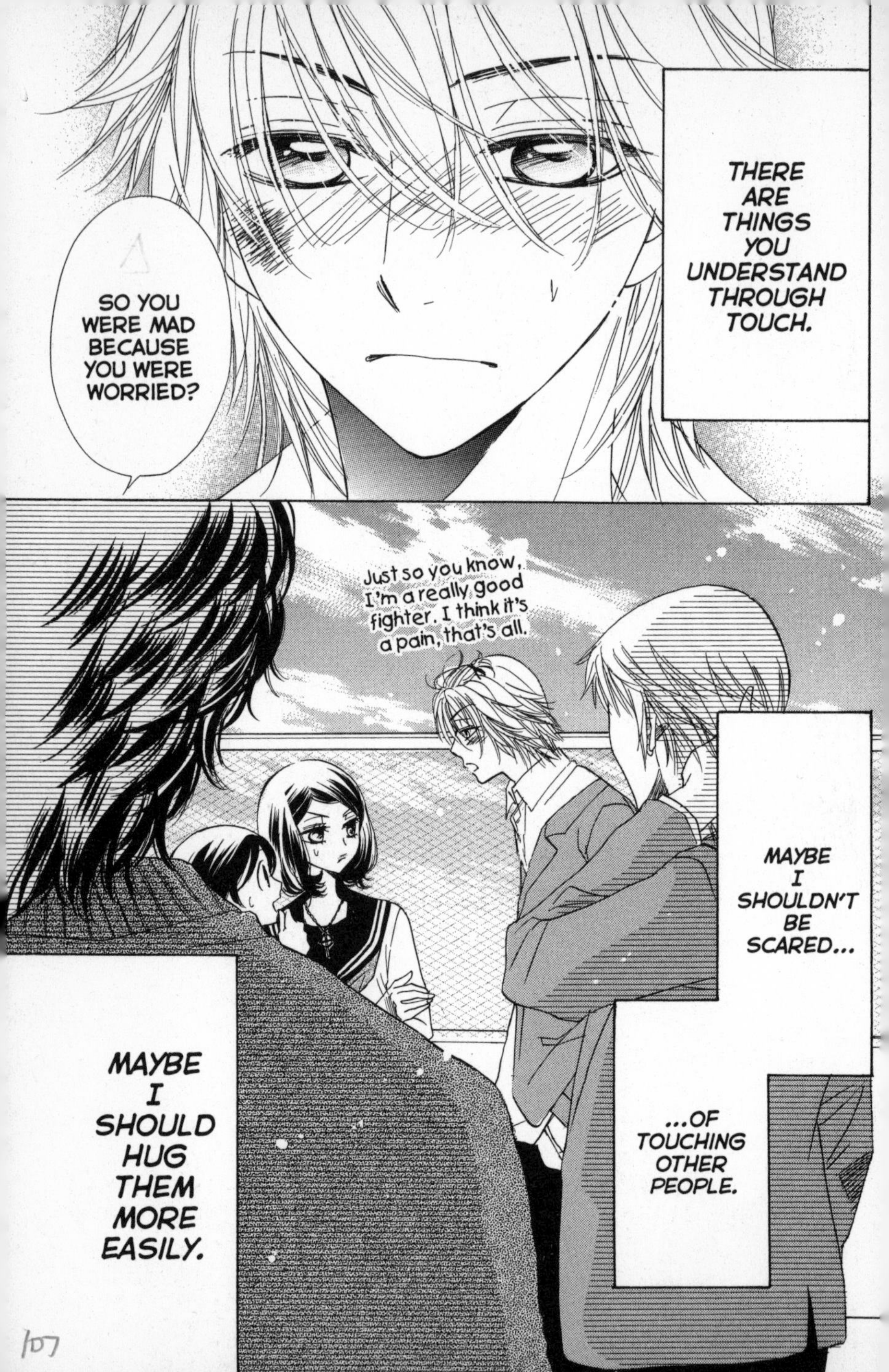
THERE ARE THINGS YOU UNDERSTAND THROUGH TOUCH.
SO YOU WERE MAD BECAUSE YOU WERE WORRIED?
Just so you know, I'm a really good fighter. I think it's a pain, that's all.
MAYBE I SHOULDN'T BE SCARED...
...OF TOUCHING OTHER PEOPLE.
MAYBE I SHOULD HUG THEM MORE EASILY.

A Devil and Her Love Song

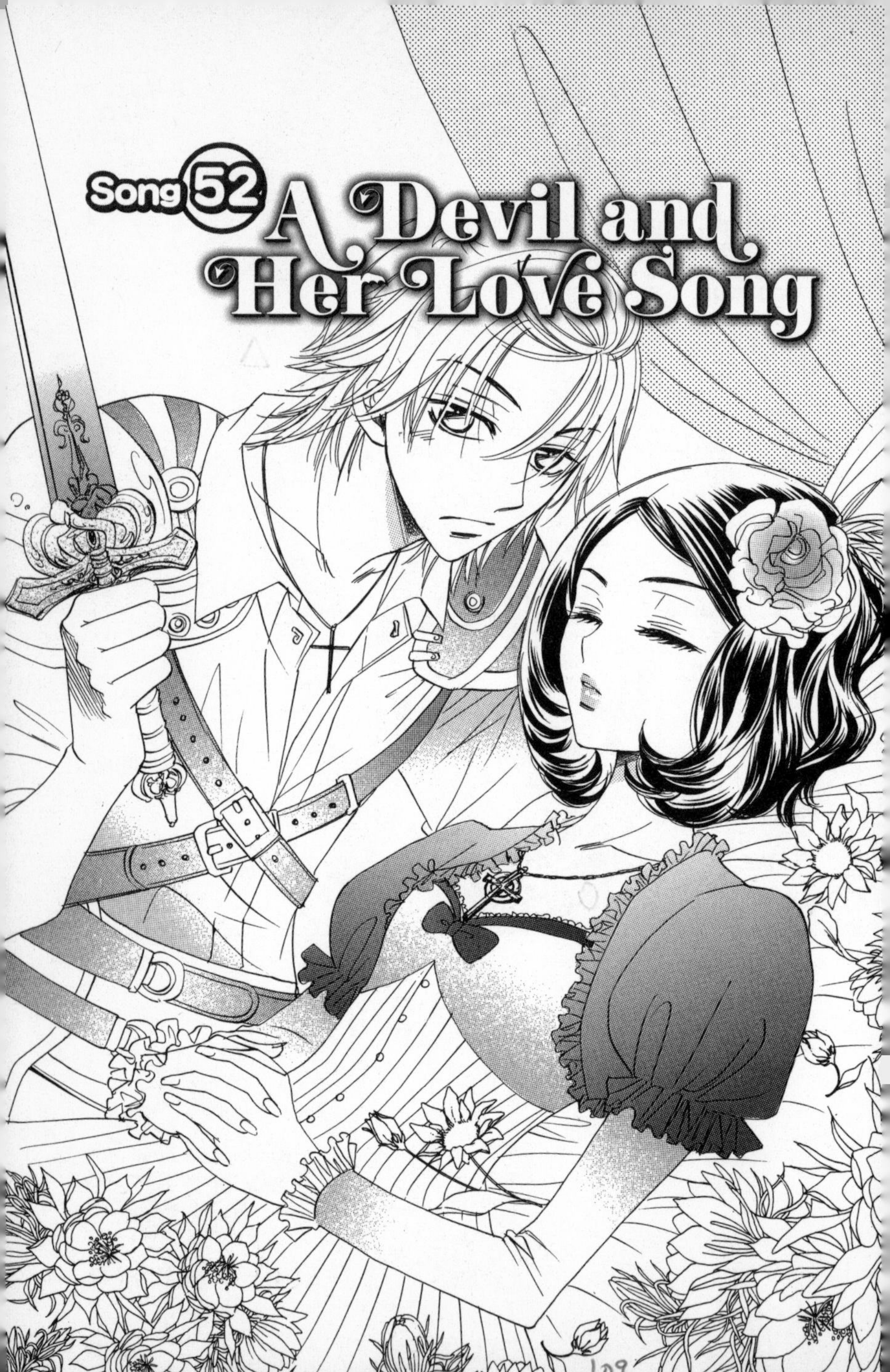
Song 52
A Devil and Her Love Song

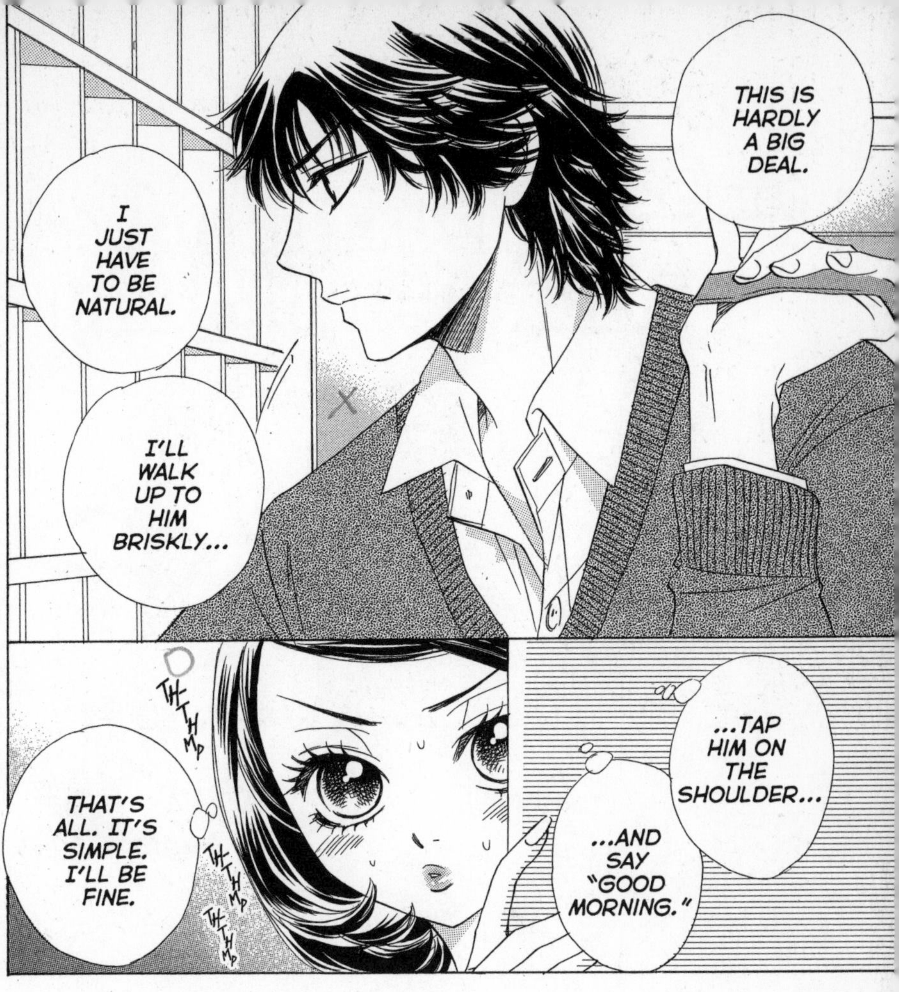
THIS IS HARDLY A BIG DEAL.
I JUST HAVE TO BE NATURAL.
I'LL WALK UP TO HIM BRISKLY...
...TAP HIM ON THE SHOULDER...
...AND SAY "GOOD MORNING."
THTHMP
THAT'S ALL. IT'S SIMPLE. I'LL BE FINE.
THTHMP
THTHMP

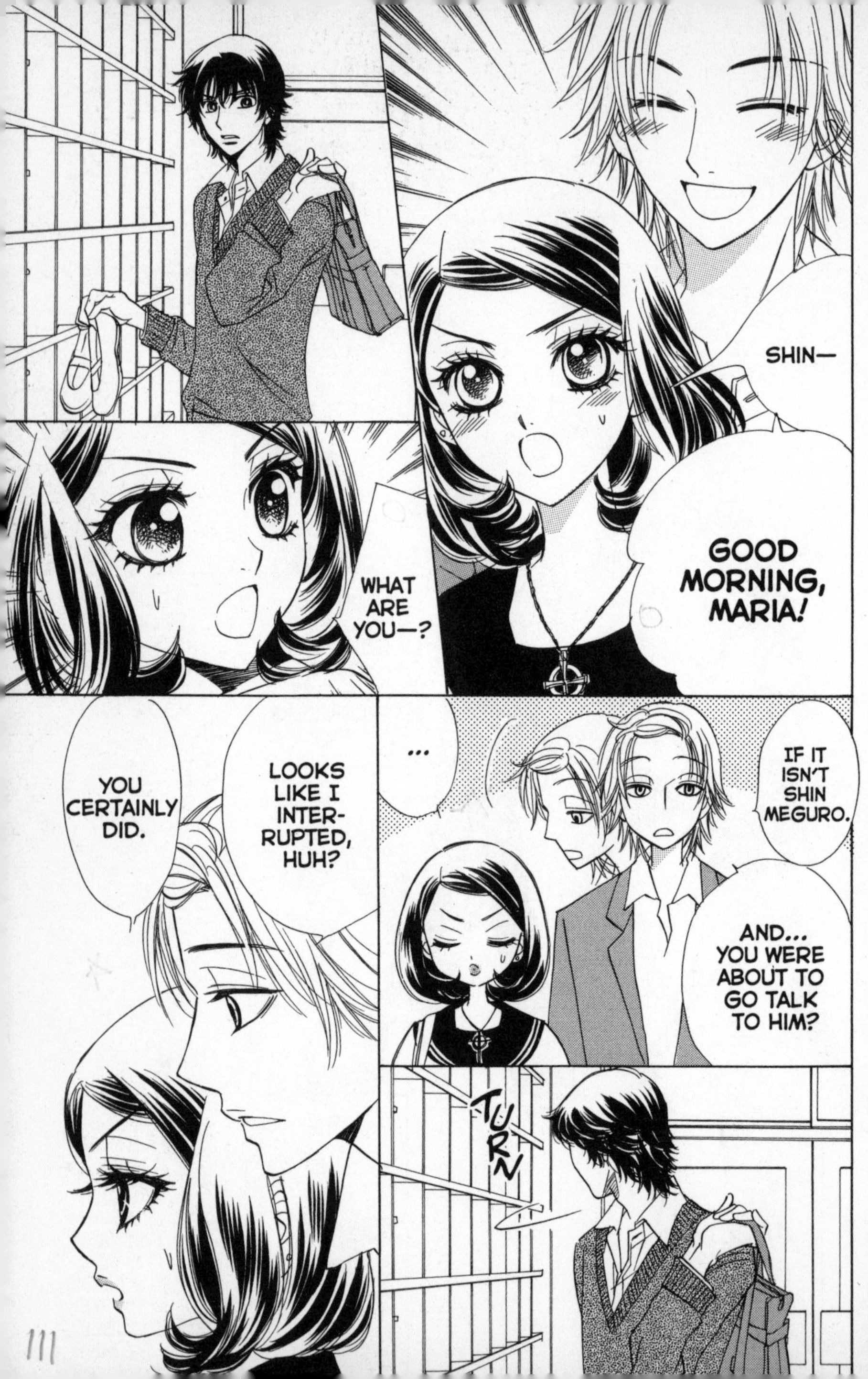
SHIN—
GOOD MORNING, MARIA!
WHAT ARE YOU—?
IF IT ISN'T SHIN MEGURO.
AND... YOU WERE ABOUT TO GO TALK TO HIM?
...
TURN
LOOKS LIKE I INTER-RUPTED, HUH?
YOU CERTAINLY DID.

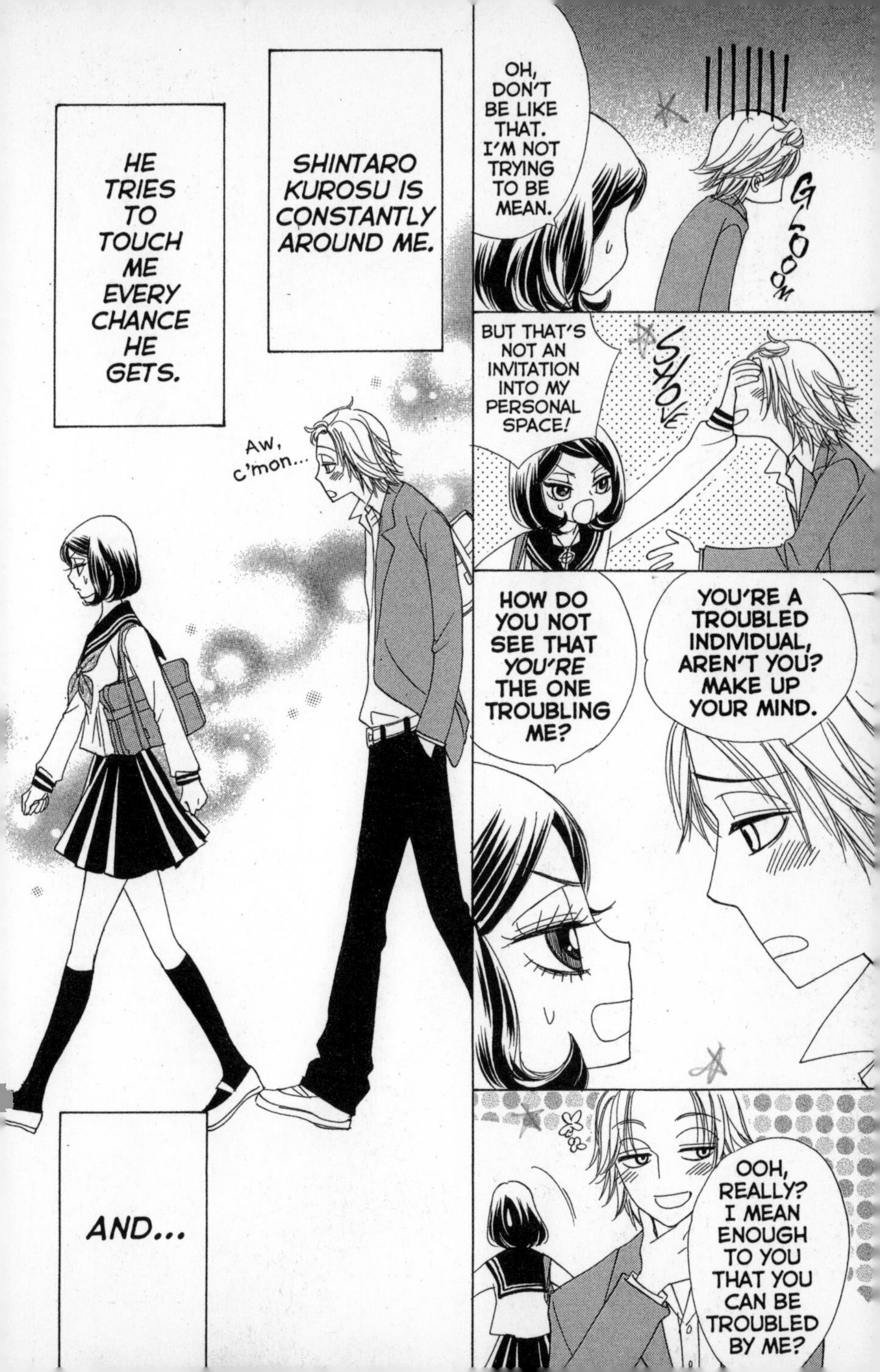
OH, DON'T BE LIKE THAT. I'M NOT TRYING TO BE MEAN.
GLOOOOM
SHOVE
BUT THAT'S NOT AN INVITATION INTO MY PERSONAL SPACE!
YOU'RE A TROUBLED INDIVIDUAL, AREN'T YOU? MAKE UP YOUR MIND.
HOW DO YOU NOT SEE THAT *YOU'RE* THE ONE TROUBLING ME?
OOH, REALLY? I MEAN ENOUGH TO YOU THAT YOU CAN BE TROUBLED BY ME?
SHINTARO KUROSU IS CONSTANTLY AROUND ME.
HE TRIES TO TOUCH ME EVERY CHANCE HE GETS.
Aw, c'mon...
AND...

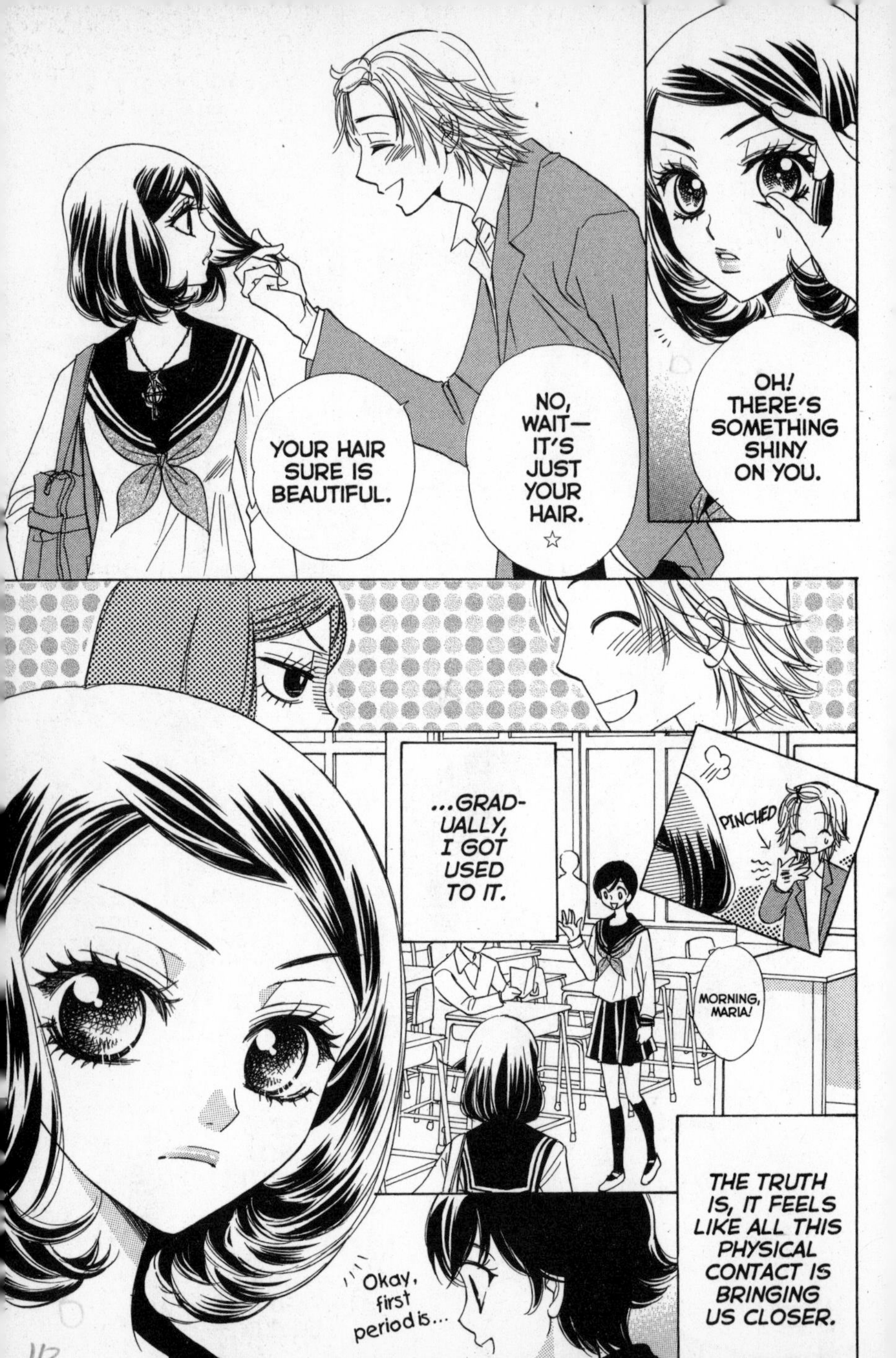
OH! THERE'S SOMETHING SHINY ON YOU.
NO, WAIT— IT'S JUST YOUR HAIR. ☆
YOUR HAIR SURE IS BEAUTIFUL.
PINCHED
MORNING, MARIA!
...GRAD- UALLY, I GOT USED TO IT.
THE TRUTH IS, IT FEELS LIKE ALL THIS PHYSICAL CONTACT IS BRINGING US CLOSER.
Okay, first period is...

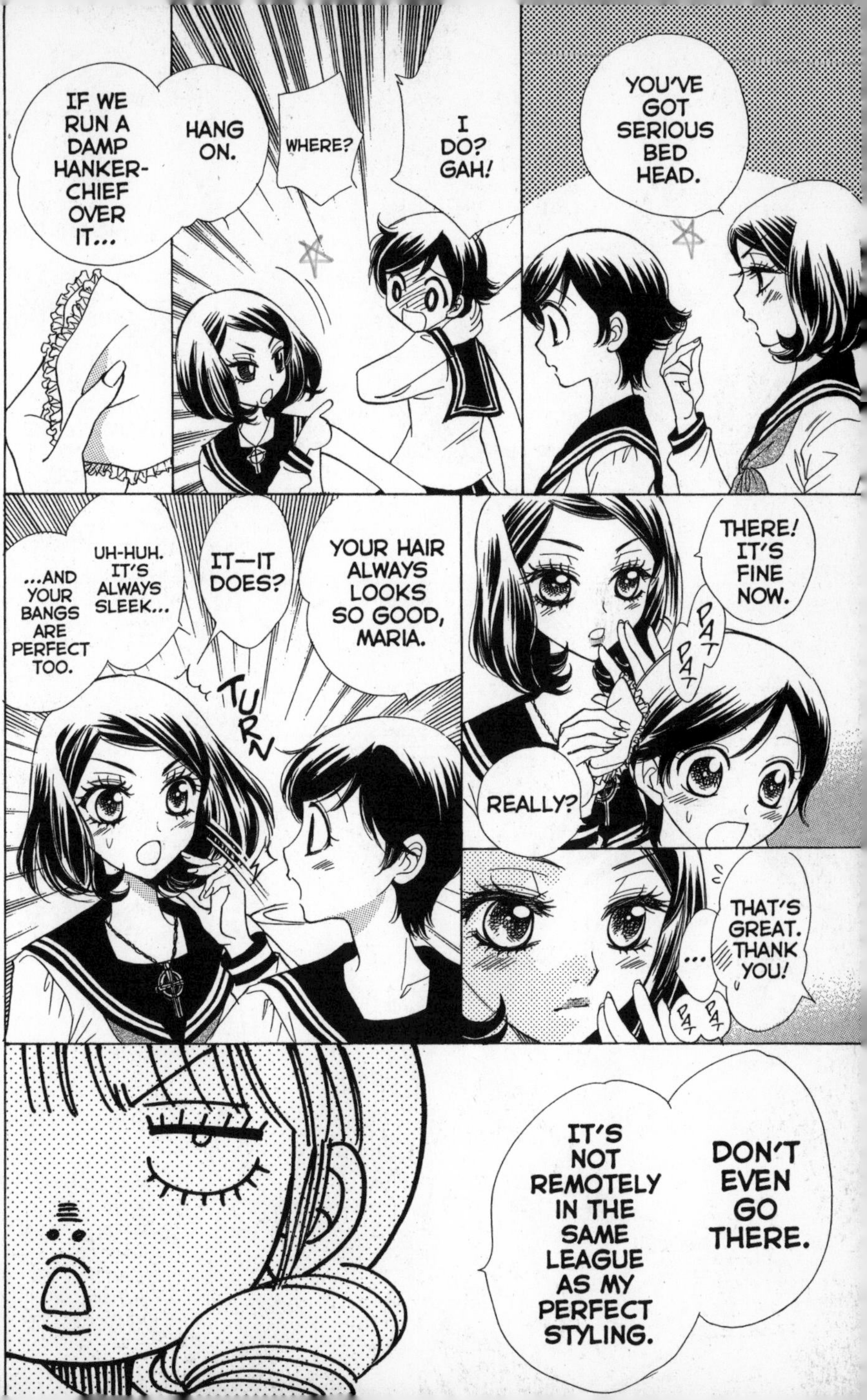
YOU'VE GOT SERIOUS BED HEAD.
I DO? GAH!
WHERE?
HANG ON.
IF WE RUN A DAMP HANKER-CHIEF OVER IT...
THERE! IT'S FINE NOW.
PAT PAT
REALLY?
THAT'S GREAT. THANK YOU!
PAT PAT
...
YOUR HAIR ALWAYS LOOKS SO GOOD, MARIA.
IT—IT DOES?
TURN
UH-HUH. IT'S ALWAYS SLEEK...
...AND YOUR BANGS ARE PERFECT TOO.
DON'T EVEN GO THERE.
IT'S NOT REMOTELY IN THE SAME LEAGUE AS MY PERFECT STYLING.

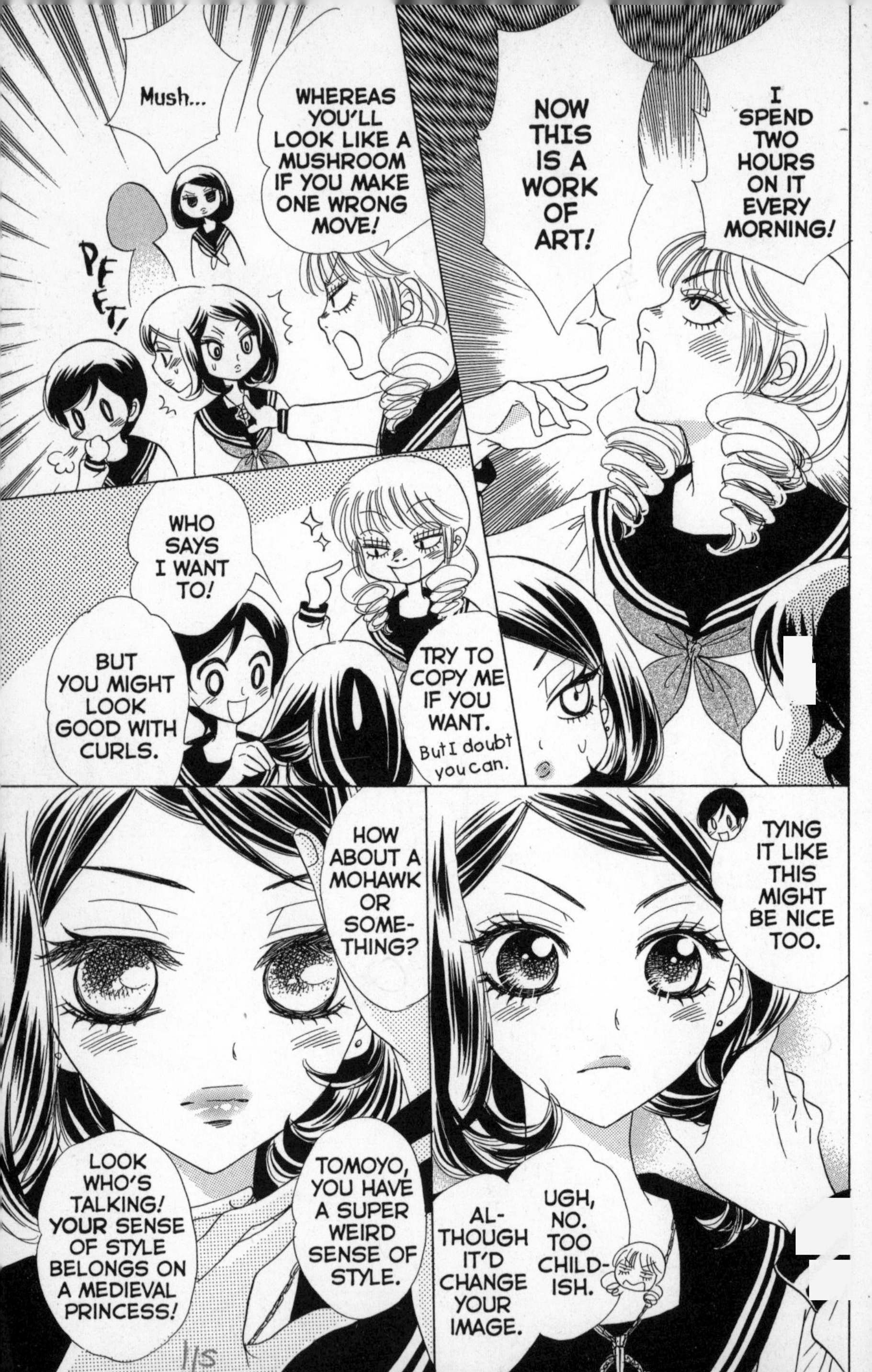
NOW THIS IS A WORK OF ART!
I SPEND TWO HOURS ON IT EVERY MORNING!
WHEREAS YOU'LL LOOK LIKE A MUSHROOM IF YOU MAKE ONE WRONG MOVE!
Mush...
PFFT!
TRY TO COPY ME IF YOU WANT.
But I doubt you can.
WHO SAYS I WANT TO!
BUT YOU MIGHT LOOK GOOD WITH CURLS.
TYING IT LIKE THIS MIGHT BE NICE TOO.
UGH, NO. TOO CHILD-ISH.
AL-THOUGH IT'D CHANGE YOUR IMAGE.
HOW ABOUT A MOHAWK OR SOME-THING?
TOMOYO, YOU HAVE A SUPER WEIRD SENSE OF STYLE.
LOOK WHO'S TALKING! YOUR SENSE OF STYLE BELONGS ON A MEDIEVAL PRINCESS!

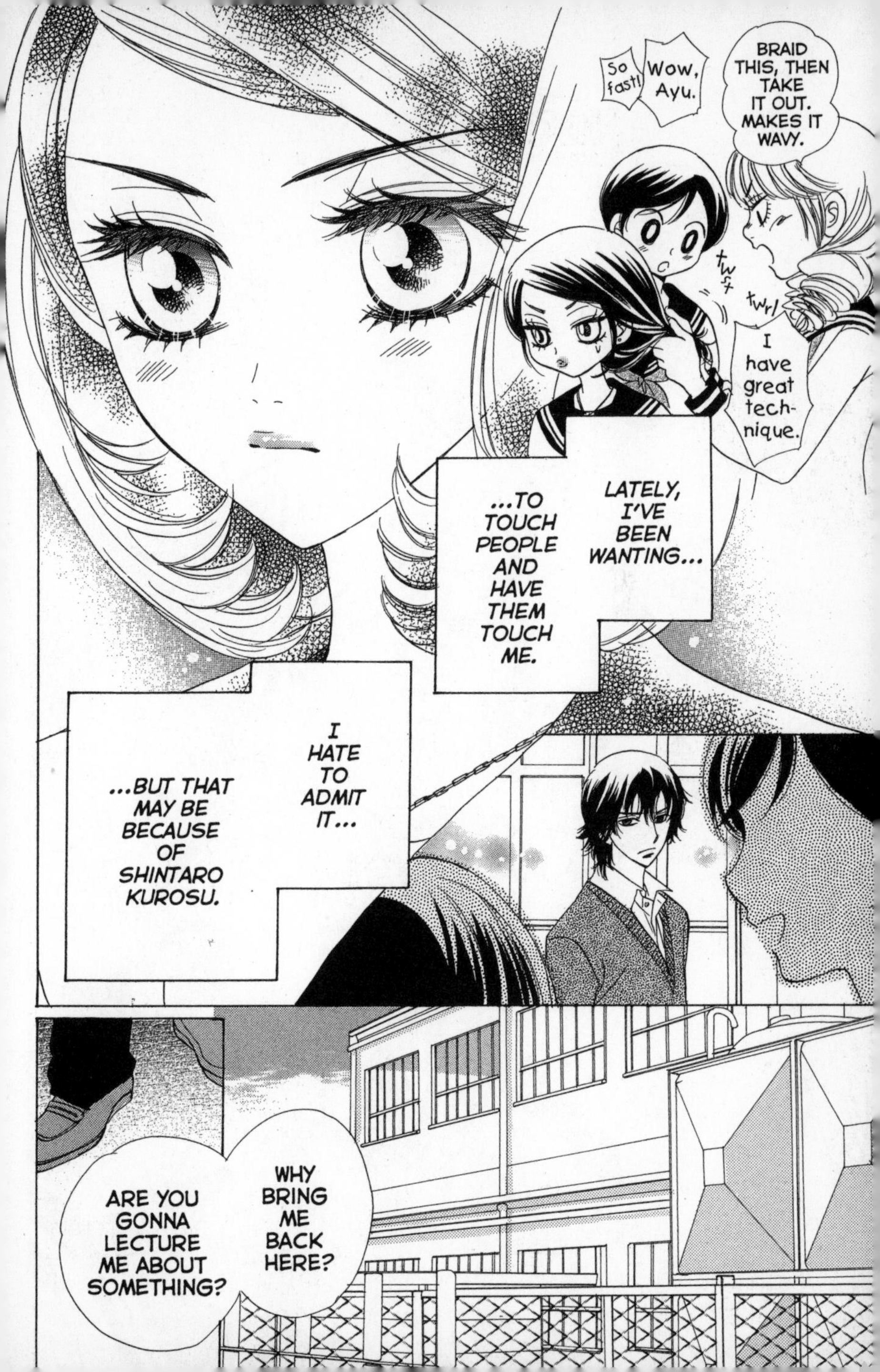
BRAID THIS, THEN TAKE IT OUT. MAKES IT WAVY.
Wow, Ayu.
So fast!
twst
twrl
I have great tech-nique.
LATELY, I'VE BEEN WANTING...
...TO TOUCH PEOPLE AND HAVE THEM TOUCH ME.
I HATE TO ADMIT IT...
...BUT THAT MAY BE BECAUSE OF SHINTARO KUROSU.
WHY BRING ME BACK HERE?
ARE YOU GONNA LECTURE ME ABOUT SOMETHING?

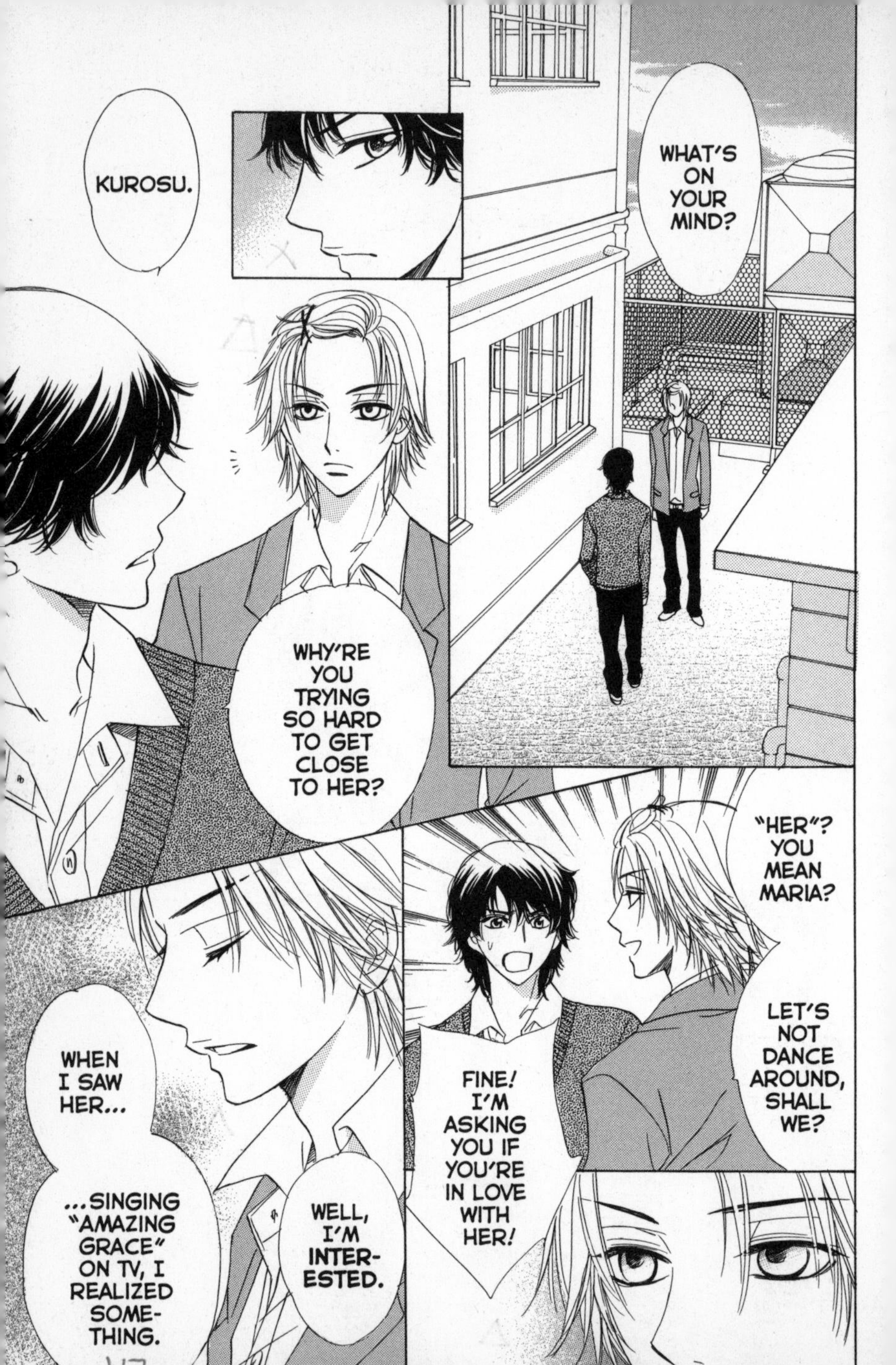
WHAT'S ON YOUR MIND?
KUROSU.
WHY'RE YOU TRYING SO HARD TO GET CLOSE TO HER?
"HER"? YOU MEAN MARIA?
LET'S NOT DANCE AROUND, SHALL WE?
FINE! I'M ASKING YOU IF YOU'RE IN LOVE WITH HER!
WELL, I'M INTER-ESTED.
WHEN I SAW HER...
...SINGING "AMAZING GRACE" ON TV, I REALIZED SOME-THING.

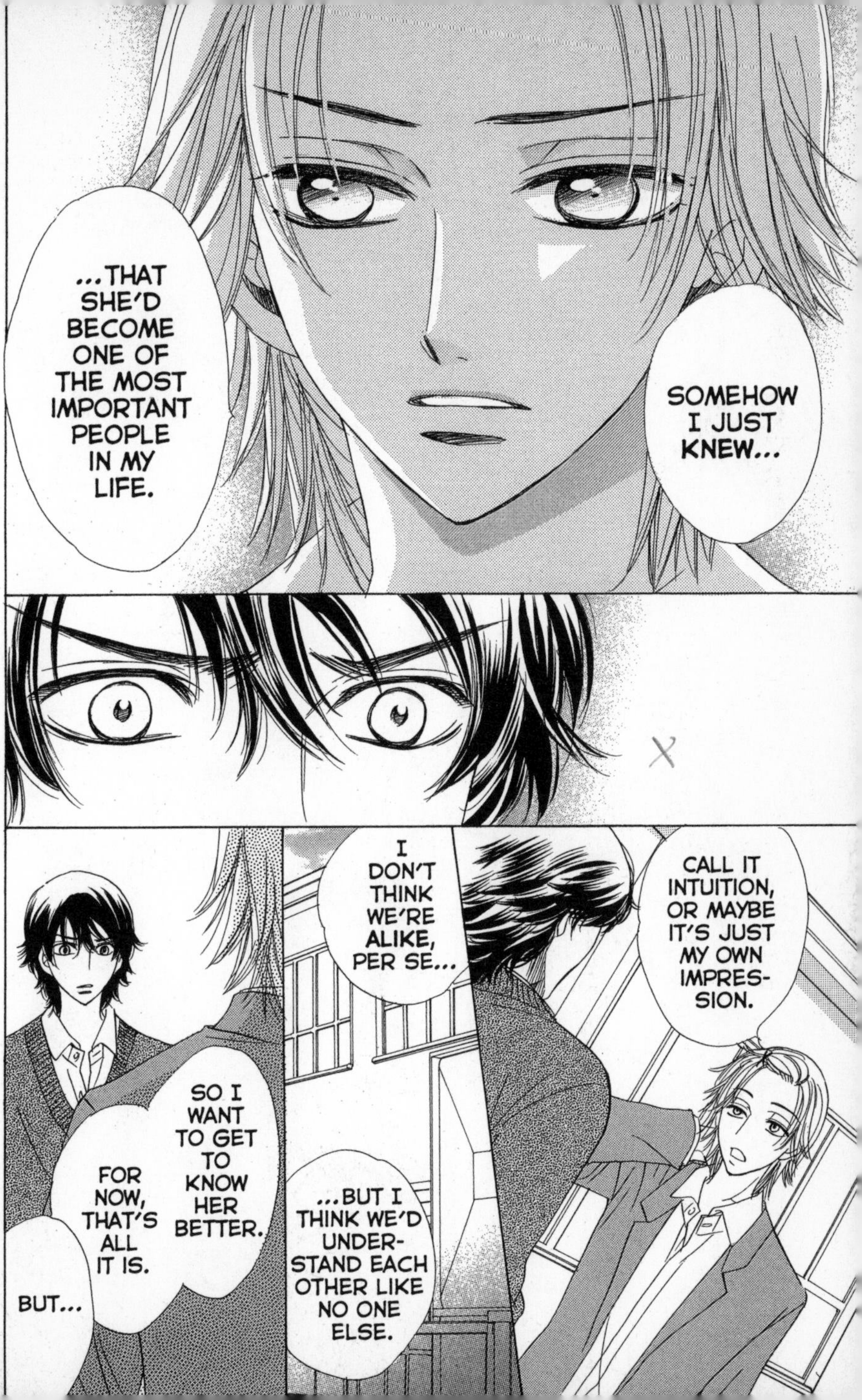
SOMEHOW I JUST KNEW...
...THAT SHE'D BECOME ONE OF THE MOST IMPORTANT PEOPLE IN MY LIFE.
CALL IT INTUITION, OR MAYBE IT'S JUST MY OWN IMPRES-SION.
I DON'T THINK WE'RE ALIKE, PER SE...
...BUT I THINK WE'D UNDER-STAND EACH OTHER LIKE NO ONE ELSE.
SO I WANT TO GET TO KNOW HER BETTER.
FOR NOW, THAT'S ALL IT IS.
BUT...

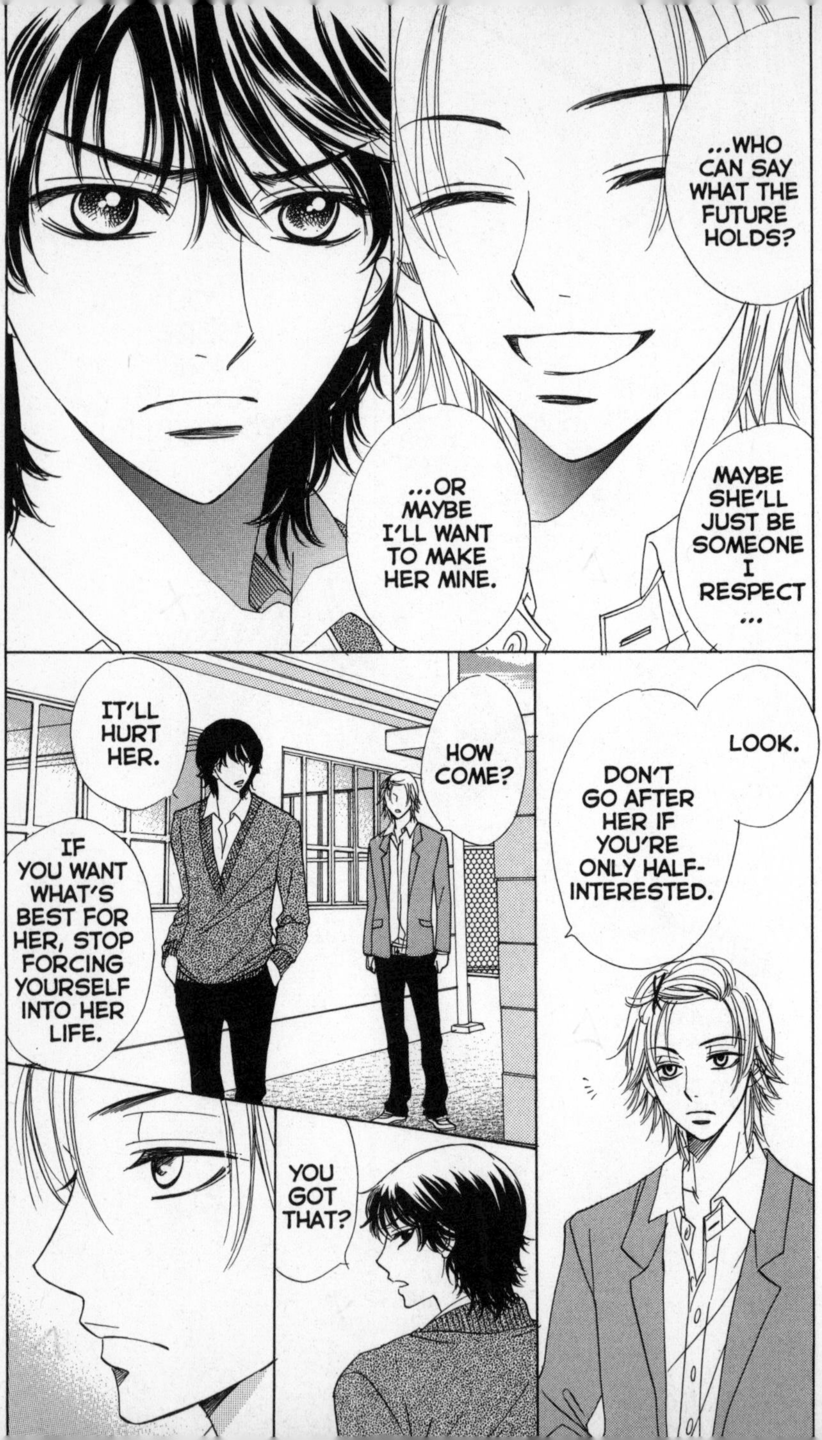
...WHO CAN SAY WHAT THE FUTURE HOLDS?
MAYBE SHE'LL JUST BE SOMEONE I RESPECT ...
...OR MAYBE I'LL WANT TO MAKE HER MINE.
LOOK.
DON'T GO AFTER HER IF YOU'RE ONLY HALF-INTERESTED.
HOW COME?
IT'LL HURT HER.
IF YOU WANT WHAT'S BEST FOR HER, STOP FORCING YOURSELF INTO HER LIFE.
YOU GOT THAT?

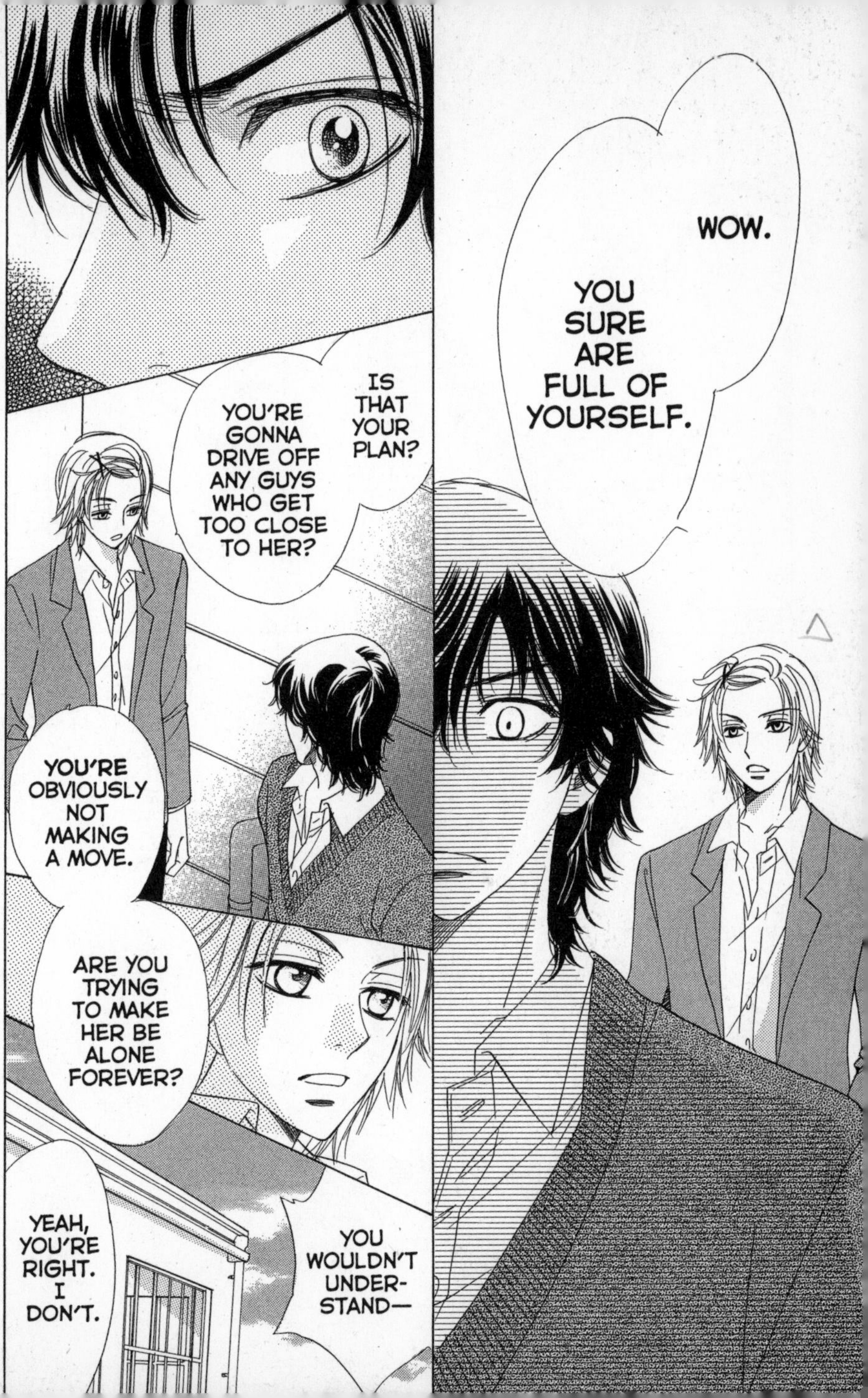
WOW.
YOU SURE ARE FULL OF YOURSELF.
IS THAT YOUR PLAN?
YOU'RE GONNA DRIVE OFF ANY GUYS WHO GET TOO CLOSE TO HER?
YOU'RE OBVIOUSLY NOT MAKING A MOVE.
ARE YOU TRYING TO MAKE HER BE ALONE FOREVER?
YOU WOULDN'T UNDER-STAND—
YEAH, YOU'RE RIGHT. I DON'T.

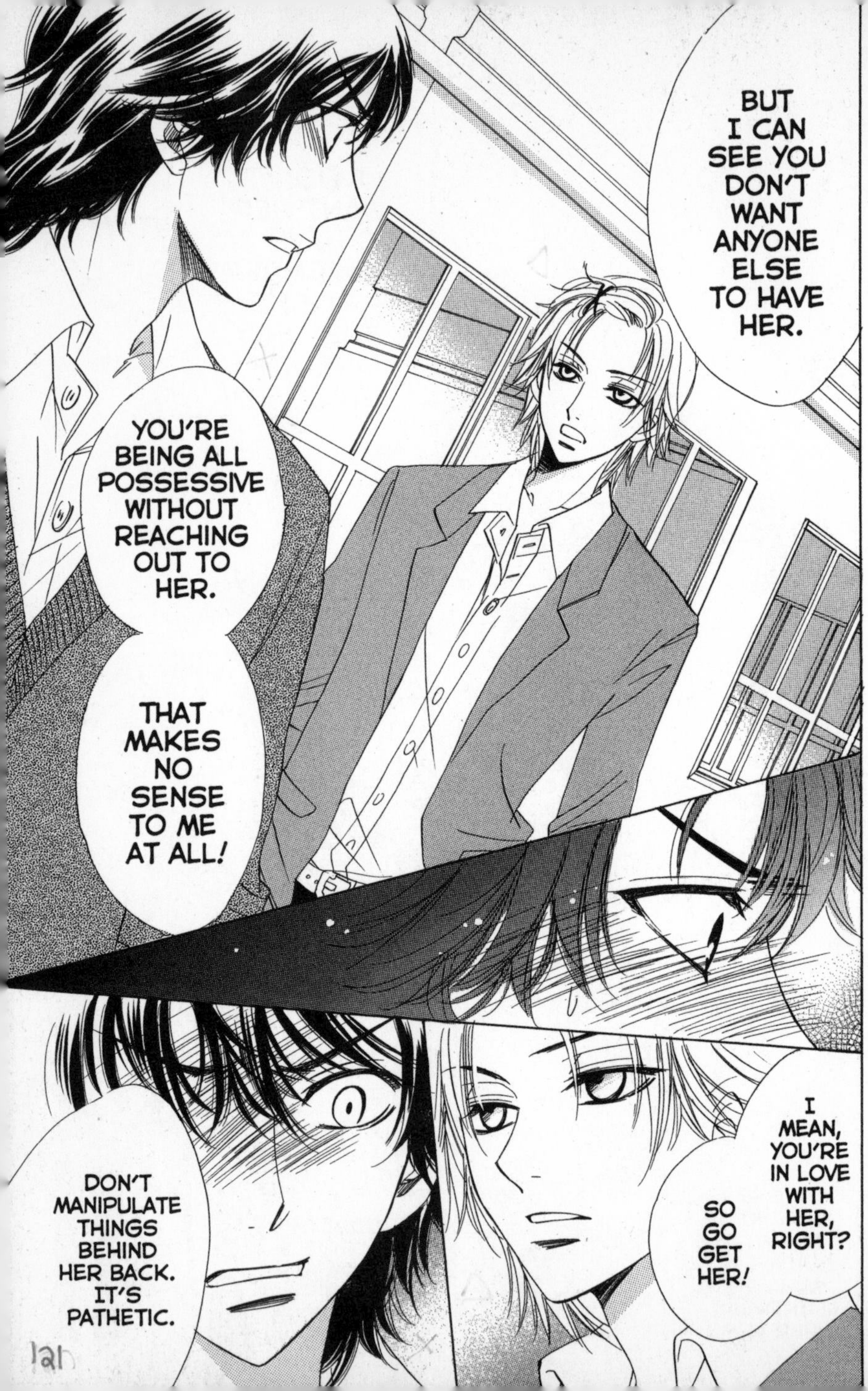
BUT I CAN SEE YOU DON'T WANT ANYONE ELSE TO HAVE HER.
YOU'RE BEING ALL POSSESSIVE WITHOUT REACHING OUT TO HER.
THAT MAKES NO SENSE TO ME AT ALL!
I MEAN, YOU'RE IN LOVE WITH HER, RIGHT?
SO GO GET HER!
DON'T MANIPULATE THINGS BEHIND HER BACK. IT'S PATHETIC.

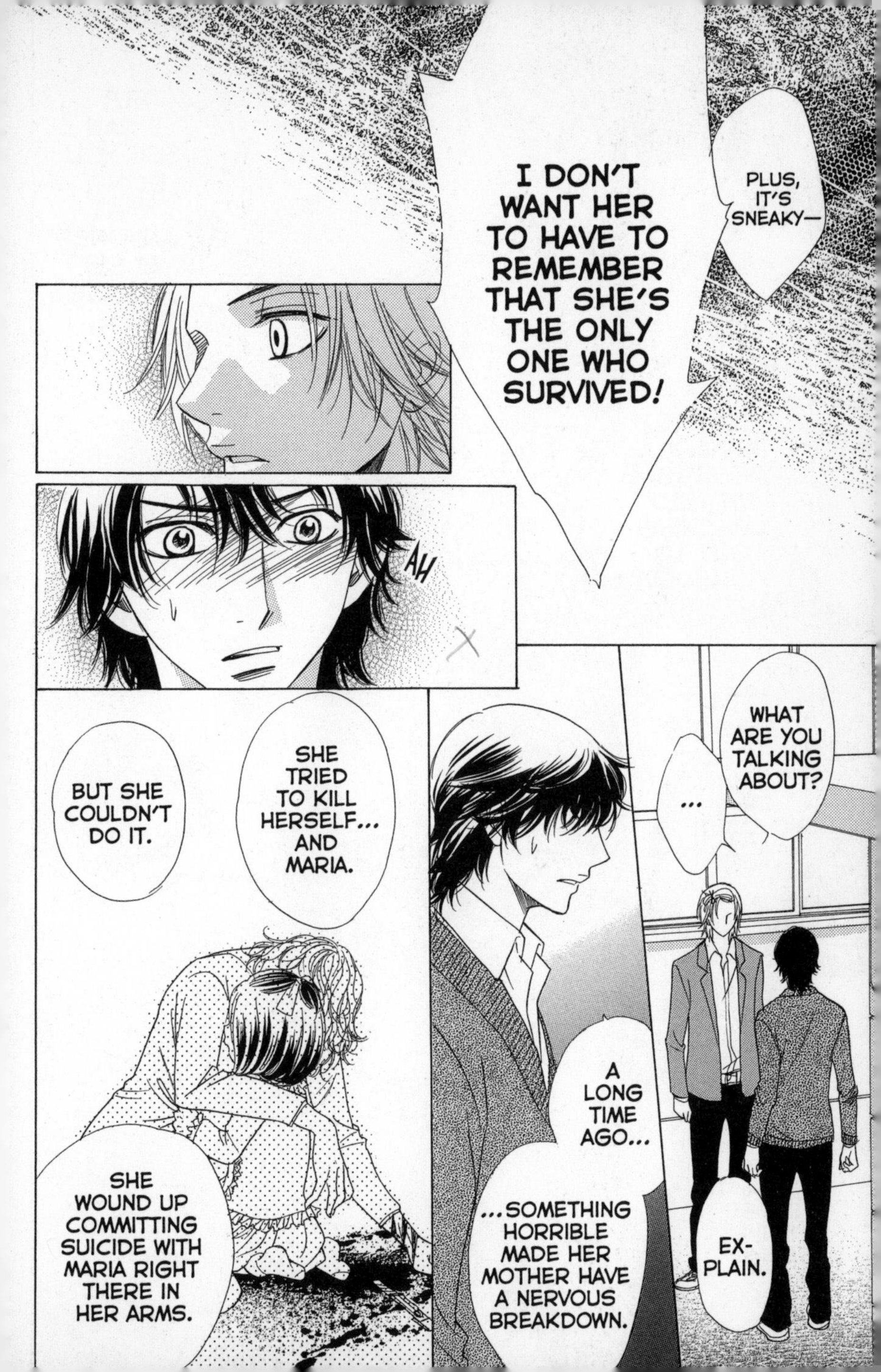
PLUS, IT'S SNEAKY—
I DON'T WANT HER TO HAVE TO REMEMBER THAT SHE'S THE ONLY ONE WHO SURVIVED!
AH
WHAT ARE YOU TALKING ABOUT?
...
EX-PLAIN.
A LONG TIME AGO...
...SOMETHING HORRIBLE MADE HER MOTHER HAVE A NERVOUS BREAKDOWN.
SHE TRIED TO KILL HERSELF... AND MARIA.
BUT SHE COULDN'T DO IT.
SHE WOUND UP COMMITTING SUICIDE WITH MARIA RIGHT THERE IN HER ARMS.

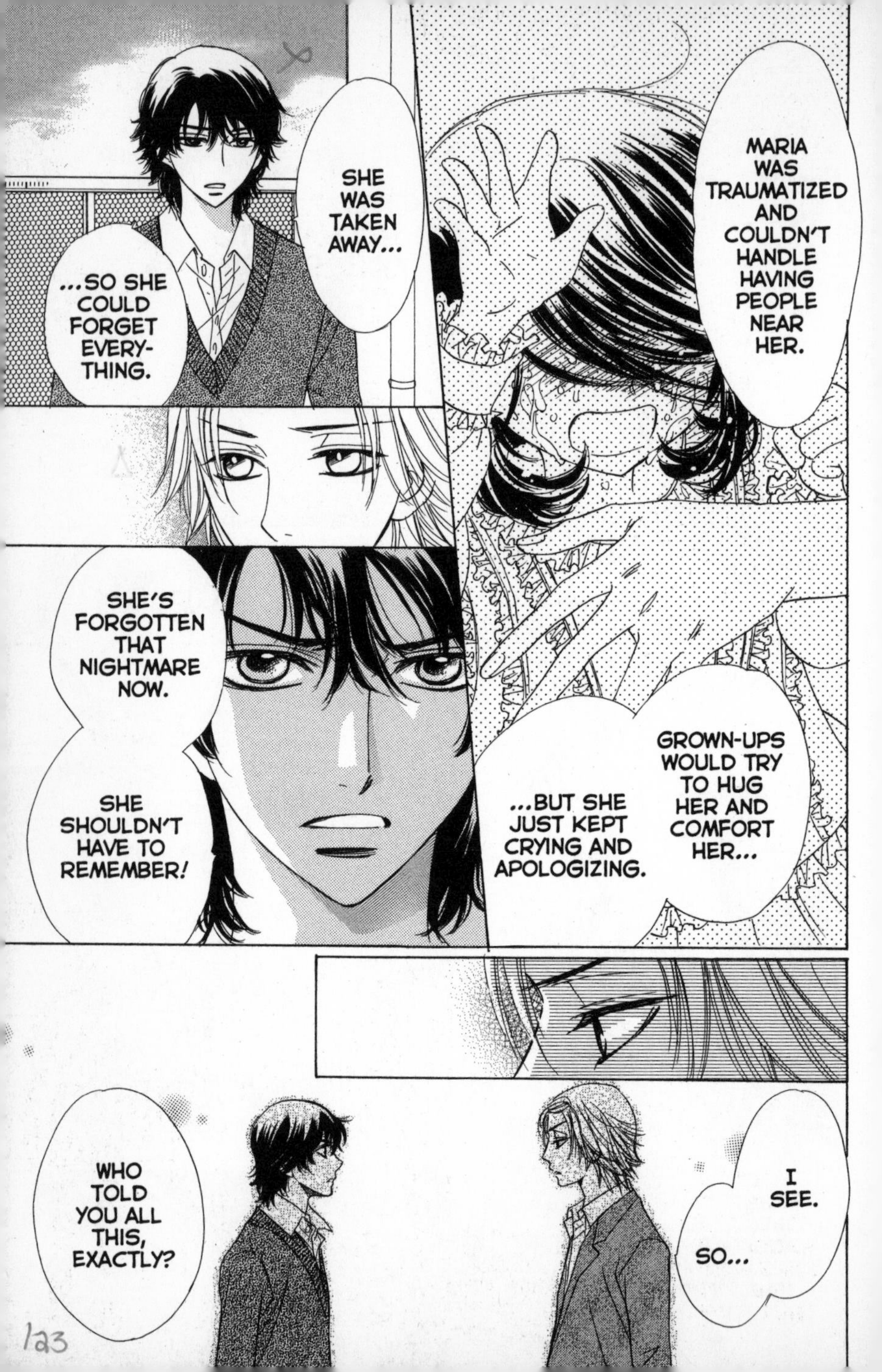
MARIA WAS TRAUMATIZED AND COULDN'T HANDLE HAVING PEOPLE NEAR HER.
GROWN-UPS WOULD TRY TO HUG HER AND COMFORT HER...
...BUT SHE JUST KEPT CRYING AND APOLOGIZING.
SHE WAS TAKEN AWAY...
...SO SHE COULD FORGET EVERY-THING.
SHE'S FORGOTTEN THAT NIGHTMARE NOW.
SHE SHOULDN'T HAVE TO REMEMBER!
I SEE.
SO...
WHO TOLD YOU ALL THIS, EXACTLY?

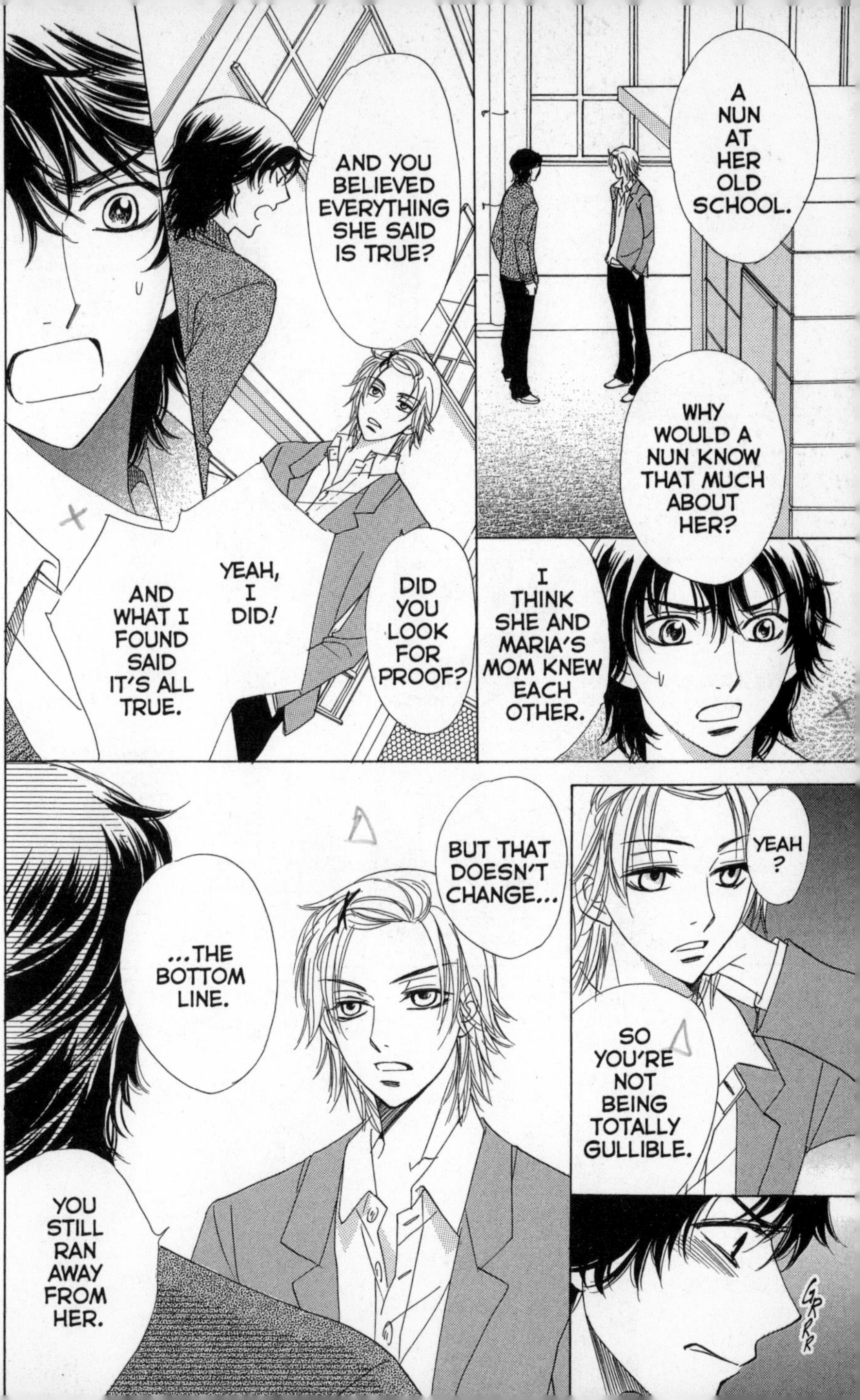
A NUN AT HER OLD SCHOOL.
WHY WOULD A NUN KNOW THAT MUCH ABOUT HER?
I THINK SHE AND MARIA'S MOM KNEW EACH OTHER.
AND YOU BELIEVED EVERYTHING SHE SAID IS TRUE?
DID YOU LOOK FOR PROOF?
YEAH, I DID!
AND WHAT I FOUND SAID IT'S ALL TRUE.
YEAH?
SO YOU'RE NOT BEING TOTALLY GULLIBLE.
GRRR
BUT THAT DOESN'T CHANGE...
...THE BOTTOM LINE.
YOU STILL RAN AWAY FROM HER.

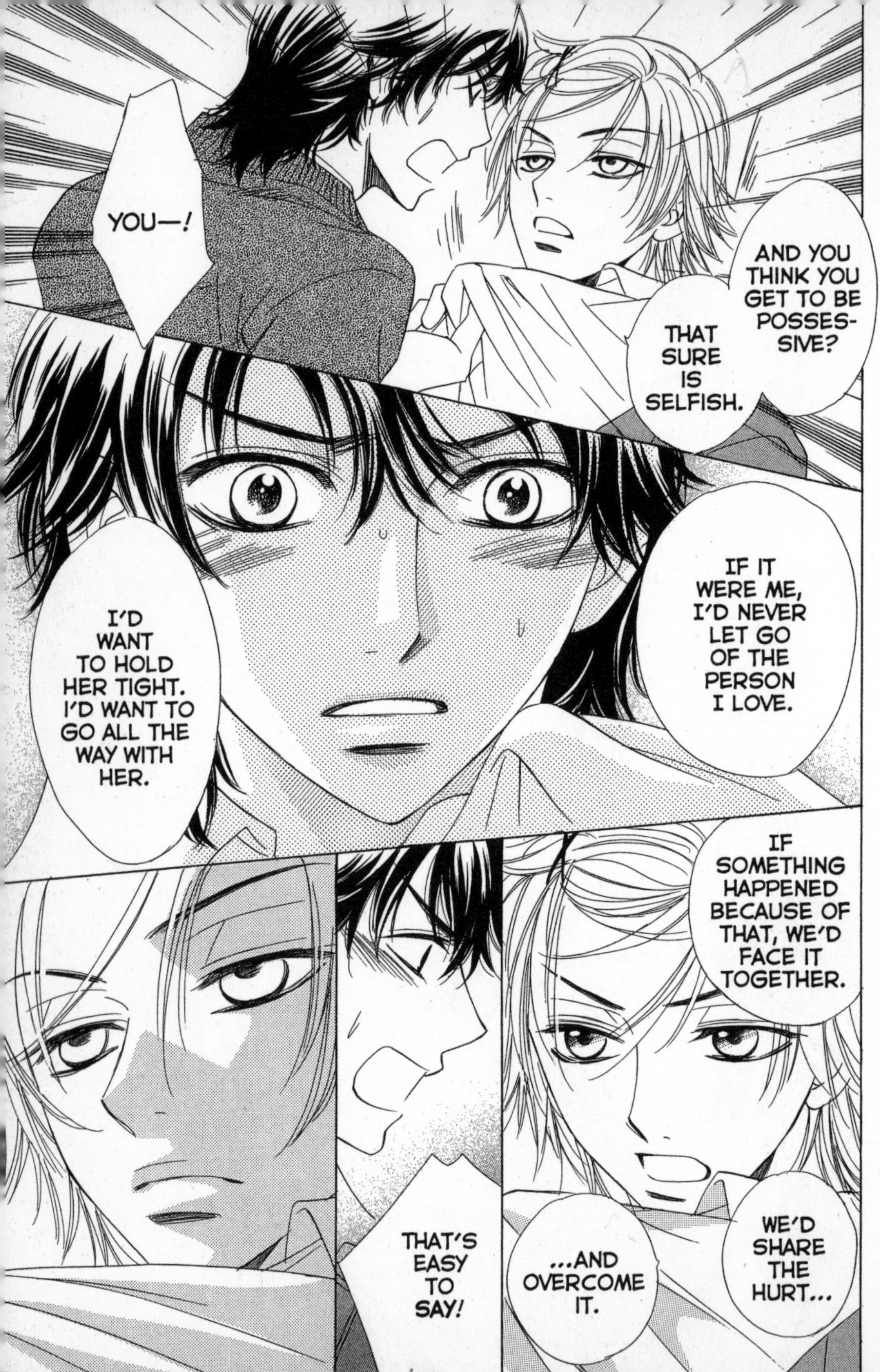
AND YOU THINK YOU GET TO BE POSSES-SIVE?
THAT SURE IS SELFISH.
YOU—!
IF IT WERE ME, I'D NEVER LET GO OF THE PERSON I LOVE.
I'D WANT TO HOLD HER TIGHT. I'D WANT TO GO ALL THE WAY WITH HER.
IF SOMETHING HAPPENED BECAUSE OF THAT, WE'D FACE IT TOGETHER.
WE'D SHARE THE HURT...
...AND OVERCOME IT.
THAT'S EASY TO SAY!

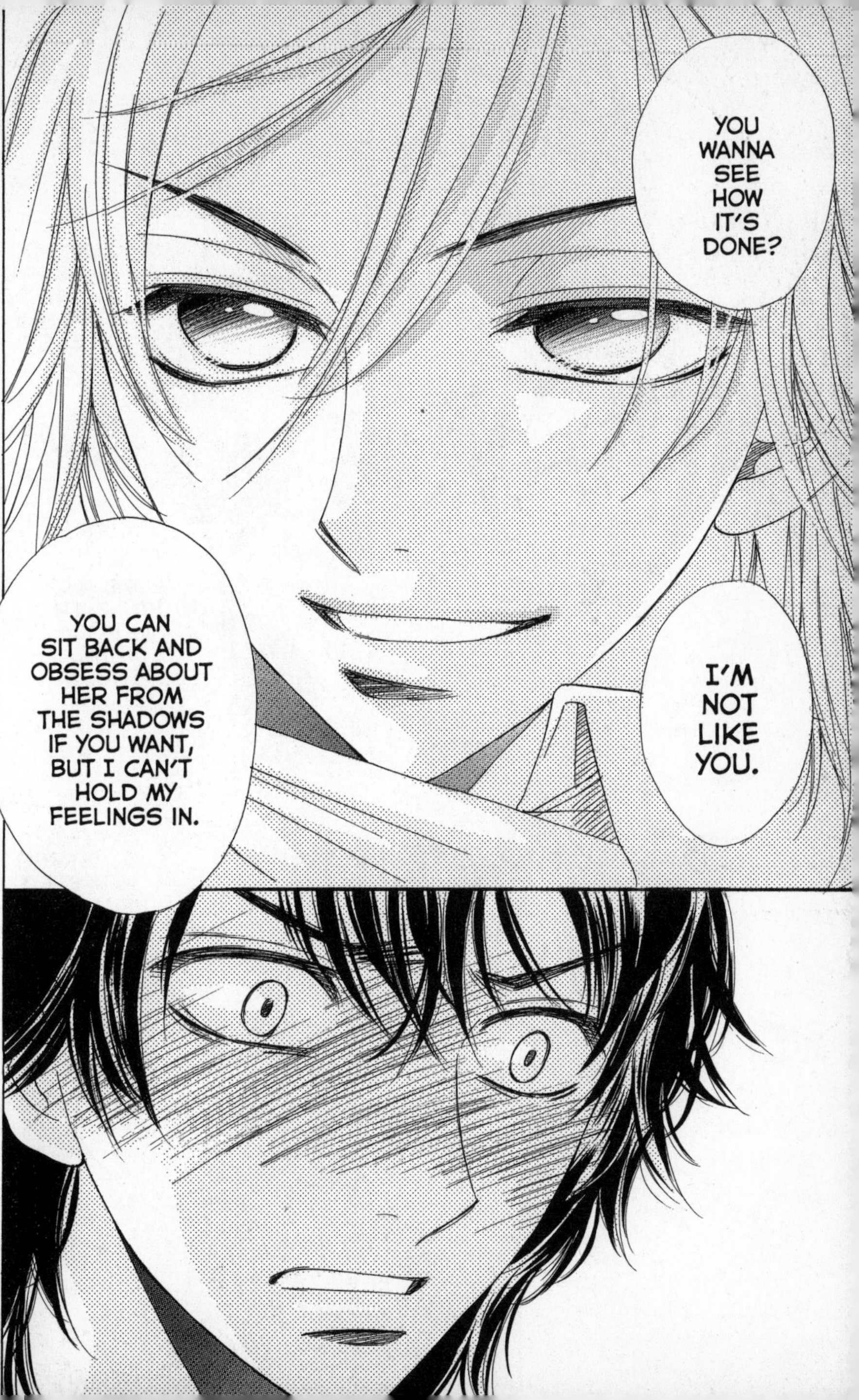
YOU WANNA SEE HOW IT'S DONE?
I'M NOT LIKE YOU.
YOU CAN SIT BACK AND OBSESS ABOUT HER FROM THE SHADOWS IF YOU WANT, BUT I CAN'T HOLD MY FEELINGS IN.

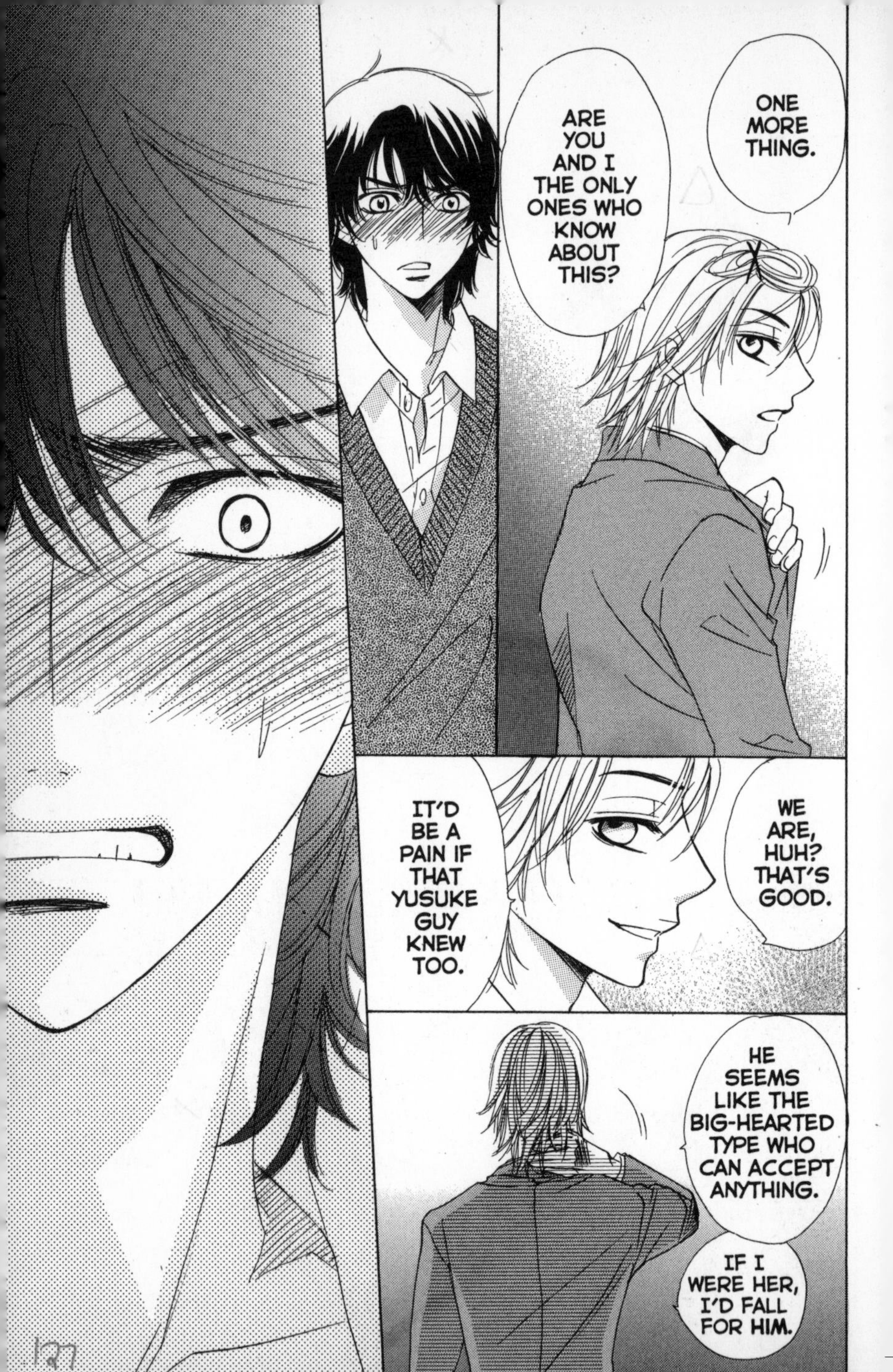
ONE MORE THING.
ARE YOU AND I THE ONLY ONES WHO KNOW ABOUT THIS?
WE ARE, HUH? THAT'S GOOD.
IT'D BE A PAIN IF THAT YUSUKE GUY KNEW TOO.
HE SEEMS LIKE THE BIG-HEARTED TYPE WHO CAN ACCEPT ANYTHING.
IF I WERE HER, I'D FALL FOR HIM.

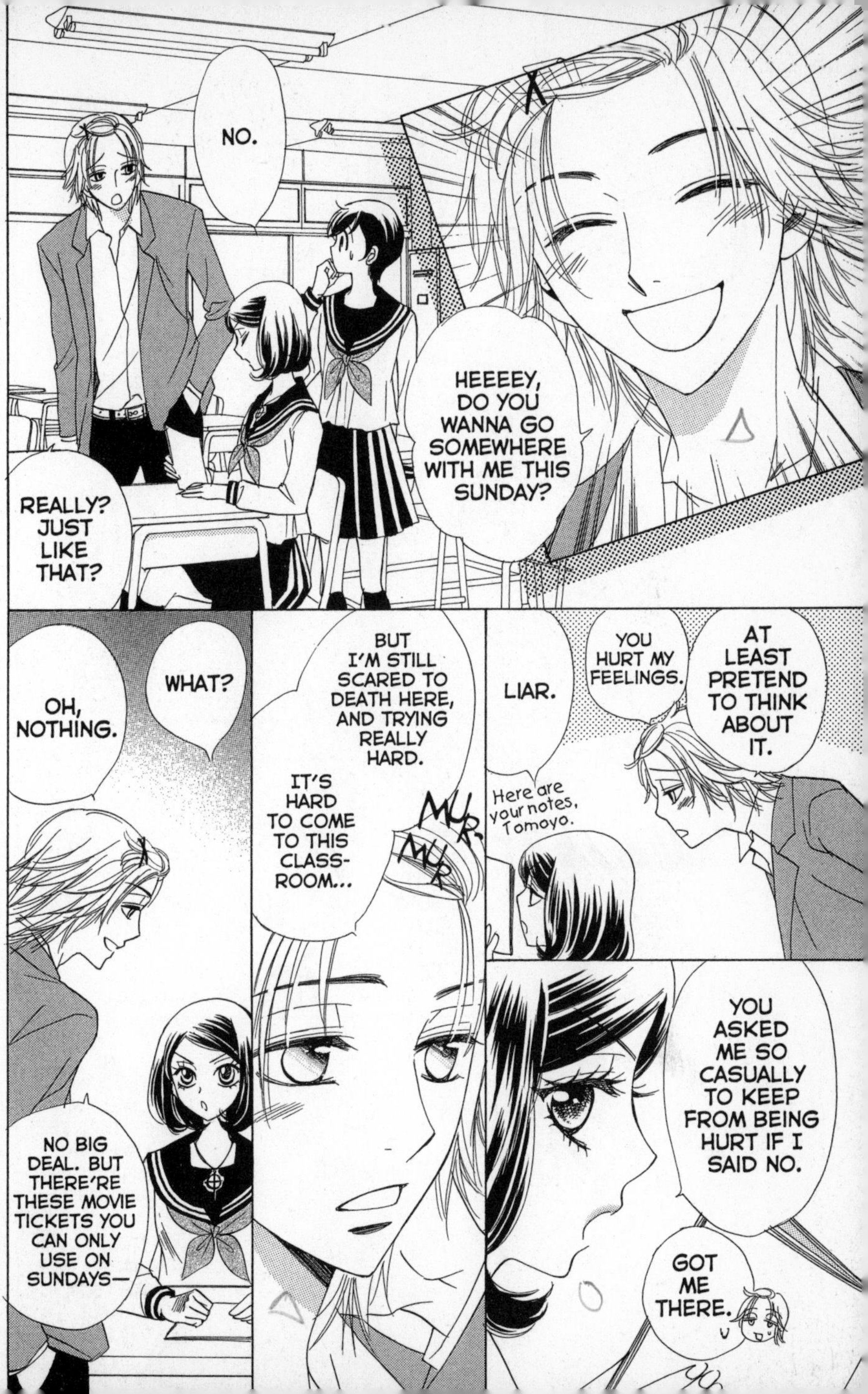
HEEEEY, DO YOU WANNA GO SOMEWHERE WITH ME THIS SUNDAY?
NO.
REALLY? JUST LIKE THAT?
AT LEAST PRETEND TO THINK ABOUT IT.
YOU HURT MY FEELINGS.
LIAR.
Here are your notes, Tomoyo.
YOU ASKED ME SO CASUALLY TO KEEP FROM BEING HURT IF I SAID NO.
GOT ME THERE.
BUT I'M STILL SCARED TO DEATH HERE, AND TRYING REALLY HARD.
MUR-MUR
IT'S HARD TO COME TO THIS CLASS-ROOM...
WHAT?
OH, NOTHING.
NO BIG DEAL. BUT THERE'RE THESE MOVIE TICKETS YOU CAN ONLY USE ON SUNDAYS—

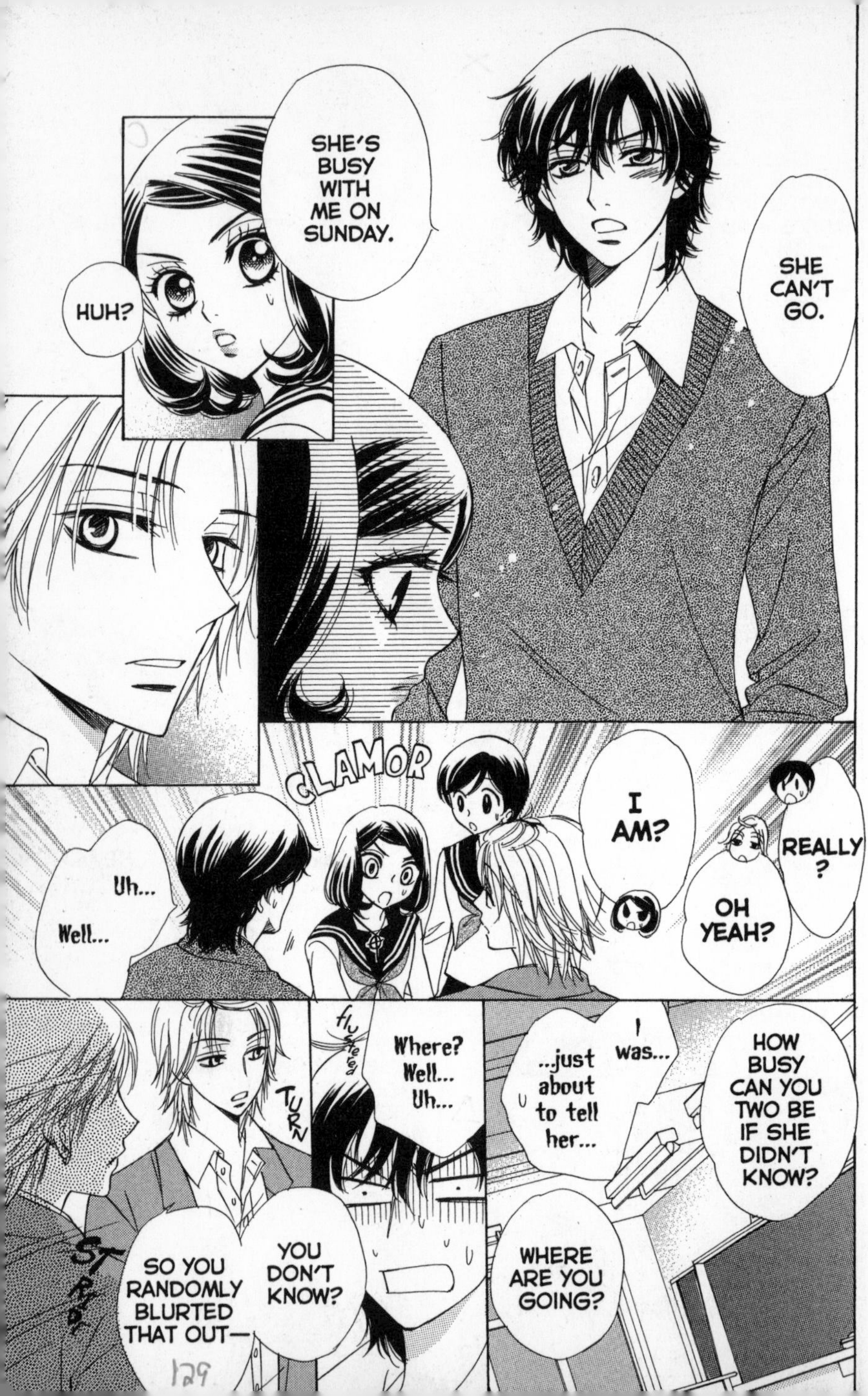

SHE CAN'T GO.
SHE'S BUSY WITH ME ON SUNDAY.
HUH?
I AM?
REALLY?
OH YEAH?
CLAMOR
Uh...
Well...
HOW BUSY CAN YOU TWO BE IF SHE DIDN'T KNOW?
I was...
...just about to tell her...
WHERE ARE YOU GOING?
flustered
Where? Well... Uh...
YOU DON'T KNOW?
TURN
SO YOU RANDOMLY BLURTED THAT OUT—
STRIDE

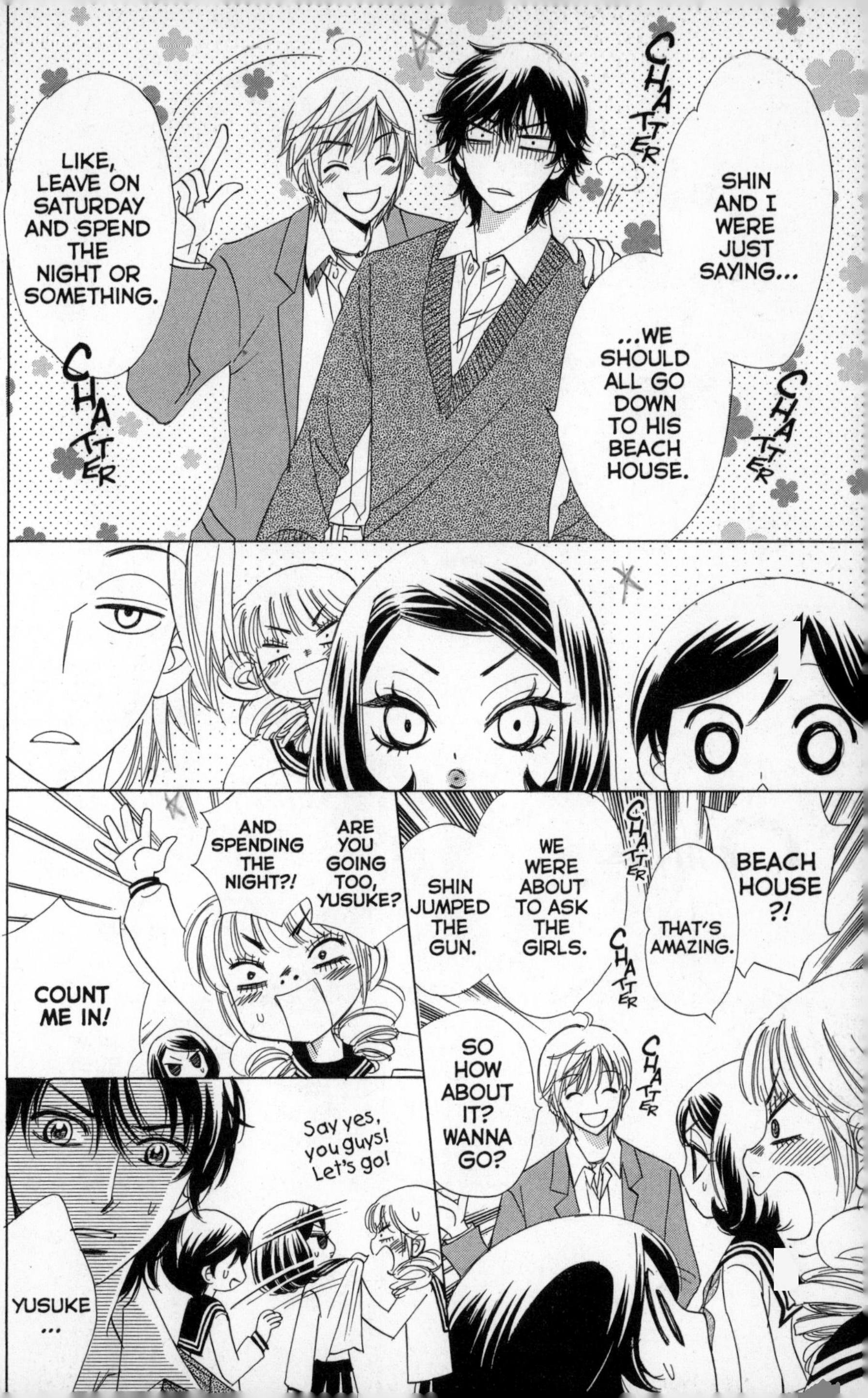
CHATTER
SHIN AND I WERE JUST SAYING...
...WE SHOULD ALL GO DOWN TO HIS BEACH HOUSE.
CHATTER
LIKE, LEAVE ON SATURDAY AND SPEND THE NIGHT OR SOMETHING.
CHATTER
BEACH HOUSE?!
THAT'S AMAZING.
CHATTER
WE WERE ABOUT TO ASK THE GIRLS.
SHIN JUMPED THE GUN.
CHATTER
SO HOW ABOUT IT? WANNA GO?
CHATTER
ARE YOU GOING TOO, YUSUKE?
AND SPENDING THE NIGHT?!
COUNT ME IN!
Say yes, you guys! Let's go!
YUSUKE ...

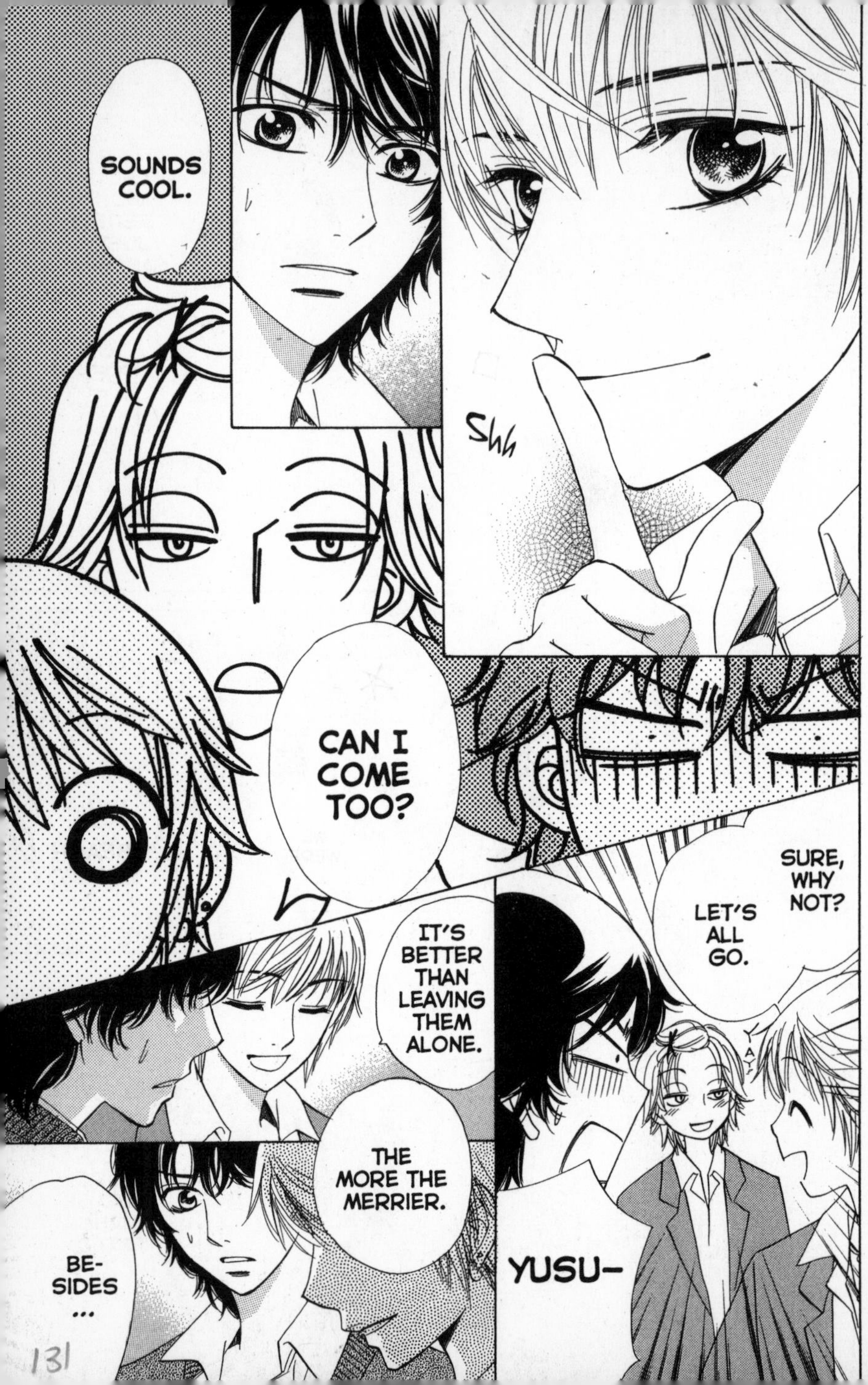
Shh
SOUNDS COOL.
CAN I COME TOO?
SURE, WHY NOT?
LET'S ALL GO.
YAY
YUSU-
IT'S BETTER THAN LEAVING THEM ALONE.
THE MORE THE MERRIER.
BE-SIDES ...

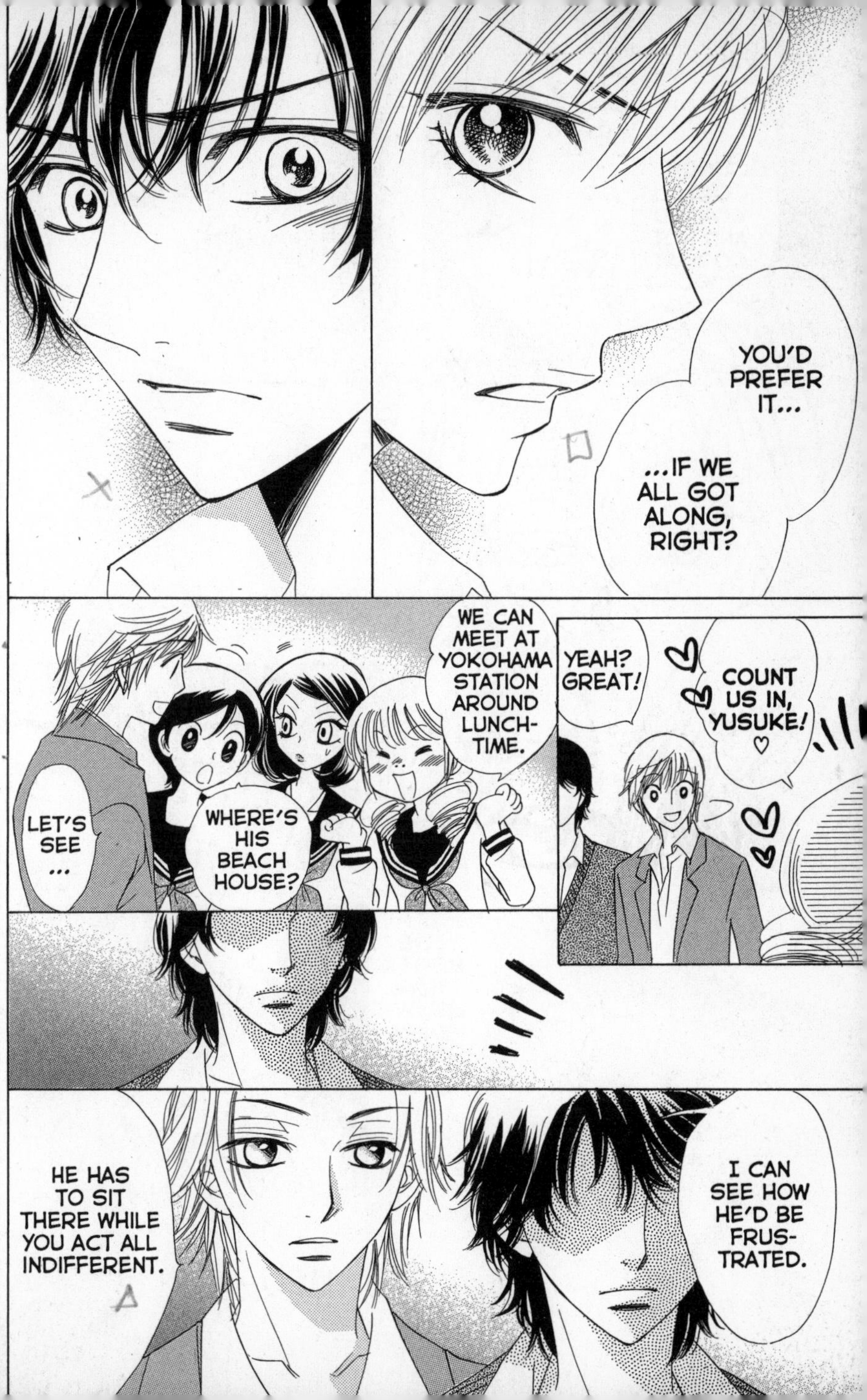
YOU'D PREFER IT...
...IF WE ALL GOT ALONG, RIGHT?
COUNT US IN, YUSUKE! ♡
YEAH? GREAT!
WE CAN MEET AT YOKOHAMA STATION AROUND LUNCH-TIME.
WHERE'S HIS BEACH HOUSE?
LET'S SEE ...
I CAN SEE HOW HE'D BE FRUS-TRATED.
HE HAS TO SIT THERE WHILE YOU ACT ALL INDIFFERENT.

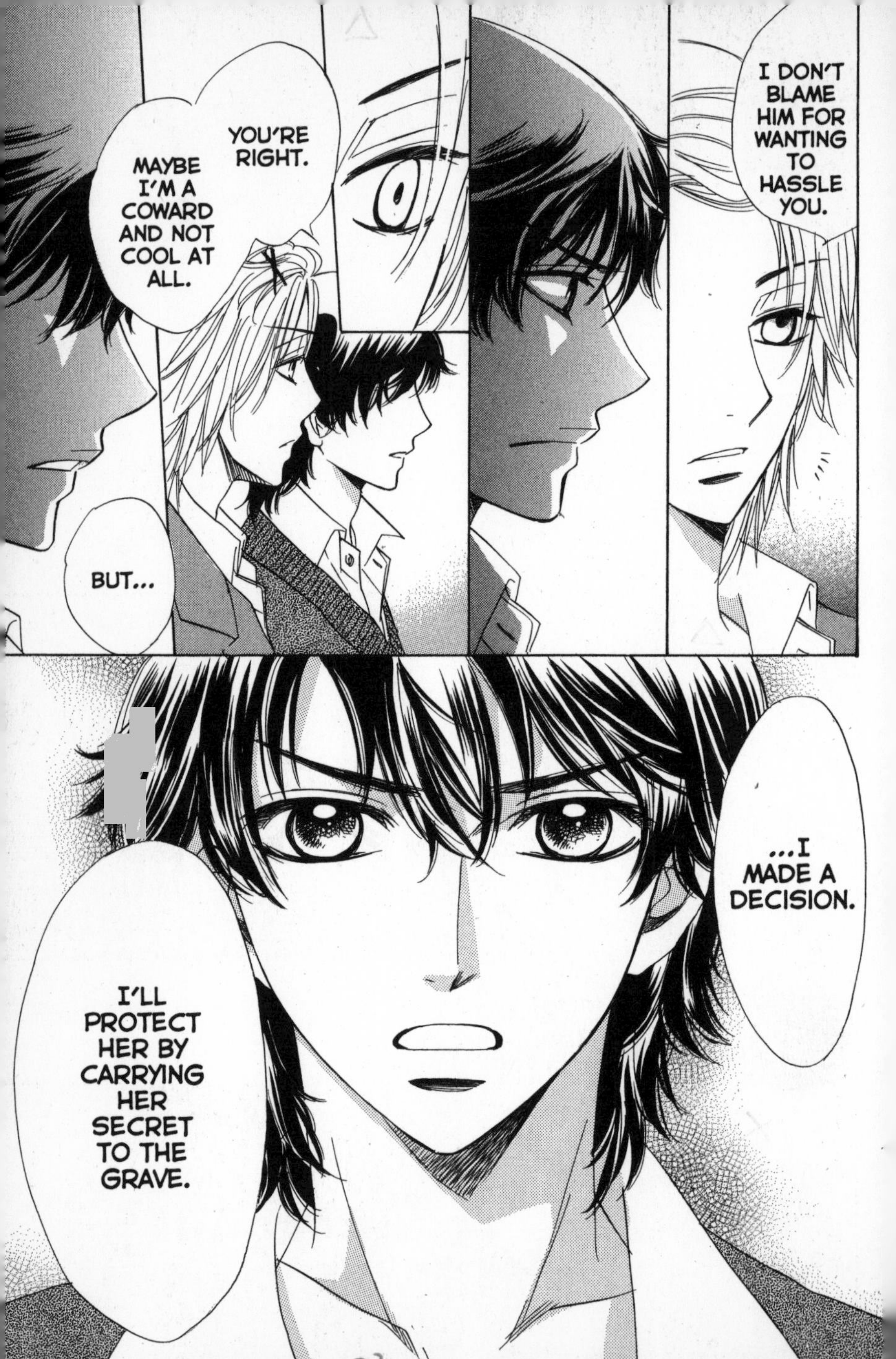
I DON'T BLAME HIM FOR WANTING TO HASSLE YOU.
YOU'RE RIGHT.
MAYBE I'M A COWARD AND NOT COOL AT ALL.
BUT...
...I MADE A DECISION.
I'LL PROTECT HER BY CARRYING HER SECRET TO THE GRAVE.

A Devil and
Her Love Song

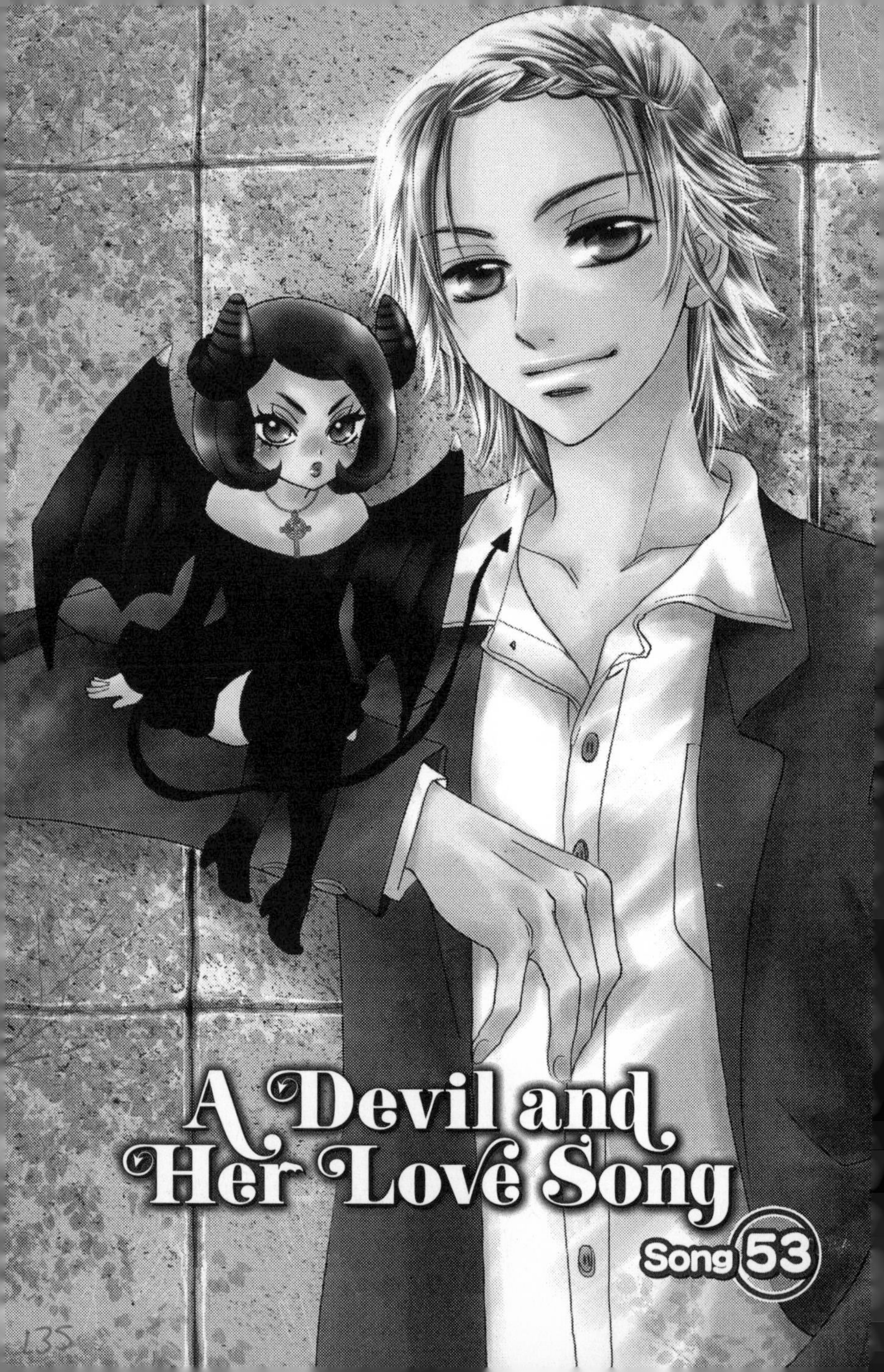
A Devil and
Her Love Song
Song 53

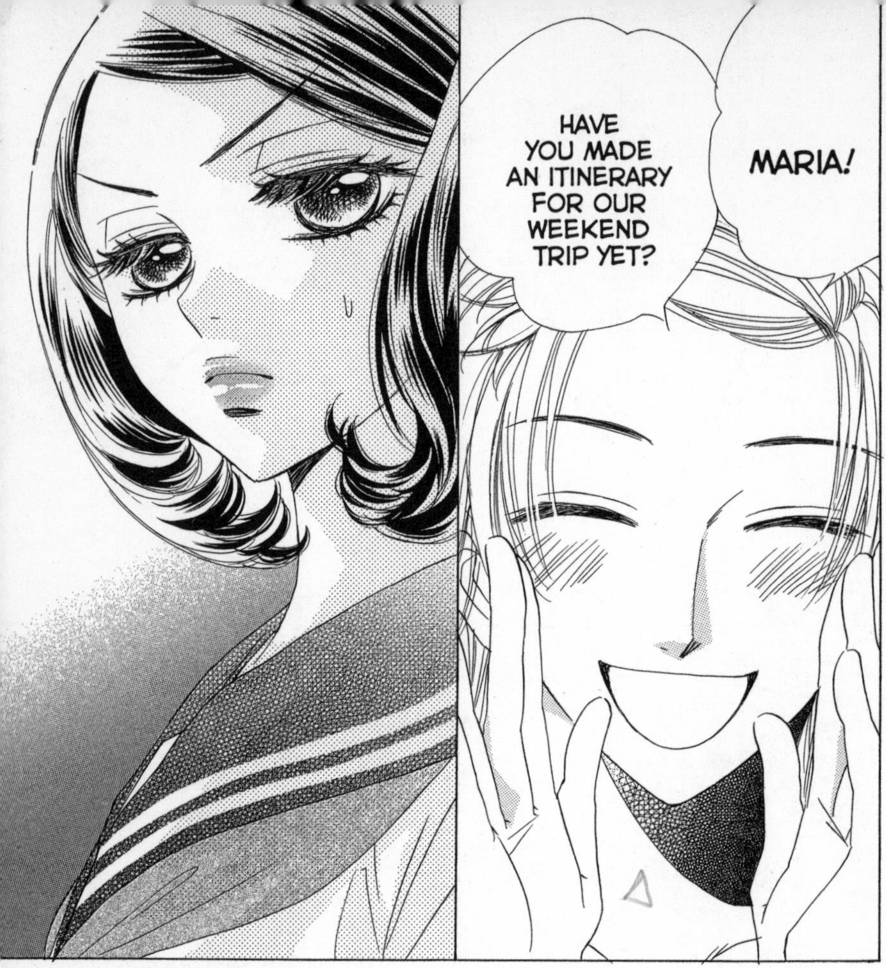
MARIA!
HAVE YOU MADE AN ITINERARY FOR OUR WEEKEND TRIP YET?

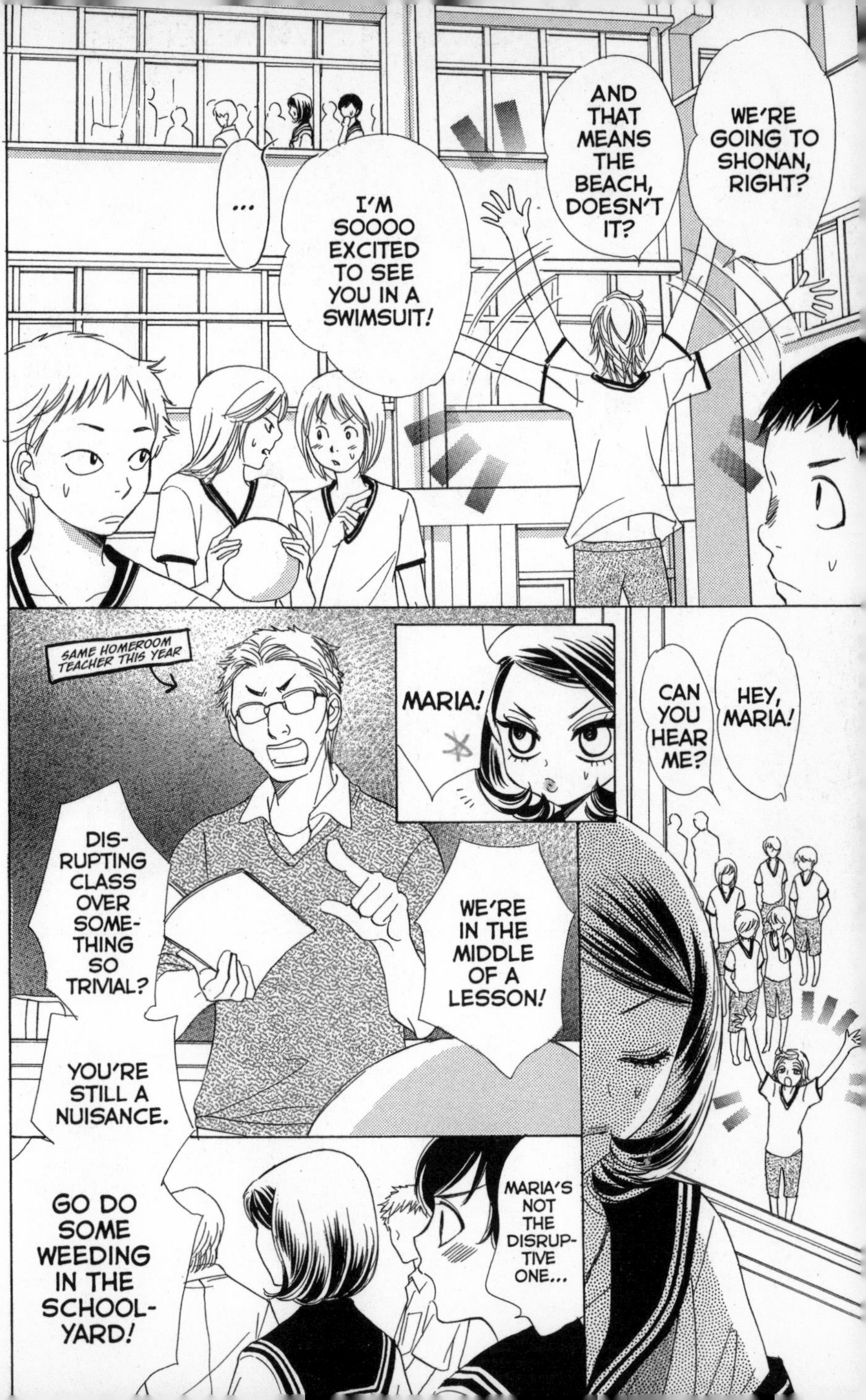

WE'RE GOING TO SHONAN, RIGHT?
AND THAT MEANS THE BEACH, DOESN'T IT?
I'M SOOOO EXCITED TO SEE YOU IN A SWIMSUIT!
...
HEY, MARIA!
CAN YOU HEAR ME?
MARIA!
SAME HOMEROOM TEACHER THIS YEAR
WE'RE IN THE MIDDLE OF A LESSON!
DIS-RUPTING CLASS OVER SOME-THING SO TRIVIAL?
YOU'RE STILL A NUISANCE.
MARIA'S NOT THE DISRUP-TIVE ONE...
GO DO SOME WEEDING IN THE SCHOOL-YARD!

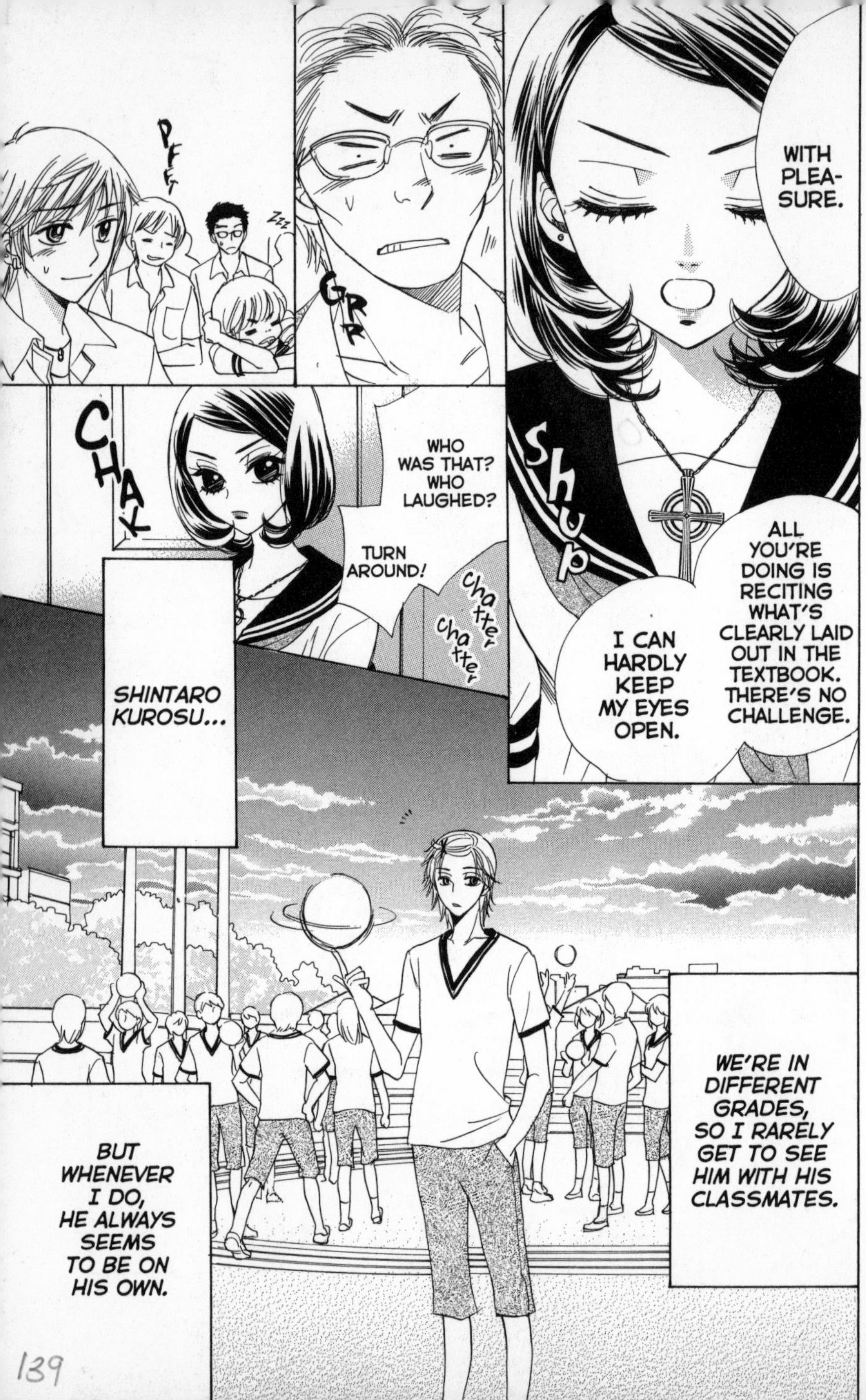
WITH PLEA-SURE.
shup
ALL YOU'RE DOING IS RECITING WHAT'S CLEARLY LAID OUT IN THE TEXTBOOK. THERE'S NO CHALLENGE.
I CAN HARDLY KEEP MY EYES OPEN.
GRR
PFFT
ZZZ
WHO WAS THAT? WHO LAUGHED?
TURN AROUND!
chatter chatter
CHAK
SHINTARO KUROSU...
WE'RE IN DIFFERENT GRADES, SO I RARELY GET TO SEE HIM WITH HIS CLASSMATES.
BUT WHENEVER I DO, HE ALWAYS SEEMS TO BE ON HIS OWN.

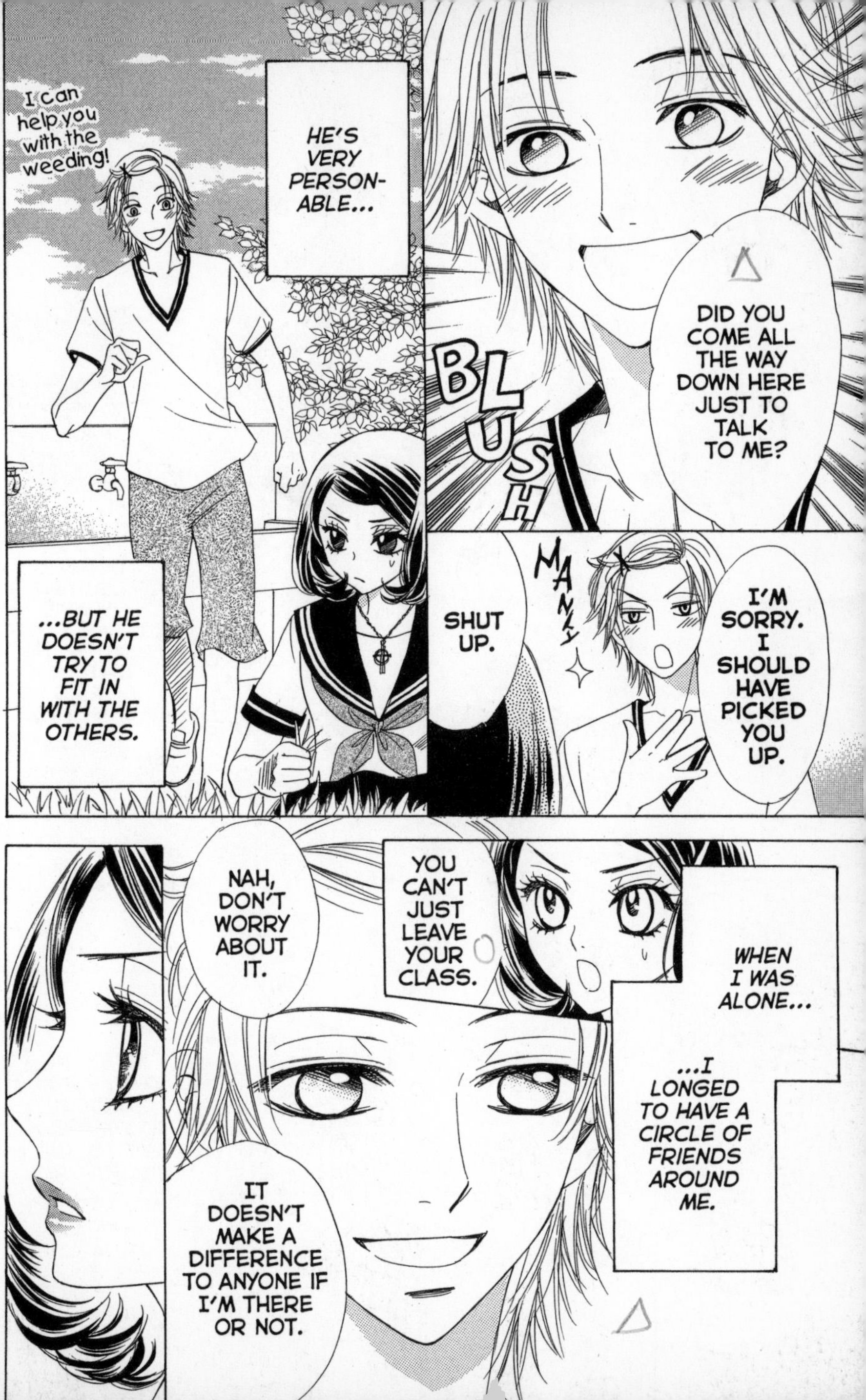

BLUSH
DID YOU COME ALL THE WAY DOWN HERE JUST TO TALK TO ME?
I'M SORRY. I SHOULD HAVE PICKED YOU UP.
MANLY
SHUT UP.
I can help you with the weeding!
HE'S VERY PERSON-ABLE...
...BUT HE DOESN'T TRY TO FIT IN WITH THE OTHERS.
YOU CAN'T JUST LEAVE YOUR CLASS.
WHEN I WAS ALONE...
NAH, DON'T WORRY ABOUT IT.
...I LONGED TO HAVE A CIRCLE OF FRIENDS AROUND ME.
IT DOESN'T MAKE A DIFFERENCE TO ANYONE IF I'M THERE OR NOT.

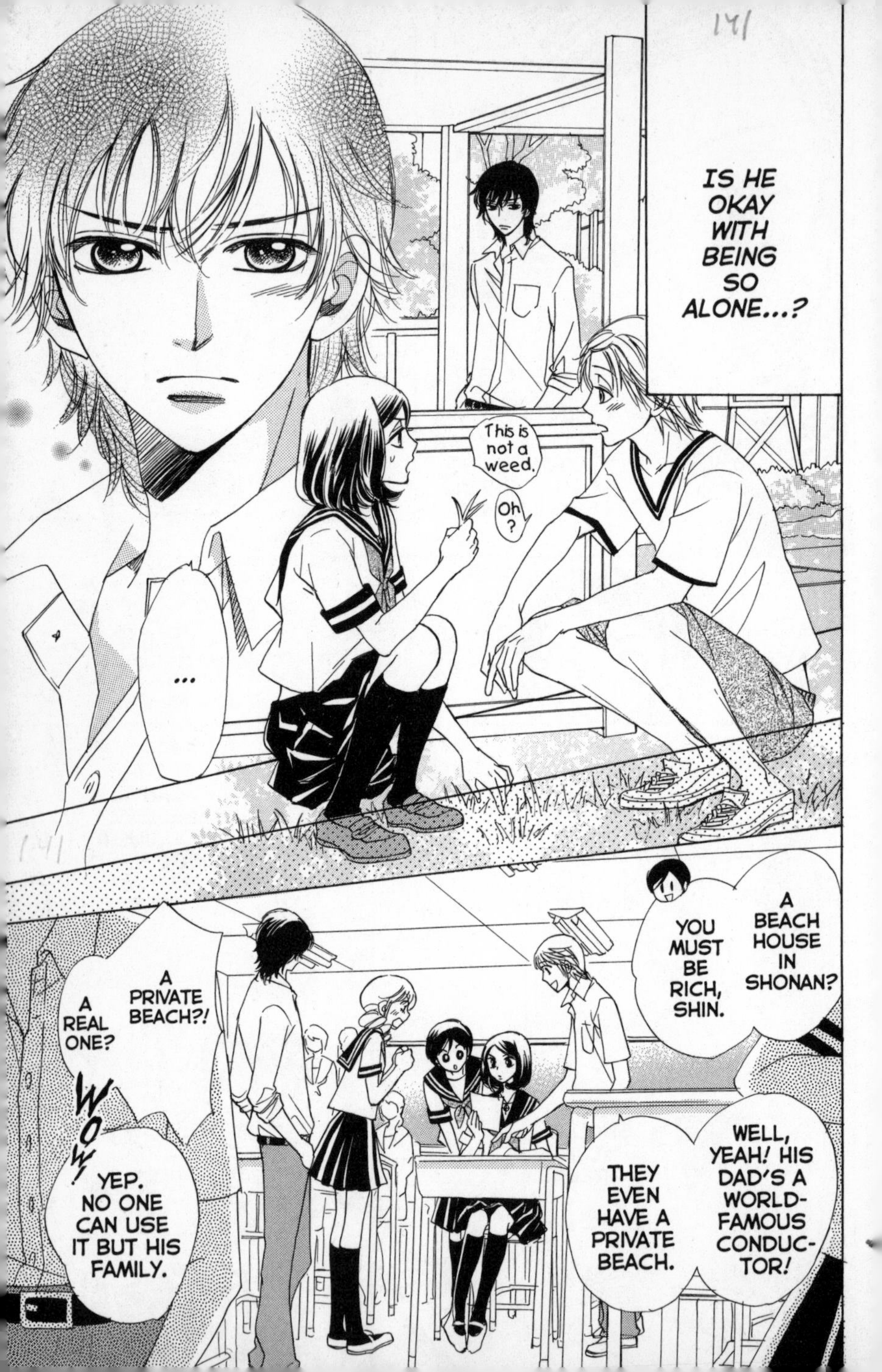
IS HE OKAY WITH BEING SO ALONE...?
This is not a weed.
Oh?
...
A BEACH HOUSE IN SHONAN?
YOU MUST BE RICH, SHIN.
WELL, YEAH! HIS DAD'S A WORLD-FAMOUS CONDUC-TOR!
THEY EVEN HAVE A PRIVATE BEACH.
A PRIVATE BEACH?!
A REAL ONE?
WOW!
YEP. NO ONE CAN USE IT BUT HIS FAMILY.

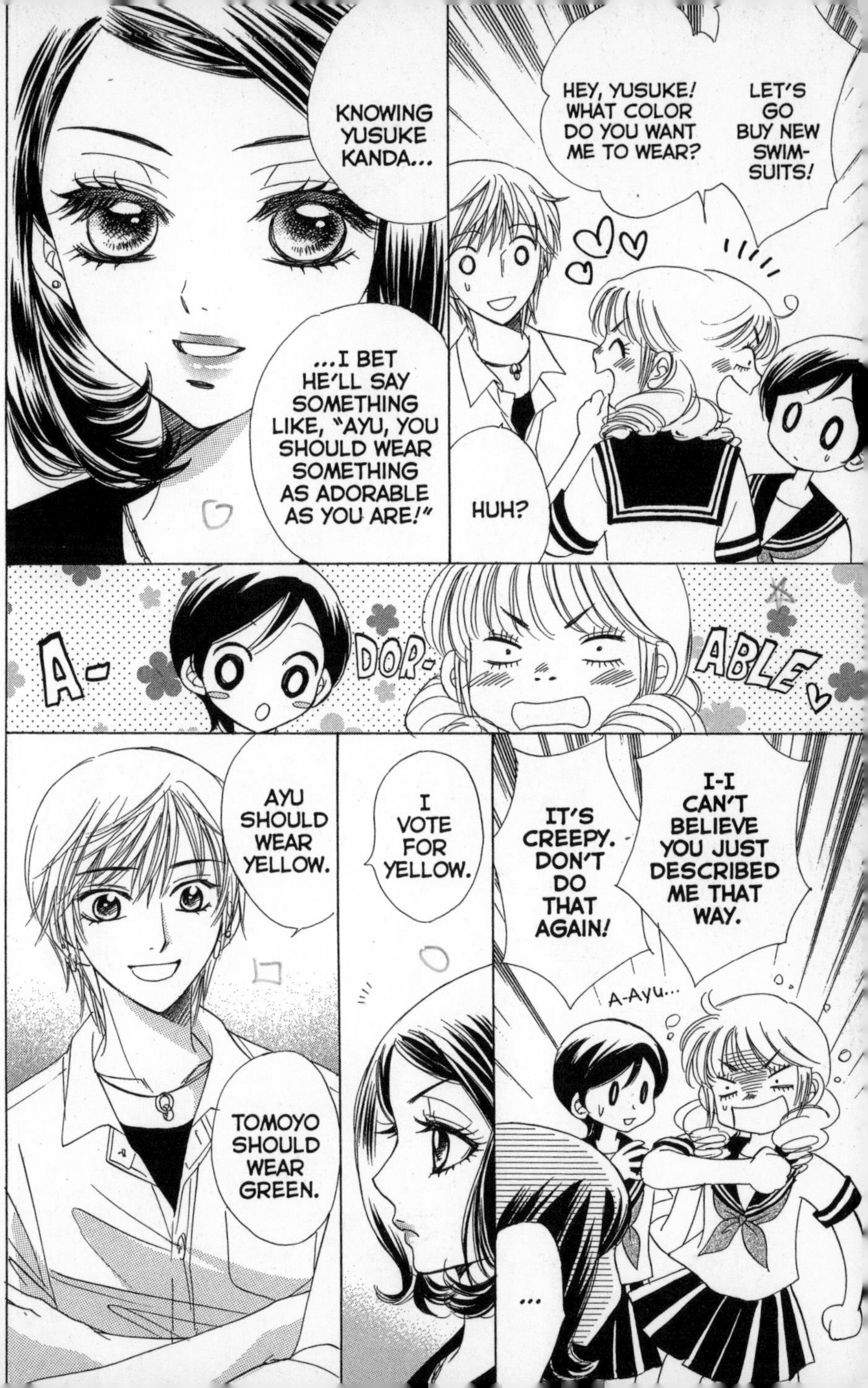
LET'S GO BUY NEW SWIM-SUITS!
HEY, YUSUKE! WHAT COLOR DO YOU WANT ME TO WEAR?
HUH?
KNOWING YUSUKE KANDA...
...I BET HE'LL SAY SOMETHING LIKE, "AYU, YOU SHOULD WEAR SOMETHING AS ADORABLE AS YOU ARE!"
A- DOR- ABLE
I-I CAN'T BELIEVE YOU JUST DESCRIBED ME THAT WAY.
IT'S CREEPY. DON'T DO THAT AGAIN!
A-Ayu...
...
I VOTE FOR YELLOW.
AYU SHOULD WEAR YELLOW.
TOMOYO SHOULD WEAR GREEN.

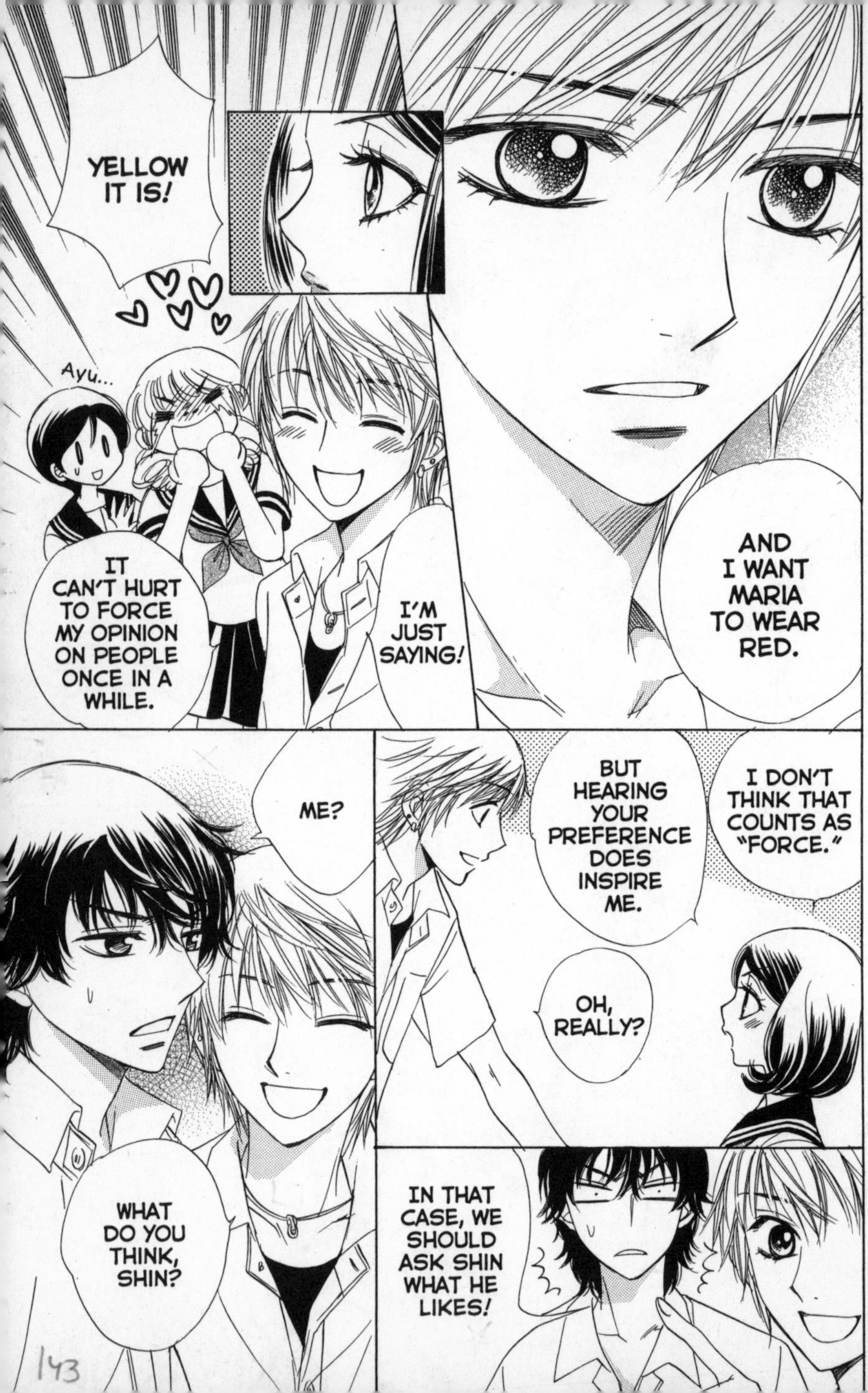
AND I WANT MARIA TO WEAR RED.
YELLOW IT IS!
Ayu...
IT CAN'T HURT TO FORCE MY OPINION ON PEOPLE ONCE IN A WHILE.
I'M JUST SAYING!
I DON'T THINK THAT COUNTS AS "FORCE."
BUT HEARING YOUR PREFERENCE DOES INSPIRE ME.
OH, REALLY?
IN THAT CASE, WE SHOULD ASK SHIN WHAT HE LIKES!
WHAT DO YOU THINK, SHIN?
ME?

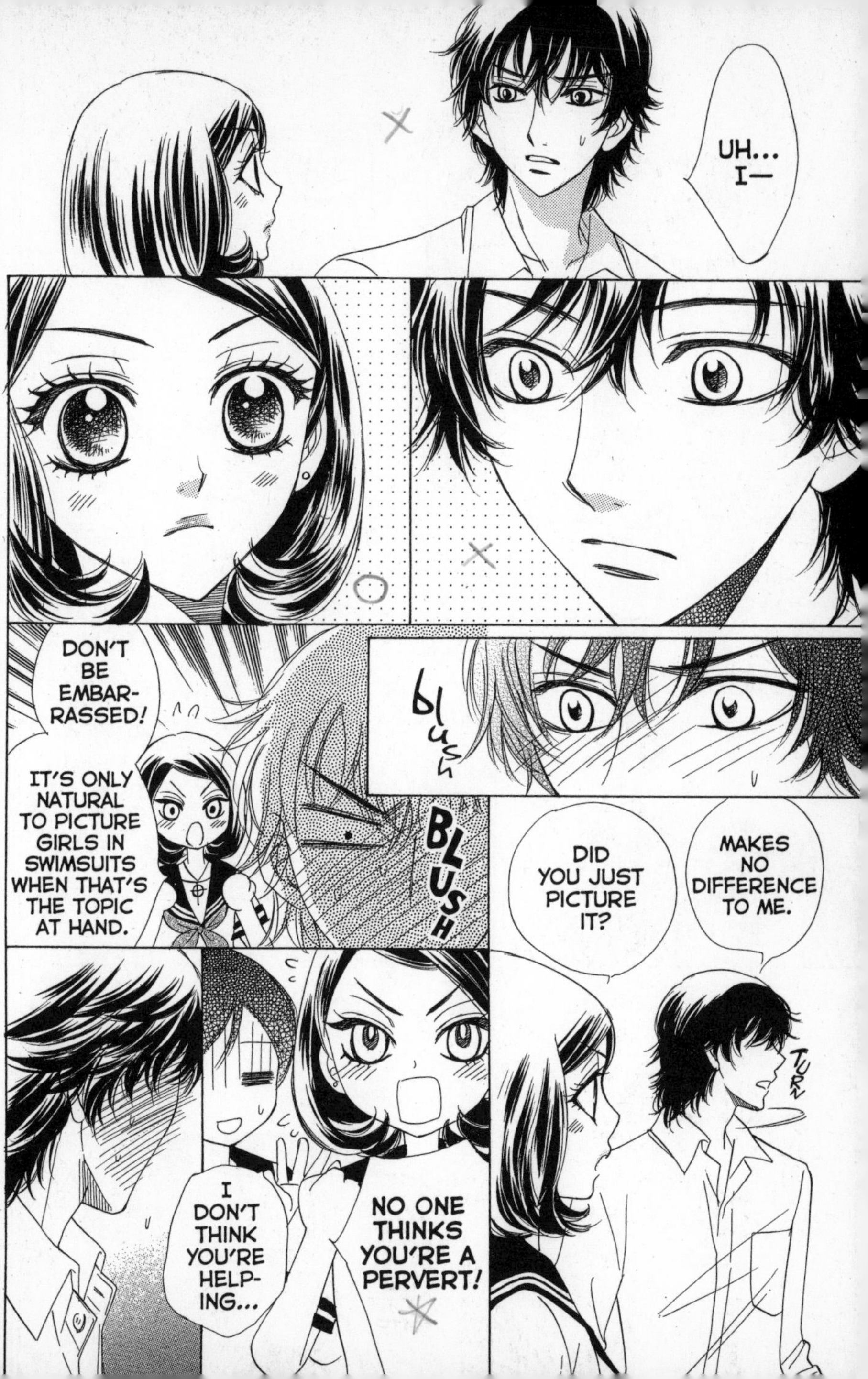
UH... I—
blush
DON'T BE EMBARRASSED!
IT'S ONLY NATURAL TO PICTURE GIRLS IN SWIMSUITS WHEN THAT'S THE TOPIC AT HAND.
BLUSH
MAKES NO DIFFERENCE TO ME.
DID YOU JUST PICTURE IT?
TURN
NO ONE THINKS YOU'RE A PERVERT!
I DON'T THINK YOU'RE HELPING...

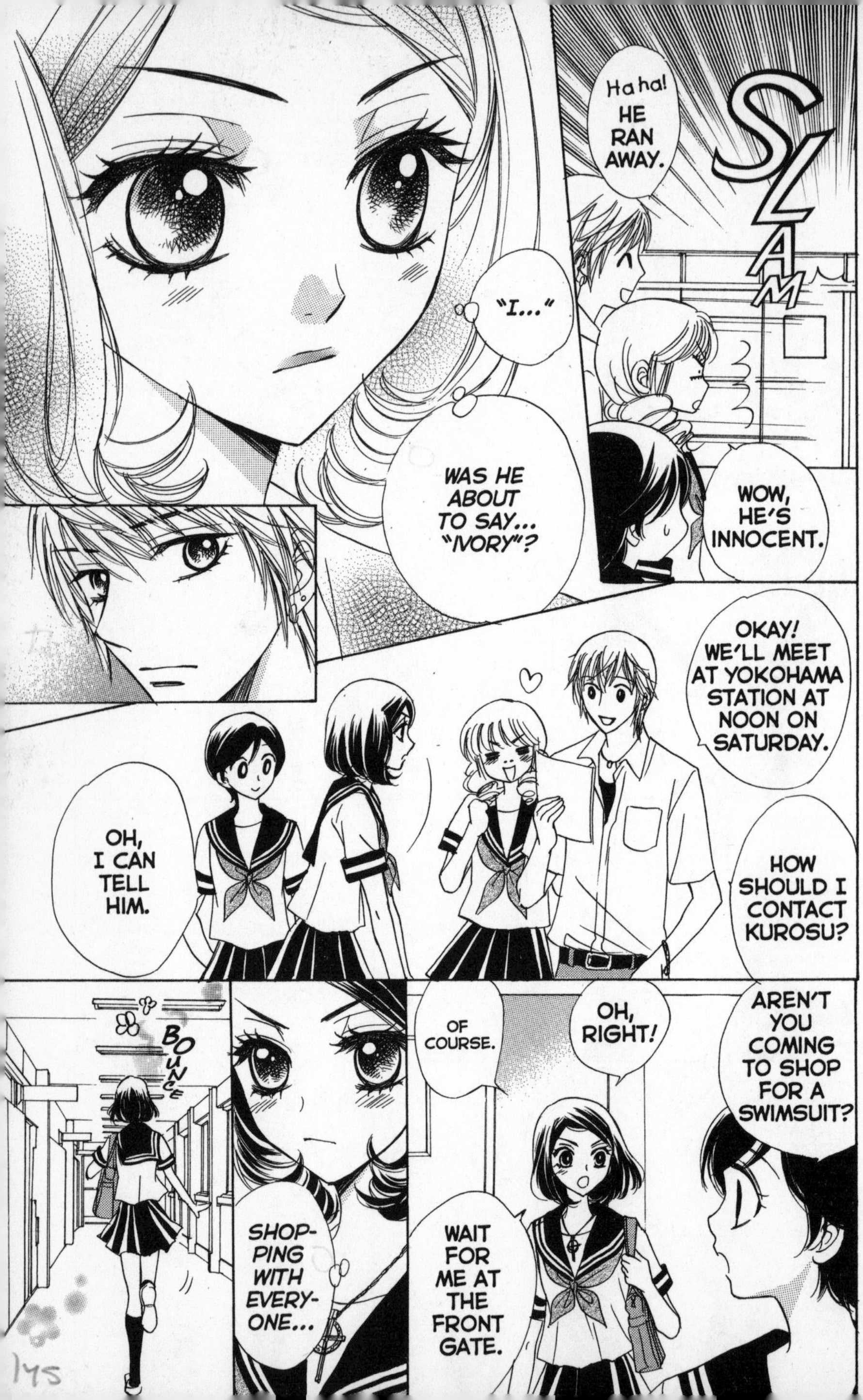
SLAM
Ha ha! HE RAN AWAY.
WOW, HE'S INNOCENT.
"I..."
WAS HE ABOUT TO SAY... "IVORY"?
OKAY! WE'LL MEET AT YOKOHAMA STATION AT NOON ON SATURDAY.
HOW SHOULD I CONTACT KUROSU?
OH, I CAN TELL HIM.
AREN'T YOU COMING TO SHOP FOR A SWIMSUIT?
OH, RIGHT!
WAIT FOR ME AT THE FRONT GATE.
OF COURSE.
SHOP-PING WITH EVERY-ONE...
BOUNCE

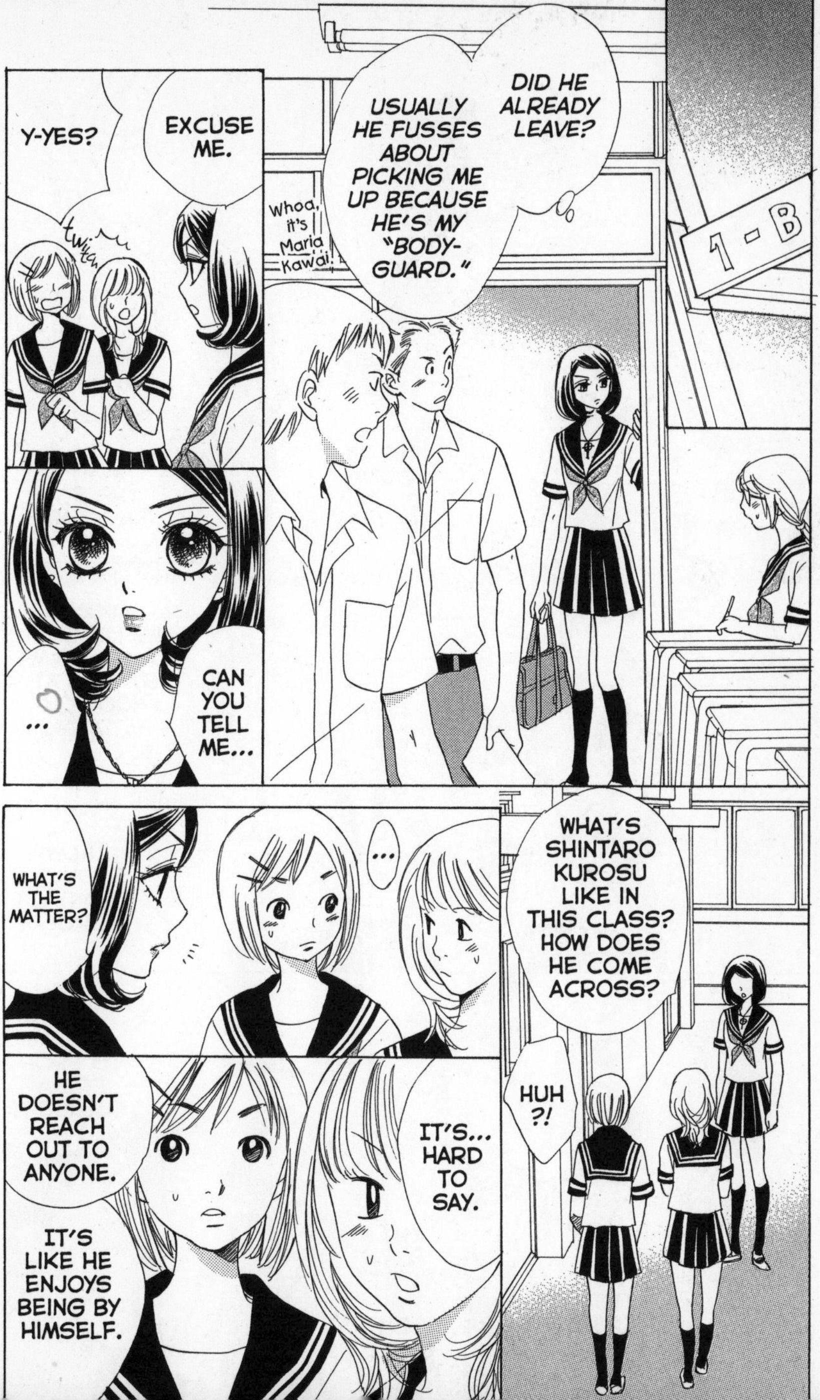
DID HE ALREADY LEAVE?
USUALLY HE FUSSES ABOUT PICKING ME UP BECAUSE HE'S MY "BODY-GUARD."
Whoa, it's Maria Kawai!
EXCUSE ME.
Y-YES?
CAN YOU TELL ME...
...
WHAT'S SHINTARO KUROSU LIKE IN THIS CLASS? HOW DOES HE COME ACROSS?
HUH?!
...
WHAT'S THE MATTER?
IT'S... HARD TO SAY.
HE DOESN'T REACH OUT TO ANYONE.
IT'S LIKE HE ENJOYS BEING BY HIMSELF.

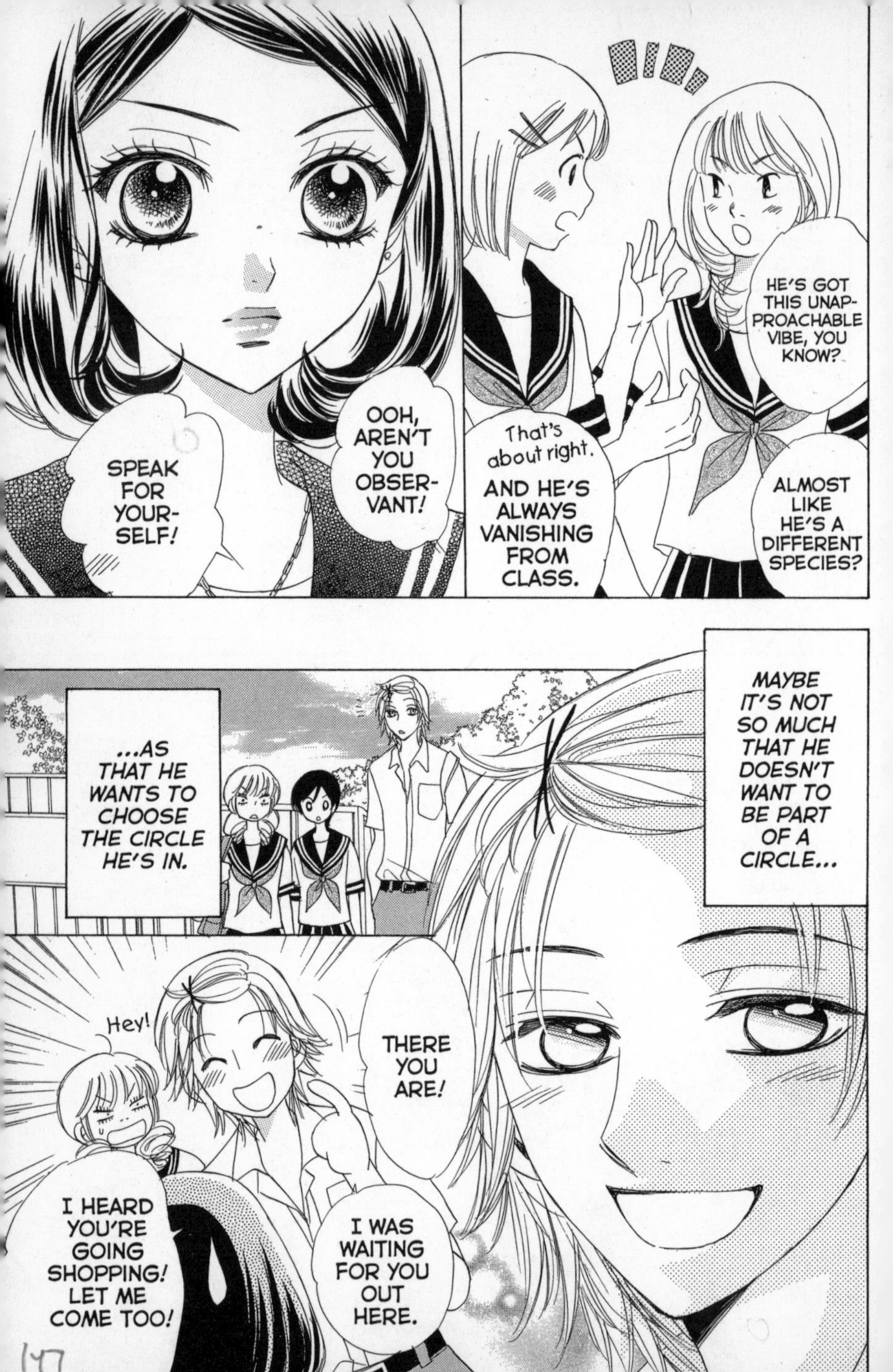
HE'S GOT THIS UNAP-PROACHABLE VIBE, YOU KNOW?
ALMOST LIKE HE'S A DIFFERENT SPECIES?
That's about right.
AND HE'S ALWAYS VANISHING FROM CLASS.
OOH, AREN'T YOU OBSERVANT!
SPEAK FOR YOUR-SELF!
MAYBE IT'S NOT SO MUCH THAT HE DOESN'T WANT TO BE PART OF A CIRCLE...
...AS THAT HE WANTS TO CHOOSE THE CIRCLE HE'S IN.
THERE YOU ARE!
I WAS WAITING FOR YOU OUT HERE.
Hey!
I HEARD YOU'RE GOING SHOPPING! LET ME COME TOO!

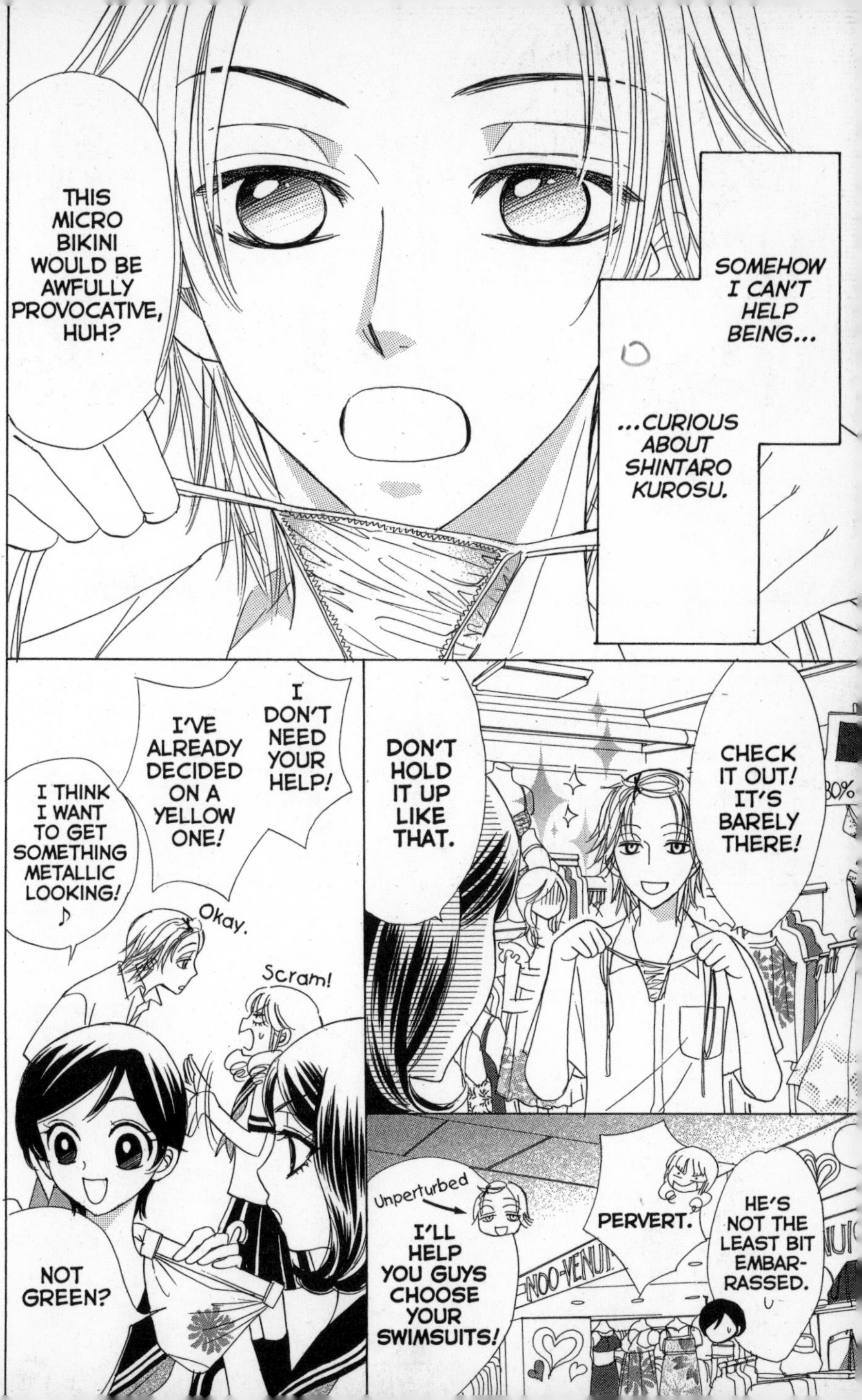
SOMEHOW I CAN'T HELP BEING...
...CURIOUS ABOUT SHINTARO KUROSU.
THIS MICRO BIKINI WOULD BE AWFULLY PROVOCATIVE, HUH?
CHECK IT OUT! IT'S BARELY THERE!
DON'T HOLD IT UP LIKE THAT.
HE'S NOT THE LEAST BIT EMBARRASSED.
PERVERT.
Unperturbed
I'LL HELP YOU GUYS CHOOSE YOUR SWIMSUITS!
I DON'T NEED YOUR HELP!
I'VE ALREADY DECIDED ON A YELLOW ONE!
I THINK I WANT TO GET SOMETHING METALLIC LOOKING! ♪
Okay.
Scram!
NOT GREEN?

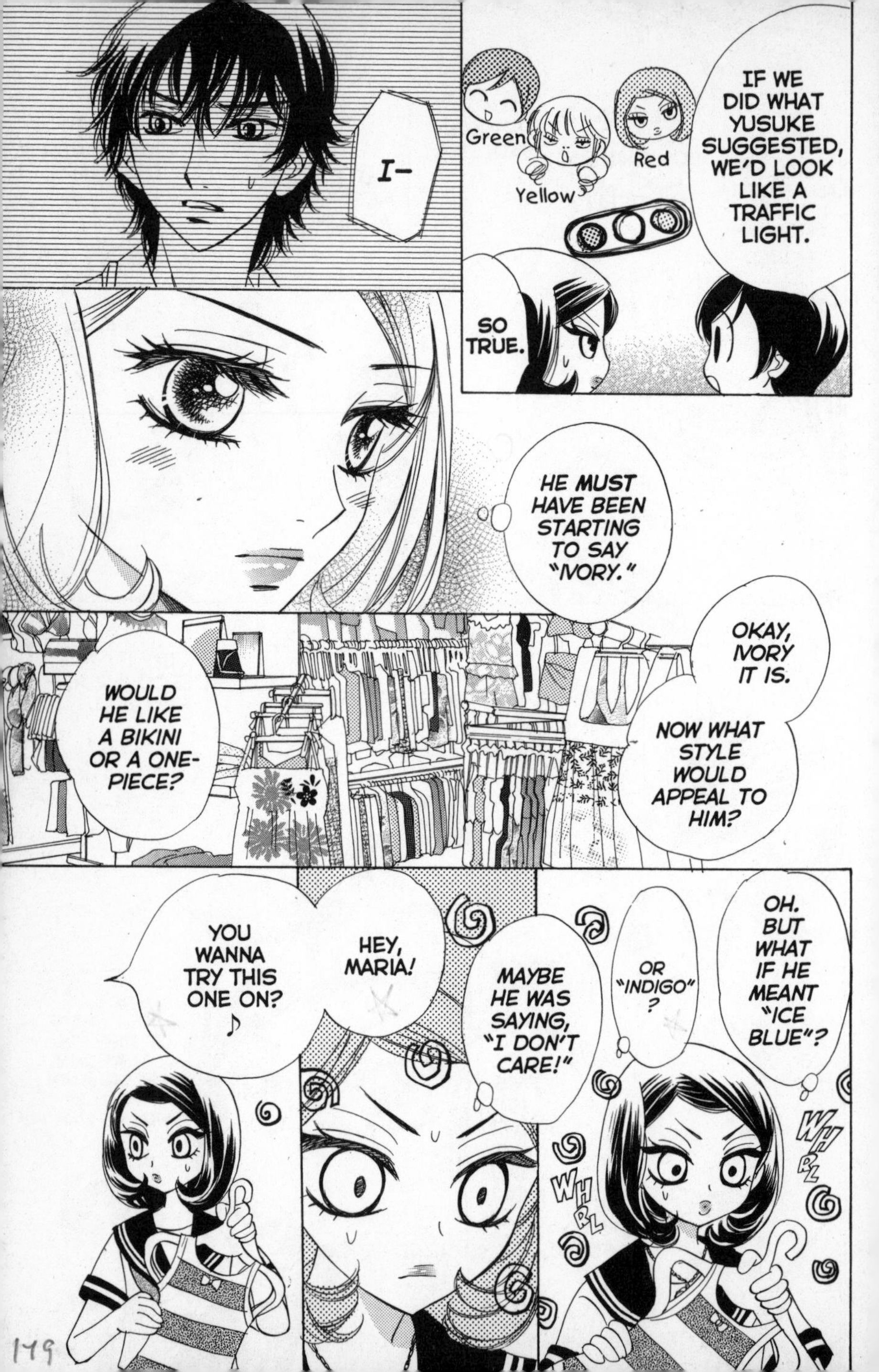
IF WE DID WHAT YUSUKE SUGGESTED, WE'D LOOK LIKE A TRAFFIC LIGHT.
Red
Green
Yellow
SO TRUE.
I–
HE MUST HAVE BEEN STARTING TO SAY "IVORY."
OKAY, IVORY IT IS.
NOW WHAT STYLE WOULD APPEAL TO HIM?
WOULD HE LIKE A BIKINI OR A ONE-PIECE?
OH. BUT WHAT IF HE MEANT "ICE BLUE"?
OR "INDIGO"?
WHRL
WHRL
MAYBE HE WAS SAYING, "I DON'T CARE!"
HEY, MARIA!
YOU WANNA TRY THIS ONE ON? ♪

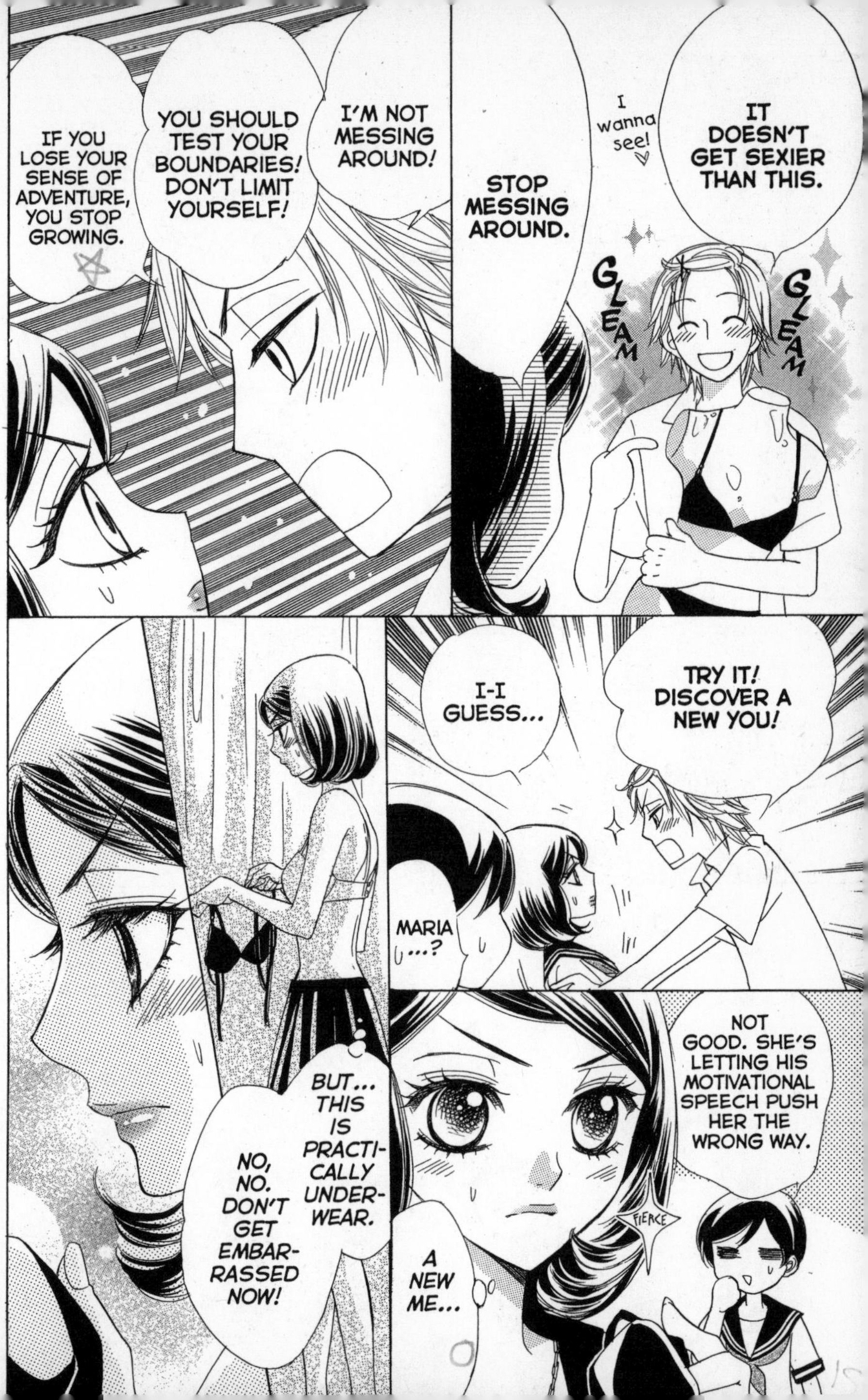
IT DOESN'T GET SEXIER THAN THIS.
I wanna see! ♡
GLEAM
GLEAM
STOP MESSING AROUND.
I'M NOT MESSING AROUND!
YOU SHOULD TEST YOUR BOUNDARIES! DON'T LIMIT YOURSELF!
IF YOU LOSE YOUR SENSE OF ADVENTURE, YOU STOP GROWING.
TRY IT! DISCOVER A NEW YOU!
I-I GUESS...
MARIA...?
NOT GOOD. SHE'S LETTING HIS MOTIVATIONAL SPEECH PUSH HER THE WRONG WAY.
FIERCE
A NEW ME...
BUT... THIS IS PRACTICALLY UNDERWEAR.
NO, NO. DON'T GET EMBARRASSED NOW!

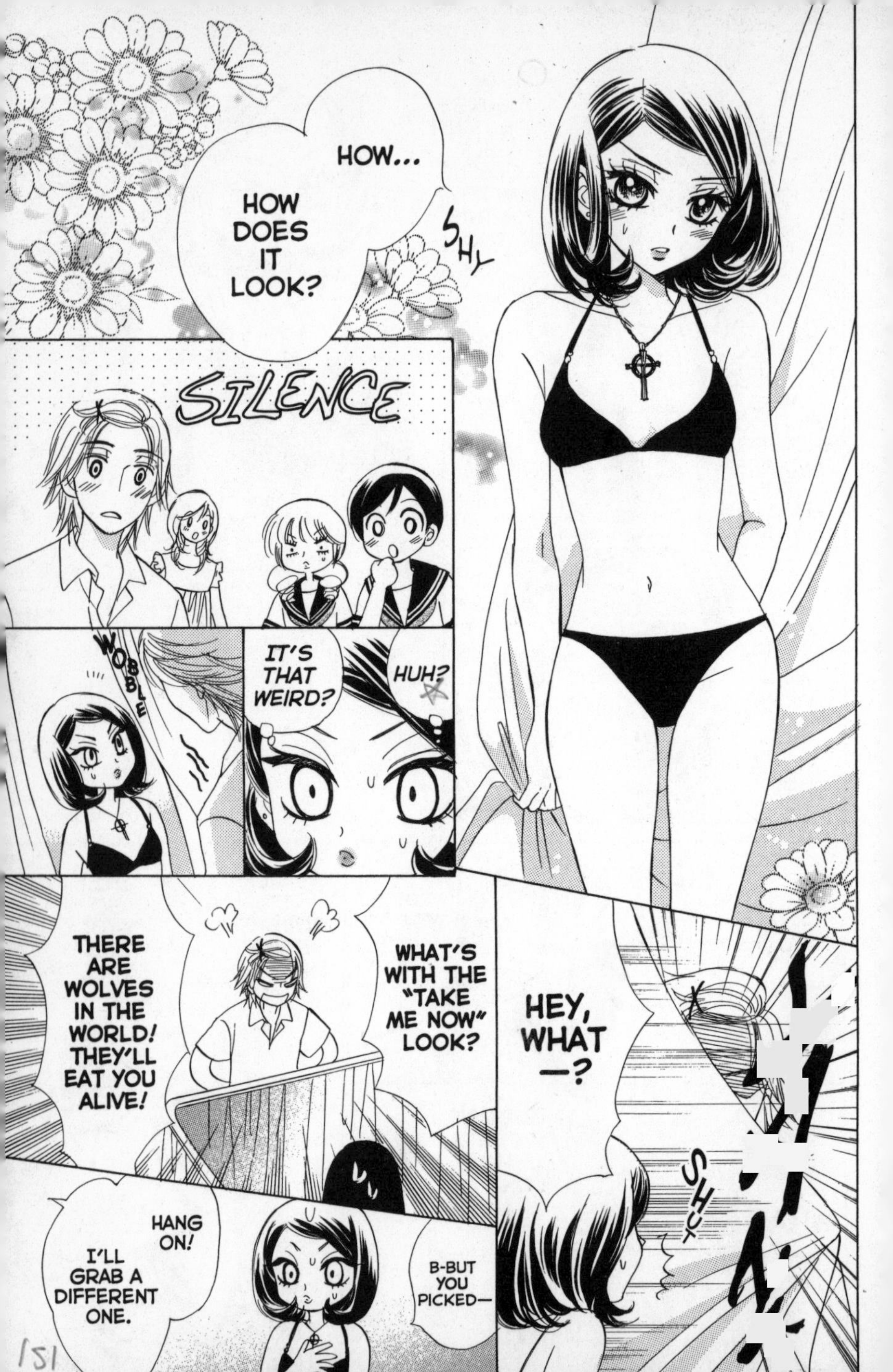
HOW...
HOW DOES IT LOOK?
SHY
SILENCE
HUH?
IT'S THAT WEIRD?
WOBBLE
HEY, WHAT—?
SHUT
WHAT'S WITH THE "TAKE ME NOW" LOOK?
THERE ARE WOLVES IN THE WORLD! THEY'LL EAT YOU ALIVE!
B-BUT YOU PICKED—
HANG ON!
I'LL GRAB A DIFFERENT ONE.

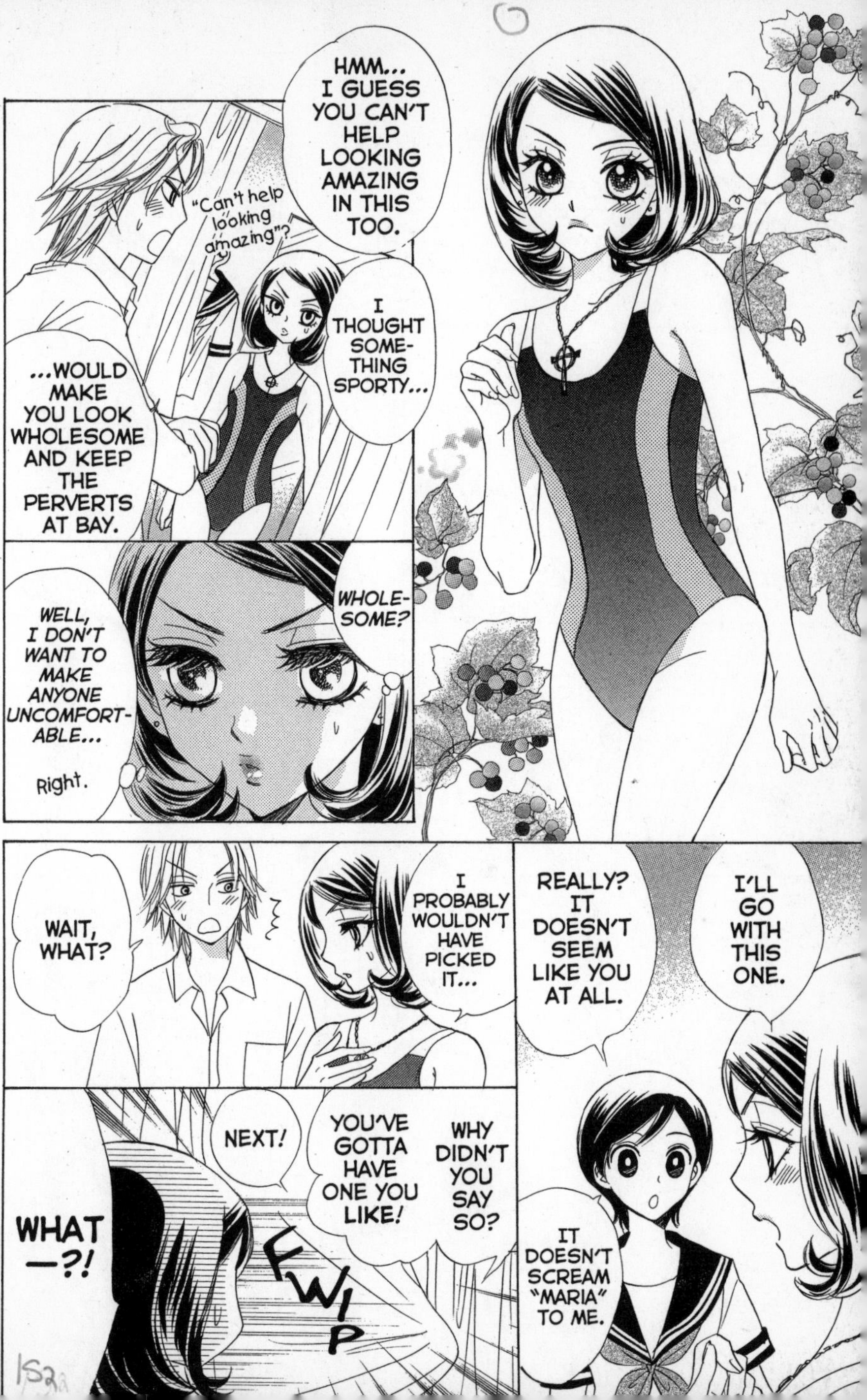
HMM... I GUESS YOU CAN'T HELP LOOKING AMAZING IN THIS TOO.
"Can't help looking amazing"?
I THOUGHT SOME-THING SPORTY...
...WOULD MAKE YOU LOOK WHOLESOME AND KEEP THE PERVERTS AT BAY.
WHOLE-SOME?
WELL, I DON'T WANT TO MAKE ANYONE UNCOMFORT-ABLE...
Right.
I'LL GO WITH THIS ONE.
REALLY? IT DOESN'T SEEM LIKE YOU AT ALL.
IT DOESN'T SCREAM "MARIA" TO ME.
I PROBABLY WOULDN'T HAVE PICKED IT...
WAIT, WHAT?
WHY DIDN'T YOU SAY SO?
YOU'VE GOTTA HAVE ONE YOU LIKE!
NEXT!
FWIP
WHAT—?!

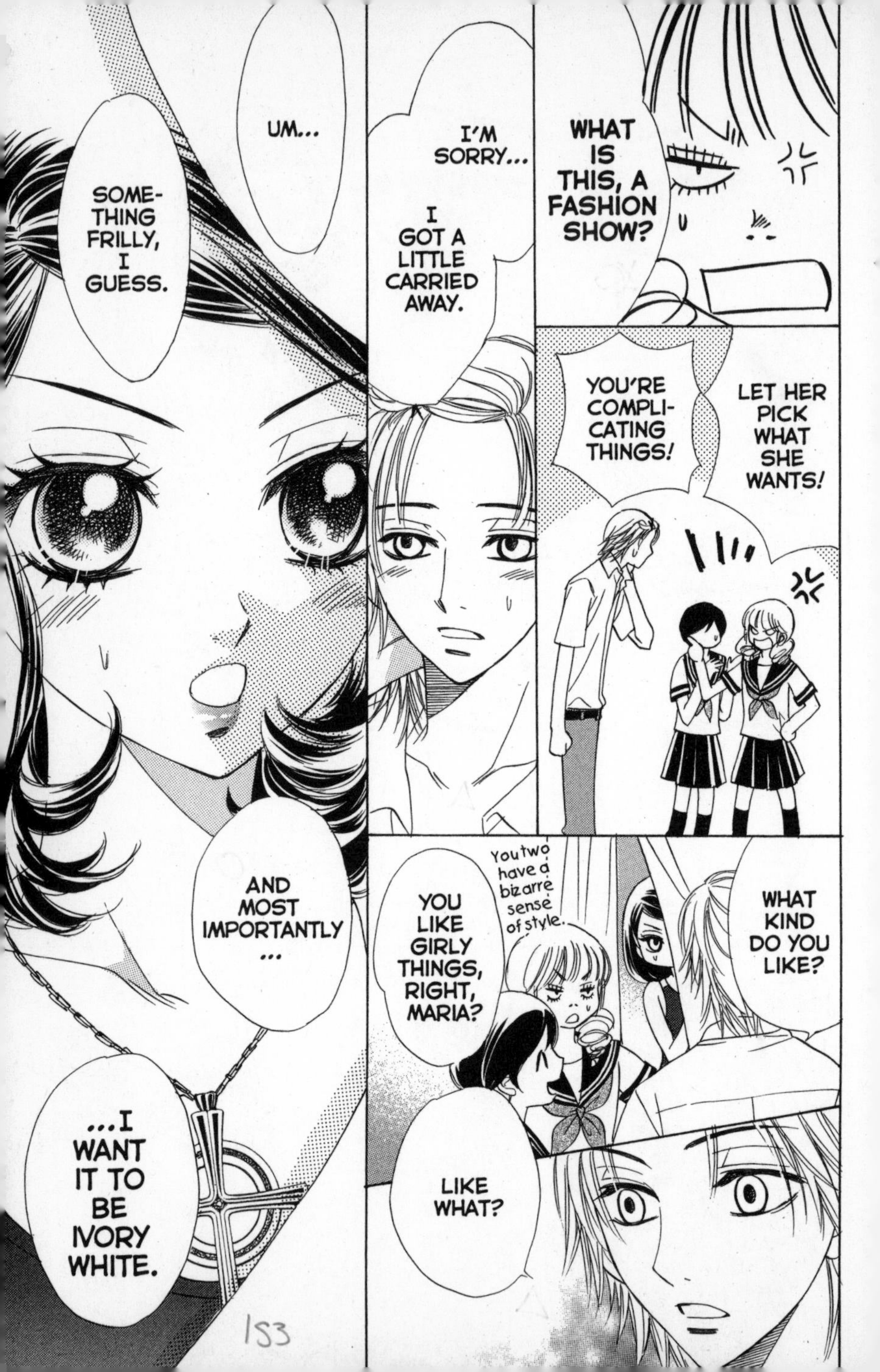
WHAT IS THIS, A FASHION SHOW?
LET HER PICK WHAT SHE WANTS!
YOU'RE COMPLICATING THINGS!
I'M SORRY...
I GOT A LITTLE CARRIED AWAY.
WHAT KIND DO YOU LIKE?
You two have a bizarre sense of style.
YOU LIKE GIRLY THINGS, RIGHT, MARIA?
LIKE WHAT?
UM...
SOMETHING FRILLY, I GUESS.
AND MOST IMPORTANTLY...
...I WANT IT TO BE IVORY WHITE.

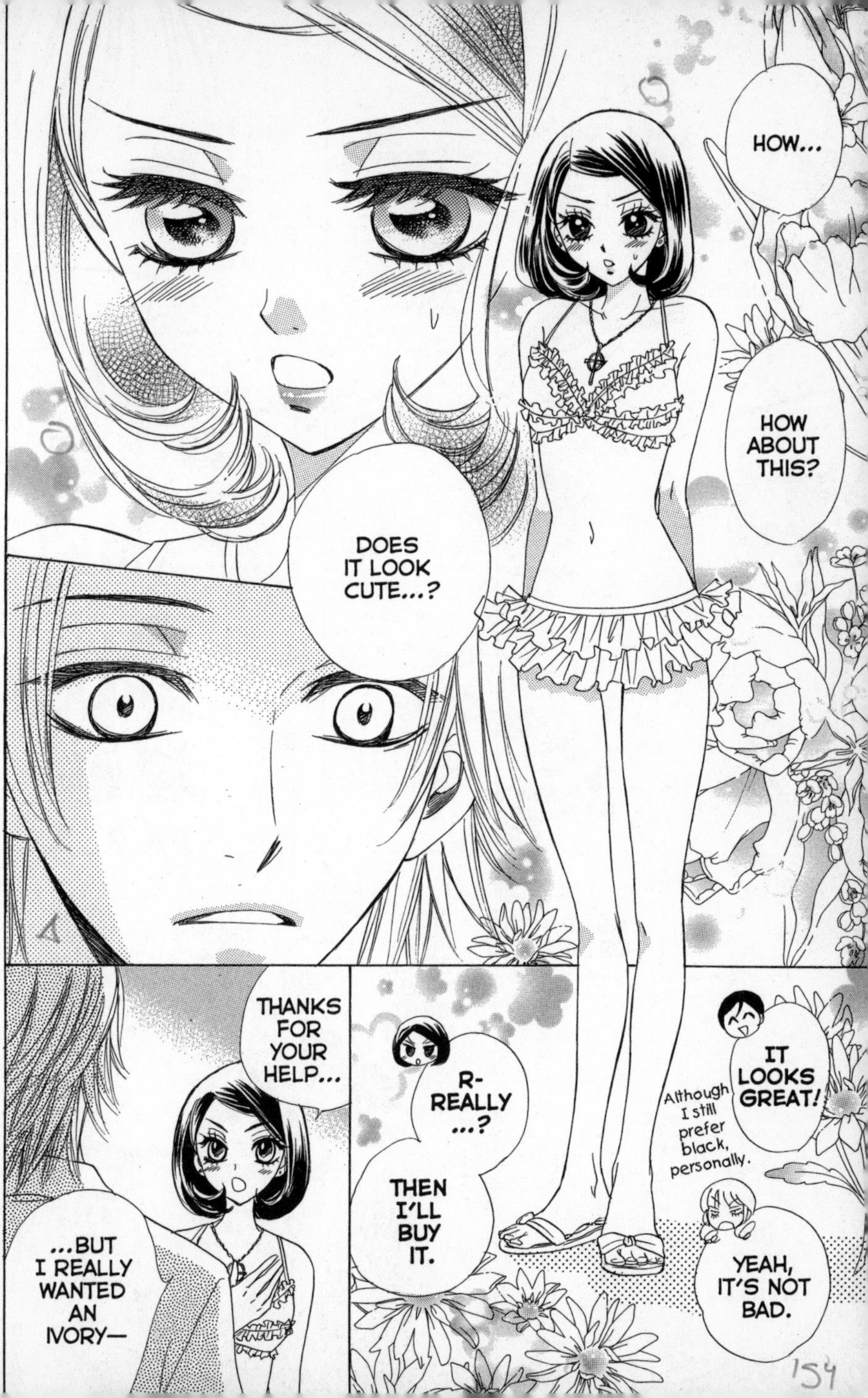
HOW...
HOW ABOUT THIS?
DOES IT LOOK CUTE...?
IT LOOKS GREAT!
Although I still prefer black, personally.
YEAH, IT'S NOT BAD.
R-REALLY...?
THEN I'LL BUY IT.
THANKS FOR YOUR HELP...
...BUT I REALLY WANTED AN IVORY—

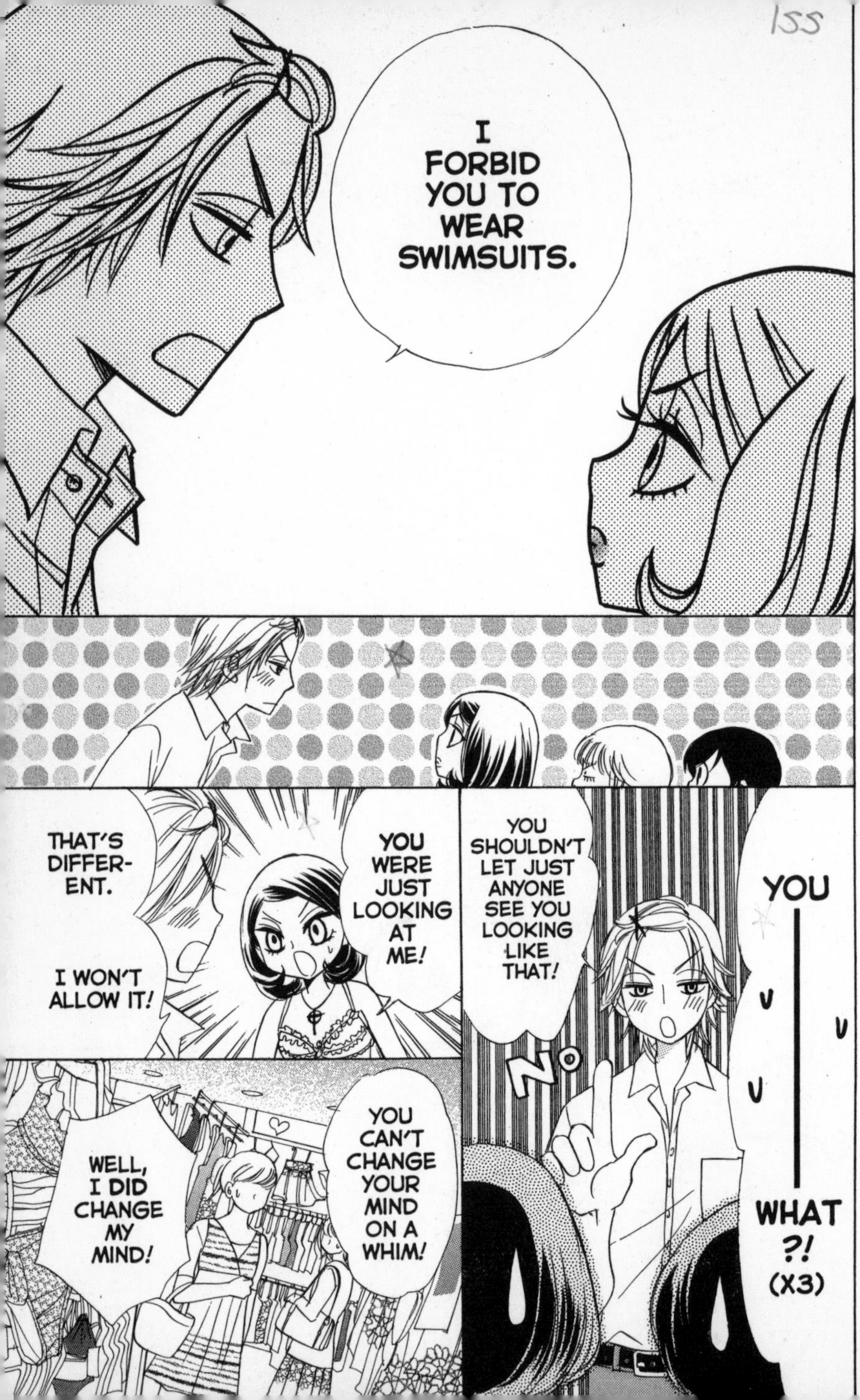
I FORBID YOU TO WEAR SWIMSUITS.
YOU—WHAT?! (X3)
YOU SHOULDN'T LET JUST ANYONE SEE YOU LOOKING LIKE THAT!
NO
YOU WERE JUST LOOKING AT ME!
THAT'S DIFFER-ENT.
I WON'T ALLOW IT!
YOU CAN'T CHANGE YOUR MIND ON A WHIM!
WELL, I DID CHANGE MY MIND!

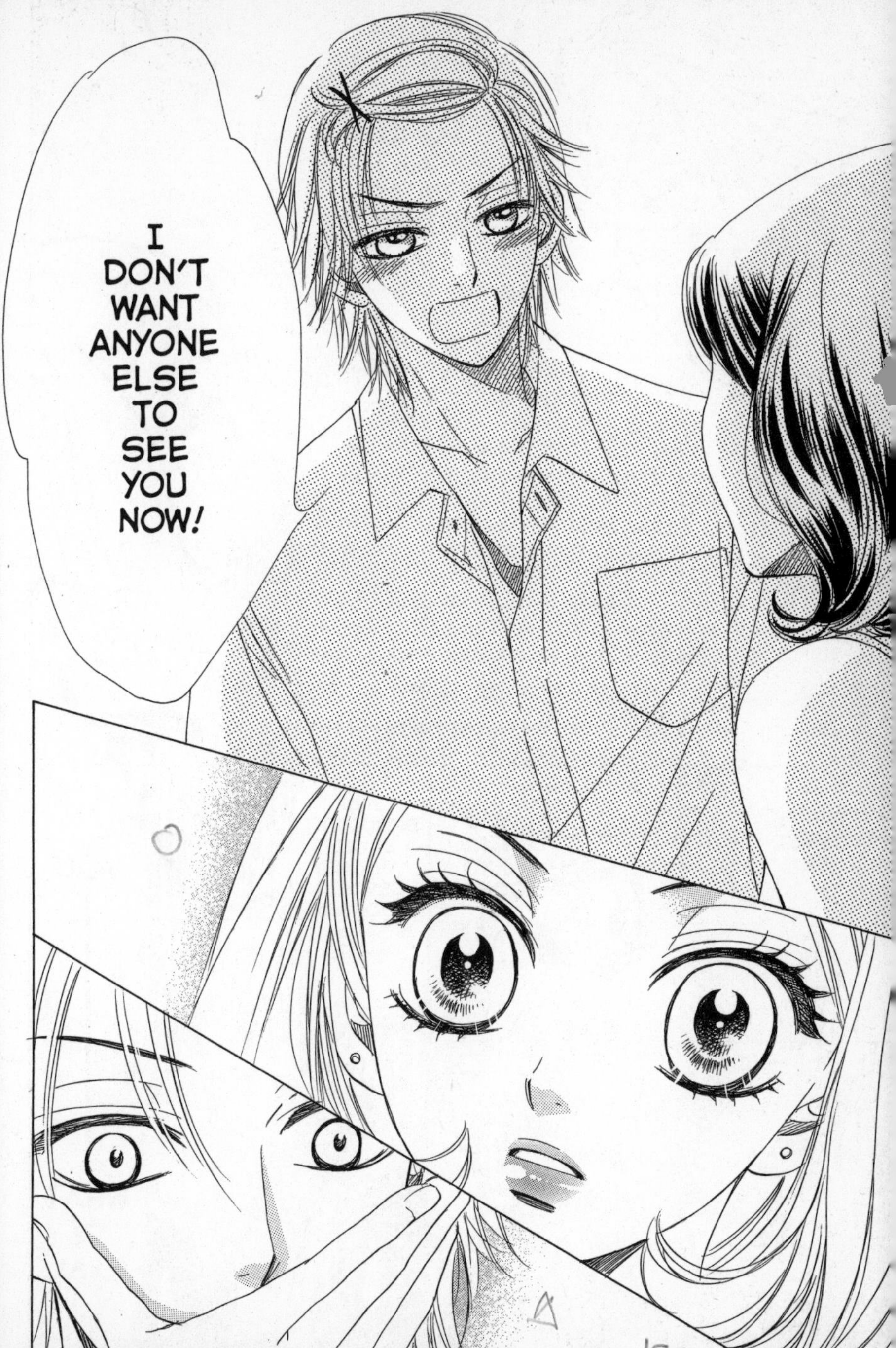
I DON'T WANT ANYONE ELSE TO SEE YOU NOW!

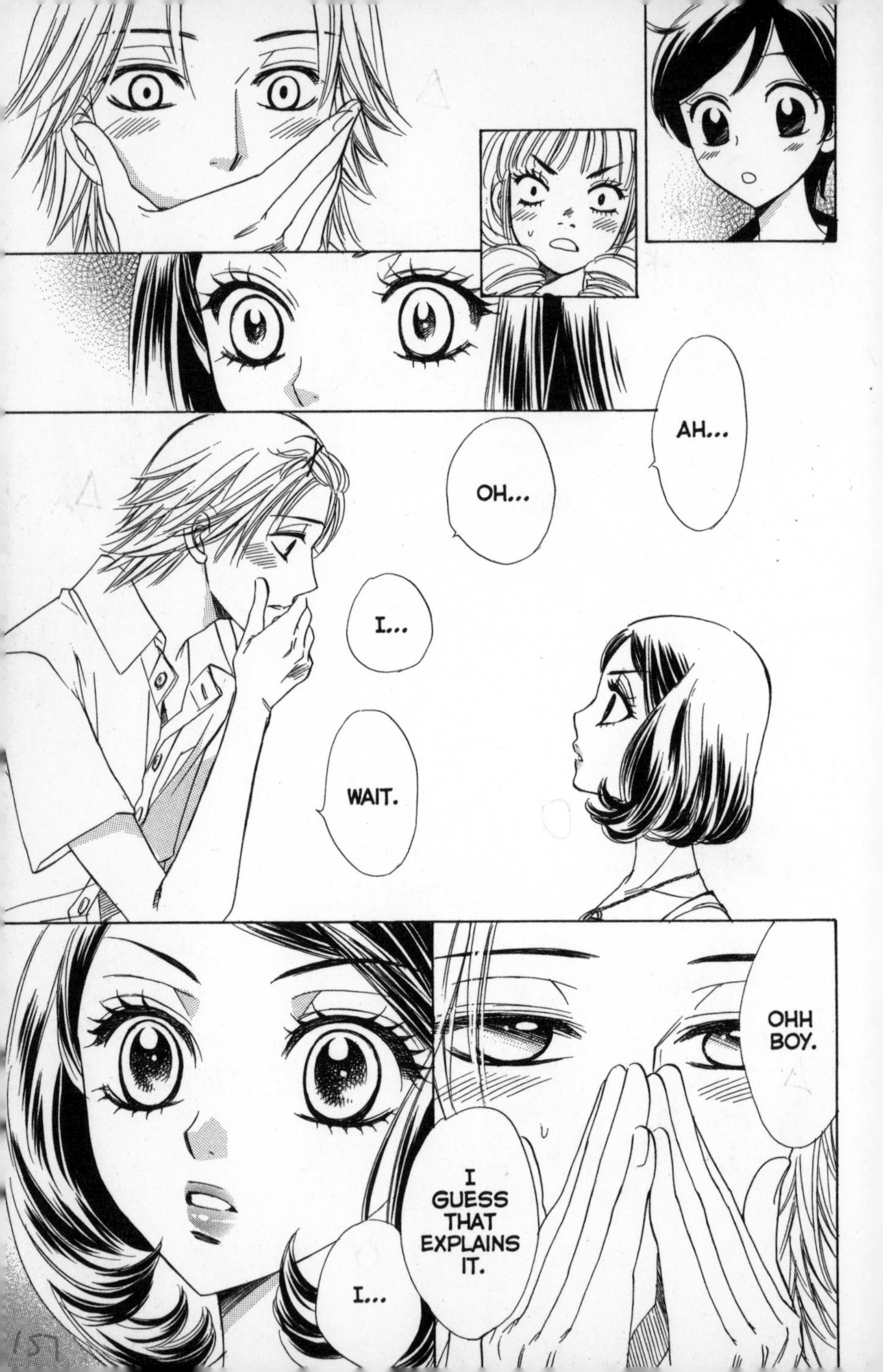
AH...
OH...
I...
WAIT.
OHH BOY.
I GUESS THAT EXPLAINS IT.
I...

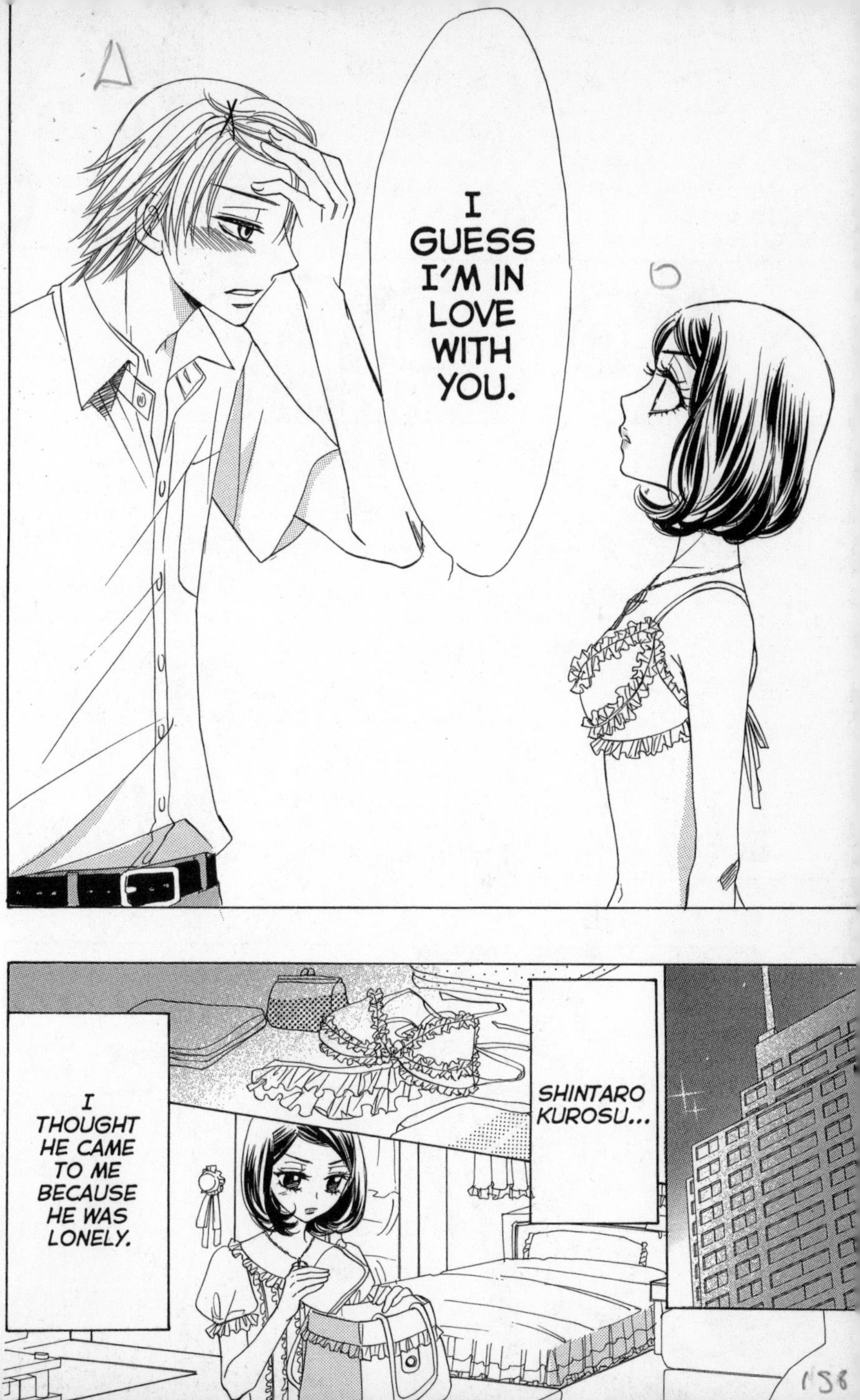
I GUESS I'M IN LOVE WITH YOU.
SHINTARO KUROSU...
I THOUGHT HE CAME TO ME BECAUSE HE WAS LONELY.

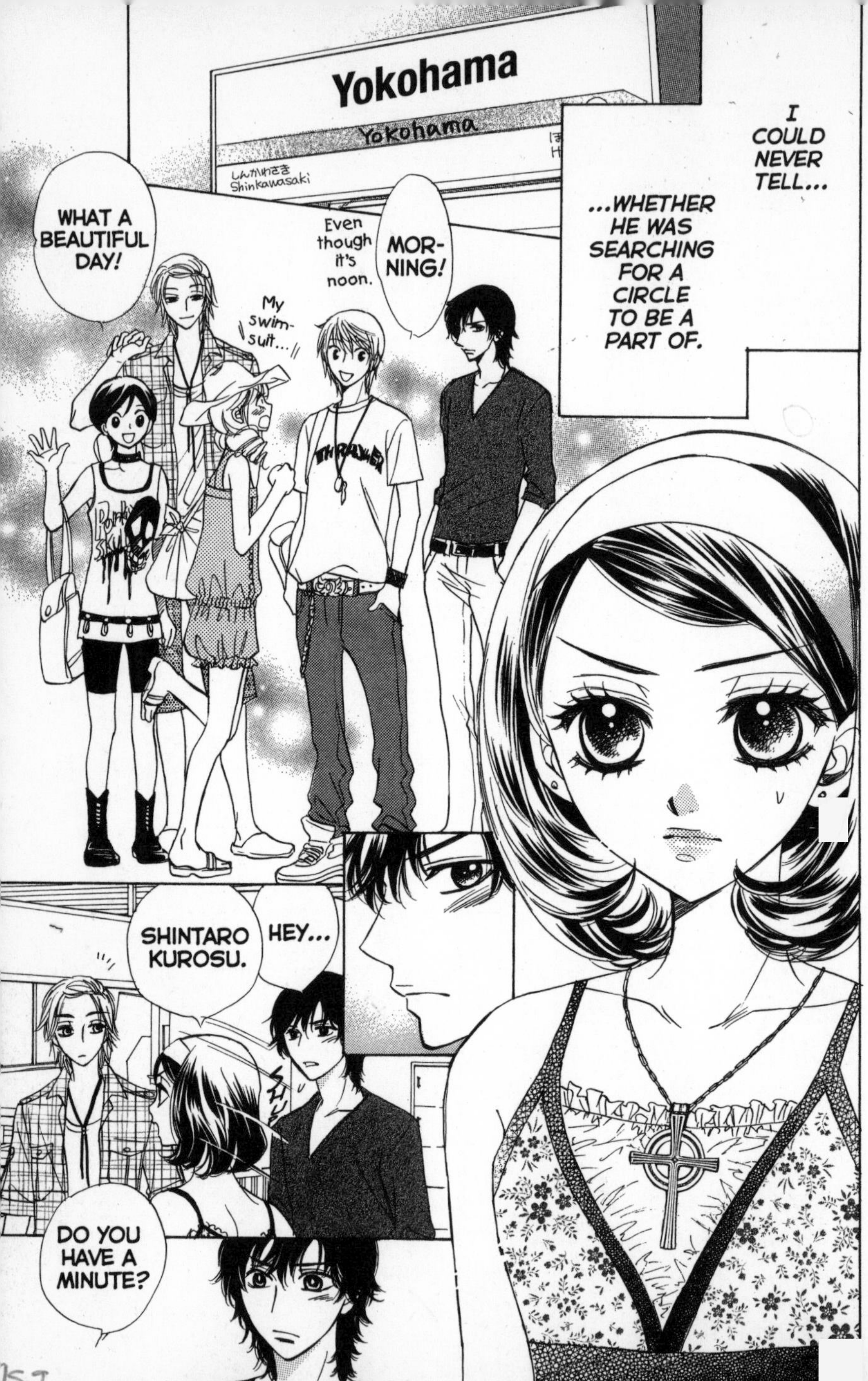
Yokohama
Yokohama
Shinkawasaki
I COULD NEVER TELL...
...WHETHER HE WAS SEARCHING FOR A CIRCLE TO BE A PART OF.
MOR-NING!
Even though it's noon.
My swim-suit...
WHAT A BEAUTIFUL DAY!
HEY...
SHINTARO KUROSU.
DO YOU HAVE A MINUTE?

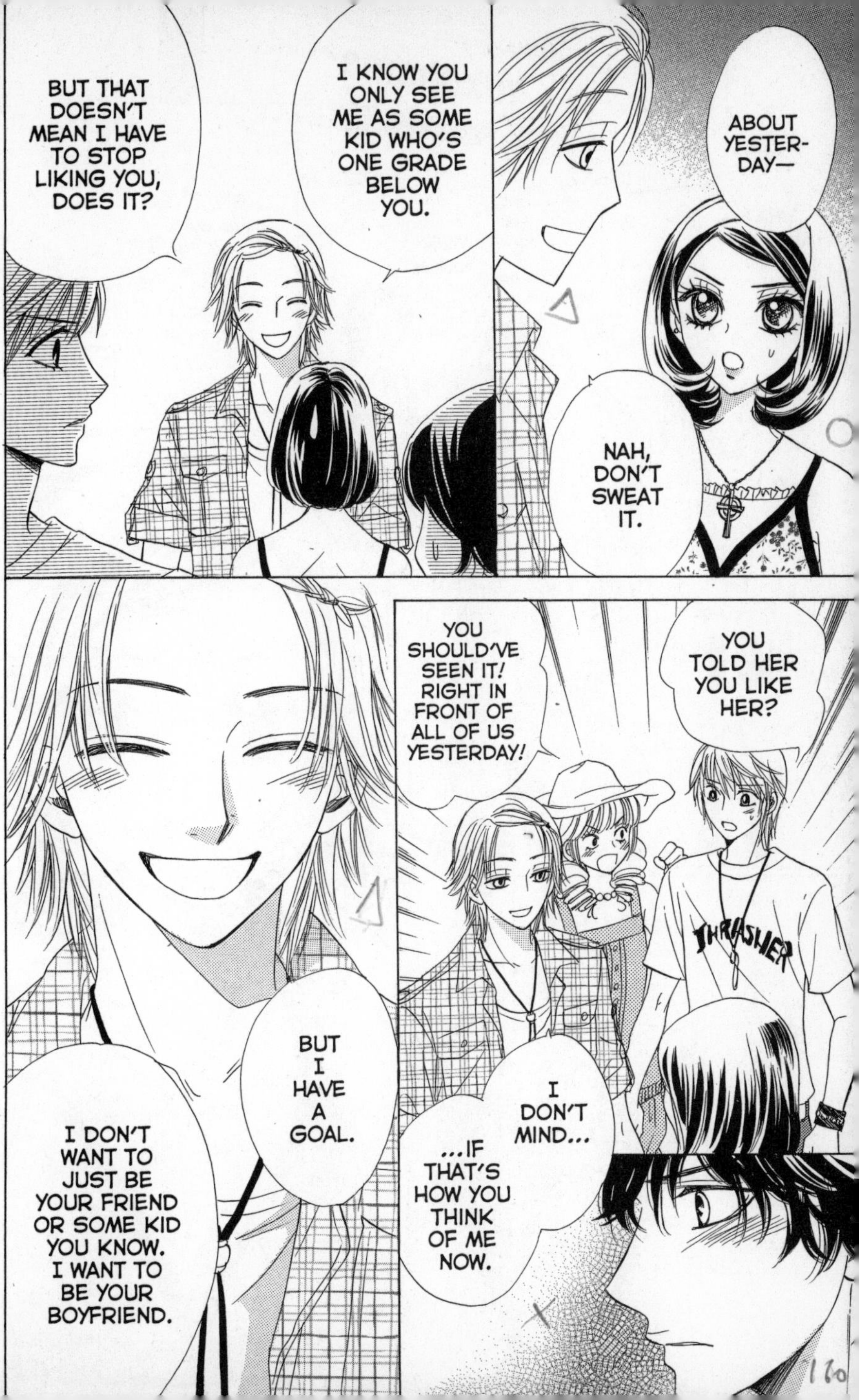
ABOUT YESTER-DAY—
NAH, DON'T SWEAT IT.
I KNOW YOU ONLY SEE ME AS SOME KID WHO'S ONE GRADE BELOW YOU.
BUT THAT DOESN'T MEAN I HAVE TO STOP LIKING YOU, DOES IT?
YOU TOLD HER YOU LIKE HER?
YOU SHOULD'VE SEEN IT! RIGHT IN FRONT OF ALL OF US YESTERDAY!
THRASHER
I DON'T MIND...
...IF THAT'S HOW YOU THINK OF ME NOW.
BUT I HAVE A GOAL.
I DON'T WANT TO JUST BE YOUR FRIEND OR SOME KID YOU KNOW. I WANT TO BE YOUR BOYFRIEND.

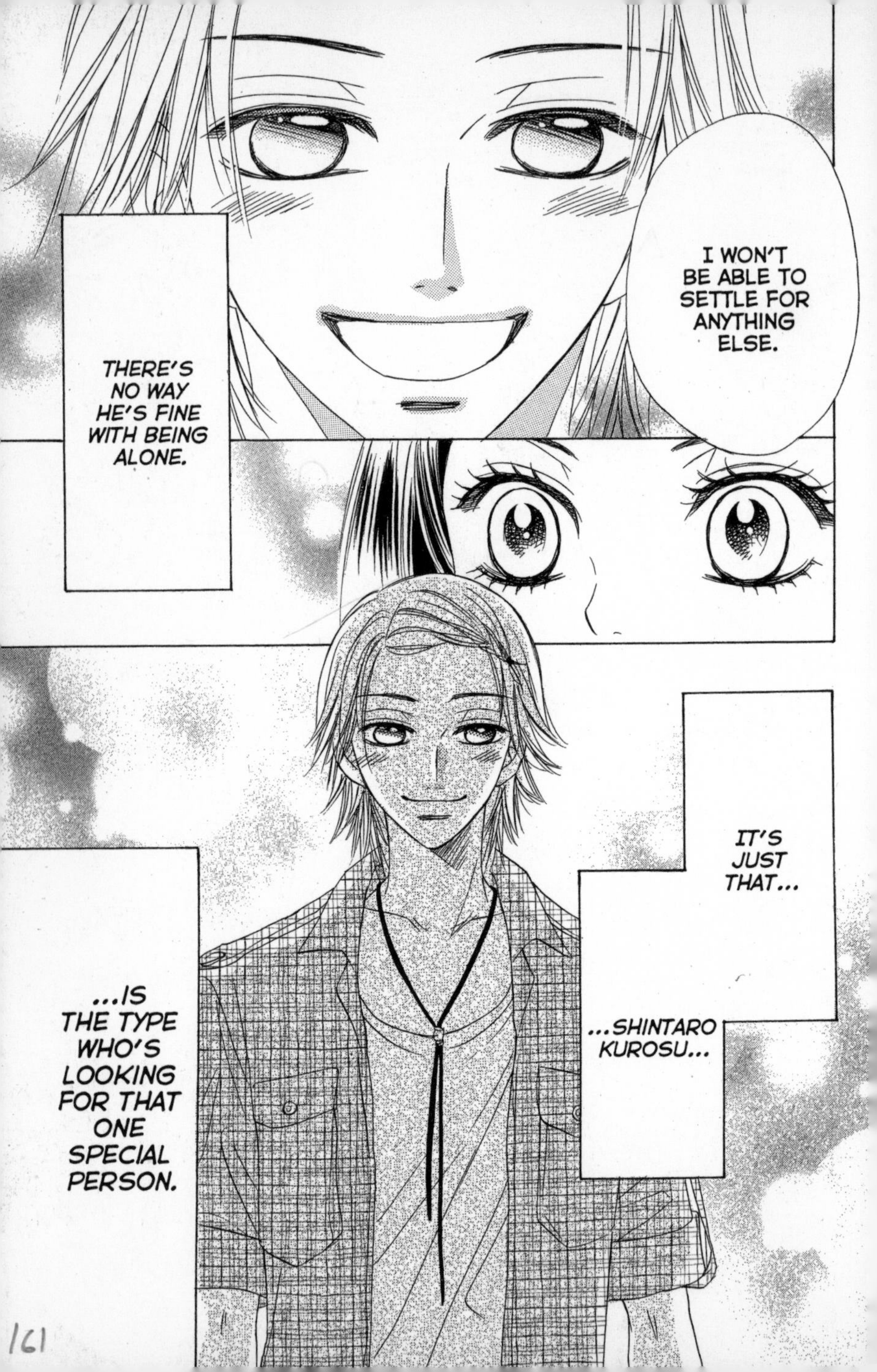
I WON'T BE ABLE TO SETTLE FOR ANYTHING ELSE.
THERE'S NO WAY HE'S FINE WITH BEING ALONE.
IT'S JUST THAT...
...SHINTARO KUROSU...
...IS THE TYPE WHO'S LOOKING FOR THAT ONE SPECIAL PERSON.

A Devil and
Her Love Song

162

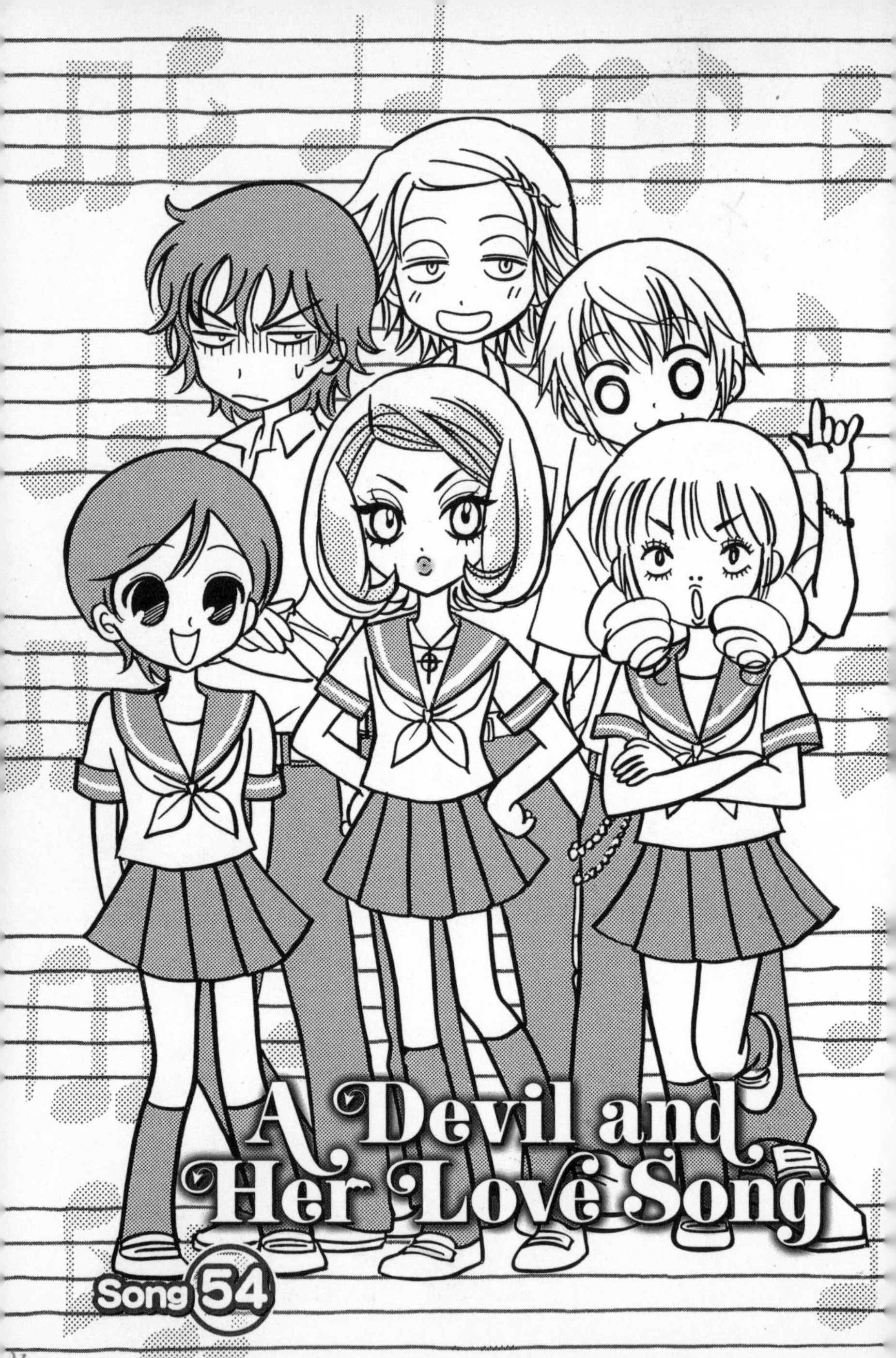
A Devil and Her Love Song
Song 54

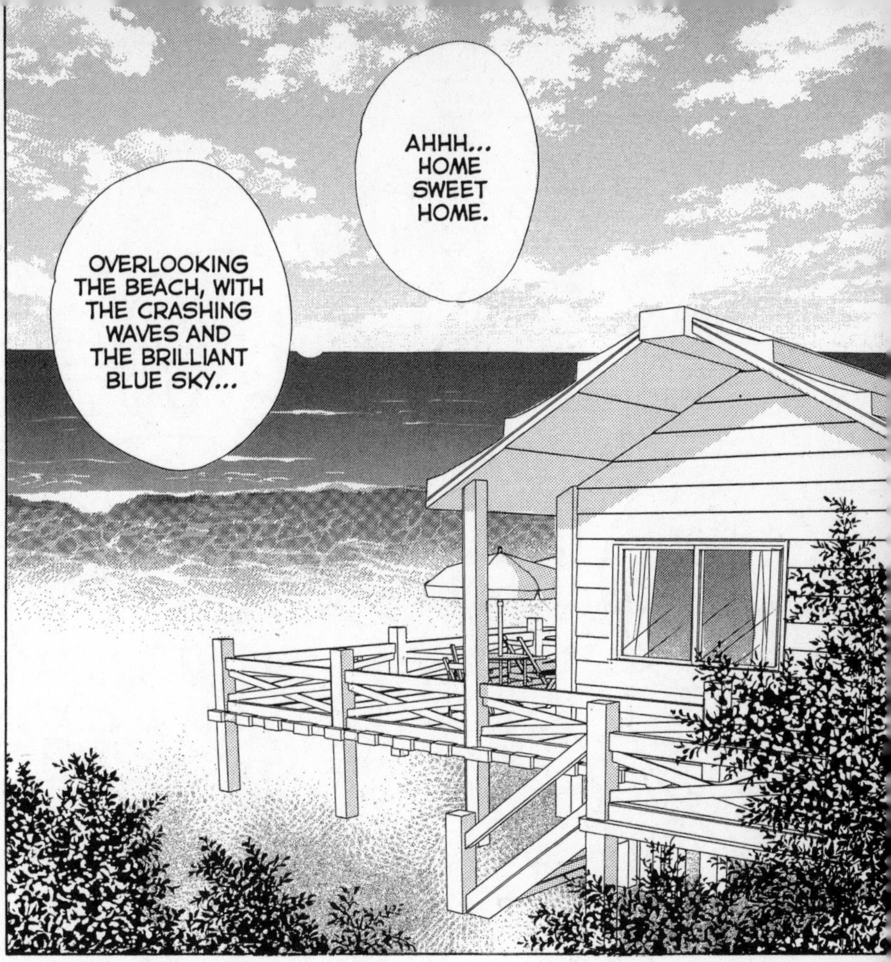
AHHH... HOME SWEET HOME.
OVERLOOKING THE BEACH, WITH THE CRASHING WAVES AND THE BRILLIANT BLUE SKY...

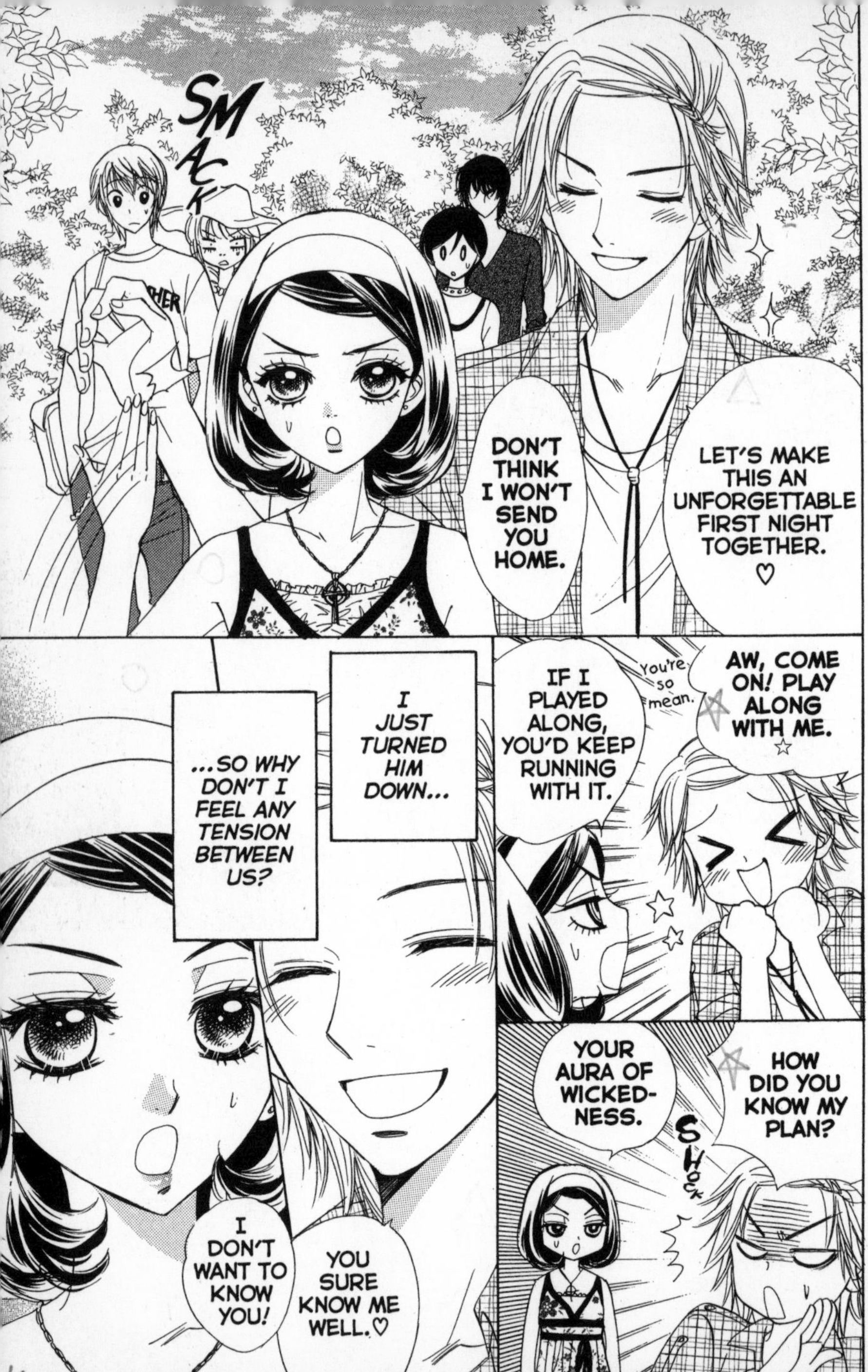
LET'S MAKE THIS AN UNFORGETTABLE FIRST NIGHT TOGETHER. ♡
DON'T THINK I WON'T SEND YOU HOME.
SMACK
AW, COME ON! PLAY ALONG WITH ME. ☆
You're so mean.
IF I PLAYED ALONG, YOU'D KEEP RUNNING WITH IT.
HOW DID YOU KNOW MY PLAN?
YOUR AURA OF WICKED-NESS.
SHOCK
I JUST TURNED HIM DOWN...
...SO WHY DON'T I FEEL ANY TENSION BETWEEN US?
YOU SURE KNOW ME WELL. ♡
I DON'T WANT TO KNOW YOU!

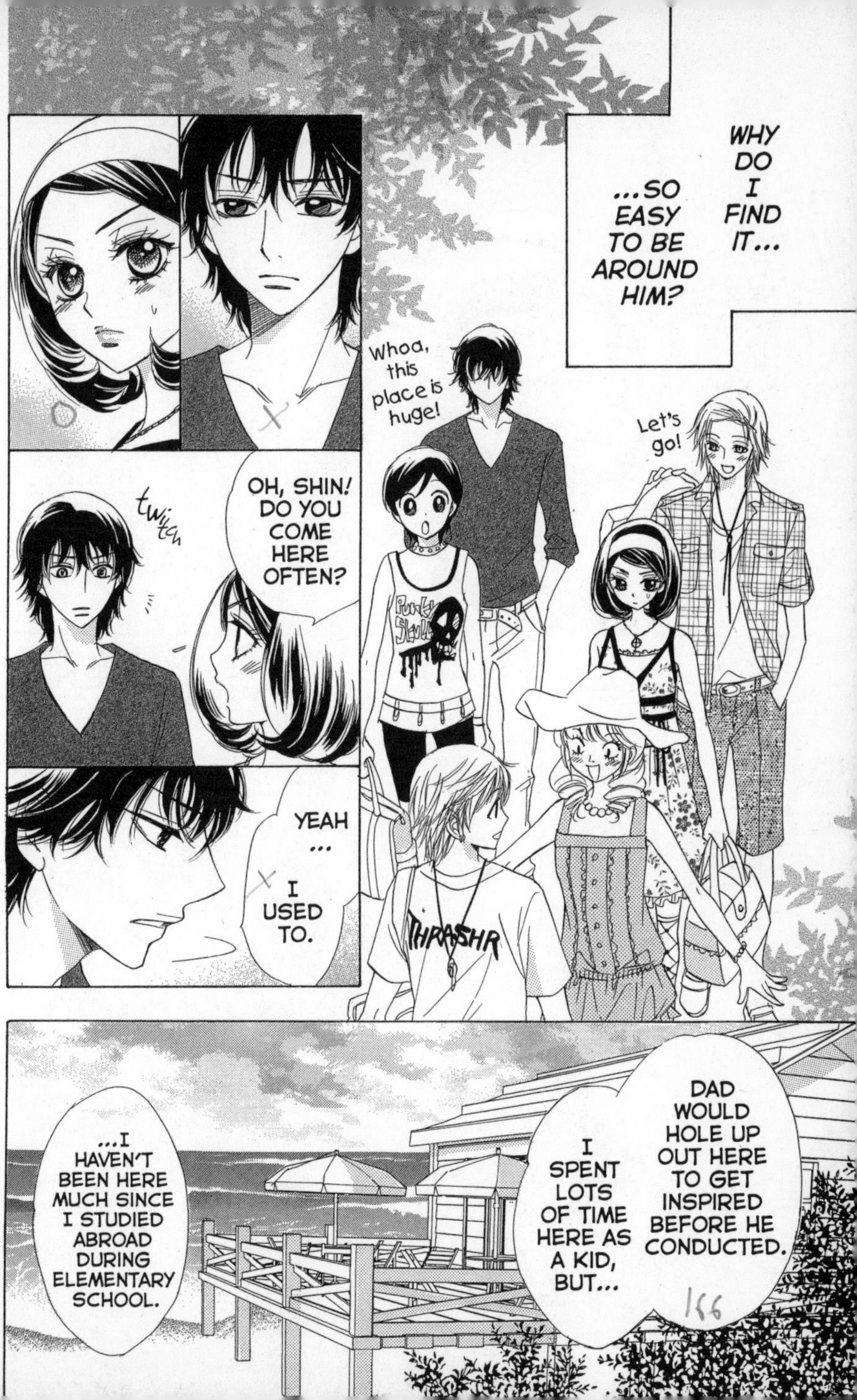
WHY DO I FIND IT...
...SO EASY TO BE AROUND HIM?
Let's go!
Whoa, this place is huge!
OH, SHIN! DO YOU COME HERE OFTEN?
twitch
YEAH... I USED TO.
DAD WOULD HOLE UP OUT HERE TO GET INSPIRED BEFORE HE CONDUCTED.
I SPENT LOTS OF TIME HERE AS A KID, BUT...
...I HAVEN'T BEEN HERE MUCH SINCE I STUDIED ABROAD DURING ELEMENTARY SCHOOL.

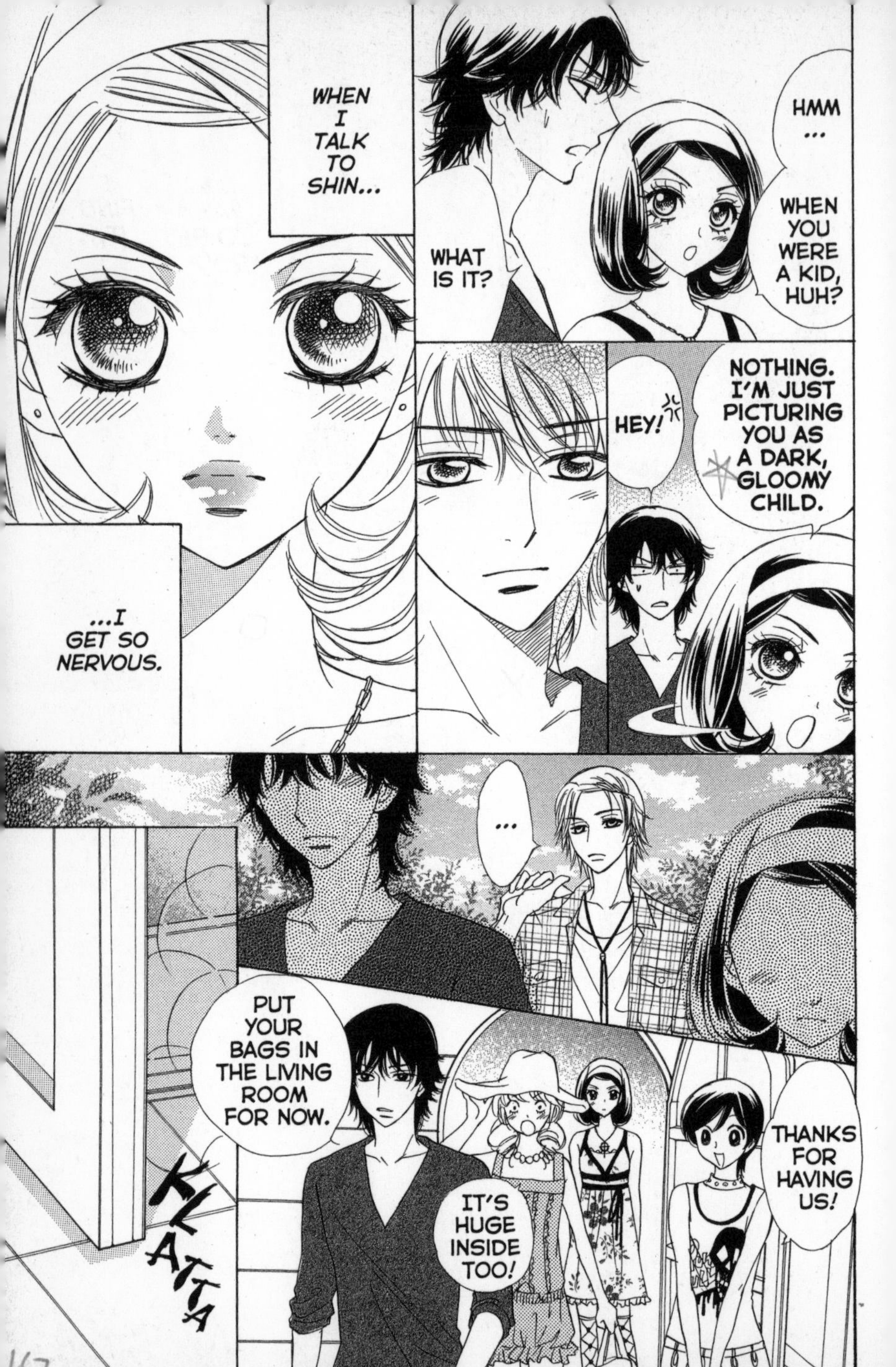
HMM...
WHEN YOU WERE A KID, HUH?
WHAT IS IT?
NOTHING. I'M JUST PICTURING YOU AS A DARK, GLOOMY CHILD.
HEY!
WHEN I TALK TO SHIN...
...I GET SO NERVOUS.
...
THANKS FOR HAVING US!
IT'S HUGE INSIDE TOO!
PUT YOUR BAGS IN THE LIVING ROOM FOR NOW.
KLATTA

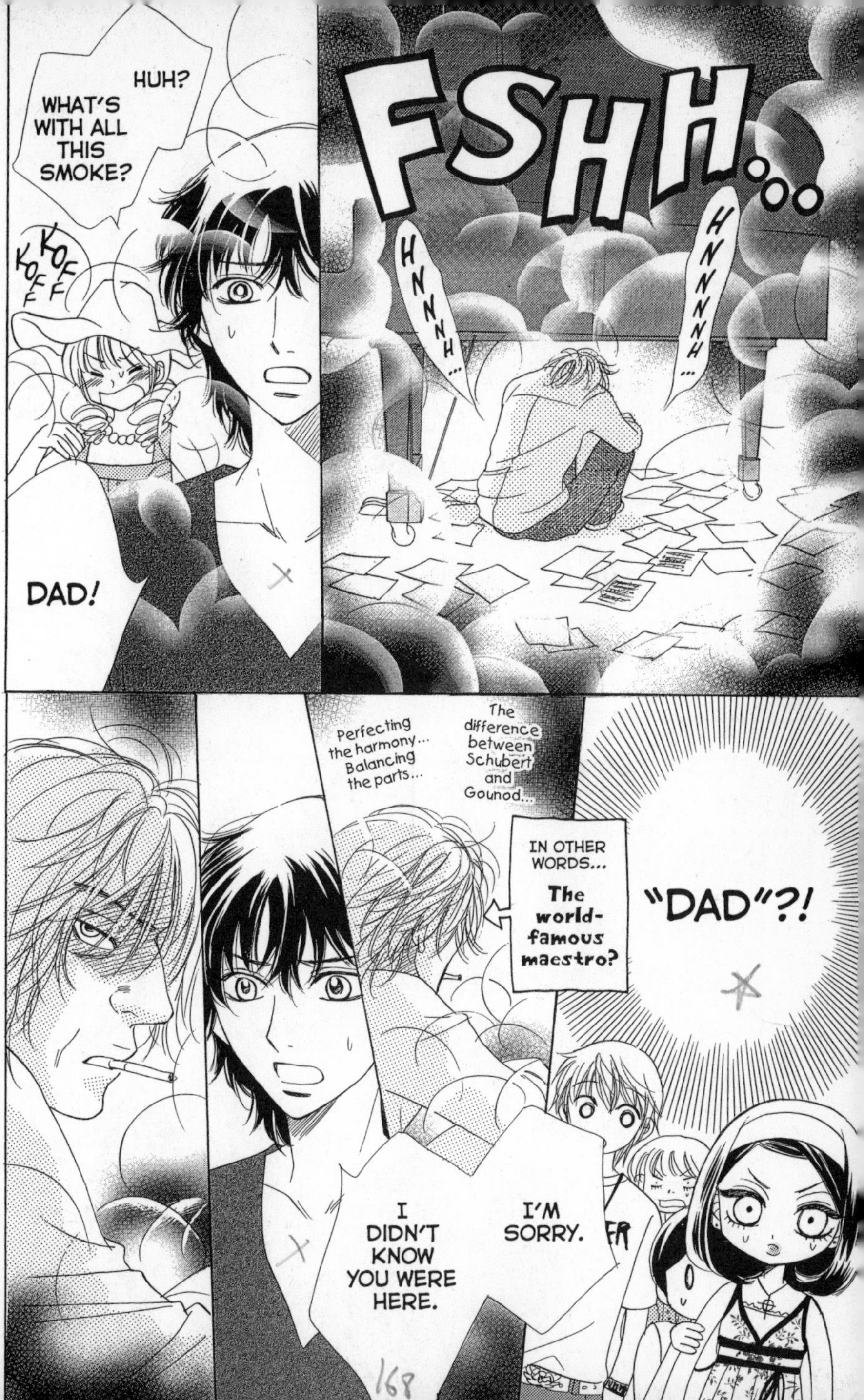
FSHH...
HNNNNNH...
HNNNH...
HUH? WHAT'S WITH ALL THIS SMOKE?
KOFF KOFF
DAD!
"DAD"?!
The difference between Schubert and Gounod...
Perfecting the harmony... Balancing the parts...
IN OTHER WORDS... The world-famous maestro?
I'M SORRY.
I DIDN'T KNOW YOU WERE HERE.

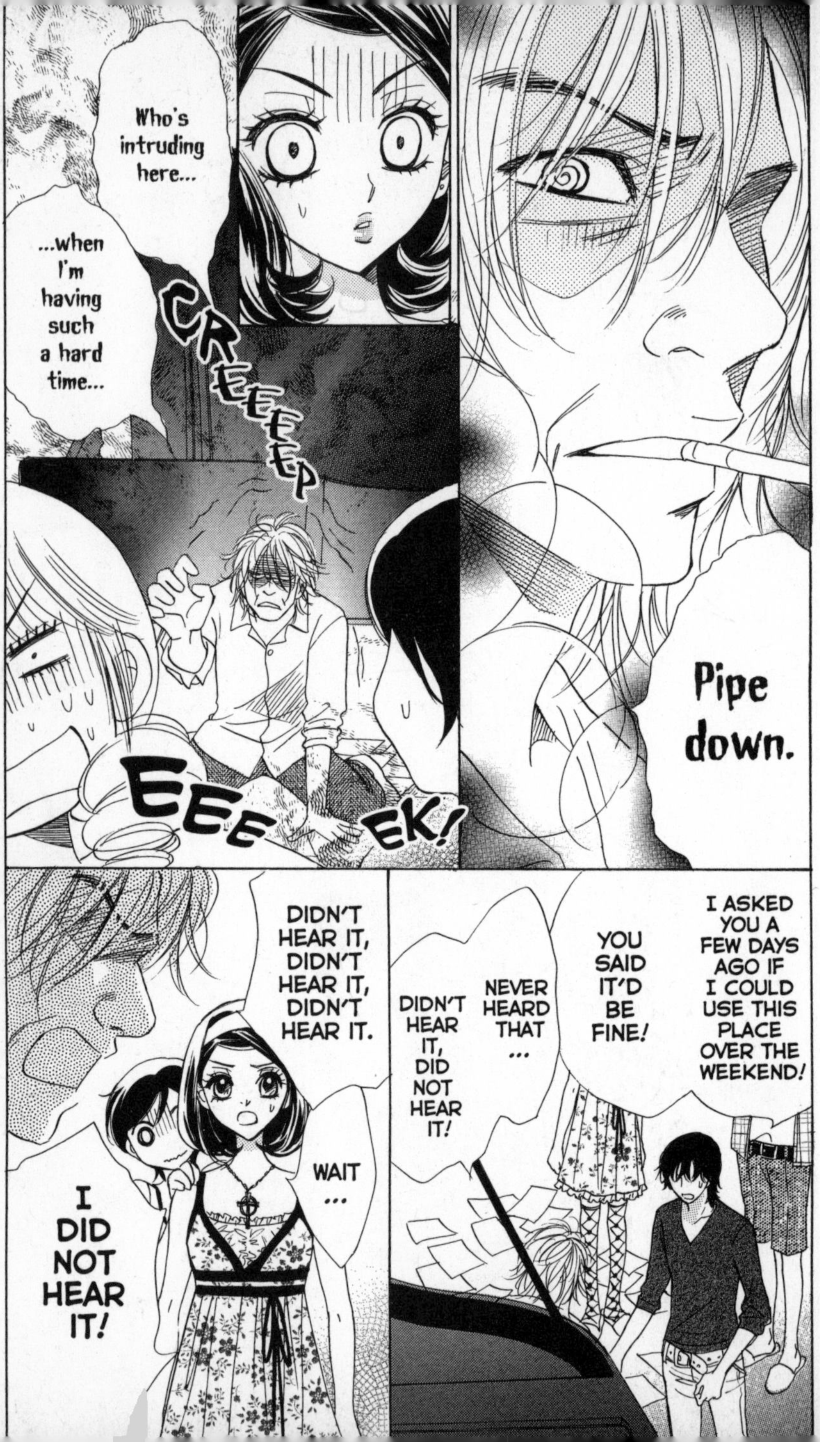
Pipe down.
Who's intruding here...
...when I'm having such a hard time...
CREEEEP
EEEEK!
I ASKED YOU A FEW DAYS AGO IF I COULD USE THIS PLACE OVER THE WEEKEND!
YOU SAID IT'D BE FINE!
NEVER HEARD THAT...
DIDN'T HEAR IT, DID NOT HEAR IT!
DIDN'T HEAR IT, DIDN'T HEAR IT, DIDN'T HEAR IT.
WAIT...
I DID NOT HEAR IT!

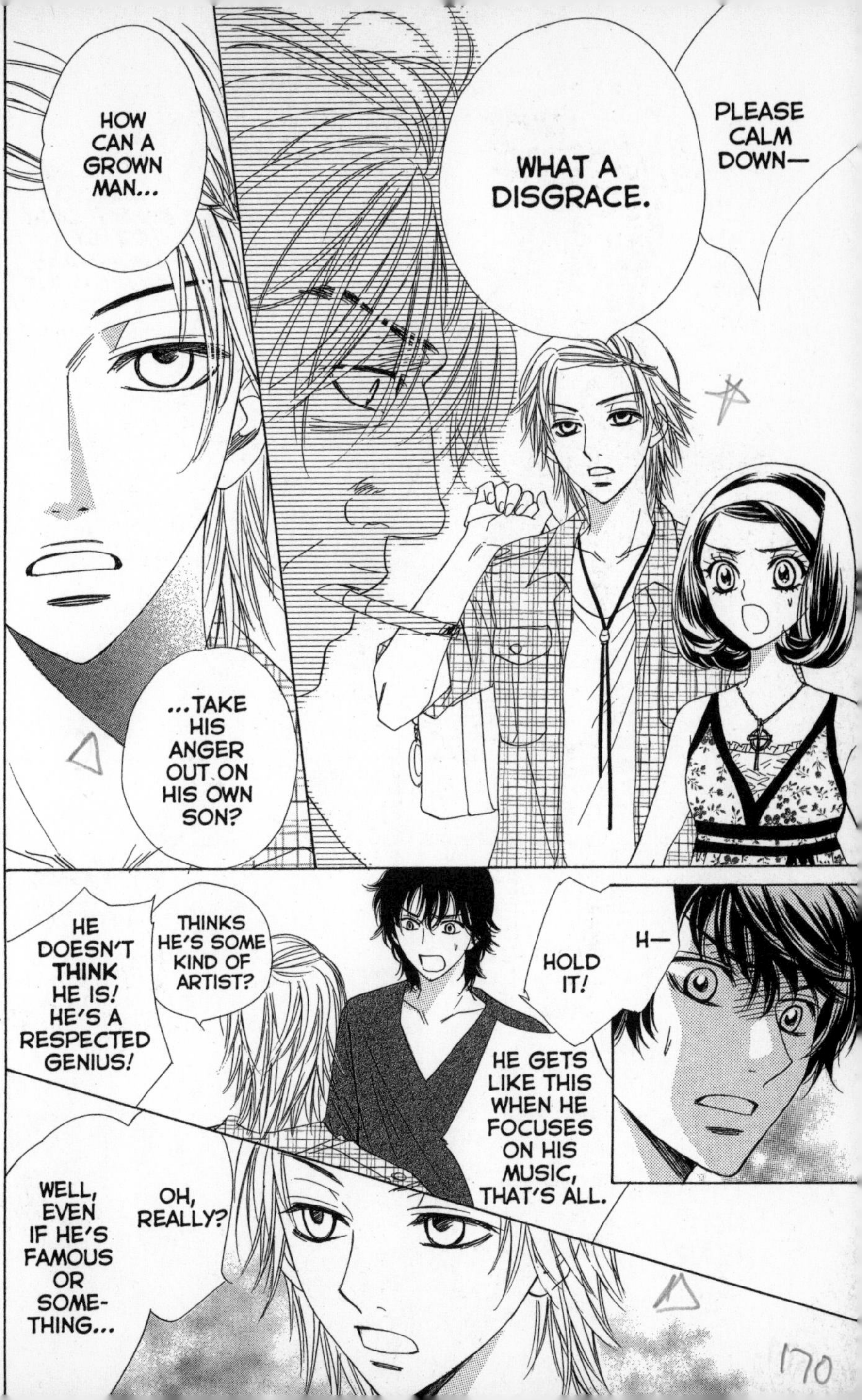
PLEASE CALM DOWN—
WHAT A DISGRACE.
HOW CAN A GROWN MAN...
...TAKE HIS ANGER OUT ON HIS OWN SON?
H—
HOLD IT!
HE GETS LIKE THIS WHEN HE FOCUSES ON HIS MUSIC, THAT'S ALL.
THINKS HE'S SOME KIND OF ARTIST?
HE DOESN'T THINK HE IS! HE'S A RESPECTED GENIUS!
OH, REALLY?
WELL, EVEN IF HE'S FAMOUS OR SOMETHING...

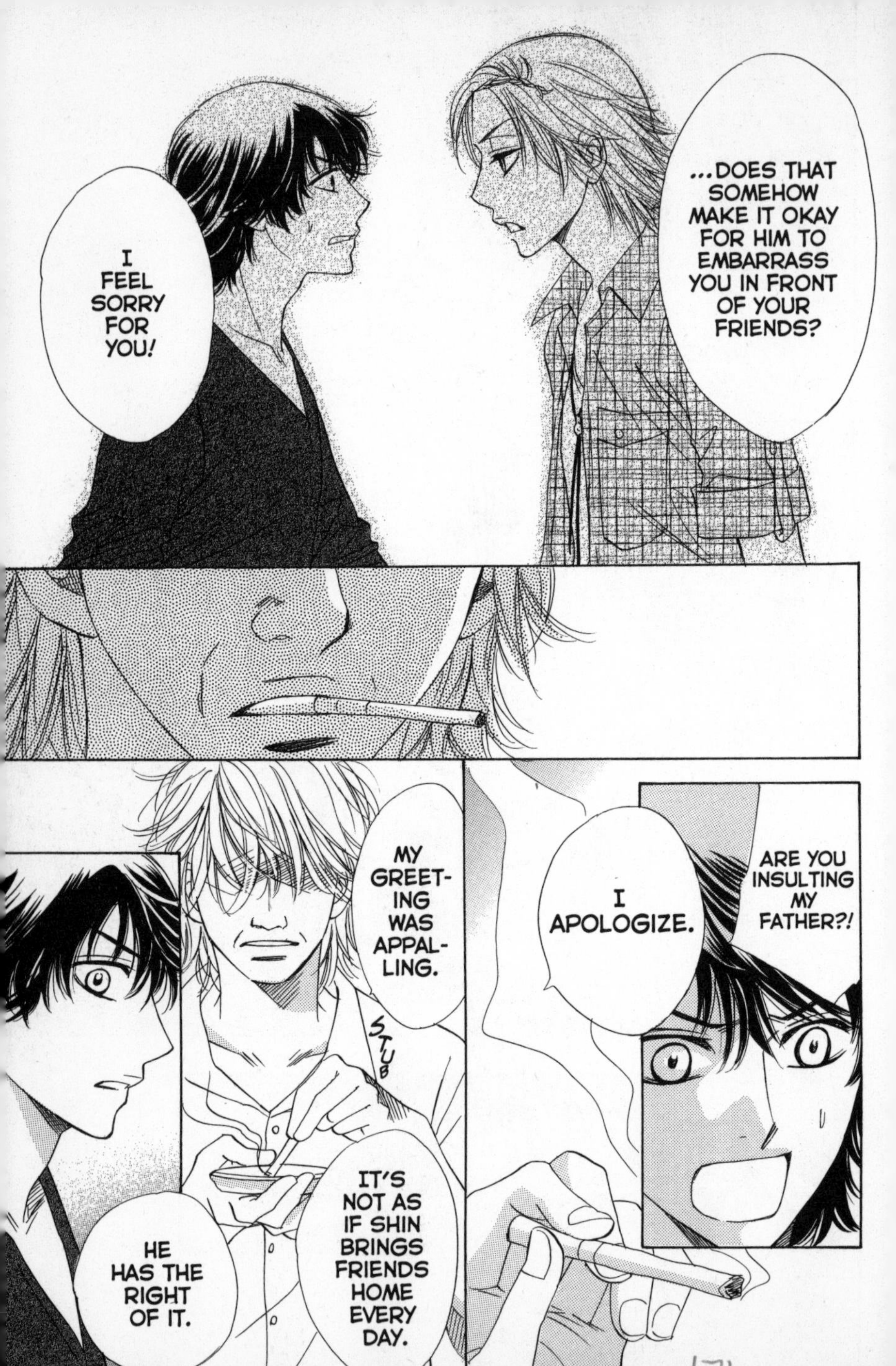
...DOES THAT SOMEHOW MAKE IT OKAY FOR HIM TO EMBARRASS YOU IN FRONT OF YOUR FRIENDS?
I FEEL SORRY FOR YOU!
ARE YOU INSULTING MY FATHER?!
I APOLOGIZE.
MY GREET-ING WAS APPAL-LING.
STUB
IT'S NOT AS IF SHIN BRINGS FRIENDS HOME EVERY DAY.
HE HAS THE RIGHT OF IT.

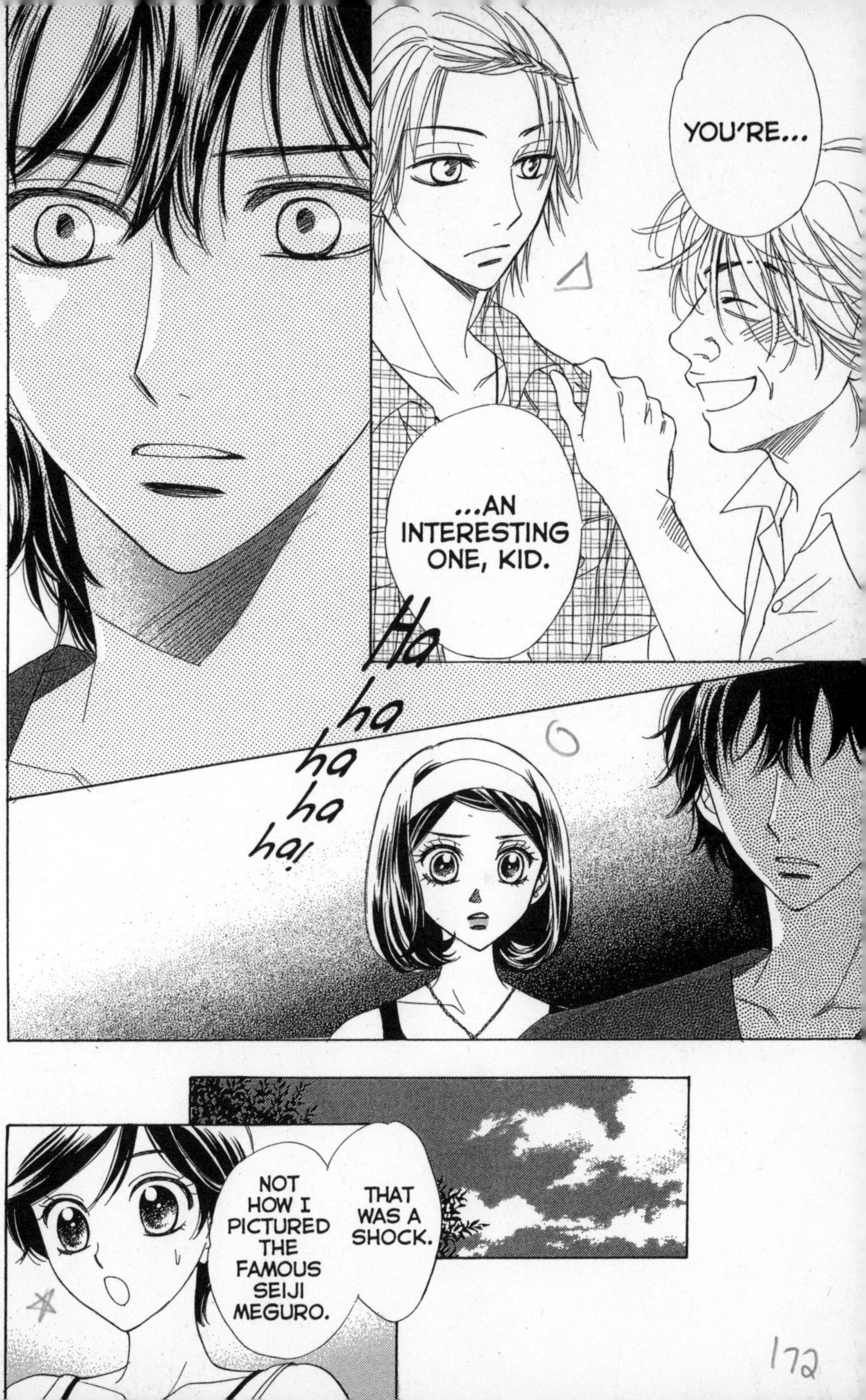
YOU'RE...
...AN INTERESTING ONE, KID.
Ha ha ha ha ha!
THAT WAS A SHOCK.
NOT HOW I PICTURED THE FAMOUS SEIJI MEGURO.

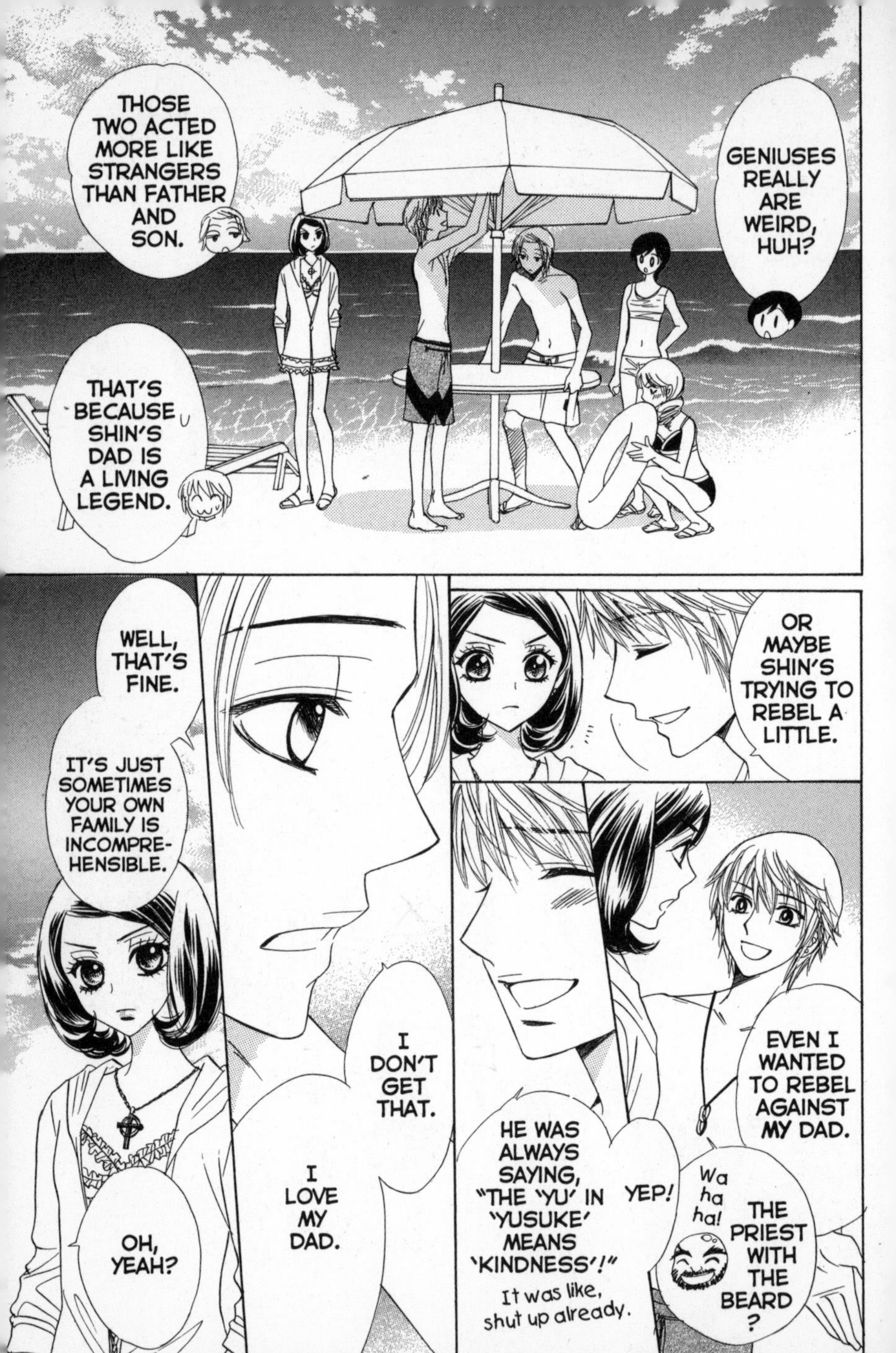
GENIUSES REALLY ARE WEIRD, HUH?
THOSE TWO ACTED MORE LIKE STRANGERS THAN FATHER AND SON.
THAT'S BECAUSE SHIN'S DAD IS A LIVING LEGEND.
OR MAYBE SHIN'S TRYING TO REBEL A LITTLE.
EVEN I WANTED TO REBEL AGAINST MY DAD.
THE PRIEST WITH THE BEARD?
Wa ha ha!
YEP!
HE WAS ALWAYS SAYING, "THE 'YU' IN 'YUSUKE' MEANS 'KINDNESS'!"
It was like, shut up already.
WELL, THAT'S FINE.
IT'S JUST SOMETIMES YOUR OWN FAMILY IS INCOMPREHENSIBLE.
I DON'T GET THAT.
I LOVE MY DAD.
OH, YEAH?

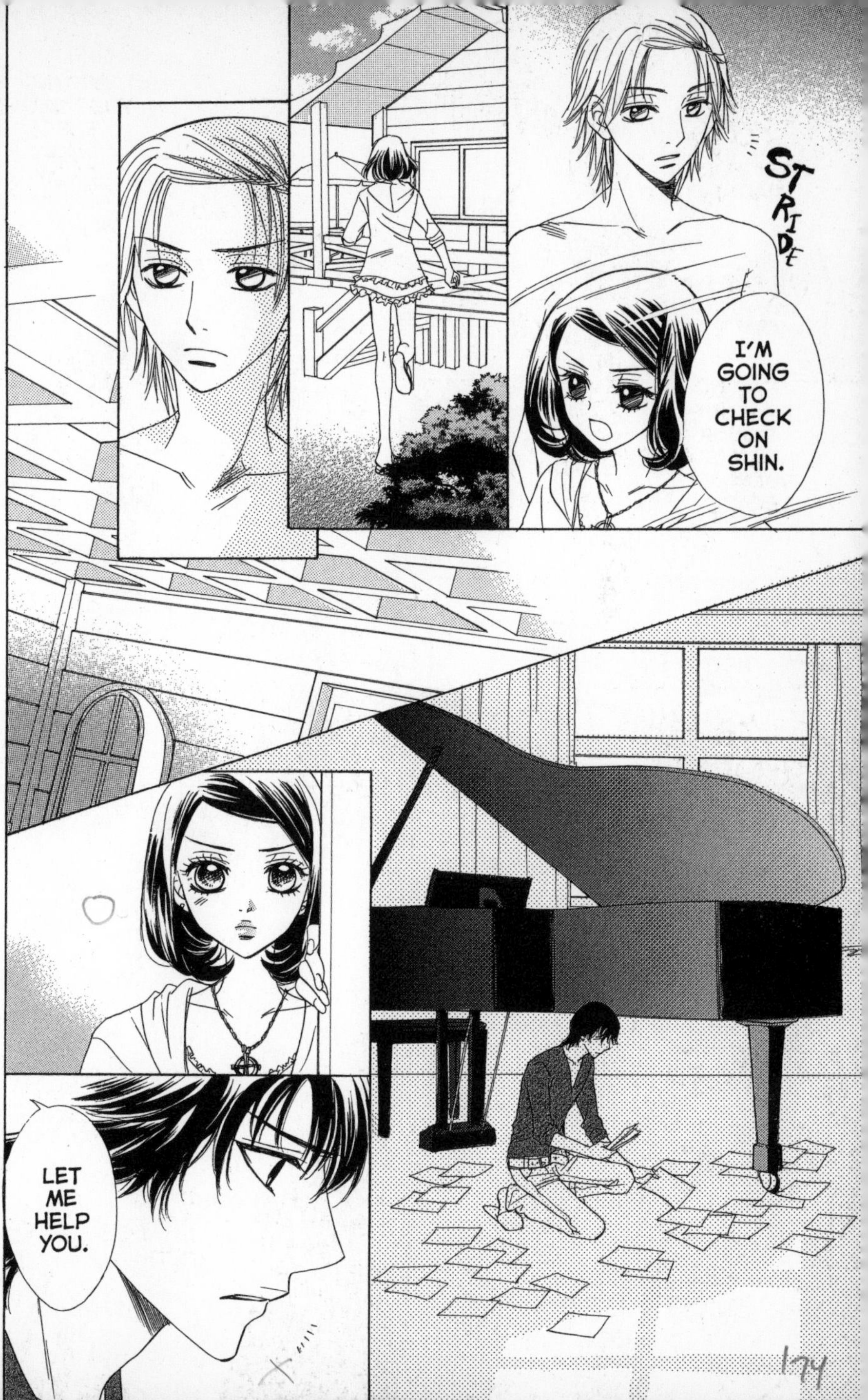
STRIDE
I'M GOING TO CHECK ON SHIN.
LET ME HELP YOU.

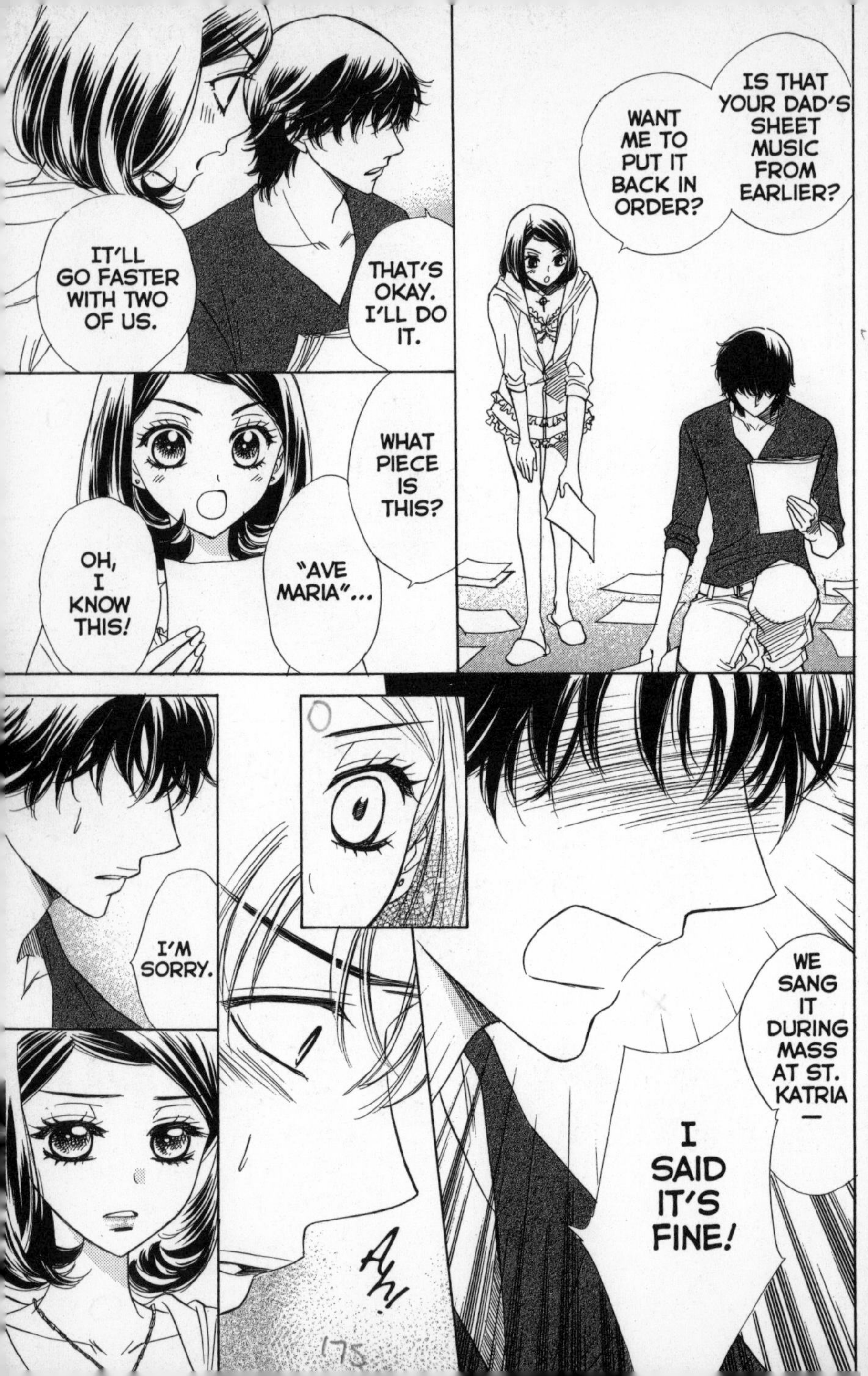
IS THAT YOUR DAD'S SHEET MUSIC FROM EARLIER?
WANT ME TO PUT IT BACK IN ORDER?
THAT'S OKAY. I'LL DO IT.
IT'LL GO FASTER WITH TWO OF US.
WHAT PIECE IS THIS?
"AVE MARIA"...
OH, I KNOW THIS!
WE SANG IT DURING MASS AT ST. KATRIA—
I SAID IT'S FINE!
AH!
I'M SORRY.

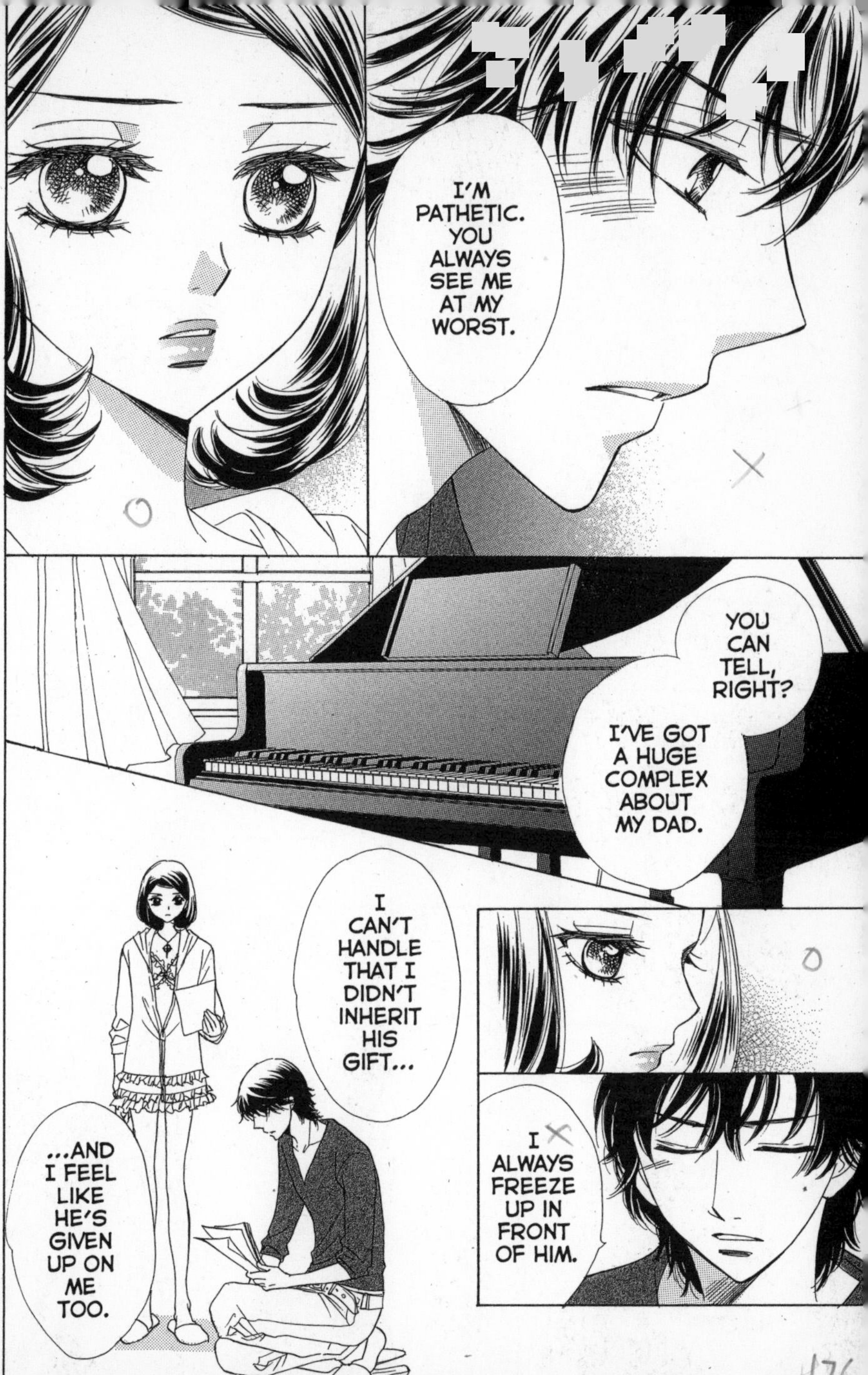
I'M PATHETIC. YOU ALWAYS SEE ME AT MY WORST.
YOU CAN TELL, RIGHT?
I'VE GOT A HUGE COMPLEX ABOUT MY DAD.
I ALWAYS FREEZE UP IN FRONT OF HIM.
I CAN'T HANDLE THAT I DIDN'T INHERIT HIS GIFT...
...AND I FEEL LIKE HE'S GIVEN UP ON ME TOO.

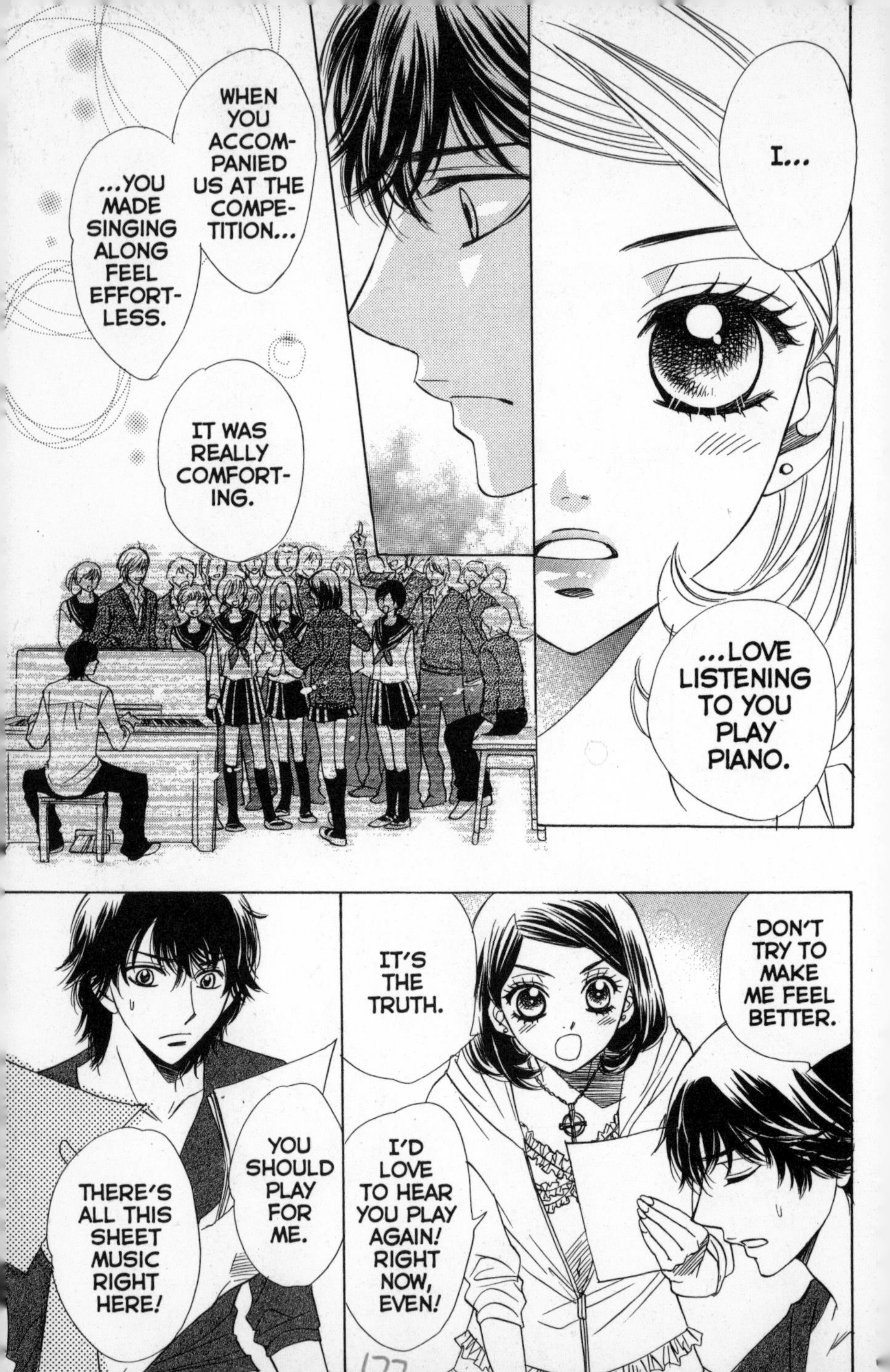
I...
...LOVE LISTENING TO YOU PLAY PIANO.
WHEN YOU ACCOMPANIED US AT THE COMPETITION...
...YOU MADE SINGING ALONG FEEL EFFORTLESS.
IT WAS REALLY COMFORTING.
DON'T TRY TO MAKE ME FEEL BETTER.
IT'S THE TRUTH.
I'D LOVE TO HEAR YOU PLAY AGAIN! RIGHT NOW, EVEN!
YOU SHOULD PLAY FOR ME.
THERE'S ALL THIS SHEET MUSIC RIGHT HERE!

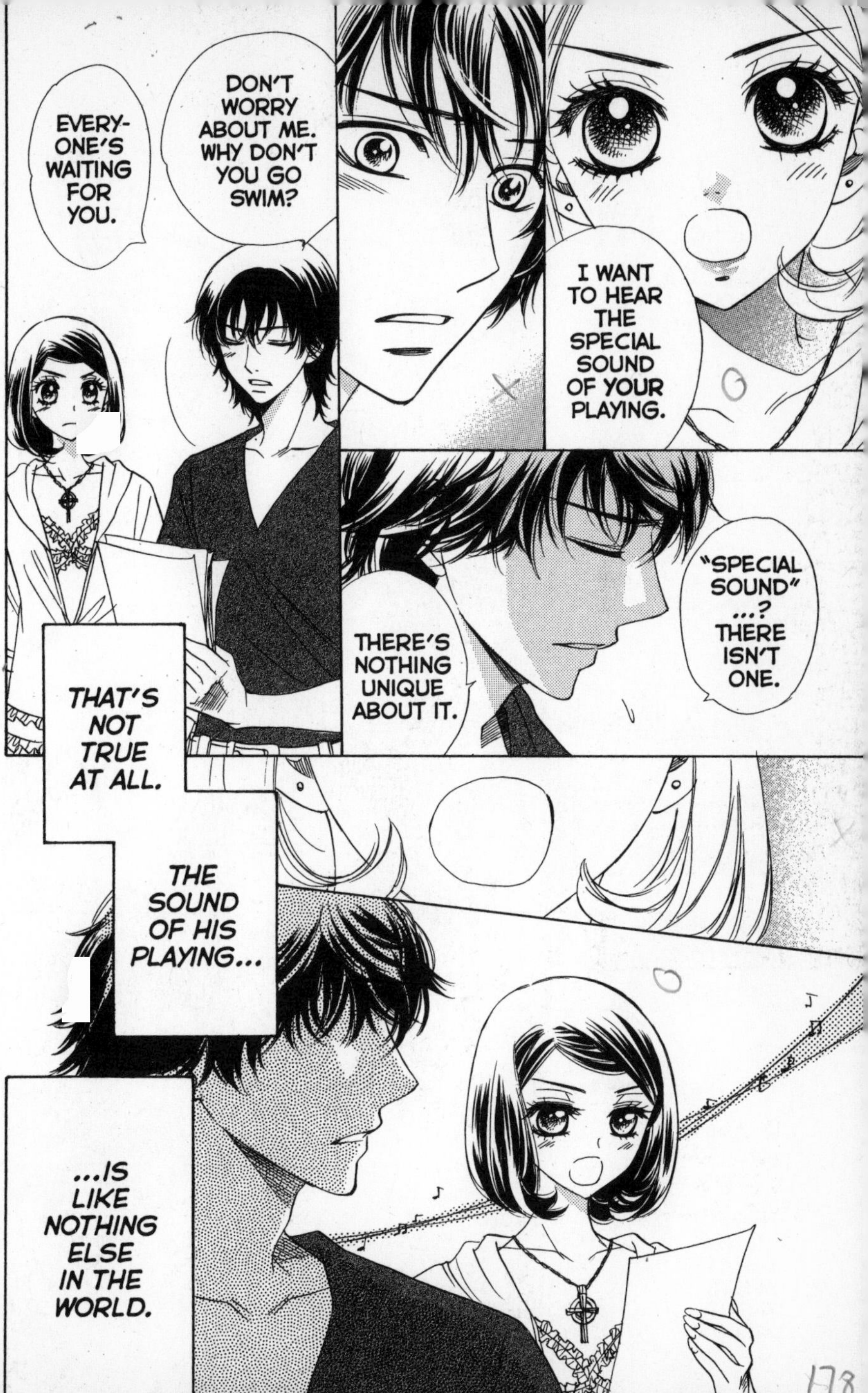
I WANT TO HEAR THE SPECIAL SOUND OF YOUR PLAYING.
"SPECIAL SOUND" ...? THERE ISN'T ONE.
THERE'S NOTHING UNIQUE ABOUT IT.
DON'T WORRY ABOUT ME. WHY DON'T YOU GO SWIM?
EVERY-ONE'S WAITING FOR YOU.
THAT'S NOT TRUE AT ALL.
THE SOUND OF HIS PLAYING...
...IS LIKE NOTHING ELSE IN THE WORLD.

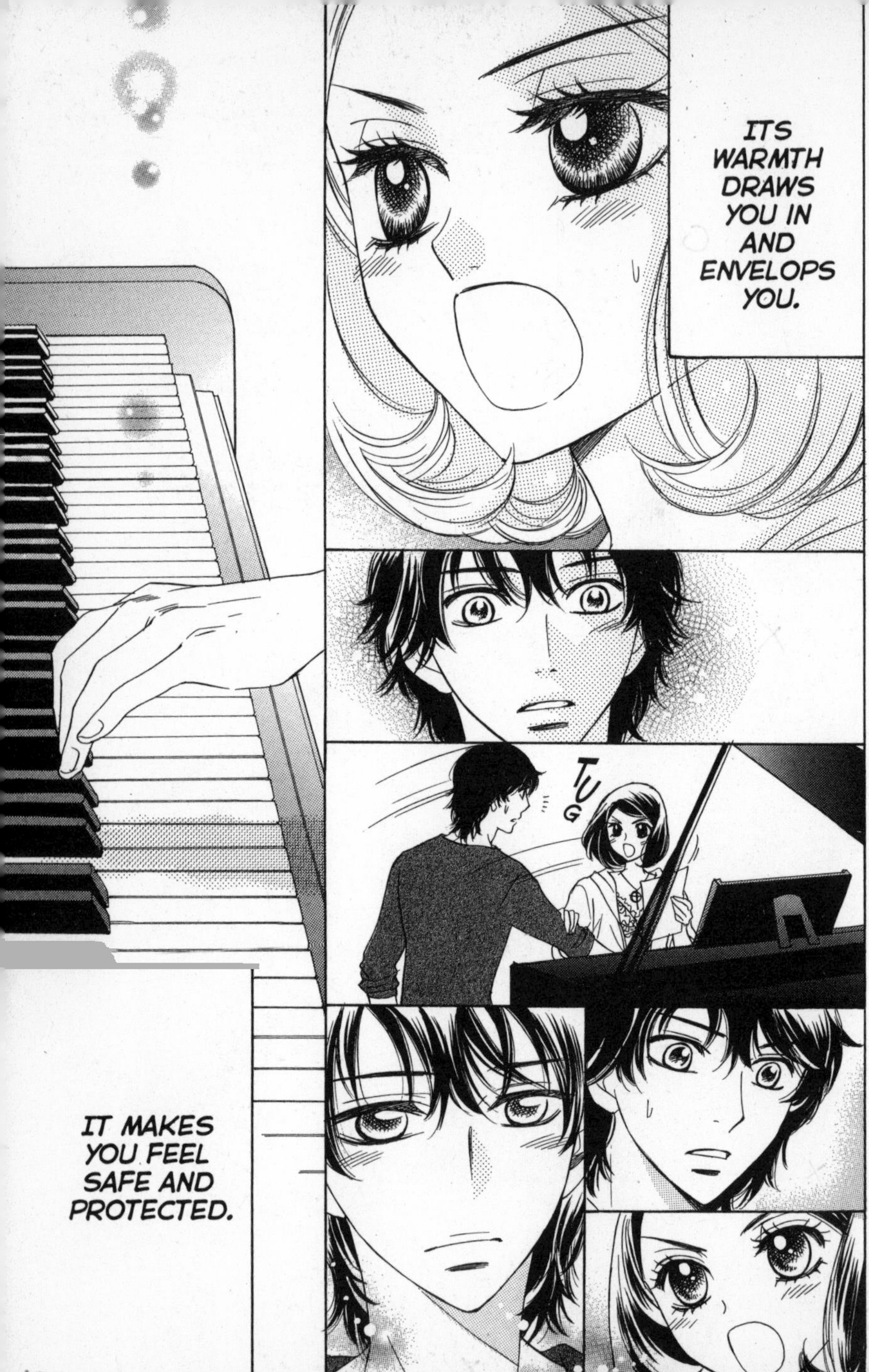
ITS WARMTH DRAWS YOU IN AND ENVELOPS YOU.
TUG
IT MAKES YOU FEEL SAFE AND PROTECTED.

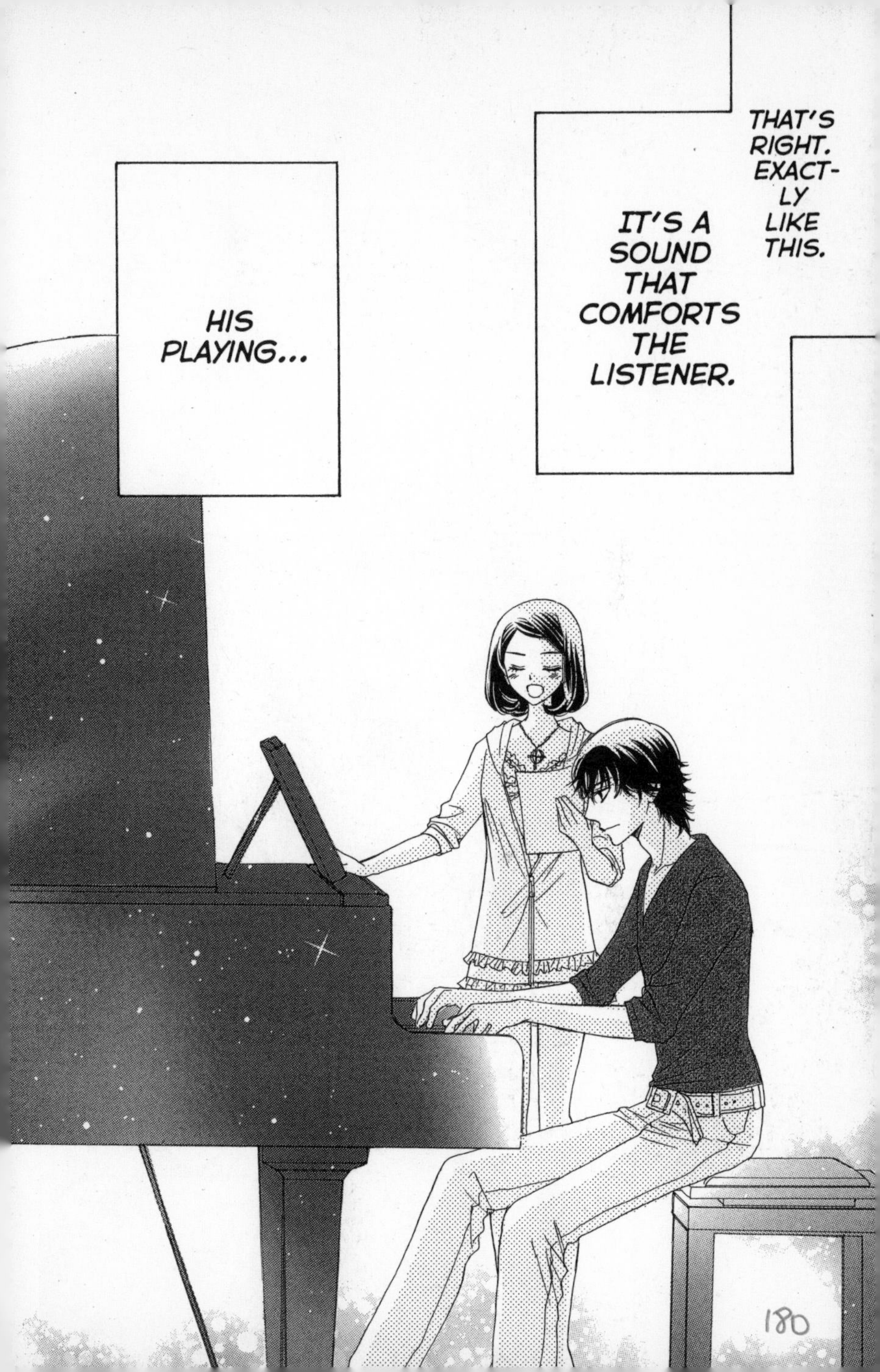
THAT'S RIGHT. EXACTLY LIKE THIS.
IT'S A SOUND THAT COMFORTS THE LISTENER.
HIS PLAYING...

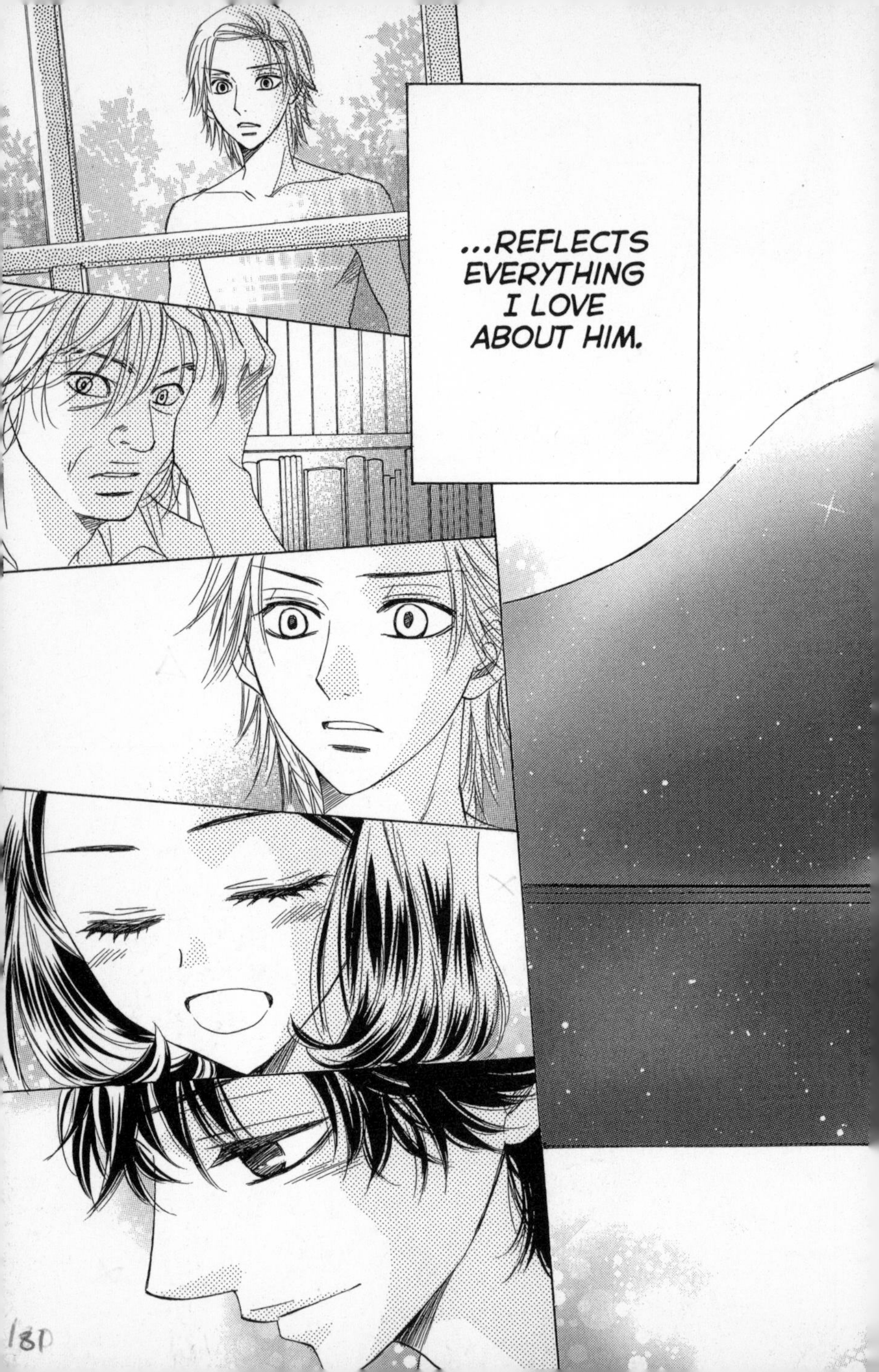
...REFLECTS EVERYTHING I LOVE ABOUT HIM.

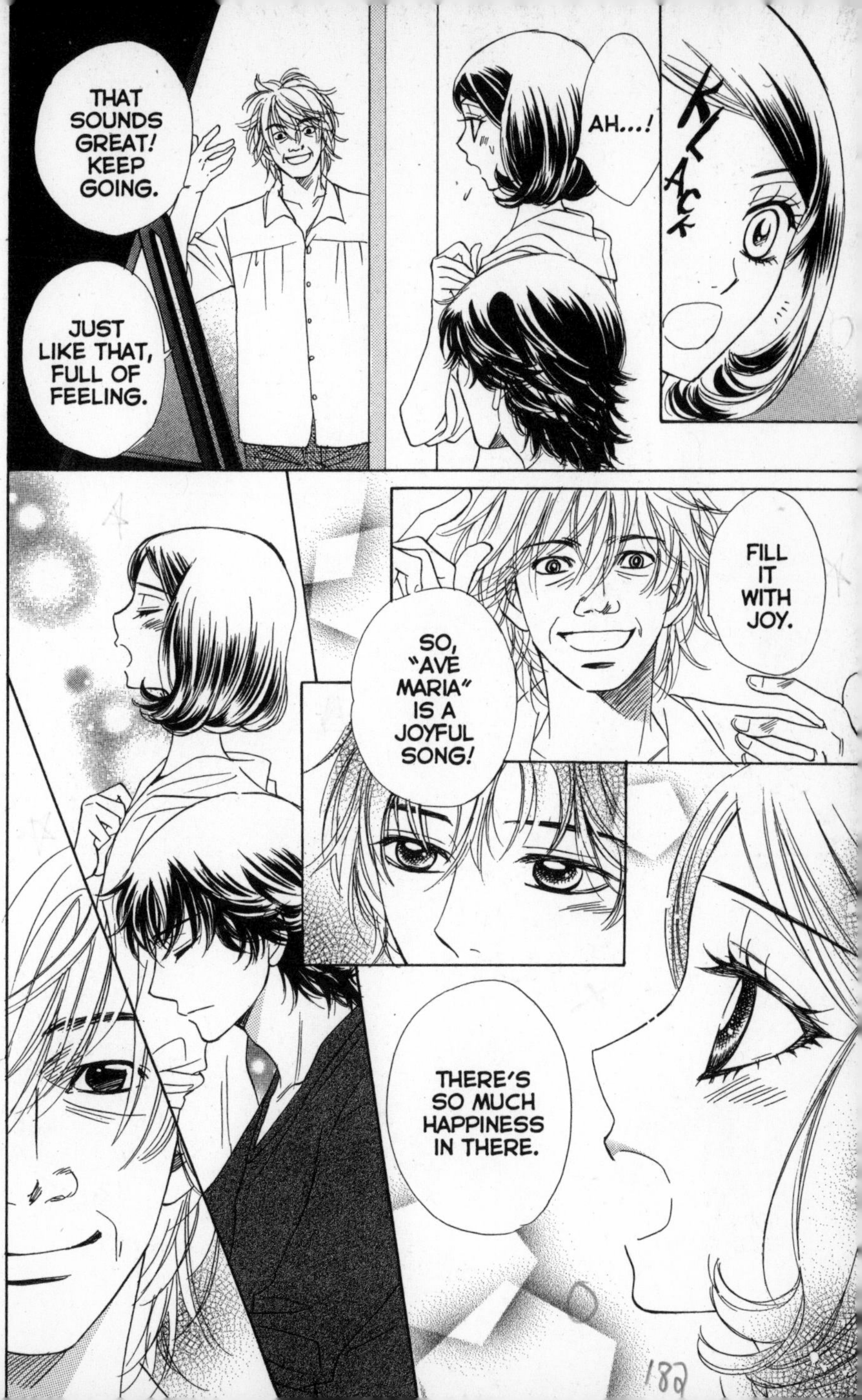
KLACK
AH...!
THAT SOUNDS GREAT! KEEP GOING.
JUST LIKE THAT, FULL OF FEELING.
FILL IT WITH JOY.
SO, "AVE MARIA" IS A JOYFUL SONG!
THERE'S SO MUCH HAPPINESS IN THERE.

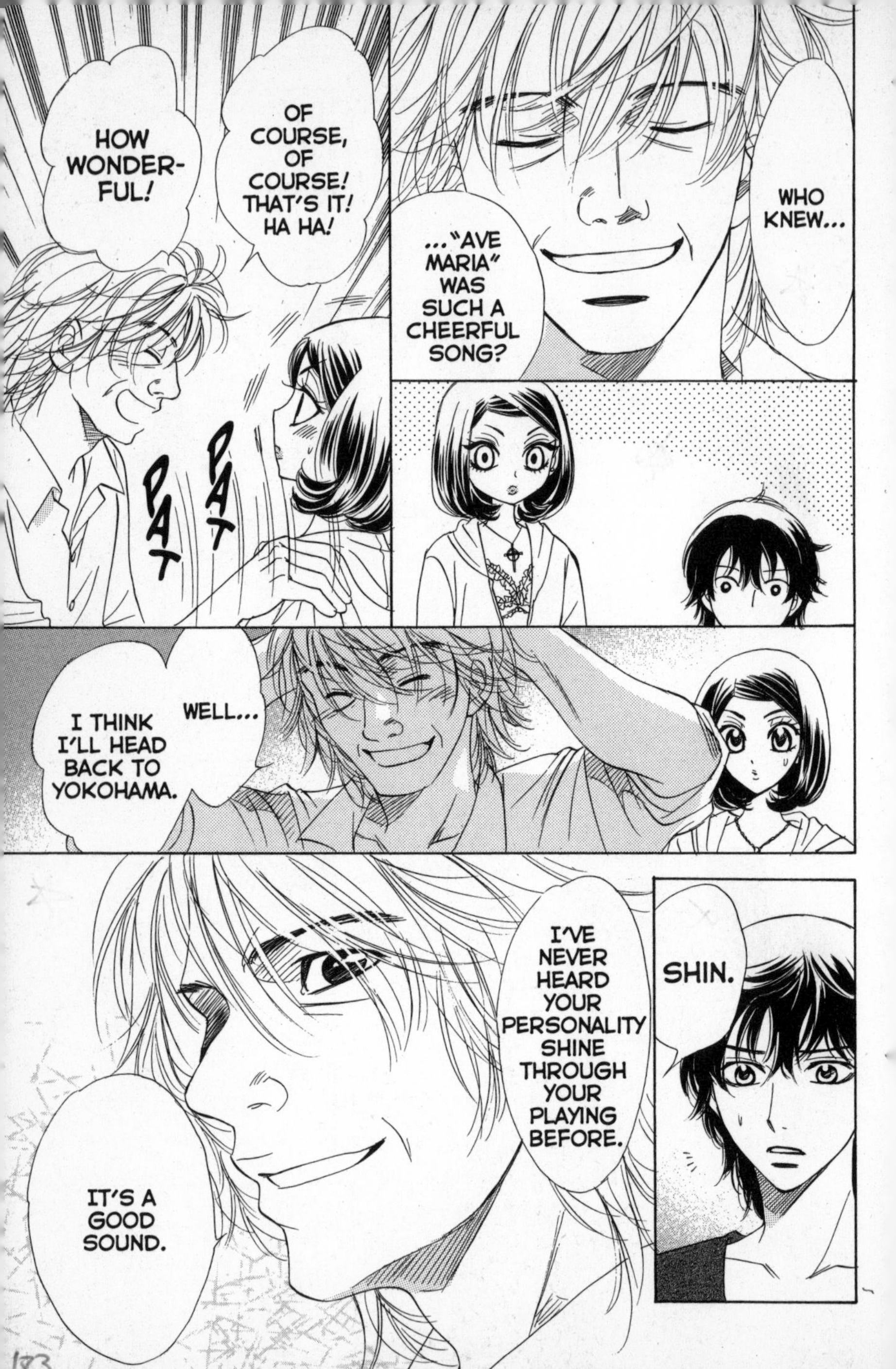
WHO KNEW...
..."AVE MARIA" WAS SUCH A CHEERFUL SONG?
OF COURSE, OF COURSE! THAT'S IT! HA HA!
HOW WONDER-FUL!
PAT PAT
WELL...
I THINK I'LL HEAD BACK TO YOKOHAMA.
SHIN.
I'VE NEVER HEARD YOUR PERSONALITY SHINE THROUGH YOUR PLAYING BEFORE.
IT'S A GOOD SOUND.

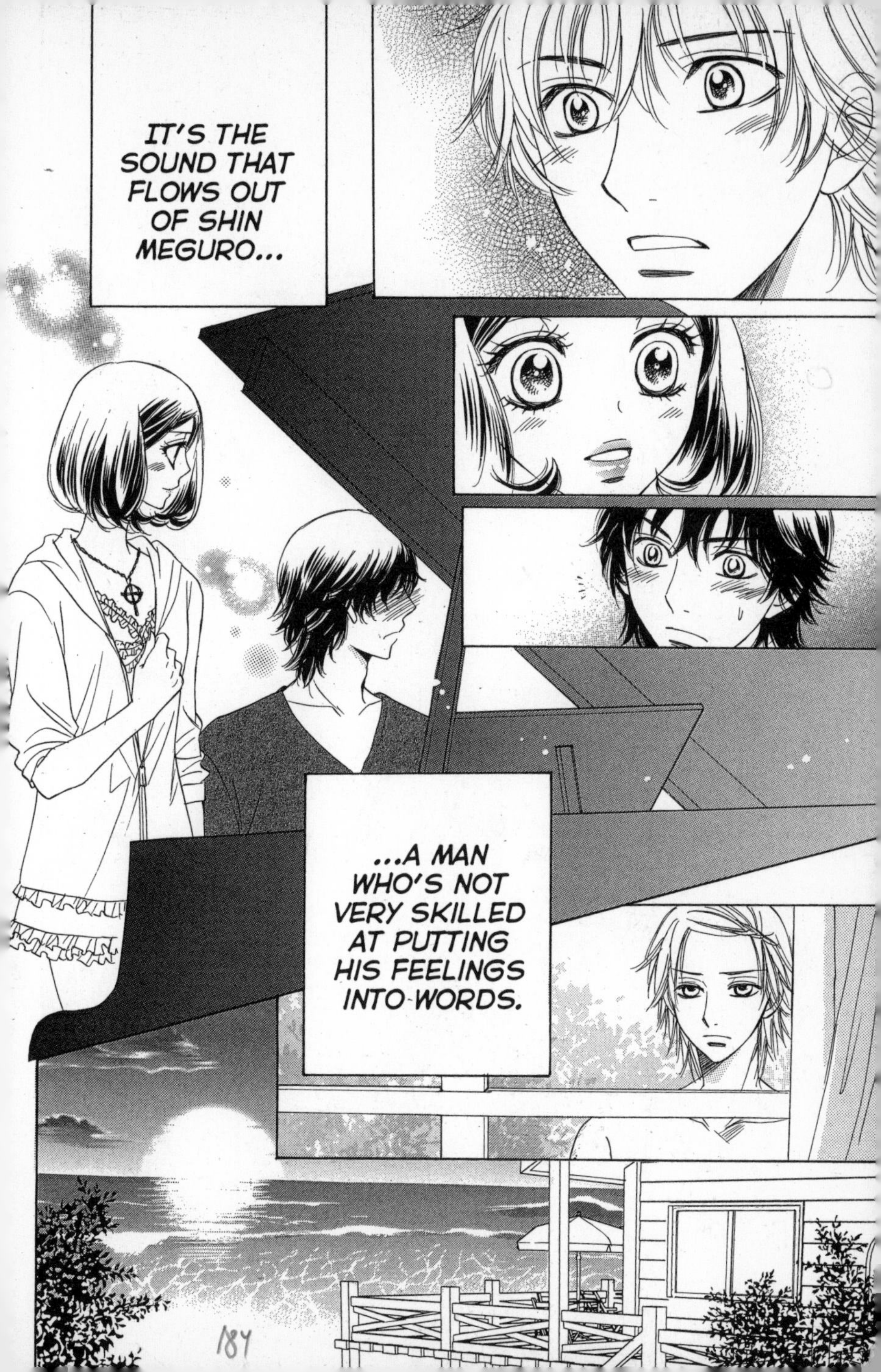
IT'S THE SOUND THAT FLOWS OUT OF SHIN MEGURO...
...A MAN WHO'S NOT VERY SKILLED AT PUTTING HIS FEELINGS INTO WORDS.

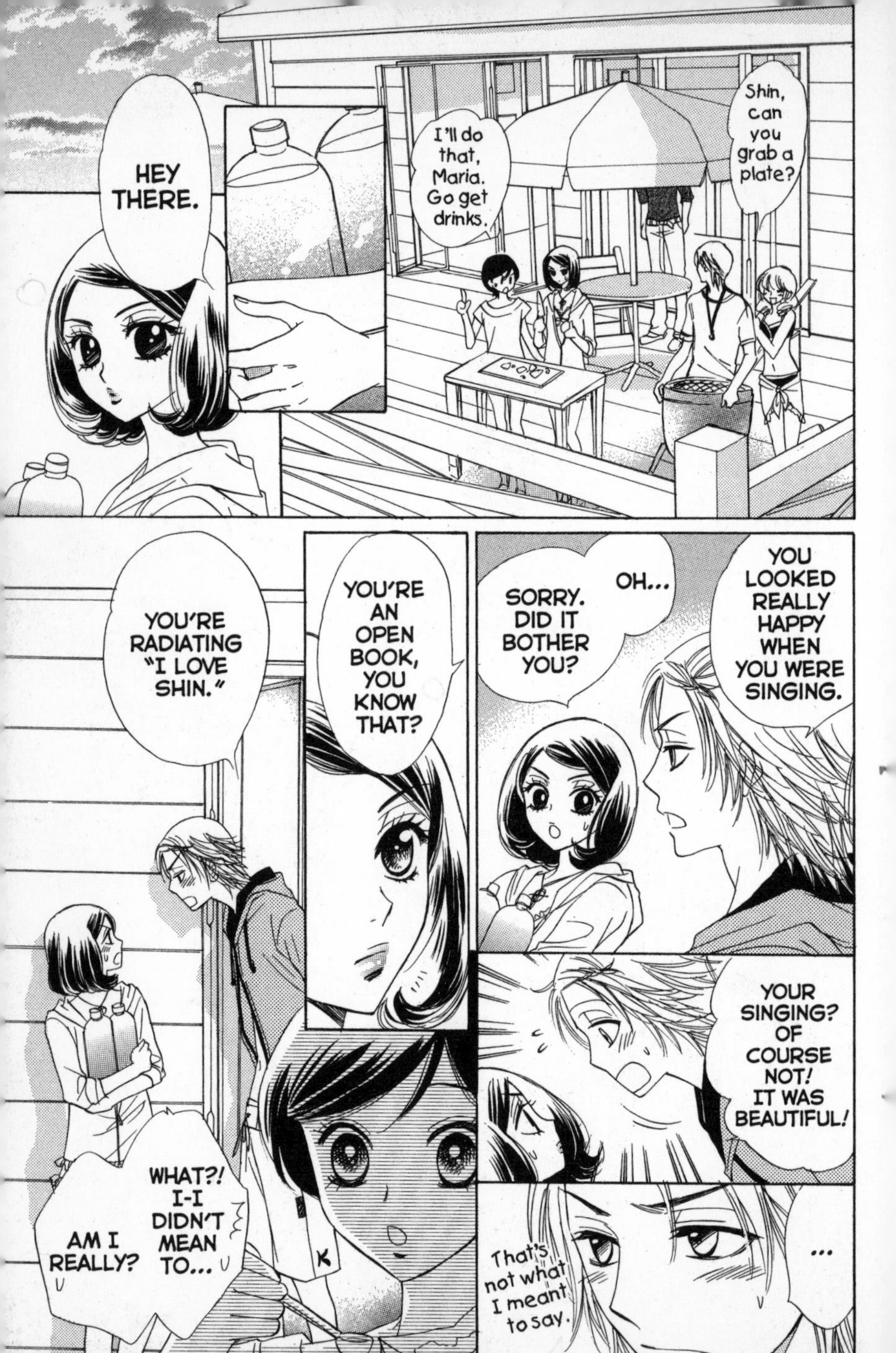
Shin, can you grab a plate?
I'll do that, Maria. Go get drinks.
HEY THERE.
YOU LOOKED REALLY HAPPY WHEN YOU WERE SINGING.
OH...
SORRY. DID IT BOTHER YOU?
YOUR SINGING? OF COURSE NOT! IT WAS BEAUTIFUL!
...
That's not what I meant to say.
YOU'RE AN OPEN BOOK, YOU KNOW THAT?
YOU'RE RADIATING "I LOVE SHIN."
WHAT?! I-I DIDN'T MEAN TO...
AM I REALLY?

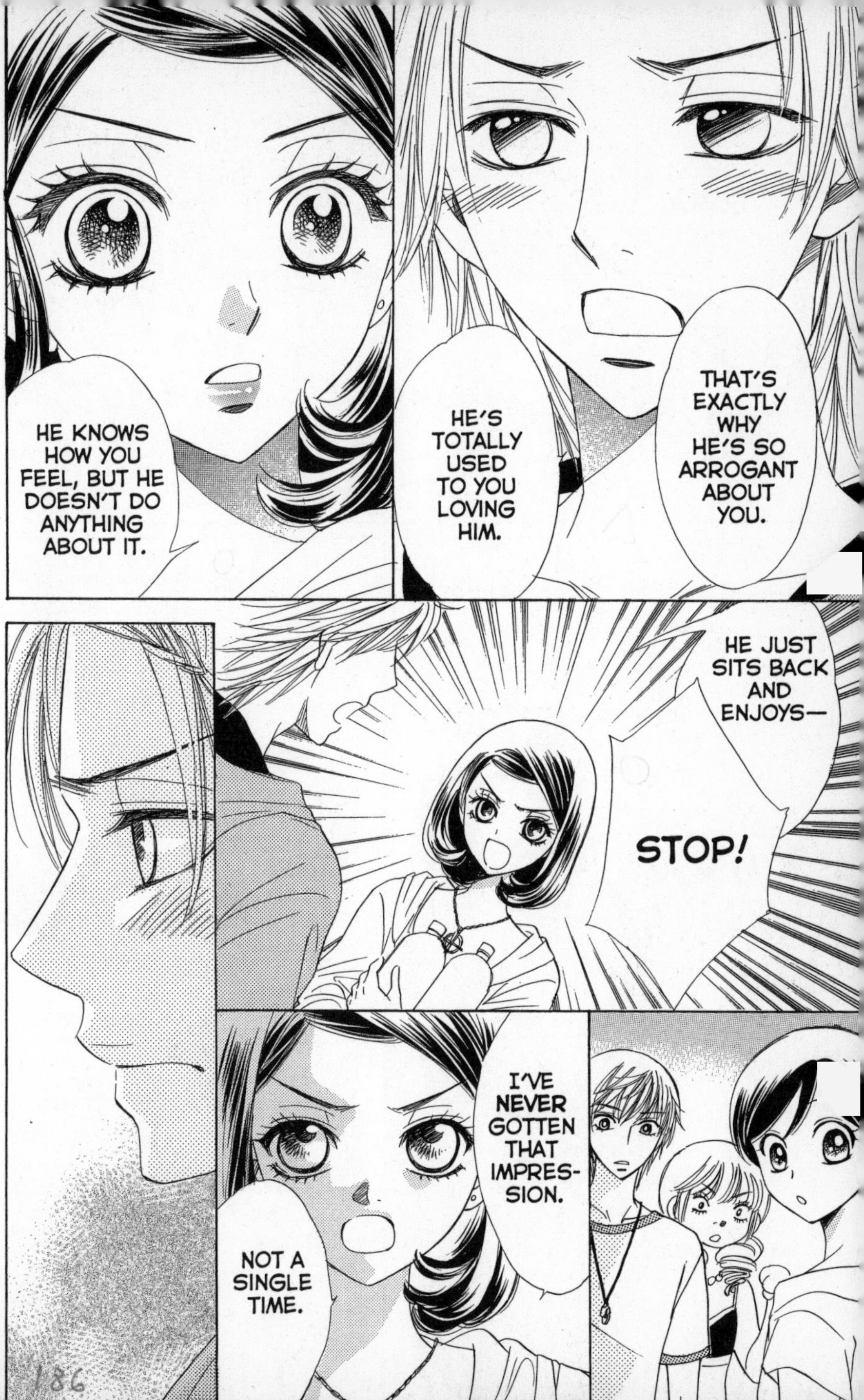
THAT'S EXACTLY WHY HE'S SO ARROGANT ABOUT YOU.
HE'S TOTALLY USED TO YOU LOVING HIM.
HE KNOWS HOW YOU FEEL, BUT HE DOESN'T DO ANYTHING ABOUT IT.
HE JUST SITS BACK AND ENJOYS—
STOP!
I'VE NEVER GOTTEN THAT IMPRESSION.
NOT A SINGLE TIME.

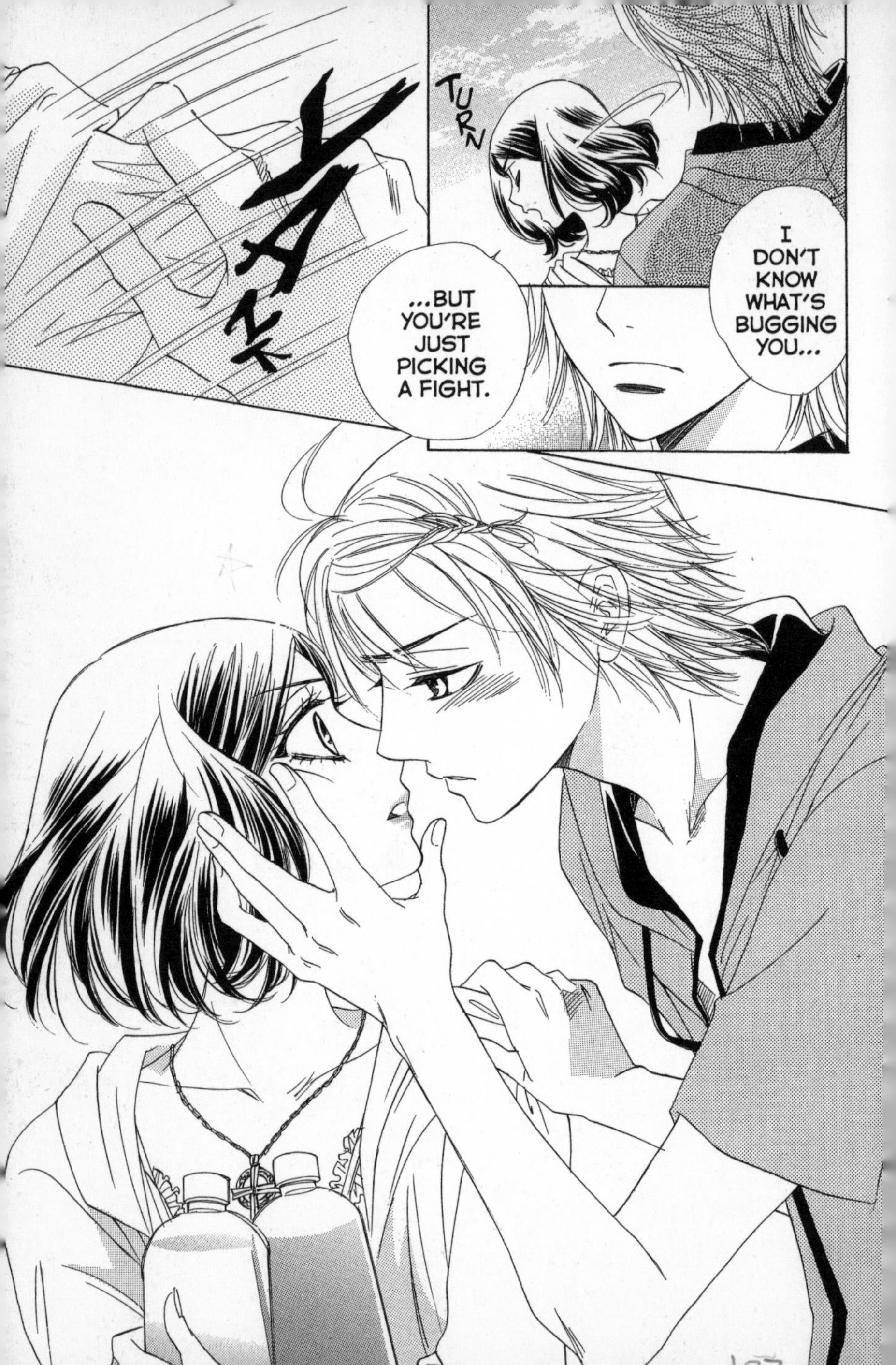
TURN
I DON'T KNOW WHAT'S BUGGING YOU...
...BUT YOU'RE JUST PICKING A FIGHT.
YANK

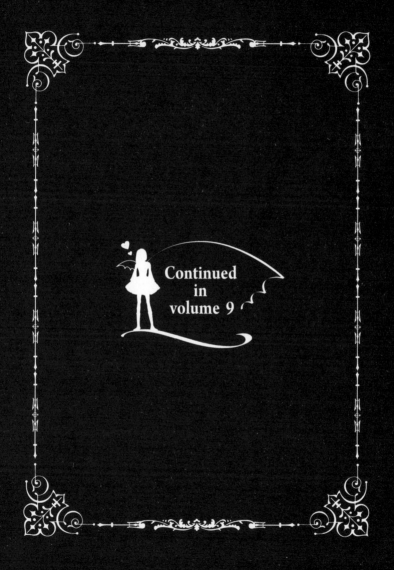

Continued
in
volume 9

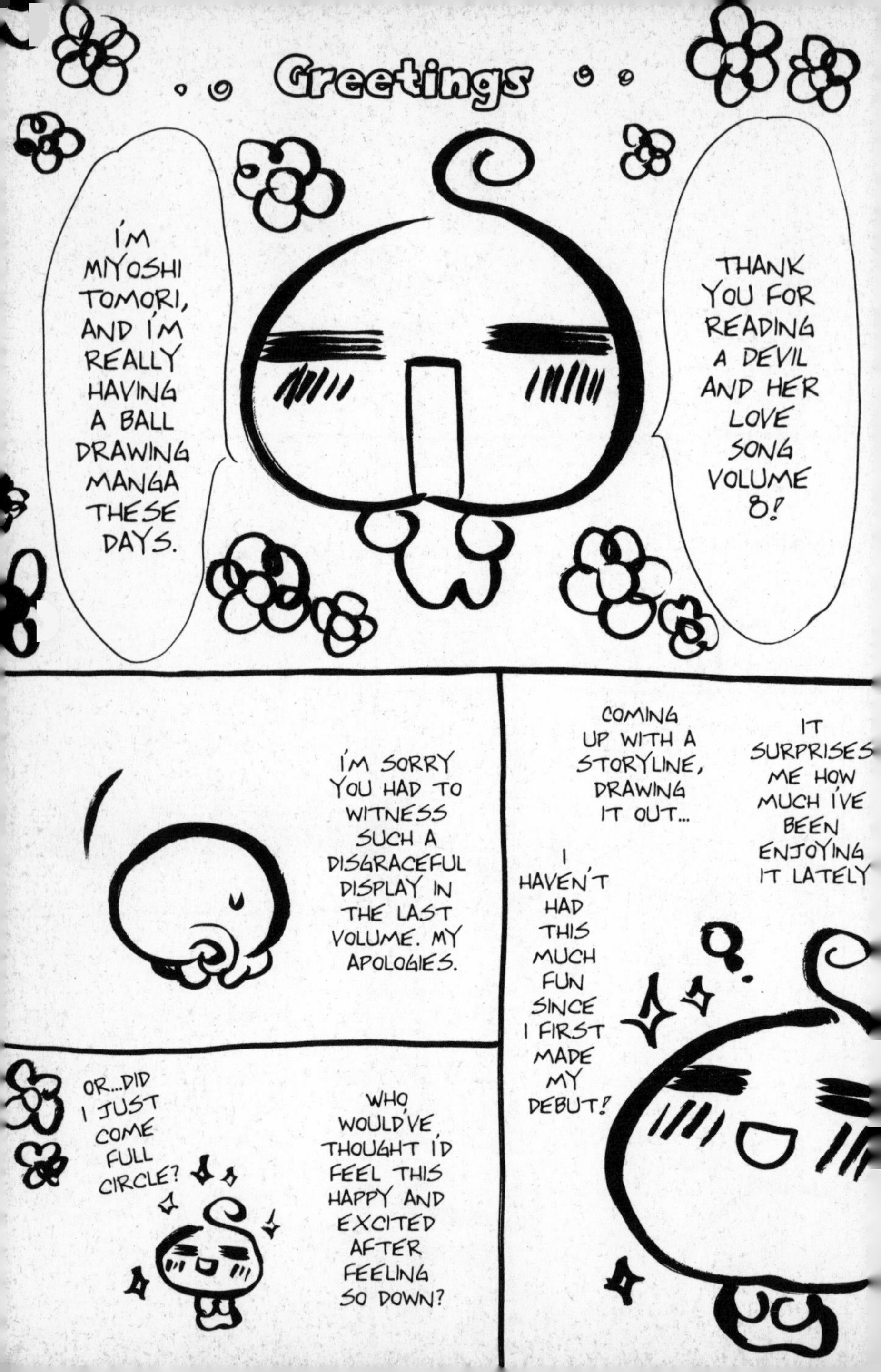
Greetings
THANK YOU FOR READING A DEVIL AND HER LOVE SONG VOLUME 8!
I'M MIYOSHI TOMORI, AND I'M REALLY HAVING A BALL DRAWING MANGA THESE DAYS.
IT SURPRISES ME HOW MUCH I'VE BEEN ENJOYING IT LATELY
COMING UP WITH A STORYLINE, DRAWING IT OUT...
I HAVEN'T HAD THIS MUCH FUN SINCE I FIRST MADE MY DEBUT!
I'M SORRY YOU HAD TO WITNESS SUCH A DISGRACEFUL DISPLAY IN THE LAST VOLUME. MY APOLOGIES.
WHO WOULD'VE THOUGHT I'D FEEL THIS HAPPY AND EXCITED AFTER FEELING SO DOWN?
OR...DID I JUST COME FULL CIRCLE?

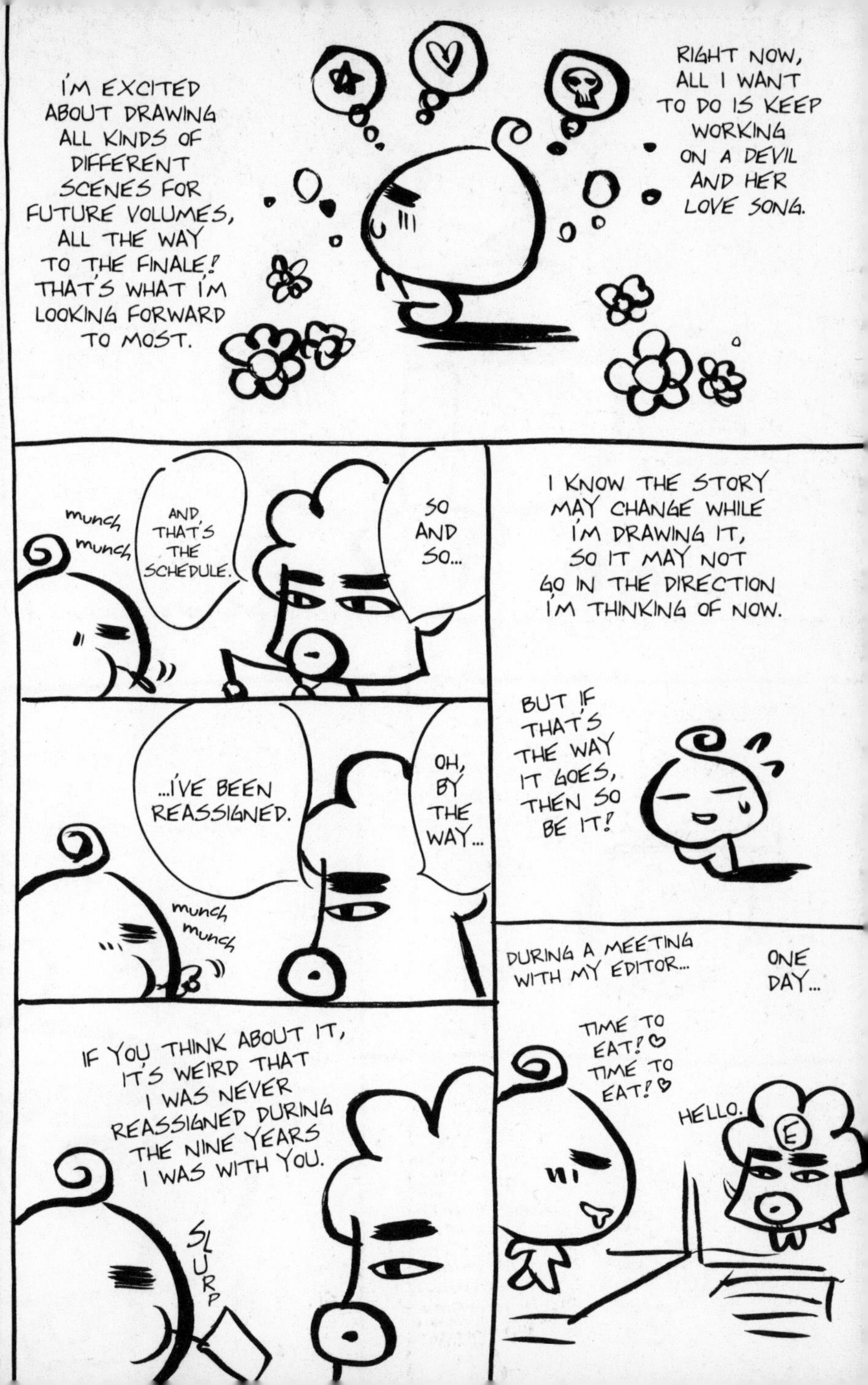
RIGHT NOW, ALL I WANT TO DO IS KEEP WORKING ON A DEVIL AND HER LOVE SONG.
I'M EXCITED ABOUT DRAWING ALL KINDS OF DIFFERENT SCENES FOR FUTURE VOLUMES, ALL THE WAY TO THE FINALE! THAT'S WHAT I'M LOOKING FORWARD TO MOST.
I KNOW THE STORY MAY CHANGE WHILE I'M DRAWING IT, SO IT MAY NOT GO IN THE DIRECTION I'M THINKING OF NOW.
BUT IF THAT'S THE WAY IT GOES, THEN SO BE IT!
ONE DAY...
DURING A MEETING WITH MY EDITOR...
TIME TO EAT! ♡ TIME TO EAT! ♡
HELLO.
SO AND SO...
AND THAT'S THE SCHEDULE.
munch munch
OH, BY THE WAY...
...I'VE BEEN REASSIGNED.
munch munch
IF YOU THINK ABOUT IT, IT'S WEIRD THAT I WAS NEVER REASSIGNED DURING THE NINE YEARS I WAS WITH YOU.
SLURP

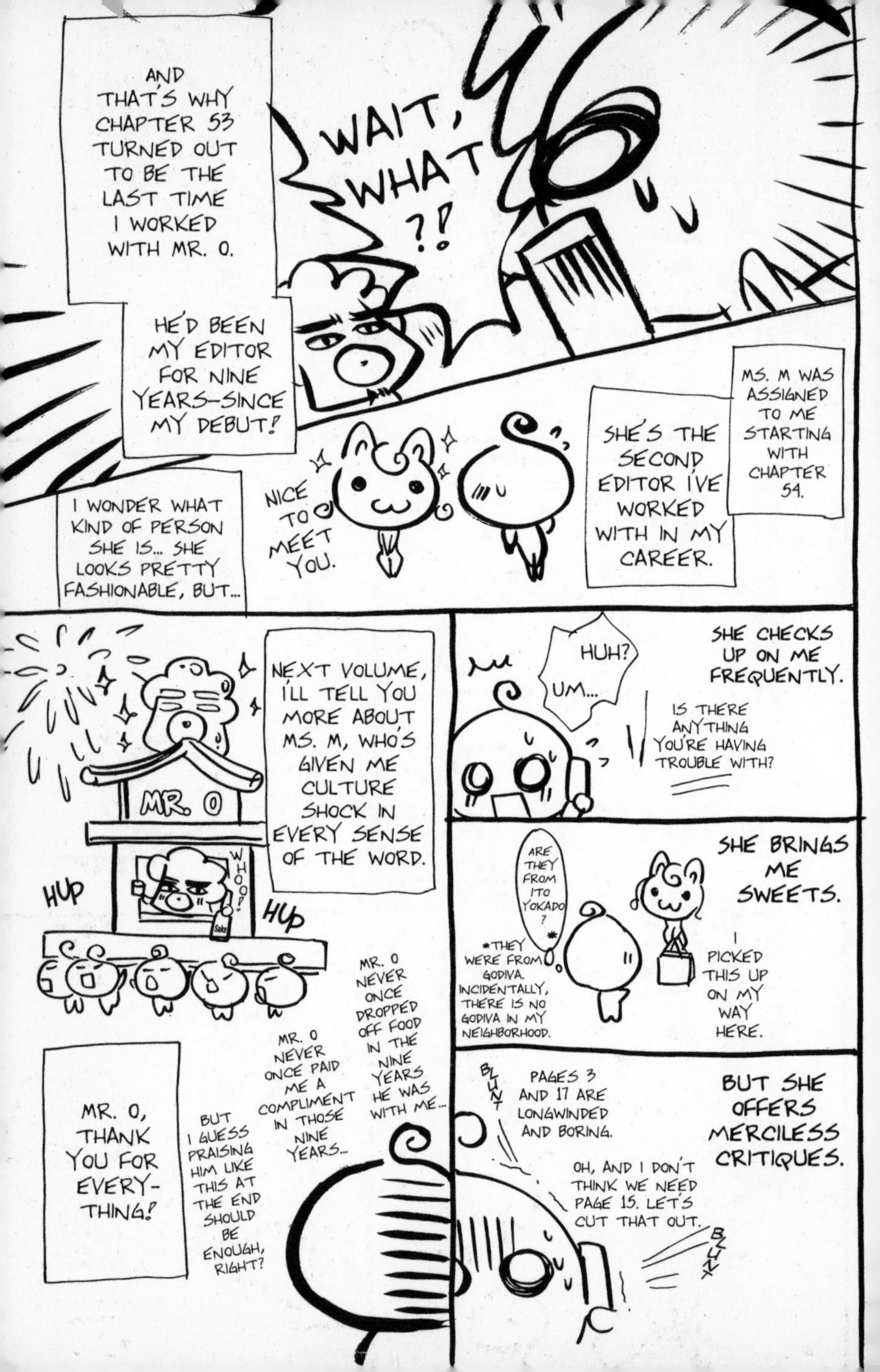
AND THAT'S WHY CHAPTER 53 TURNED OUT TO BE THE LAST TIME I WORKED WITH MR. O.
WAIT, WHAT ?!
HE'D BEEN MY EDITOR FOR NINE YEARS—SINCE MY DEBUT!
MS. M WAS ASSIGNED TO ME STARTING WITH CHAPTER 54.
SHE'S THE SECOND EDITOR I'VE WORKED WITH IN MY CAREER.
NICE TO MEET YOU.
I WONDER WHAT KIND OF PERSON SHE IS... SHE LOOKS PRETTY FASHIONABLE, BUT...
SHE CHECKS UP ON ME FREQUENTLY.
IS THERE ANYTHING YOU'RE HAVING TROUBLE WITH?
HUH?
UM...
SHE BRINGS ME SWEETS.
I PICKED THIS UP ON MY WAY HERE.
ARE THEY FROM ITO YOKADO?
*THEY WERE FROM GODIVA. INCIDENTALLY, THERE IS NO GODIVA IN MY NEIGHBORHOOD.
BUT SHE OFFERS MERCILESS CRITIQUES.
PAGES 3 AND 17 ARE LONGWINDED AND BORING.
BLUNT
OH, AND I DON'T THINK WE NEED PAGE 15. LET'S CUT THAT OUT.
BLUNT
NEXT VOLUME, I'LL TELL YOU MORE ABOUT MS. M, WHO'S GIVEN ME CULTURE SHOCK IN EVERY SENSE OF THE WORD.
MR. O
WHOO?!
HUP
HUP
Sake
MR. O NEVER ONCE DROPPED OFF FOOD IN THE NINE YEARS HE WAS WITH ME...
MR. O NEVER ONCE PAID ME A COMPLIMENT IN THOSE NINE YEARS...
BUT I GUESS PRAISING HIM LIKE THIS AT THE END SHOULD BE ENOUGH, RIGHT?
MR. O, THANK YOU FOR EVERY-THING!

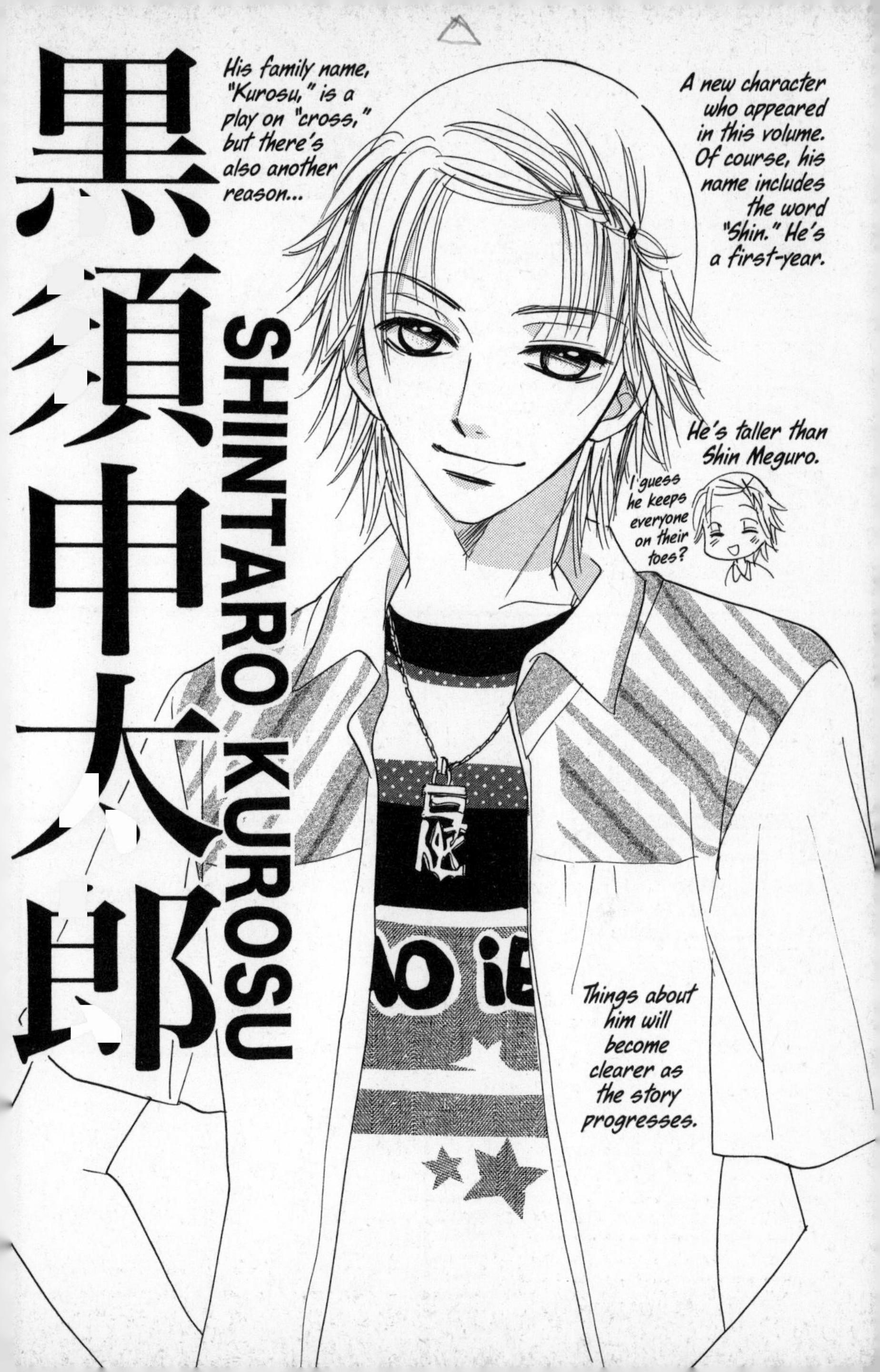
A new character who appeared in this volume. Of course, his name includes the word "Shin." He's a first-year.
He's taller than Shin Meguro.
I guess he keeps everyone on their toes?
Things about him will become clearer as the story progresses.
His family name, "Kurosu," is a play on "cross," but there's also another reason...
SHINTARO KUROSU
黒須申太郎

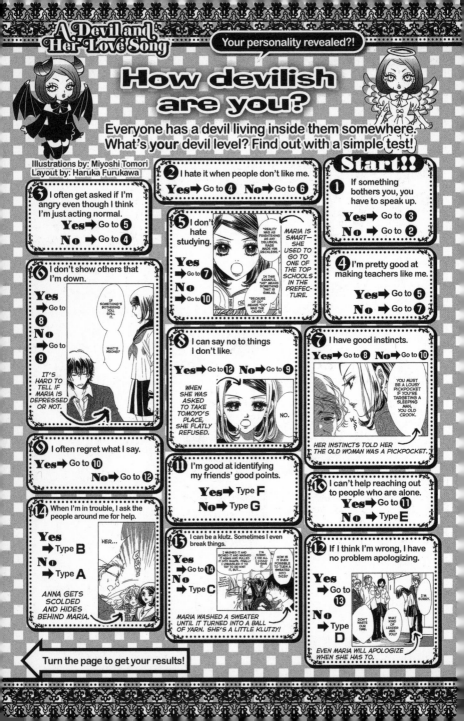

A Devil and Her Love Song

Your personality revealed?!

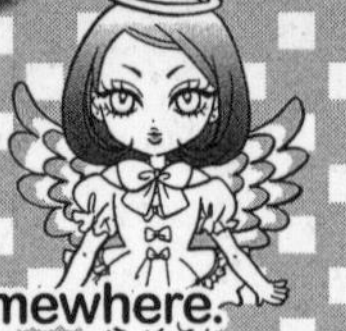

How devilish are you?

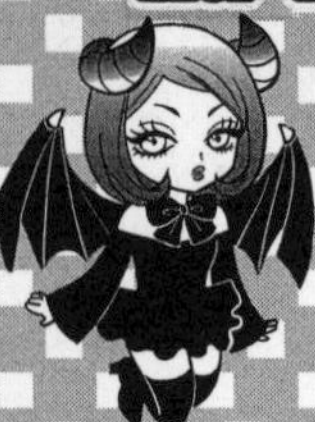

Everyone has a devil living inside them somewhere. What's your devil level? Find out with a simple test!

Illustrations by: Miyoshi Tomori
Layout by: Haruka Furukawa

Start!!

1 If something bothers you, you have to speak up.
Yes → Go to 3
No → Go to 2

2 I hate it when people don't like me.
Yes → Go to 4 No → Go to 6

3 I often get asked if I'm angry even though I think I'm just acting normal.
Yes → Go to 5
No → Go to 4

4 I'm pretty good at making teachers like me.
Yes → Go to 5
No → Go to 7

5 I don't hate studying.
Yes → Go to 7
No → Go to 10

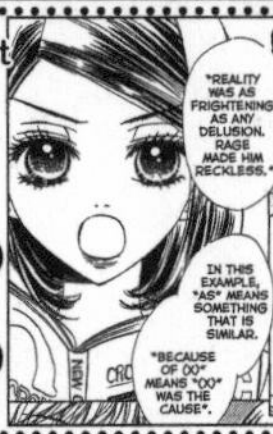
"REALITY WAS AS FRIGHTENING AS ANY DELUSION. RAGE MADE HIM RECKLESS."
IN THIS EXAMPLE, "AS" MEANS SOMETHING THAT IS SIMILAR.
"BECAUSE OF OO" MEANS "OO" WAS THE CAUSE".

MARIA IS SMART—SHE USED TO GO TO ONE OF THE TOP SCHOOLS IN THE PREFECTURE.

6 I don't show others that I'm down.
Yes → Go to 8
No → Go to 9

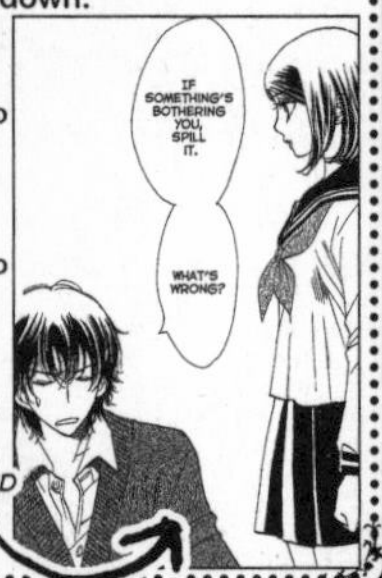
IF SOMETHING'S BOTHERING YOU, SPILL IT.
WHAT'S WRONG?

IT'S HARD TO TELL IF MARIA IS DEPRESSED OR NOT.

7 I have good instincts.
Yes → Go to 8 No → Go to 10

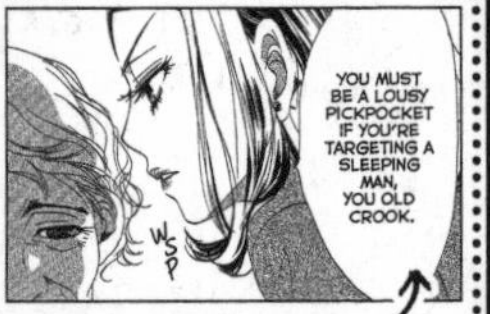
YOU MUST BE A LOUSY PICKPOCKET IF YOU'RE TARGETING A SLEEPING MAN, YOU OLD CROOK.
WSP

HER INSTINCTS TOLD HER THE OLD WOMAN WAS A PICKPOCKET.

8 I can say no to things I don't like.
Yes → Go to 12 No → Go to 9

WHEN SHE WAS ASKED TO TAKE TOMOYO'S PLACE, SHE FLATLY REFUSED.

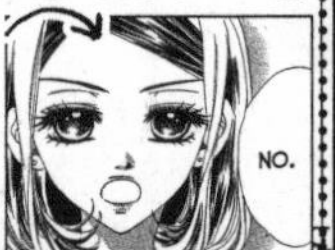
NO.

9 I often regret what I say.
Yes → Go to 10
No → Go to 12

10 I can't help reaching out to people who are alone.
Yes → Go to 11
No → Type E

11 I'm good at identifying my friends' good points.
Yes → Type F
No → Type G

12 If I think I'm wrong, I have no problem apologizing.
Yes → Go to 13
No → Type D

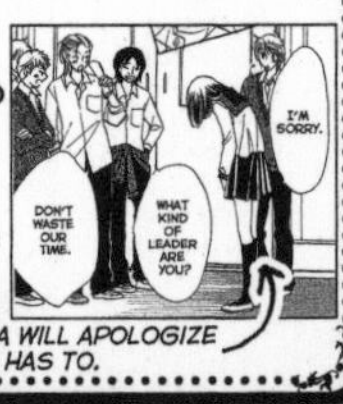
I'M SORRY.
WHAT KIND OF LEADER ARE YOU?
DON'T WASTE OUR TIME.

EVEN MARIA WILL APOLOGIZE WHEN SHE HAS TO.

13 I can be a klutz. Sometimes I even break things.
Yes → Go to 14
No → Type C

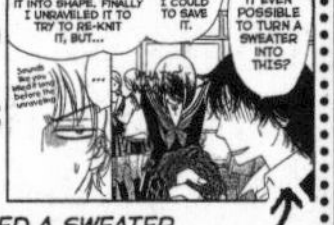
HOW IS IT EVEN POSSIBLE TO TURN A SWEATER INTO THIS?
I'M SORRY. I DID ALL I COULD TO SAVE IT.
I WASHED IT AND IRONED IT AND WASHED IT AGAIN AND PULLED IT INTO SHAPE. FINALLY I UNRAVELED IT TO TRY TO RE-KNIT IT, BUT...
...

MARIA WASHED A SWEATER UNTIL IT TURNED INTO A BALL OF YARN. SHE'S A LITTLE KLUTZY!

14 When I'm in trouble, I ask the people around me for help.
Yes → Type B
No → Type A

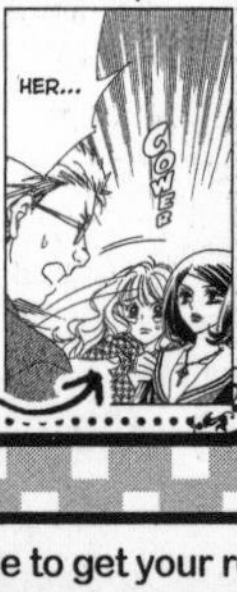
HER...
GOWER

ANNA GETS SCOLDED AND HIDES BEHIND MARIA.

Turn the page to get your results!

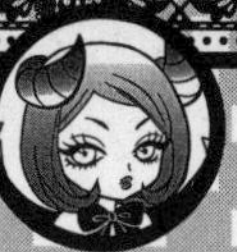

Results

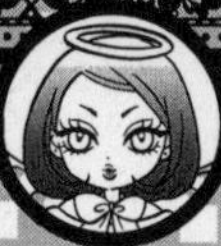

Find out which *A Devil and Her Love Song* character you're most like!

Type A Character

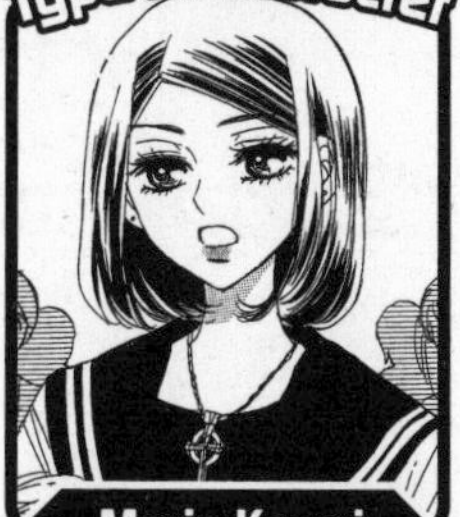

Maria Kawai

Partly because of her harsh looks, even kind words sound scary coming out of Maria's mouth! (*Ha ha.*)That trait earned her the nickname "Devil Maria."

You're not trying to be mean, but sometimes you make other people cry. You think you're acting nicely, but people are afraid of you. Does this happen to you?! You have a high devil score because it comes naturally to you—so naturally that you're not even aware of it! It might be a good idea to reflect on your behavior every so often.

TYPE A

DEVIL LEVEL 90%

Type B Character

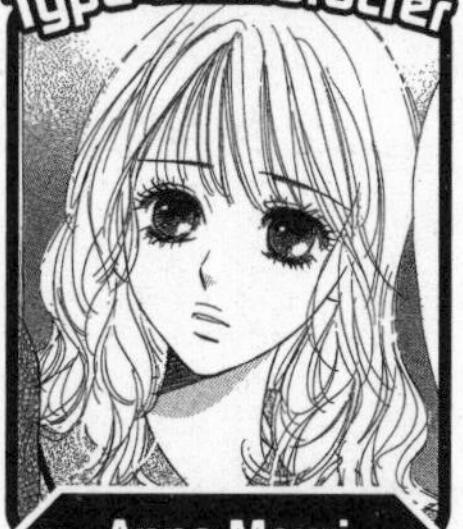

Anna Mouri

People who don't know her well may think of her as a helpless girl, but the truth is she's very strong! Her personality is almost as strong as Maria's.

You think nothing of pretending to cry if it's to protect yourself. Not only that, you secretly laugh at people who are fooled by your act. But with this much devil in you, you'll have no problem surviving the harsh world we live in.

TYPE B

DEVIL LEVEL 85%

Type C Character

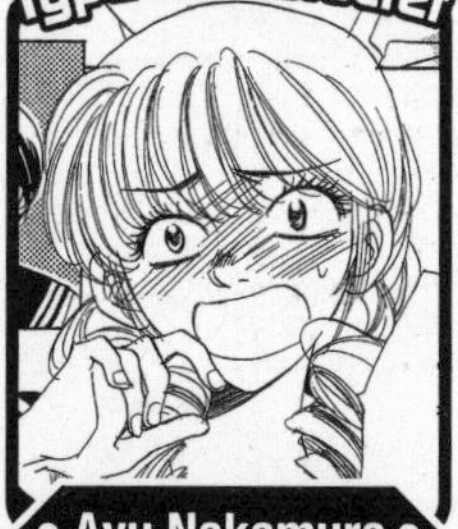

Ayu Nakamura

When Maria first came to the school, Ayu regarded her as an enemy and bullied her relentlessly. But her attitude changed after Maria said things that made her reconsider her outlook! Now the two of them are friends.

You won't rest until you totally destroy your enemies and anyone who stands in your way! But you're not the cerebral type who comes up with cunning plans, so sometimes you panic when the results aren't what you expected. But somehow, no one can resent your behavior. (*Heh.*)

TYPE C

DEVIL LEVEL 60%

TYPE D — DEVIL LEVEL 40%

Type D Character

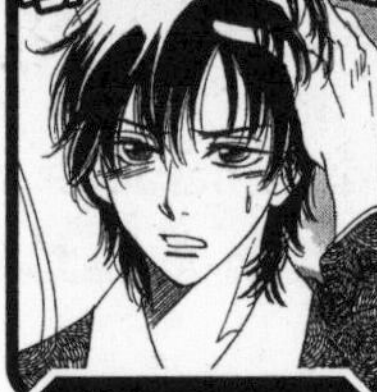

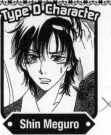

• Shin Meguro •

He always cuts class, and he comes across as though he doesn't care about anyone else. But the truth is he cares deeply about his friends and is always paying attention, whether it seems that way or not.

Your harsh words and cool demeanor may leave people thinking you're scary. But the reality is that you have a pure heart. You tend to act tough to hide your awkwardness, but there are people who recognize your kindness.

TYPE E — DEVIL LEVEL 30%

Type E Character

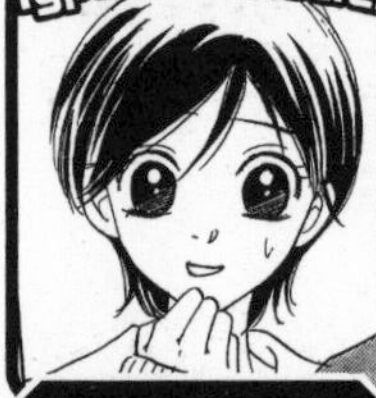

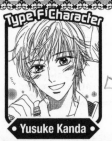

• Tomoyo Kohsaka •

She always hid her true feelings behind a smile, but ever since she met Maria, she's changed. These days she's able to calmly observe people.

It's human nature to get upset or irritated at other people sometimes. But you can't help feeling like you need to hide the small devil that lives in your heart. Because you usually try to repress those feelings, they may all break free occasionally and freak people out.

TYPE F — DEVIL LEVEL 5%

Type F Character

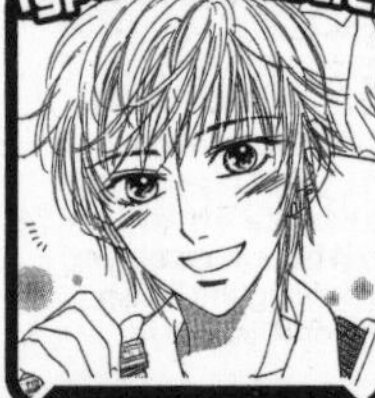

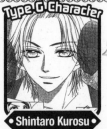

• Yusuke Kanda •

He's kind to everyone and popular with the girls, but because he tries to please everyone, he has a hard time making close friends. He thinks his own sweetness isn't real.

You can be friends with everyone! You're good-natured and popular in your class. But maybe you're such a nice person that you don't make much of an impression on other people. You should try showing the mean or cool side of you once in a while so there's more of a contrast in your personality. That might make you even more appealing!

TYPE G — DEVIL LEVEL 90%

Type G Character

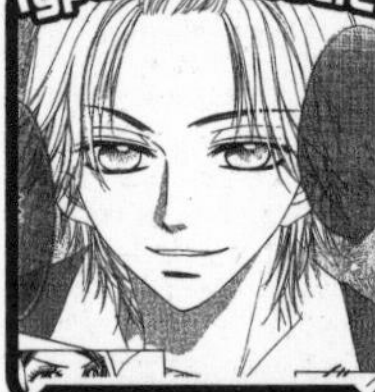

• Shintaro Kurosu •

He's pure to the point of cluelessness sometimes. He doesn't get discouraged easily, and he can change the situation with his positive attitude.

You tend to speak your mind to everyone. What you see is what you get, since you wear your feelings on your sleeve. But that trait may make people tire of you because they're at the mercy of your emotions, which can be exhausting. Some people may have fallen victim to you without you even realizing it!

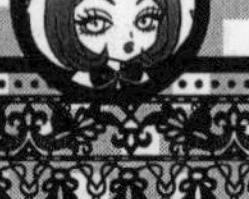

How big is the devil that lives in your heart? If you have a high level of devilishness, be careful!

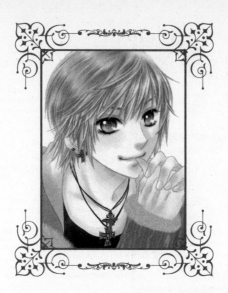

Lately, I'm really into collecting stationery goods and accessories with a butterfly motif. Butterfly magnets are especially pretty, and a colorful swarm of them now adorn my desk. As I gloat over their beauty, I also find it troubling that I keep stabbing my fingers on their sharp wings made of steel...

–Miyoshi Tomori

Miyoshi Tomori made her debut as a manga creator in 2001, and her previous titles include *Hatsukare* (First Boyfriend), *Tongari Root* (Square Root), and *Brass Love!!* In her spare time she likes listening to music in the bath and playing musical instruments.

A DEVIL AND HER LOVE SONG

Volume 8
Shojo Beat Edition

STORY AND ART BY
MIYOSHI TOMORI

English Adaptation/Ysabet MacFarlane
Translation/JN Productions
Touch-up Art & Lettering/Monalisa de Asis
Design/Courtney Utt
Editor/Amy Yu

AKUMA TO LOVE SONG © 2006 by Miyoshi Tomori
All rights reserved. First published in Japan in 2006
by SHUEISHA Inc., Tokyo.
English translation rights arranged
by SHUEISHA Inc.

Printed in the U.S.A.

Published by VIZ Media, LLC
P.O. Box 77010
San Francisco, CA 94107

10 9 8 7 6 5 4 3 2 1
First printing, April 2013

www.viz.com   www.shojobeat.com

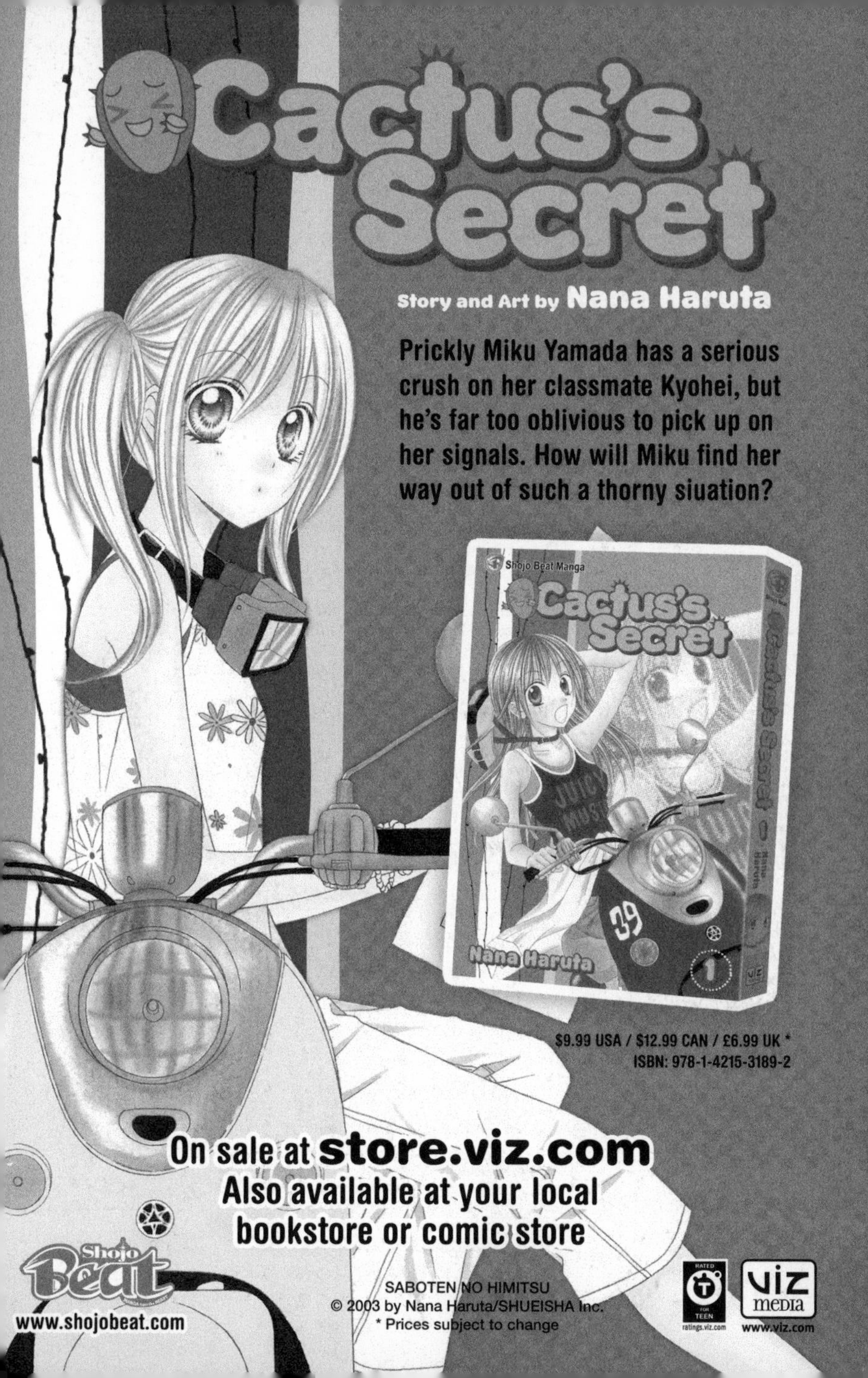
Cactus's Secret
Story and Art by Nana Haruta
Prickly Miku Yamada has a serious crush on her classmate Kyohei, but he's far too oblivious to pick up on her signals. How will Miku find her way out of such a thorny siuation?
Shojo Beat Manga
Cactus's Secret
Nana Haruta
1
$9.99 USA / $12.99 CAN / £6.99 UK *
ISBN: 978-1-4215-3189-2
On sale at store.viz.com
Also available at your local bookstore or comic store
Shojo Beat
www.shojobeat.com
SABOTEN NO HIMITSU
© 2003 by Nana Haruta/SHUEISHA Inc.
* Prices subject to change
RATED T FOR TEEN
ratings.viz.com
VIZ media
www.viz.com

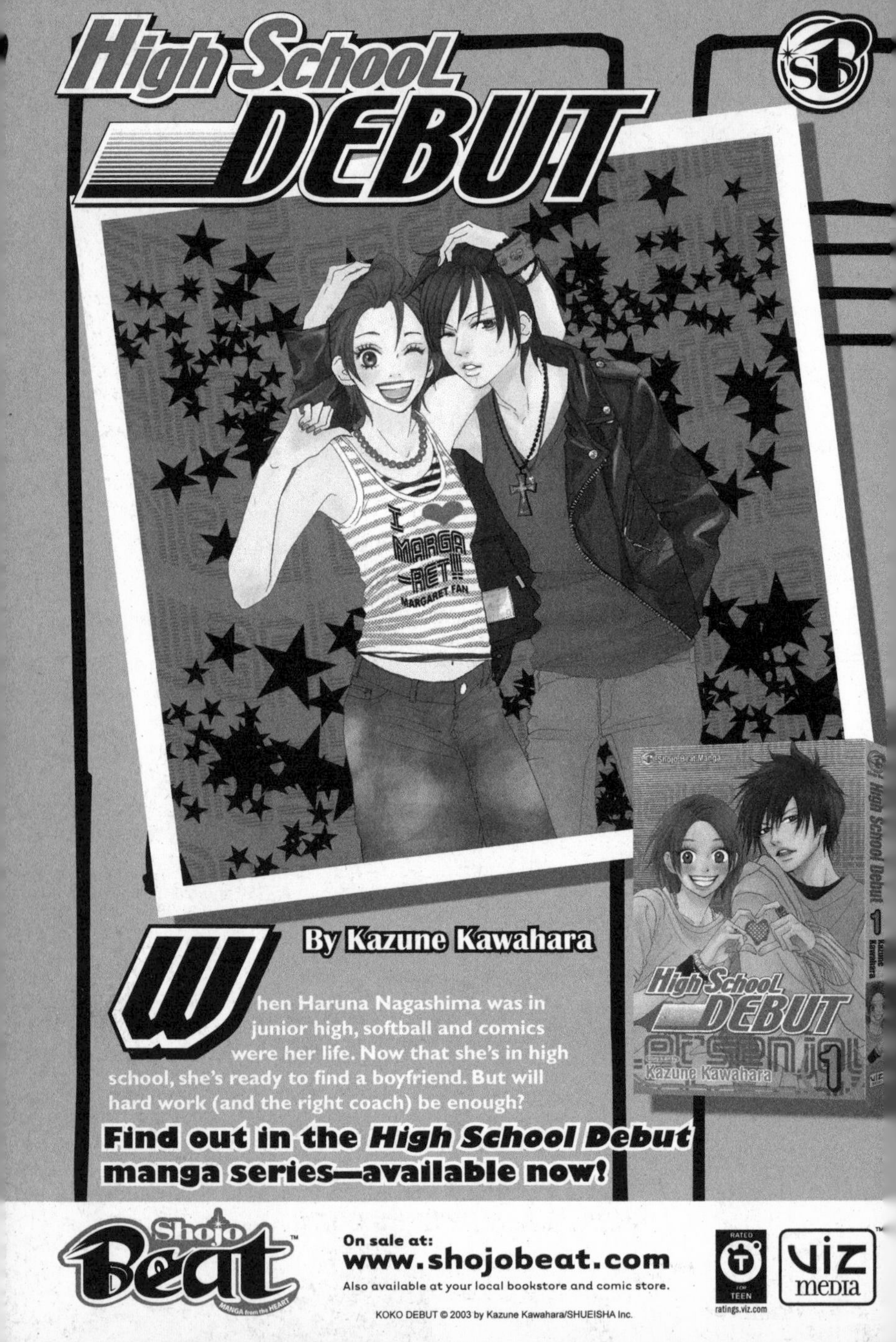
High School DEBUT
By Kazune Kawahara
When Haruna Nagashima was in junior high, softball and comics were her life. Now that she's in high school, she's ready to find a boyfriend. But will hard work (and the right coach) be enough?
Find out in the *High School Debut* manga series—available now!
Shojo Beat Manga
High School Debut 1
Kazune Kawahara
Shojo Beat™
MANGA from the HEART
On sale at:
www.shojobeat.com
Also available at your local bookstore and comic store.
RATED T FOR TEEN
ratings.viz.com
VIZ media™
KOKO DEBUT © 2003 by Kazune Kawahara/SHUEISHA Inc.

Surprise!

You may be reading the wrong way!

It's true: In keeping with the original Japanese comic format, this book reads from right to left—so action, sound effects, and word balloons are completely reversed. This preserves the orientation of the original artwork—plus, it's fun! Check out the diagram shown here to get the hang of things, and then turn to the other side of the book to get started!

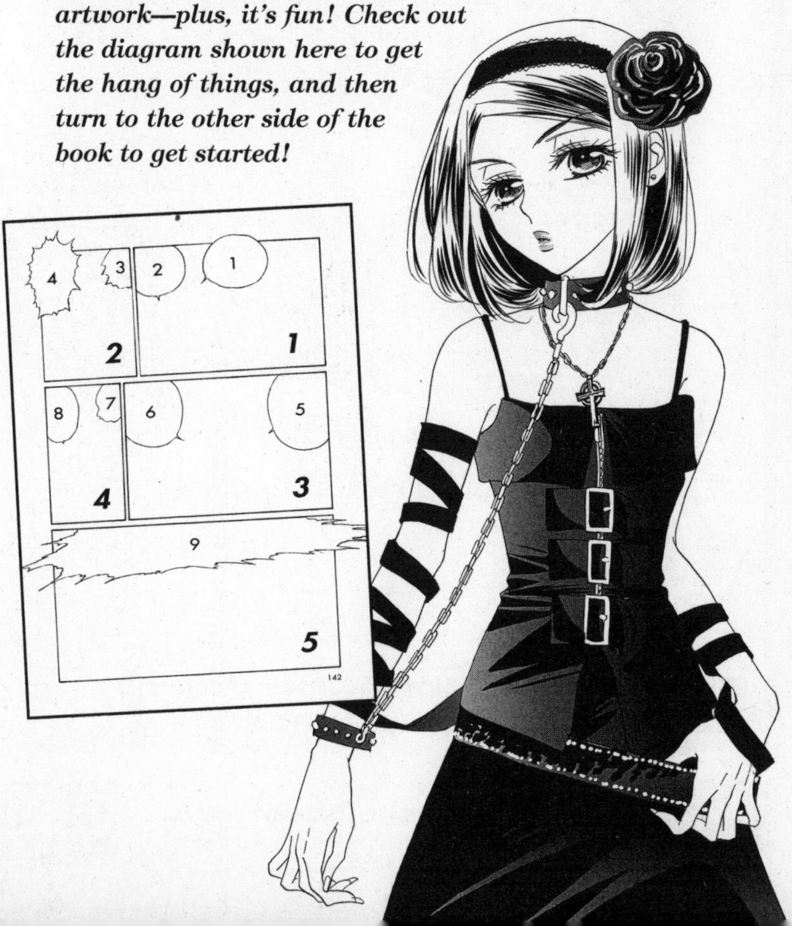
1
2
1
3
4
2
5
6
3
7
8
4
9
5
142